SOCIAL EXCLUSION OF YOUTH IN EUROPE
The Multifaceted Consequences of Labour Market Insecurity

Edited by
Marge Unt, Michael Gebel, Sonia Bertolini,
Vassiliki Deliyanni-Kouimtzi, and Dirk Hofäcker

P

First published in Great Britain in 2023 by

Policy Press, an imprint of
Bristol University Press
University of Bristol
1-9 Old Park Hill
Bristol
BS2 8BB
UK
t: +44 (0)117 374 6645
e: bup-info@bristol.ac.uk

Details of international sales and distribution partners are available at
policy.bristoluniversitypress.co.uk

© Bristol University Press 2023

The digital PDF and ePub versions of this title are available Open Access and distributed under the terms of the Creative Commons Attribution-NonCommercial-NoDerivatives 4.0 International license (https://creativecommons.org/licenses/by-nc-nd/4.0/) which permits reproduction and distribution for non-commercial use without further permission provided the original work is attributed.

British Library Cataloguing in Publication Data
A catalogue record for this book is available from the British Library

ISBN 978-1-4473-5872-5 hardcover
ISBN 978-1-4473-5873-2 paperback
ISBN 978-1-4473-5874-9 OA ePub
ISBN 978-1-4473-5875-6 OA ePdf

The right of Marge Unt, Michael Gebel, Sonia Bertolini, Vassiliki Deliyanni-Kouimtzi and Dirk Hofäcker to be identified as editors of this work has been asserted by them in accordance with the Copyright, Designs and Patents Act 1988.

All rights reserved: no part of this publication may be reproduced, stored in a retrieval system, or transmitted in any form or by any means, electronic, mechanical, photocopying, recording, or otherwise without the prior permission of Bristol University Press.

Every reasonable effort has been made to obtain permission to reproduce copyrighted material. If, however, anyone knows of an oversight, please contact the publisher.

The statements and opinions contained within this publication are solely those of the editors and contributors and not of the University of Bristol or Bristol University Press. The University of Bristol and Bristol University Press disclaim responsibility for any injury to persons or property resulting from any material published in this publication.

Bristol University Press and Policy Press work to counter discrimination on grounds of gender, race, disability, age and sexuality.

Cover design: Hayes Design
Front cover image: © Rea Antoniou

Contents

List of figures and tables	v
List of abbreviations	vii
Notes on contributors	ix
Preface and acknowledgements	xv

1   Introduction: Youth transitions in times of labour market insecurity   1
Michael Gebel, Marge Unt, Sonia Bertolini, Vassiliki Deliyanni-Kouimtzi, and Dirk Hofäcker

PART I   Labour market insecurity and youth well-being and health

2   Effects of unemployment and insecure jobs on youth well-being in Europe: economic development and business cycle fluctuations   31
Olena Nizalova, Gintare Malisauskaite, Despoina Xanthopoulou, Katerina Gousia, and Christina Athanasiades

3   Health effects of unemployment in couples: does becoming unemployed affect a young partner's health?   58
Anna Baranowska-Rataj and Mattias Strandh

4   Multiple routes to youth well-being: a qualitative comparative analysis of buffers to the negative consequences of unemployment   81
Triin Lauri and Marge Unt

5   Experiencing unemployment and job insecurity in two European countries: German and Italian young people's well-being and coping strategies   112
Christoph Schlee, Rosy Musumeci, and Chiara Ghislieri

PART II   Labour market insecurity and youth autonomy

6   Meanings of work in the narratives of Italian, Estonian, and Polish young people who experience labour market insecurity   139
Eve-Liis Roosmaa, Epp Reiska, Jędrzej Stasiowski, Sonia Bertolini, and Paola Maria Torrioni

7   Housing autonomy of youth in Europe: do labour and housing policies matter?   166
Valentina Goglio and Sonia Bertolini

| 8 | Is housing autonomy still a step towards adulthood in a time of job insecurity?
Sonia Bertolini, Rosy Musumeci, Christina Athanasiades, Anastasia Flouli, Lia Figgou, Vassiliki Deliyanni-Kouimtzi, Veneta Krasteva, Maria Jeliazkova, and Douhomir Minev | 192 |
|---|---|---|
| 9 | Becoming economically autonomous: young people in Italy and Poland in a time of job insecurity
Antonella Meo, Valentina Moiso, Jędrzej Stasiowski, and Zofia Włodarczyk | 214 |
| 10 | The role of informal social support for young people in unemployment and job insecurity in Italy, Estonia, and Germany
Antonella Meo, Roberta Ricucci, Christoph Schlee, Jelena Helemäe, and Margarita Kazjulja | 239 |
| 11 | How young people experience and perceive labour market policies in four European countries
Roberta Ricucci, Chiara Ghislieri, Veneta Krasteva, Maria Jeliazkova, Marti Taru, and Magdalena Rokicka | 263 |

PART III Labour market insecurity and the socio-economic consequences for youth

| 12 | Can labour market policies protect unemployed youth from poverty? A cross-European comparison
Małgorzata Kłobuszewska, Marta Palczyńska, Magdalena Rokicka, Jędrzej Stasiowski, Kadri Täht, and Marge Unt | 295 |
|---|---|---|
| 13 | Unemployment and job precariousness: material and social consequences for Greek and Italian youth
Lia Figgou, Martina Sourvinou, Christina Athanasiades, Valentina Moiso, and Rosy Musumeci | 315 |
| 14 | Syntheses of long-term socio-economic consequences of insecure labour market positions for youth in Europe
Dirk Hofäcker, Sina Schadow, and Janika Kletzing | 340 |
| 15 | Conclusions: Integrating perspectives on youth transitions and the risk of social exclusion
Sonia Bertolini, Vassiliki Deliyanni-Kouimtzi, Michael Gebel, Dirk Hofäcker, and Marge Unt | 362 |

Index	378

List of figures and tables

Figures

1.1	Theoretical multilevel model	9
2.1	Moderating effects of macroeconomic indicators on well-being in men	46
2.2	Moderating effects of macroeconomic indicators on well-being in women	47
4.1	Estimated effect of unemployment on life satisfaction	90
4.2	Outcome dimension (LS), explanatory conditions and chosen crossover points	96
4.3	Sufficient routes to two alternatively calibrated outcomes and cases that can be explained by these	102
7.1	Average marginal effect (AME) of being unemployed (vs employed) on housing autonomy	176
7.2	Indicators of employment protection legislation (EPL) and average marginal effect (AME) of being unemployed on housing autonomy	177
7.3	Indicators for expenditure on housing policies (rent benefits, housing benefits, housing and social exclusion benefits) and average marginal effect (AME) of being unemployed on housing autonomy	181
12.1	Household financial indicators by employment and household type	304
14.1	General importance attributed to savings in European countries: young people (15–39 years) versus full (non-retired) sample in 2008	343
14.2	Own savings to live comfortably in old age: young people (15–29 years) versus full (non-retired) sample in 2006	344
14.3	Consideration of employment uncertainty in public pension systems: composite index	348

Tables

2.1	Descriptive statistics for the samples (by gender)	42
2.2	Effect of micro- and macroindicators and their interactions on young male and female well-being (Model 1)	44

2.3	Effect of micro- and macroindicators and their interactions on young male and female well-being (Model 2)	48
3.1	Impact of individual and partner's unemployment on self-rated health among young men and women – results from panel data models	64
3.2	Results for mediating role of reduced household income and partner's health	66
3.3	Results for moderating factors: gender-role attitudes and work ethics	67
3.4	Sample structure – means and proportions	69
3.5	Distribution of contextual variables across countries	71
3.6	Results for moderating factors: gender-role attitudes and social norm of unemployment	72
3.7	Results for additional analyses combining individual and partners' labour market status	73
3.8	Results for additional analyses using fixed effects for years of survey	74
4.1	Dimensions included in the configurational comparison	91
4.2	Dimensions included in the analysis: raw and calibrated data	93
4.3	Truth table: empirical linkages between countries' combinations of institutional and contextual characteristics and outcomes	99
4.4	Sufficient routes to outcomes	100
6.1	Summary of concepts regarding meanings of work	142
6.2	Characterisation of national context (2015)	147
6.3	Sample description	148
7.1	List of macrolevel indicators	175
7.2	Second step regression for macrolevel indicators of EPL and the association between unemployment and housing autonomy; linear regression coefficients	179
7.3	Second step regression for macrolevel indicators of housing policies and the association between unemployment and housing autonomy; linear regression coefficients	183
8.1	Number of interviewees by age and housing status	198
11.1	Number of interviewees according to involvement in ALMPs	271
12.1	Summary statistics of dependent variables	303
12.2	Summary statistics of independent variables	303
12.3	Economic situation of unemployed youth: moderating role of PLMP and ALMP (all households)	305
12.4	Economic situation of unemployed youth: moderating role of PLMP and ALMP (households without parents)	307

List of abbreviations

AG	generosity of ALMP
AI	investment orientation of ALMP
ALMP	active labour market policy or programme
AP	active labour market policy
CEE	Central and Eastern European
COR	conservation of resources
EPL	employment protection legislation
ESS	European Social Survey
EU	European Union
EUIF	Estonian Unemployment Insurance Fund
EU-SILC	European Union Statistics on Income and Living Conditions
EVS	European Values Study
FA	extended family model
GDP	gross domestic product
HP	Hodrick-Prescott
ILO	International Labour Organization or Office
LLSI	limiting long-standing illness
LM	labour market
LMP	labour market policy or programme
LS	life satisfaction
NEET	not in education, employment or training
PC	PLMP coverage
PG	PLMP generosity
PLMP	passive labour market policy or programme
PPP	purchasing power parity
PPS	power purchasing standards
PRI	proportional reduction in inconsistency
QCA	qualitative comparative analysis
UE	aggregate unemployment
UIF	Unemployment Insurance Fund
UR	unemployment rate
YGS	Youth Guarantee Scheme

Country codes

AT	Austria
BE	Belgium
BG	Bulgaria

CZ	Czech Republic
DE	Germany
DK	Denmark
EE	Estonia
EL	Greece
ES	Spain
FI	Finland
FR	France
HU	Hungary
IE	Ireland
IT	Italy
LT	Lithuania
LV	Latvia
NL	Netherlands
PL	Poland
PT	Portugal
RO	Romania
SK	Slovakia
UK	United Kingdom

Level of education

LE	low level of education, ISCED scale levels 0–2
ME	medium level of education, ISCED scale levels 3–4
HE	high level of education, ISCED scale levels 5–8

Employment status

NCJ	non-contractual job
NEET	not in education, employment or training
PE	permanent employment
TE	temporary employment
U	unemployment

Notes on contributors

Christina Athanasiades is Associate Professor of Counselling Psychology at the Department of Psychology, Aristotle University of Thessaloniki, Greece. Her research focuses on school (career) counselling, school bullying, gender equality issues, and violence against women.

Anna Baranowska-Rataj is Associate Professor at the Department of Sociology and Centre for Demographic and Ageing Research (CEDAR), Umeå University, Sweden. Her research interests concern processes at the intersections of the labour market as well as health and well-being of family members.

Sonia Bertolini is Associate Professor at the Department of Cultures, Politics and Society, University of Turin, Italy, where she teaches sociology of work. Her research interests include youth labour market entry, female labour market participation, labour market flexibilisation, and transition to adult life.

Vassiliki Deliyanni-Kouimtzi is Professor Emeritus of the School of Psychology, Aristotle University of Thessaloniki, Greece. Her teaching and research interests have been in the areas of gender and education, youth studies, and women's studies. She is the author of several books and articles in both English and Greek.

Lia Figgou is Associate Professor of Social Psychology at the School of Psychology, Aristotle University of Thessaloniki, Greece. Her research interests lie in the study of intergroup relations, discrimination, and social exclusion through qualitative research methods.

Anastasia Flouli is a PhD student at the School of Psychology, Aristotle University of Thessaloniki, Greece. Her research interests include gender equality issues, sex-based violence, feminist psychology, and qualitative research methods.

Michael Gebel is Professor of Methods of Empirical Social Research at the University of Bamberg, Germany. His research focuses on the transition to adulthood, atypical employment, unemployment, international comparative research, and quantitative methods.

Chiara Ghislieri is Associate Professor of Work and Organisational Psychology at the University of Turin, Italy. Her research interests include the work–family balance, well-being at work, leadership and followership, and vocational guidance.

Valentina Goglio is a postdoctoral fellow at the Department of Cultures, Politics and Society, University of Turin, Italy. Her research interests lie at the intersection between education and the labour market dealing with the organisation of higher education systems, digital higher education, skills, and the labour market situation of youth.

Katerina Gousia is a research associate at the School of Social Policy, Sociology and Social Research, University of Kent, England. Her research interests include labour economics and the economics of ageing and long-term care.

Jelena Helemäe is a senior research fellow at the Institute of International Social Studies, Tallinn University, Estonia. Her research focuses on social mobility, ethnic inequality, and gender inequality.

Dirk Hofäcker is Professor of Quantitative Methods of Social Research at the University of Duisburg-Essen, Germany. His main research interests include comparative welfare state and labour market research, social inequality, social security, and pensions.

Maria Jeliazkova is Associate Professor of Sociology at the Institute of Philosophy and Sociology of the Bulgarian Academy of Sciences, Bulgaria. She works in the fields of anti-poverty strategies, employment and unemployment, inequalities, and welfare.

Margarita Kazjulja is a research fellow at the Institute of International Social Studies, Tallinn University, Estonia. Her research interests include education and different aspects of social stratification in the labour market.

Janika Kletzing was scientific assistant at the Institute for Social Work and Social Policy at the University of Duisburg-Essen, Germany, until 2018.

Małgorzata Kłobuszewska is an economist (PhD, University of Warsaw) and researcher at the Educational Research Institute University of Warsaw, Poland. She specialises in applied micro-econometric analysis in the field of the economics of education and labour. Her research interests include parental expenditure on education, vocational education, and youth in the labour market.

Veneta Krasteva is Associate Professor of Sociology at the Institute of Philosophy and Sociology in the Bulgarian Academy of Sciences, Bulgaria. Her main research interests include poverty and social exclusion, employment and unemployment, social policies, and welfare reforms.

Triin Lauri is Associate Professor of Public Policy and researcher at Tallinn University, Estonia. Her main research interests include comparative social policy and policy, politics, and the distributional effects of social investment policies in Baltic countries.

Gintare Malisauskaite is a research associate at the Personal Social Services Research Unit in the School of Social Policy, Sociology and Social Research, University of Kent, England. Her research interests include healthcare policy evaluations and the economics of ageing and long-term care.

Antonella Meo is Associate Professor of Sociology at the University of Turin, Italy. Her main research interests include social vulnerability and inequality dynamics, poverty and social exclusion, social policies, and local welfare.

Douhomir Minev is a professor with a Doctor of Science in Sociology and a PhD in Economics. He works in the fields of economic and social development, social risks and the knowledge society, and has long-term experience in reviewing, analysing, and making recommendations on public policies.

Valentina Moiso is Assistant Professor of Sociology at the Department of Cultures, Politics and Society, University of Turin, Italy. Her research interests include household finance and social vulnerability, economic socialisation and the social construction of money practices, as well as Islamic finance.

Rosy Musumeci is Assistant Professor of the Sociology of Cultural and Communication Processes at the Department of Cultures, Politics and Society, University of Turin, Italy. Her research interests include the work–life balance with particular regard to the transition to parenthood, youth working careers, as well as gender imbalances in careers and academic institutions.

Olena Nizalova is a senior research fellow (Associate Professor) in Health Economics at the University of Kent, England. Her research interests include the interaction between the labour market, family responsibilities, and health outcomes.

Marta Palczyńska is an economist at the Institute for Structural Research and a PhD student at the SGH Warsaw School of Economics, Poland. Her work focuses on the analysis of skills and gender wage gaps, educational mismatches, and the evaluation of youth labour market policies.

Epp Reiska graduated in sociology with an MA and works as a research assistant at the Institute of International Social Studies, Tallinn University, Estonia. Her main tasks include providing administrative support for the institute's research projects and managing the journal *Studies of Transition States and Societies* published by the institute.

Roberta Ricucci is Associate Professor of the Sociology of International Mobility at the University of Turin, Italy. Her research focuses on migration and Muslims, immigrant children's education and socio-economic inclusion, as well as identity-building processes and religiousness in the diaspora.

Magdalena Rokicka is an economist (PhD, University of Essex), and a former assistant professor at the Educational Research Institute, University of Warsaw, Poland. She specialises in quantitative methods of data analysis. Her research interests include applied micro-econometric analysis of education, labour market, time use, and gender-related issues.

Eve-Liis Roosmaa is a researcher and lecturer in sociology at the Institute of International Social Studies and School of Governance, Law, and Society, Tallinn University, Estonia. Her main research interests are in education, lifelong learning, and the labour market in different institutional contexts.

Sina Schadow is a research fellow at the University of Kassel, Germany, in the Institute of Economic and Vocational Education. Her research interests include youth unemployment, social inequality, welfare policies and social security systems, and qualitative methods.

Christoph Schlee is a research associate and PhD student in methods of empirical social research at the Department of Sociology, University of Bamberg, Germany. His research focuses on unemployment, atypical employment, transition to adulthood, and qualitative research methods.

Martina Sourvinou is a PhD student at the School of Psychology, Aristotle University of Thessaloniki, Greece. Her research interests include the social psychology of citizenship, politics, and qualitative research methods.

Jędrzej Stasiowski is a sociologist and research assistant at the Educational Research Institute, University of Warsaw, Poland. His research interests include graduate tracking, evaluation of educational and labour market policies, life course transitions, unemployment, and social exclusion.

Mattias Strandh is Professor of Social Work at Umeå University and at the Centre for Research on Child and Adolescent Mental Health, Karlstad University, Sweden. His research interests include the interrelationship between health, school outcomes, and unemployment as well as the microlevel impact of policy and policy configurations.

Marti Taru works as a researcher at Tallinn University, Estonia. His main areas of interest are employment, active labour market policies, social inclusion and exclusion, young people and public policy, and the evaluation of public policies.

Paola Maria Torrioni is Associate Professor at the Department of Cultures, Politics, and Society, University of Turin, Italy, where she teaches family, gender, and socialisation. Her research interests include gender and family, welfare policies and cultural processes, transition to parenthood, and ageing.

Kadri Täht is Associate Professor and Senior Researcher at Tallinn University, Estonia. Her main research interests include labour market transitions and interactions between work and family.

Marge Unt is Professor of Comparative Sociology and Head of the Institute of International Social Studies, Tallinn University, Estonia. Her main research interests include life course transitions in comparative perspective, and especially the transition to adulthood, as well as labour market research.

Zofia Włodarczyk is a PhD candidate in the Department of Sociology with designated emphasis on human rights at the University of California, Davis, USA. Her research interests include gender in Central and Eastern Europe, women's rights, migration, and domestic violence.

Despoina Xanthopoulou is Associate Professor of Organisational Psychology at the School of Psychology, Aristotle University of Thessaloniki, Greece. Her research interests include job (re)design, job and personal resources, well-being, and recovery from job demands.

Preface and acknowledgements

This book is being finalised in the middle of the COVID-19 crisis that is putting so much pressure on health care systems, changing global value chains and shaking global labour markets. This is placing the most vulnerable groups – and these also include youth – at a higher risk of social exclusion. Youth is a generation at the turning point in their personal lives at a time when their social contacts and access to the labour market are being severely disrupted by lockdown measures in the pandemic. This volume brings together spirited academic discussions and the diligent work of scholars across Europe who have been researching and reflecting on the implications of labour market insecurity since the Great Recession in 2008–09 and the subsequent debt crisis, and drawing lessons that are highly relevant in the current situation.

The book is one of the milestones marking a long academic journey. The academic community contributing to this volume consists of researchers based in Bulgaria, Estonia, Germany, Greece, Italy, Poland, Sweden, Ukraine, and the United Kingdom (UK). The chapters of this book are only a small part of the vast output of the project 'Social Exclusion of Youth in Europe: Cumulative Disadvantage, Coping Strategies, Effective Policies, and Transfer' (EXCEPT). An extensive list of working papers, policy briefs, links to academic publications, videos, and photos is available on the project website: except-project.eu. Thank you to all who contributed, all members of the EXCEPT project, experts, policymakers, advisory board members, and youth organisations who have formed a great academic community and made such an exciting and productive project. Since 2018, the European Cooperation in Science and Technology (COST) Action 'Transdisciplinary solutions to cross sectoral disadvantage in youth (YOUNG-IN)' has provided a major framework to expand the geographical scope and continue academic exchange on youth facing the risk of social exclusion. We are grateful to YOUNG-IN Coordinator Prof. Anu Toots and all colleagues from 33 countries for the enriched discussions and feedback that helped us greatly when finalising the chapters for the edited volume.

In the course of this extended journey, some steps especially need to be highlighted. We kicked off discussion about this book in June 2015 in Tallinn at the first meeting of EXCEPT at which the foundations of the project were agreed and the first heated debates on qualitative comparative methodology were held. In October 2015, we met up in Turin to agree on the set-up of our pan-European qualitative study aiming to give voice especially to youth in precarious situations. We found that we were able to reach a fertile compromise in bringing together different approaches to qualitative research. The next step in our journey was the meeting at Bamberg in February 2016 where we drew on excellent policy insights from many academics including our advisory board members Professor Jale Tosun (Coordinator of CUPESSE, University of Heidelberg) and Ruth Santos-Brien (Programme Director of Public Policy, ICF). This meeting also marked the clear dedication of our project to more responsible research by prioritising the involvement of youth and also deciding to hold future meetings in places where young people face especially high labour market insecurity in the form of high youth unemployment. We are grateful that we were able to meet in Sofia in September 2016 and in Warsaw in February 2017 to discuss results on how policies moderate the effect of labour market insecurity and whether one can detect scarring effects over the life course. We also especially want to thank our advisory board member Dr Caroline Dewilde (Coordinator of HOWCOME, University of Tilburg) for her valuable feedback on our analysis of youth autonomy. The last major project consortium meeting took place in Thessaloniki in August 2017. We are grateful to the major policy forum and our advisory board members Dr Vanessa Di Paola and Dr Virginie Mora (Aix–Marseille University) for productive discussion of the findings gained from the rich interviews with youth in nine European countries including Bulgaria, Estonia, Germany, Greece, Italy, Poland, Sweden, Ukraine, and the UK. The next meeting in Catania in April 2018 provided a further round of feedback from editors. We thank all involved in the kind hosting of project meetings and the spirit-raising social events at Tallinn University, Turin University, Bamberg University, the Institute of the Study of Societies and Knowledge of the Bulgarian Academy of Sciences, the Educational Research Institute, and Aristotle University of Thessaloniki. Especially now, in the era of virtual meetings, we realise just how much physical presence helps in triggering new ideas, engaging in heated debates when discussing the ongoing work, and gaining invaluable feedback, all of which helps to refine ideas and methodologies and maintain a high level of motivation.

We have been really blessed to be able to meet in person not only with our co-researchers but also youth workers and policymakers across Europe, including the Ukraine. We express our gratitude to Olena Nizalova and Rowena Merritt for leading the outstanding dissemination of our work resulting in a fact sheet published by the

EU Commission, *Making research results work for society: sharing knowledge and informing policy*, in which the EXCEPT project was mentioned as a good example of a project that is successful in reaching out to policymakers.

Some of the book chapters have been presented at numerous international conferences and expert seminars including a special session at the Work, Employment and Society conference at the University of Leeds, UK, in 2016, together with the EU-funded Strategic Transitions for Youth Labour in Europe (STYLE) and CUPESSE projects; at the expert group meeting, *The role of families and family policy in supporting youth transitions*, at Doha International Family Institute, Qatar, 2018; an employment seminar at the International Labour Office, Geneva, Switzerland; and a special symposium at the 36th International Labour Process Conference in Buenos Aires, Argentina, 2018. Our research was enriched by exchange with the EU-funded CatchEyoU (Constructing AcTive CitizensHip with European Youth) project and by our Norway-based sister project NEGOTIATE-research.no (Negotiating Early Job Insecurity and Labour Market Exclusion in Europe). We also benefited greatly from further discussions and exchange about some of the book chapters at meetings of the YOUNG-IN network in Thessaloniki, Greece and in Valletta, Malta in 2019.

This book would not have been possible without generous support from the European Union's Horizon 2020 research and innovation programme under grant agreement No 649496 (EXCEPT) and from COST Action CA17114 (YOUNG-IN). European funding made it possible to carry out truly comparative research, gain insights from country experts, and give voice to youth by carrying out qualitative interviews in nine countries. We are deeply indebted for the careful guidance, support, and encouragement provided across the project and beyond by our project officer at the Research Executive Agency, Kerstin Wilde. The views expressed here are those of the authors and do not necessarily reflect the official opinions of the European Union.

Maybe even more importantly, European Union funding enabled us to build up a spirited research community and develop close personal friendships across Europe. The editors of this book became 'infected' with comparative research as PhD students while participating in large-scale research projects led by Professors Hans Peter Blossfeld and Irena Kogan, and we hope we have spread this positive 'virus' to young scholars. It is such a great pleasure to see how a project like this can contribute to the creation of a pan-European academic community and inspire numerous brilliant young researchers to continue in comparative research.

In this research, we have learned a lot from young people who have experienced job exclusion and labour market insecurity. We express our deepest gratitude to the 386 young persons who shared their life worlds and dreams via in-depth interviews as they made their way towards adulthood; to all the others who participated at rant box, graffiti wall, and numerous other events; and to those who reviewed the key findings of the project and wrote a summary for other young people. At the beginning of each section of the volume, you will see a photo taken by a young person that was submitted to the EXCEPT photo competition 'Youth Vision: Becoming adult today'. We thank all the young people who actively took part and sent in 117 photos showing visually what becoming an adult means for young people today. These photos were exhibited at Bamberg University, Germany, at the Estonian Presidency of the Council of the EU conference 'European Research Excellence – Impact and Value for Society' and at Tallinn University, Estonia; at the Museum of Work History, Turin, Italy; at a parliamentary reception in the House of Commons, London, UK; at the Educational Research Institute, Warsaw, Poland; at the 16th Conference of the Hellenic Psychological Society in Thessaloniki, Greece; at the workshop 'Uncertain pensions – lesser pensions' at Duisburg-Essen University, Germany; and at the Estonian Liaison Office for the EU Framework Programme for Research and Technological Development in Brussels, Belgium, between 2016 and 2019. We hope the findings of this book will contribute to a broader understanding of the life experiences of those young persons who fail to gain a stable foothold in the labour market, and be of benefit to policymakers in their work to empower the next generation through life course policies.

We cannot conclude without a note on the 'EXCEPT kids': nine babies were born to researchers during the lifetime of the EXCEPT project. They are all too vibrant proof of the ability to combine research and family transitions, and we hope that the energy we put into understanding and explaining the consequences of labour market insecurity will help to fine-tune policy interventions for their generation.

The editors are grateful to the contributors for their diligent work and patience in responding to our numerous requests for revisions to their manuscripts. Many thanks to Epp Reiska and Léa Gérard for research assistance during the editing process. Jonathan Harrow's careful and critical editing ensured the quality of language in our

Preface and acknowledgements

publication. Importantly, the staff at Policy Press, particularly Laura Vickers-Rendall, provided great support throughout the production of this book, and we are also thankful to the anonymous reviewers for very helpful comments.

As editors, we were inspired by the topic, the approach, the rich data, and the great pan-European academic community. Therefore, we have brought together the main results in one volume to facilitate the dissemination of our findings on vulnerable youth life courses embedded in their country context, characterised by different institutional, structural, and cultural frames of reference.

Thank you to all who shared this stimulating academic journey!

Marge Unt, Sonia Bertolini, Vassiliki Deliyanni-Kouimtzi,
Michael Gebel, and Dirk Hofäcker
Pärnu, Turin, Thessaloniki, Bamberg,
and Duisburg-Essen, January, 2021

EXCEPT project has received funding from the European Union's Horizon 2020 research and innovation programme under grant agreement No. 649496.

This publication is based upon work from COST Action YOUNG-IN, supported by COST (European Cooperation in Science and Technology).

1

Introduction: Youth transitions in times of labour market insecurity

Michael Gebel, Marge Unt, Sonia Bertolini,
Vassiliki Deliyanni-Kouimtzi, and Dirk Hofäcker

Description of the problem and research questions

Labour market insecurities are widespread among young people in Europe, and they represent a key challenge to society. Comparative research has shown that, across Europe, youth often experience labour market exclusion in terms of periods of unemployment and episodes of being not in employment, education, or training (NEET) (Eurofound, 2012; Dietrich, 2013; Lange et al, 2014; O'Reilly et al, 2015; Rokicka et al, 2018). Moreover, if young people actually do find a job, they often face job insecurity in the form of temporary jobs (Baranowska and Gebel, 2010; Karamessini et al, 2019; Passaretta and Wolbers, 2019). Indeed, labour market insecurities hit young people more often than the rest of the population in Europe (Breen, 2005; Baranowska and Gebel, 2010).

However, counter to the rhetoric in public and political debates, trend studies cannot confirm a general increase in youth NEET and temporary employment over time (Gebel and Giesecke, 2016). Instead, there are strong cyclical components, because youth are affected specifically by business cycle fluctuations (Dietrich, 2013; Lange et al, 2014). They were affected particularly during crises such as the 2008 financial crisis and the subsequent debt and Eurozone crises (Choudhry et al, 2012; Marques and Hörisch, 2020). Such crises are expected to have a potentially detrimental effect on the future of these young people in the form of 'scar effects' (Unt and Täht, 2020). Indeed, concerns have been raised as to whether the so-called Great Recession has produced a 'lost generation' of young people (Hur, 2018). It is still too early to assess the full impact of the current COVID-19 pandemic on youth labour markets, but indications suggest that it is giving rise to the most severe economic recession for decades in most European countries, and prevailing uncertainty about prospects and projections give great cause for concern.

European comparative research has highlighted that the extent of youth labour market problems varies widely across countries (Saar et al, 2008; Karamessini et al, 2019; O'Reilly et al, 2019a, 2019b; Dvouletý et al, 2020). Previous research has revealed that this cross-country variation can be related to differences in the structural, institutional, and cultural contexts across Europe. In this respect, policies come into play that modify contexts in such a way that they improve youth labour market chances (Lahusen et al, 2013; Caliendo and Schmidl, 2016; Hora et al, 2019).

Since the 1990s and particularly following the financial crisis in 2008, this problem has been a high priority for policymakers at both national and European levels, and numerous initiatives have been developed to overcome it. For example, the Europe 2020 strategy makes explicit reference to promoting youth employment chances through better education policies. The Youth on the Move flagship initiative aims to improve the qualifications and labour market integration of youth (European Commission, 2010a) and the European Social Fund Youth Opportunities Initiative has promoted vocational and apprenticeship training for youth to support smooth transitions from education to work (European Commission, 2011). In 2012, the EU launched the Youth Guarantee Scheme (YGS) which promised to offer good quality jobs or education opportunities (for example apprenticeships) for young people facing labour market problems (Eichhorst and Rinne, 2017; Escudero and Mourelo, 2017). In 2016, the YGS was extended to support school-to-work transition under the Investing in Europe's Youth programme, and also to provide better opportunities through education and training systems, and learning mobility (European Commission, 2016). The YGS, as an open method of coordination, does not prescribe one common active labour market policy (ALMP), but calls for alignment to specific local circumstances and mutual learning (Tosun et al 2017; Tosun et al, 2019a). In their European comparative study, Tosun et al (2019a) have shown that the YGS led to some catching-up and convergence with regard to the sectoral coverage of active labour market policies, but also to divergence in the number of policies. Regarding the risks of social exclusion, the Europe 2020 strategy integrated guidelines for economic and employment policies that also propagated active inclusion policies for vulnerable young people. Next to the EU-level initiatives, a large array of policy measures in different education, labour market, and social policy fields exist on national and regional levels that aim to improve youth labour market integration and social inclusion.

Against this background, the first central research question emerging in this book asks about *the consequences of labour market insecurities for young people*. The book addresses the multifaceted consequences that arise on the individual level, in order to find out what the implications are for the young persons affected. To capture this multidimensionality, research is framed in the field of social exclusion. The concept of social exclusion is particularly relevant for youth and has been on the agenda of European social policies for some time. One example is the Europe 2020 flagship initiative European Platform against Poverty and Social Exclusion (European Commission, 2010b). Specifically, the researchers in this book investigate the implications of experiencing individual labour market insecurities for the subjective well-being and health of young people, their chances of gaining autonomy through leaving the parental home, of gaining economic independence from parents, as well as their short-, medium-, and long-term economic situation in terms of their risk of poverty and material deprivation, together with their eligibility for social security. This comprehensive view offers an opportunity to identify the complex interrelationships and potential risks of cumulative disadvantage.

The second central research question relates to the *coping strategies and compensatory mechanisms that facilitate social inclusion for disadvantaged youth*. While it is important to understand what the consequences of labour market insecurity are, it is also important to understand what can be done to mitigate negative consequences (O'Rand, 2009). Mitigation can function on various levels. This book refers to coping strategies and compensatory mechanisms on the microlevel and the mesolevel. First of all, the young person who is affected has the agency to deal with the emerging problems and try to mitigate the consequences or find ways to compensate for the negative effects of experiencing labour market insecurity. Moreover, family members, friends, and local communities and neighbourhoods can step in and help young people who are in need (Tosun et al, 2019b; Tosun et al, 2021). Finally, other mesolevel actors which the young person has to deal with or contacts voluntarily such as public employment agencies can also intervene to provide help (Shore and Tosun, 2019).

On the macrolevel, policies are designed to help mitigate the risks of social exclusion that may arise in response to labour market insecurities (Lahusen et al, 2013; Caliendo and Schmidl, 2016). This leads to the third central research question: *Which policies are effective in mitigating the negative effects of labour market insecurity*? Because this book studies the multifaceted consequences of labour market insecurity for the risk of social exclusion, it is important to investigate the various policy fields that exist to address specific social exclusion risks. This complements the great majority of studies on how policies can reduce youth labour market problems by investigating which policies can actually help those young people who are currently affected by labour market insecurity. As long as youth labour market problems continue to exist, it is also necessary to know how to help young people who are affected.

In sum, this book addresses the following three central research questions:

1. What are the multifaceted consequences on the individual level of labour market insecurities for young people's risk of social exclusion?
2. What coping strategies and compensatory mechanisms on the individual level and the mesolevel facilitate social inclusion for disadvantaged youth?
3. Which policies are effective in terms of mitigating the negative effects of labour market insecurities on young people's risk of social exclusion?

The following section briefly reviews the state of the art regarding comparative research on youth labour market insecurities and explains the present innovative contribution of this edited volume to the existing literature and its main research aims. The next section introduces the multilevel theoretical model that acts as the conceptual and theoretical backbone of this book. This is followed by an explanation of the multimethod comparative approach adopted in this European project. The final section outlines the structure of the book and the individual chapters.

State of the art, innovative contribution, and main aims

There have been several European comparative studies on various determinants of individual-level labour market insecurity. These include, for example, the major volumes by O'Reilly et al (2019a, 2019b) which offer a systematic comparison of European youth labour markets. Moreover, based on three-generational interviews in eleven European countries, Tosun et al (2019b, 2021) have substantially increased knowledge on the role and intergenerational transmission of values and norms as important supply-side determinants of youth labour market chances. Based on the same data, Dvouletý et al (2020) have documented a variety of individual-level and family background variables as predictors of unemployment in young adults. There is also a long tradition of European comparative studies on the macrolevel determinants of individual-level labour market insecurity that emphasise the role of economic and other structural conditions such as globalisation, youth cohort size, educational expansion, or occupational upgrading (Gangl, 2002; Lange et al, 2014); the education and training system (Shavit and Müller, 1998; Müller and Gangl, 2003; Kogan et al, 2011); labour market regulation and institutions (Breen, 2005; Baranowska and Gebel, 2010; Barbieri et al, 2016; Gebel and Giesecke, 2016); and active and passive labour market policies (ALMPs and PLMPs) (Hvinden et al, 2019a; Marques and Hörisch, 2020).

However, there is much less European comparative research on the consequences of individual-level labour market insecurity for young people. Notable exceptions are Blossfeld et al's (2005) comparative studies on the effects of temporary employment and unemployment on the timing of leaving the parental home, and Hvinden et al's (2019b) work on the multitude of effects of job insecurity on well-being, drug use, and later wage consequences. In a comparative qualitative study of six European countries, Kieselbach et al (2001) provided in-depth insights into the social exclusion experiences of long-term unemployed youth. Moreover, there are a few comparative studies on the moderating role of social inequality, education policies, labour market conditions, and institutions in aggravating or mitigating the job insecurity effect (Stasiowski and Kłobuszewska, 2018; Högberg et al, 2019a, 2019b; Täht et al, 2020).

Thus, previous research has focused mainly on the drivers of youth labour market problems. However, given that despite all political efforts many young people experience labour market insecurity, it is not only the drivers but also the consequences that have become a growing concern. Given that the youth transition period is a central stage which affects every aspect of the individual's future life course, this key topic urgently warrants further attention. This book addresses exactly this research gap by studying the *multifaceted consequences of labour market insecurities on risks of social exclusion*. Specifically, as mentioned before, it investigates how individual-level labour market insecurities affect the subjective well-being and health of young people, their chance of gaining autonomy by leaving the parental home, their chance of gaining economic independence from parents, as well as their short-, medium-, and long-term economic situation in terms of their risk of poverty and material deprivation, together with their eligibility for social security. In this way, the book overcomes the limitations of previous research that focused on single dimensions, and it adds new evidence on dimensions that have not yet been in the spotlight of research. Nonetheless, it has to be acknowledged that there are further dimensions of social exclusion in terms of, for example, deviant behaviour, social participation, and political participation, however it goes beyond the scope of this book to focus on an in-depth understanding of these dimensions.

Moreover, the book augments the existing literature by conducting empirical analyses that are framed in a *common theoretical multilevel model*. The backbone of this model is the microlevel analysis of the effects of labour market insecurities on various risks of social exclusion in a dynamic and life course perspective. Following the seminal study by Gallie and Paugam (2000), the social consequences of labour market exclusion should be understood as a dynamic process of social exclusion acting as a downward spiral of progressive disadvantages. Thus, next to approaching the issue of youth social exclusion from a standard cross-sectional social-indicator-based perspective, the book seeks to gain new insights by analysing the timing, ordering, and causal interrelationships of youth experiences of labour market insecurities and various other dimensions of social exclusion from a dynamic individual-level perspective. This dynamic process perspective is complemented with a life course perspective by providing an analysis of the short-and long-term consequences of labour market insecurity for multiple risks of social exclusion for young people. Regarding the mesolevel in terms of families/households, communities, and organisations (firms, public employment agencies, and so on), the book studies how these other actors either support young people in mitigating or compensating for the negative effects of labour market insecurities or in some circumstances worsen their situation. Similarly, it investigates how the institutional, structural, and cultural macrolevel context either buffers or worsens the effects of labour market insecurities on risks of social exclusion.

On the macrolevel, the specific objective of the book is to study contextual effects, particularly the role of *labour market, economic, family, housing, and social policies* in aggravating or mitigating the negative effects of labour market insecurities. Whereas previous policy-related research has looked mainly at the effects of policies on labour market insecurity itself, this book adds another important perspective by focusing on the moderating role of policies on the effects of labour market insecurity on young people's risk of social exclusion. Previous research is also partly challenged, because policies can have different effects as a driver of insecurities or as a moderator of the consequences of insecurities. Based on multilevel analyses, this book highlights relevant policy conclusions, outlining the context and policies supporting young people in disadvantaged labour market positions. Whereas some chapters single out the effects of specific policies by taking a macroindicator approach, other chapters aim to understand the combined effect of policies by using a country-typology approach.

Another specific aim and contribution of this book is its *multimethod and European comparative approach*. European comparative research has highlighted that the extent of labour market problems for young people varies widely across countries (for example, Blossfeld et al, 2008, 2011; O'Reilly et al, 2015; Tosun et al, 2019b, 2021). This book uses a multimethod design to study how the consequences of labour market problems differ across Europe. Whereas such a design is not innovative per se, the rigorous implementation of a European comparative design in each chapter is one of the book's original contributions. Chapters providing comparative quantitative analyses of European microdata use empirical multilevel analyses to quantify the moderating role of the macrolevel context and, specifically, the effects of policies. The unique innovation lies in the chapters applying a European comparative qualitative approach (Bertolini et al, 2018). This is an especially valuable contribution, given the almost complete lack of comparative qualitative literature on young people's perceptions of labour market exclusion and job insecurity. Thus, it overcomes the limits of previous qualitative research that focused on single countries and aims to generate new findings by listening to the voice of young people in various European countries.

Theoretical multilevel model

This book focuses on *young people*, using the terms *youth* and *young adults* as synonyms. Static age definitions (for example, 15–24 years) as commonly imposed are not practicable for the present research purposes. Given the research interest in the consequences of labour market integration problems, it is necessary to investigate young people who have already left the education system, and this does not apply to all members of a specific age group. Because the labour market entry process has been delayed in recent decades due to educational expansion (Buchmann and Kriesi, 2011), a low upper age limit cannot be imposed. It would systematically exclude young people who have experienced higher education. Because the book also aims to investigate labour market integration problems and the consequences these have for young people with higher education, it applies a higher upper age limit. Moreover, given the interest in both the short- and long-term consequences of labour market problems in the early career stage, it is also necessary to look at a longer period following the transition from education to work. Hence, the book follows the life course paradigm and considers life course events and their consequences from an individual *dynamic perspective* (Elder et al, 2004; Mayer, 2009).

The individual-level dynamic perspective is also highly relevant when studying *social exclusion as a dynamic process* (Gallie et al, 2003). The book studies social exclusion from a life course perspective, looking not only at the short term but also at the medium- and long-term consequences for later life periods. The dynamic process and life course perspectives are crucial to better detecting mechanisms that could combat or compensate for youth social exclusion.

Following insights from previous research (Gallie et al, 2003), in this book, social exclusion is understood as a *multidimensional concept* that entails economic, social, and psychological consequences. Whereas labour market exclusion can be seen as part of the broader concept of social exclusion, this dimension is singled out as a key explanatory variable because of the interest in the impact of labour market exclusion on other dimensions of social exclusion which are treated as outcome variables. As mentioned earlier, the focus is on the subjective well-being and health of young adults, their chances of gaining autonomy by leaving the parental home, their chances of gaining economic independence from parents and forming their own families, as well as their short- and long-term economic situation in terms of risks of poverty and material deprivation, together with their eligibility for social security.

Another important aspect of life course theory that is taken into account here is that individual agency and life courses are socially embedded in higher-level contexts. The individual agency of young people is bound closely to the opportunities and constraints in their family, friends, and community. At the same time, families, schools, companies, youth centres, and public employment agencies are constrained in their opportunities and choices by the institutional, structural, and cultural macrocontext at the national level. National level policies influence and are influenced by EU-level initiatives through the set of programmes and measures such as the YGS. Figure 1.1 illustrates the *theoretical multilevel model* in this respect.

The microlevel context

The book analyses the effect of labour market exclusion and job insecurity on various dimensions of social exclusion on the microlevel.

Figure 1.1: Theoretical multilevel model

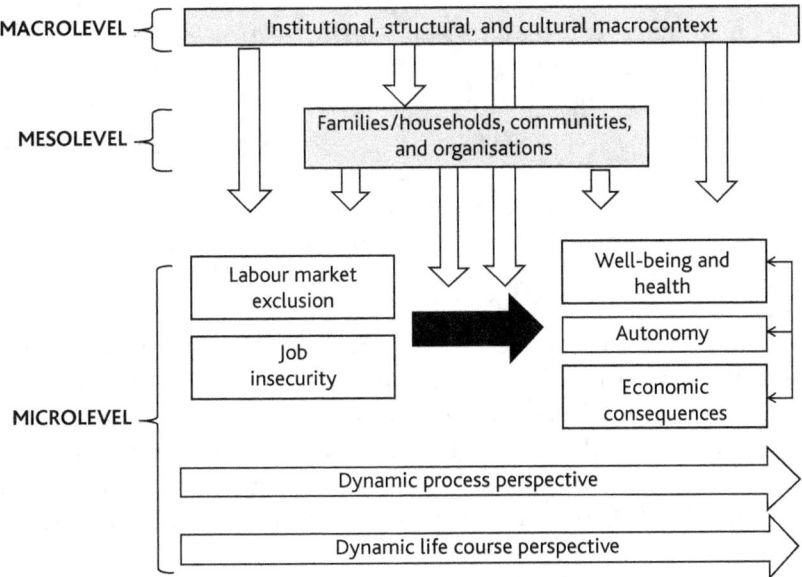

Source: Author's own

From a life course perspective, this addresses the important aspect of intraindividual spillover effects, because it investigates how one life domain (work) affects other life domains. Some chapters also investigate crossover effects – that is, interindividual effects of the life course of one person on the life course of another person. In general, on the individual level, it is important to analyse the decisions of individual agents who make choices and reach compromises regarding different alternatives and the implications that arise from these. It is also relevant to understand the subjective perspectives of young people and how they perceive and cope with the consequences of labour market insecurities.

Labour market exclusion and job insecurity are the key microlevel explanatory variables. *Labour market exclusion* is defined here as NEET (Eurofound, 2012). Overcoming the shortcomings of the stricter concept of *youth unemployment* (young people who are not employed but are available and actively searching for work), the NEET concept also makes it possible to capture youth who become discouraged and give up any job search as well as inactive persons who cannot or do not want to work. The analyses here acknowledge this heterogeneity within the NEET group (Eurofound, 2012). They do not apply a broader conception that defines labour market exclusion as also being part of the secondary labour market segment – that is, as being excluded from good jobs in the primary segment. This is because this aspect is already partly covered in the definition of job insecurity.

Regarding the theoretical concept of *job insecurity*, the book distinguishes between objective and subjective job insecurity (de Witte, 2010). For example, questions about the fear or expectations of job loss in the near future can be used as measures of the subjective feeling of job insecurity. Objective indicators relate to the type of contract such as temporary work contracts, temporary agency work, seasonal/casual work, or non-contractual informal work arrangements that are all usually accompanied by a high risk of job loss (Barbieri, 2009; Kalleberg, 2009).

The two major concepts of labour market exclusion and job insecurity are subsumed under the overarching concept of *labour market insecurity*. Hence, this key concept is defined on the individual level, because of the interest in the individual-level consequences of experiencing labour market insecurities. Moreover, labour market insecurities also come into play as a macrolevel factor that will be explained later.

On the individual level, various consequences of labour market insecurity for social exclusion are considered. The outcomes under scrutiny in the current project are young people's subjective well-being and health, autonomy and socio-economic situation. The key dependent variables are defined in the following paragraphs. The individual chapters of this book apply specific theories in order to explain how individual labour market insecurities affect the outcome dimensions.

From a conceptual point of view, a specific definition of *subjective well-being* is applied that includes a cognitive (that is, global judgements of life satisfaction) and an affective component of positive feelings (happiness) and negative feelings (sadness) (Diener, 2009). The book does not apply a wider definition of well-being including such aspects as material living conditions and individual economic and financial situations, because these dimensions are covered by other outcome variables. Regarding *health*, both subjective and objective indicators are used to rate the physical and psychological health status of young people (Jylhä, 2009).

Autonomy is conceptualised as housing and economic autonomy from the parental household. Broader conceptions of economic self-sufficiency also emphasise financial independence from the welfare state (Tosun et al, 2019b, 2021). Leaving the parental home and establishing an independent household can be regarded as one of the most important requirements for *housing autonomy* and achieving the status of an autonomous adult. Leaving the home of origin is a key marker of the transition to adulthood (Corijn and Klijzing, 2001). It implies not only housing independence but also greater social autonomy for young people (Billari, 2004). However, housing autonomy does not necessarily coincide with economic independence (Walther, 2006; Baranowska-Rataj et al, 2015). Hence, *economic autonomy* is considered as a second autonomy concept. This is a self-assessment of whether a young person's personal economic resources are sufficient to meet her or his own needs. Thus, economic autonomy is not dependent on a fixed threshold, but on the relative coherence between economic resources and needs. A low level of autonomy often implies economic dependence on the family (in terms of transfers) and/or the state (in terms of social benefits).

The socio-economic situation is also considered as a multidimensional phenomenon. Disadvantage may take different forms: On the one hand, it may refer to aspects of *income poverty* – that is, falling below an income threshold considered to reflect poverty (Sen, 1983). On the other hand, it may reflect *deprivation* in consumption levels in multiple domains (Nolan and Whelan, 1996). The aim here is to investigate socio-economic disadvantage from both an individual perspective (focusing on individual work or transfer income) and a household perspective (focusing on the material deprivation of the entire household in which a young person is living). Objective deprivation indicators will be contrasted with European young adults' subjective perceptions of their socio-economic situation. Furthermore, analyses are not restricted to the immediate socio-economic consequences of labour market uncertainty, but also investigate its impact in the medium and long term. In terms of long-term effects, one interest is in whether and to what extent young adults are able to make provision for social security and pensions, both publicly funded and private.

The moderating mesolevel context

On the *mesolevel*, the family is a central institution. Life course research emphasises that individual lives are strongly linked to those of relevant others such as parents, siblings, partners, friends, and neighbours (Mayer, 2009). This is expressed by the principle of *linked lives* which states that lives are interdependent and influenced by networks (Elder et al, 2004). Specifically, it is assumed that the resources and attitudes of the family of origin (parents, siblings, and relatives) and the family of destination (partner and partner's family) are relevant. Tosun et al (2019b, 2021) emphasise the role of values, personality traits, self-efficacy, subjective norms, and entrepreneurial orientation that are transmitted from parents to children and shown to be of great importance for youth labour market chances. In the literature on the transition to adulthood, it becomes evident that the family of origin plays an important role, influencing all the different components of the process such as the transition to work, to independence from the parental family, to personal autonomy, to sexuality, partnership, and parenthood, as well as to citizenship (Arnett, 2000).

Moreover, communities and organisations also come into play on the mesolevel. For example, schools and work environments have major socialising functions for young persons (Kraaykamp et al, 2019). Public employment services are important state organisations that should support and guide youth who face labour market problems (Shore and Tosun, 2019).

Thus, the mesolevel affects the probability of labour market insecurity as well as the outcome variables of interest – that is, individual health, well-being, autonomy, and socio-economic situation. However, the particular interest here is in the moderating effect of the mesolevel on the effects of labour market insecurity on the social exclusion outcome dimensions. In this regard, mesolevel actors are expected to play a central role for young people who are coping with the individual consequences of labour market insecurities. The individual chapters analysing the moderating mesocontext provide specific theoretical arguments on the causal mechanisms for moderating effects.

The moderating macrolevel context

Young people's individual life courses are socially embedded in the *institutional, structural, and cultural macrocontext*. This defines the set of opportunities and constraints that young people face when making their life course decisions and transitions (Leisering, 2003; Mayer, 2004; Blossfeld et al, 2005, 2008; Buchmann and Kriesi, 2011). The macrocontext varies across countries and, depending on the extent of federal state structures, also across regions within countries. Although the book refers to some EU policy initiatives that target youth, it does not address the role of the EU directly, because EU policies usually impact on individuals indirectly via national policies. The macrocontext influences the probability of young people experiencing labour market insecurities as well as the outcome variables. However, the particular interest here lies in its moderating effect – that is, how contextual factors moderate the individual-level effects of labour insecurities on the outcomes. From a multilevel analysis perspective, this represents a cross-level interaction – that is, how the *effect* of a microlevel variable on another microlevel variable is moderated by a macrolevel variable. The individual book chapters analysing the moderating macrocontext provide specific theoretical arguments on the causal mechanisms for moderating effects.

In terms of *structural factors,* the focus is on aggregate economic and labour market conditions. Economic conditions are best captured by the level of gross domestic product (GDP) and its growth rate. Business cycle fluctuations are also separated from long-term economic growth trends. In this way, the book also captures the role of the economic recession. Labour market conditions can be measured by the aggregate unemployment rate on the (national) macrolevel that may moderate the effects of individual-level labour market insecurity.

Regarding *institutional factors,* the book follows the example of earlier research (Blossfeld et al, 2005; Hora et al, 2019) and investigates the simultaneous influence of various policy dimensions. One important dimension is public regulation of the labour market. This is often conceptualised as employment protection regulation for regular work contracts and collective dismissals as well as the regulation of fixed-term contracts and temporary agency work. Another important dimension is active labour market policies such as further training measures, public job creation measures, counselling, and job search assistance provided by public employment services along with social work measures. Furthermore, the book analyses the role of PLMPs in relation to the generosity of unemployment benefits and social assistance (coverage, duration, and level of benefits). Public support for people in need also includes public social services such as provision of public employment services, childcare, healthcare, and social housing. Because the book also investigates housing autonomy, housing policy is also seen as a potential moderator of the individual-level effect of labour market insecurities on housing autonomy. Another institutional dimension of support is family allowances. For example, young people's parents may qualify for family allowances to support their children, or young people who have already formed a family may qualify for family allowances themselves. Finally, social security programmes targeted at later phases, such as social security and pension programmes, may be just as relevant to young people, given that people are increasingly expected to start saving for such programmes at an early stage in their working lives, and labour market uncertainty may keep young people from making such savings.

In terms of *cultural factors,* next to country differences in cultural norms on gender and gender-specific welfare state arrangements, the book considers the interregional differences in the functioning of the family. Scholars have identified considerable diversity in European family systems. They have contrasted family patterns in North-Western Europe, in which relationships between family members have grown weaker over the centuries, with those in Southern Europe, which are based on strong ties between family members (Papadopoulos and Roumpakis, 2013). There are also diverse patterns in Eastern Europe: some countries, such as Estonia, have an early home-leaving culture similar to Northern Europe; others, such as Croatia and Slovakia, have a late home-leaving culture similar to Southern Europe; whereas other Eastern European countries fall in between (Eurostat, 2020). Sociological research has often focused on how the family functions in Southern European cultures, highlighting its important role in offering affective and instrumental support for its members, because the family is considered to be the main provider of welfare in society. As a result of the 2008–09 financial crisis, these long-established patterns of intergenerational transfers and solidarities, which have played key roles in the transition to adulthood, may no longer remain intact – a phenomenon that can have dramatic consequences in young people's lives (Chisholm and Deliyianni-Kouimtzis, 2014).

Analytical perspectives of this book

The contributions to this book are guided by the novel multilevel theoretical model outlined in this section.

In general, all chapters take a cross-country comparative perspective, but they differ in their approach to studying the moderating influence of the macrocontext. Some chapters take a quantitative comparative approach and use macroindicators to figure out the effects of specific variables in the macrocontext. Other chapters summarise the macrocontext in typologies such as welfare state typologies (Esping-Andersen, 1990) in order to capture the joint effect of a combined set of structural, institutional, and cultural configurations.

In terms of the timing of these analyses, what all chapters have in common is that they analyse the experiences of youth in a period of financial crisis that includes *recession and austerity measures* in some countries, especially in South-Eastern Europe. Many countries have responded to recent crises by cuts in public spending and retrenchments of their welfare state, also referred to as austerity policies. The generosity of public benefits has been reduced, eligibility conditions have been tightened, and private responsibility for ensuring an individual's own welfare has been promoted. The findings presented in this book reflect these general circumstances in countries that are affected in different ways by economic recession and austerity measures.

It is important to note that the aim of this book is not to 'test' the multilevel and multidimensional theoretical model developed here or its components and relations in any strict sense. Such an endeavour is clearly beyond the scope of a single edited volume. Instead, the book aims to take the model as a conceptual 'umbrella' for several exemplary analyses, focusing on different outcome variables (health and well-being, autonomy, and socio-economic situation), analysing different sets of countries, and applying different methodologies (discussed in the following section). In doing so, it provides first insights into the usefulness of this new theoretical model. At the same time, it may be seen as an invitation to further scholars to apply this model in their own research.

Multimethod European comparative approach

A major goal of this book is to investigate the influence of the macrocontext using a *multi-method and European comparative approach*. Hence, it engages in comparative research by means of systematic quantitative or qualitative comparisons designed to determine the moderating influence of the macrocontext. This comparative approach is not based on a country case study design focusing on individual countries, because the interest is not in the features of a country itself; and it does not try to provide a full description of each country case. This is also the reason why the selection of countries differs between chapters. Countries are chosen systematically for their ability to cast light on the impact of the macrocontext on the specific topic under investigation. In general, one can distinguish two comparative approaches in such systematic investigations.

Chapters using *quantitative comparative analysis* apply statistical multilevel analyses on comparative microdata (Bryan and Jenkins 2016) to quantify the moderating role of the macrolevel context – specifically, the effects of policies. In order to attain a high degree of freedom for this statistical approach, chapters in which quantitative analysis is applied try to maximise the number of countries to be studied given data limitations. In the *indicator-based approach*, the complex macrocontext is broken down into separate dimensions that are operationalised as macroindicators with the aim of isolating the effect of the respective macrovariable. The isolation of the effect of the variable of interest is done by statistically controlling for other confounding macrovariables. In the *typology-based approach*, typologies of welfare regimes are applied to quantify the impact of bundles of structural, institutional, and cultural context factors.

In chapters using qualitative methods for comparative analysis, a number of approaches are taken. A specific *statistical approach*, qualitative comparative analysis (QCA), is used for comparative welfare state research (Emmenegger et al, 2013). Based on logical inference, combinations of macrocontext conditions are sought that determine the outcome of interest. In the *case-oriented approach*, a limited number of countries is investigated in a so-called small-N comparison (Ebbinghaus 2005). Depending on the design of the study, countries may be chosen that are known to be similar in many respects (most similar cases) or those with a particularly low degree of similarity (most different cases). The inclusion of particularly striking individual cases (deviant or extreme cases) can also be useful for testing theoretical assumptions. Justification is made either based on specific macrocontext conditions or by applying existing typologies of countries based on clusters of macrocontext conditions.

The qualitative versus quantitative comparative approach is also mirrored in the type of analyses on the individual level. Some chapters follow the *quantitative approach on the individual level* when studying individual-level effects of labour market insecurity on various outcome dimensions. Statistical techniques of multivariate data analysis are used to control for confounding variables on the microlevel in order to isolate the effect of labour market insecurity. Other chapters follow a qualitative approach on the individual level.

All these chapters draw on in-depth qualitative interviews that were collected in the framework of the Horizon 2020-funded EXCEPT project in which the editors and authors were engaged over several years (see, for details, Bertolini et al, 2018). The aim of this qualitative study was to gain a better understanding of the situation of youth experiencing labour market insecurity in different contexts, and especially to gain insights into how young people self-perceive their situation in different life domains and how they cope with risks of social exclusion. The unique qualitative comparative data make it possible to learn from the often overlooked and unheard voices and subjective perspectives of young people themselves. The interviews provide an in-depth understanding of how disadvantaged young people perceive their social situation and try to cope with it in different economic, institutional, and cultural environments.

A total of 386 interviews were conducted with youth from nine European countries representing different macrocontexts: Bulgaria, Estonia, Germany, Greece, Italy, Poland, Sweden, the Ukraine, and the UK. The samples were recruited using criteria which aimed to guarantee comparability but also to tap into national specificities. The sample in each country was composed of young people aged 18–30 years but with an oversampling of those aged 18–24 years in one of the following occupational conditions: NEET, temporary workers, or non-contractual workers. In addition, young people with permanent jobs were included as contrasting cases. All educational levels were represented with an oversampling of young people with a low level of education.[1] At least half of the respondents were directly involved in ALMPs or PLMPs. The sample was balanced for gender and it included minority ethnic and/or migrant groups. In terms of regional coverage, at least two different areas (big cities and small towns or villages or rural areas) with different macrostructural regional characteristics were taken into account. Furthermore, specificities of each country were considered by identifying risk groups and oversampling specific categories.

The organisation and analysis of this vast and rich qualitative interview material required the construction and adoption of common methodological tools and procedures among all nine EXCEPT country teams. This work was the final output of an intensive and complex three-year process structured in the following steps: (a) the common definition of the tools among the qualitative researchers involved: in particular, the outline of the semi-structured interview, the national sampling plans, the codebook to codify transcriptions of the interviews, and the outline of a synopsis to summarise the main issues in each interview; (b) the fieldwork in the nine countries in order to collect 386 face-to-face, semi-structured interviews with young people following the sampling plan; and (c) the analysis of the interviews in each country and writing of national reports.

The method applied to the interview data in each country was thematic analysis. This uses a categorising strategy as a procedure for encoding qualitative information. Thematic analysis involves searching across a data set (that is, a number of interviews) to find repeated patterns of meaning (Boyatzis, 1998; Braun and Clarke, 2006; Grunow and Evertsson, 2016). In order to identify themes (and subthemes), researchers in the EXCEPT project were advised (a) to use both an inductive (bottom-up) and a deductive (top-down) approach – that is, to rely both on the data (what the participants/individuals actually say) as well as on theory; and (b) to use both a semantic approach (which means to look at the explicit, surface meanings of the data) and a latent approach (to examine underlying ideas, assumptions, and conceptualisations).

Structure of the book and outline of the chapters

As well as this introductory chapter, the book is framed by a concluding chapter (Chapter 15) that synthesises the main empirical findings, addresses issues associated with effective policymaking, and identifies future directions for research. In between, the thematic chapters (Chapters 2 to 14) are structured in three general parts representing *three key outcome dimensions on the individual level* identified in the multilevel theoretical model described earlier in this chapter, each of which subsumes various, strongly interrelated subdimensions. One unifying element of all three parts is that the key microvariables of interest refer to labour market insecurities such as unemployment, NEET, or job insecurity.

Part I unites studies on the consequences of labour market insecurities for health (Chapters 3 [Baranowska-Rataj and Strandh], and 5 [Schlee et al]) and subjective well-being such as happiness (Chapters 2 [Nizalova et al] and 5 [Schlee et al]) and life satisfaction (Chapters 2 [Nizalova et al], 4 [Lauri and Unt], and 5 [Schlee et al]). Digging deeper into the mechanisms of how labour market insecurity relates to self-perception, Chapter 6 (Roosmaa et al) focuses on the ways in which young people in different national contexts construct the meaning of work and their expectations towards work embedded in their personal labour market experiences.

Part II combines strongly interrelated topics of job insecurity and different types of autonomy associated with transitions to adulthood. In particular, Chapters 7 (Goglio and Bertolini) and 8 (Bertolini et al) examine housing autonomy and how it varies in different institutional contexts. Chapter 9 (Meo et al) scrutinises how young people define and gain economic independence in different contexts. Digging deeper into the mechanisms, Chapter 10 (Meo et al) investigates the role of informal support from family, close friends, and wider social networks in the process of gaining autonomy; and Chapter 11 (Ricucci et al) elaborates on how labour market policy measures are subjectively perceived and assessed by young people in their transition to the labour market.

Part III addresses the socio-economic consequences in terms of subjective and objective individual-level and household-level poverty and material deprivation (Chapters 12 [Kłobuszewska et al] and 13 [Figgou et al]), and social security (Chapter 14 [Hofäcker et al]). In previous literature, the topics of poverty and material deprivation have often been considered together due to their strong interrelationship. Adding the social security dimension to poverty and material deprivation makes sense, because in EU welfare states, social security is an important aspect of the medium- and long-term socio-economic situation of a person; even though the guarantee of one's individual welfare has increasingly become the responsibility of (young) individuals themselves.

Given that all chapters apply a cross-country comparative design, they all test the *moderating macrolevel context* as outlined in our multilevel model mentioned earlier. Various chapters use quantitative comparative analysis methods in this regard. For example, taking an indicator-based quantitative approach, Chapter 2 (Nizalova et al) in Part I studies how a country's macroeconomic situation, in terms of its unemployment rate and GDP, moderates the effect of individual unemployment and job insecurity on unhappiness and life dissatisfaction. Chapter 7 (Goglio and Bertolini) in Part II investigates the role of institutional configurations such as the level of employment protection legislation for regular and for temporary contracts and the level of public expenditure on housing policies with regard to the effect of unemployment and job insecurity on the timing of housing autonomy. Following a typology-based quantitative approach, Chapter 3 (Baranowska-Rataj and Strandh) in Part I analyses how the effect of individual unemployment on a partner's health is moderated by the type of welfare regime.

The other chapters use qualitative comparative analysis methods. Chapter 4 (Lauri and Unt) in Part I uses QCA to disentangle the importance of particular combinations of institutional factor (ALMPs and PLMPs, and family regime) and structural factors (unemployment rate) as moderators of the individual-level relationship between unemployment and well-being. All remaining chapters use a case-oriented qualitative approach to focus on the small-N comparison of two to four of the countries in which the EXCEPT qualitative interviews were conducted. Systematic comparisons are used to plot the role of various structural, institutional, and cultural macrocontext conditions. For instance, Chapter 8 (Bertolini et al) and Chapter 9 (Meo et al) in Part II investigate the meaning of and the strategies used to gain housing and economic autonomy among young people facing job insecurity in light of the different institutional arrangements in each country. Chapter 10 (Meo et al) of Part II shows the mediating role of informal social support in this process and how it relates to formal welfare provisions. Chapter 11 (Ricucci et al) in Part II investigates how the effect of unemployment on the economic situation of youth is moderated by ALMPs and PLMPs. Chapter 13 (Figgou et al) in Part III explores social and material consequences of young people's unemployment and job precariousness in light of the different economic situations and socio-economic policies in selected countries. In particular, it explores the ways in which participants construct their experience of labour market exclusion and uncertainty and represent their implications in their private and social life.

Some chapters also address the important issue of the moderating *mesolevel context* as outlined in the multilevel model described earlier in this chapter. For example, Chapter 5 (Schlee et al) addresses the role of mesolevel coping strategies in managing potential negative effects of unemployment and job insecurity on well-being. Taking into account that patterns of psychological behaviour cannot be understood solely from the point of view of the individual but have to be explained through reference to the mesolevel of society, the authors of this qualitative research chapter examine the role of mesolevel components in dealing with job insecurity, anxiety, and distress. Chapter 11 (Ricucci et al) delivers insights into the role of public employment agencies and other mesolevel actors directly involved in delivery of ALMP measures. Drawing on qualitative data, the chapter attempts to gain a better understanding of the ways in which young people deal with state policies and the related services these offer in order to ameliorate their access to the job market and their life conditions. Another perspective on the mesolevel is taken in Chapter 3 (Baranowska-Rataj and Strandh) which investigates the adverse effects of individual unemployment on the closest family members – that is, the partners – by exploring the mediating role of the family context and close relationships when dealing with the negative consequences of unemployment on young people's well-being.

Each thematic part also reflects the methodological structure of the chapters, because each part has both quantitative and qualitative chapters. The following briefly introduces the data sources for the thematic chapters. These include various European microdata sets: the European Social Survey (ESS) (Chapter 2 [Nizalova et al]); the European Statistics on Income and Living Conditions (EU-SILC) (Chapters 3 [Baranowska-Rataj and Strandh], 4 [Lauri and Unt], 7 [Goglio and Bertolini], and 12 [Kłobuszewska et al]). Chapter 14 (Hofäcker et al) is based on desk research and qualitative expert interviews. The remaining Chapters 5 (Schlee et al), 6 (Roosmaa et al), 8 (Bertolini et al), 9 (Meo et al), 10 (Meo et al), 11 (Riccucci et al), and 13 (Figgou et al) used the rich qualitative research material from EXCEPT semi-structured interviews.

The present edited volume brings together the work of a group of international scholars across Europe who have been researching and reflecting on the implications of labour market insecurity on young people's lives. Combining comparative research with quantitative and qualitative data, the book contributes to a better understanding of the changing social and economic conditions that emerge in Europe by taking respectful account of what young people, as social actors, have to say about their life experience.

Note

[1] In each qualitative chapter part of the sample of interviews is used. The subsample analysed is specified at the beginning of each qualitative chapter. Please note that the quotations of the interviews in the qualitative chapters are identified by: pseudonyms, sex (M/F), age (in years), level of education (based on ISCED scale – LE [low level ISCED 0-2], ME [medium level ISCED 3-4], HE [high level ISCED 5-8]), employment status (NCJ [non-contractual job], TE [temporary employment], PE [permanent employment], U [unemployed], NEET [not in education, employment or training]), and country code.

References

Arnett, J.J. (2000) 'Emerging adulthood: a theory of development from the late teens through the twenties', *American Psychologist*, 55(5): 469–80.

Baranowska, A. and Gebel, M. (2010) 'The determinants of youth temporary employment in the enlarged Europe: do labour market institutions matter?', *European Societies*, 12(3): 367–90.

Baranowska-Rataj, A., Bertolini, S., Ghislieri, C., Meo, A., Moiso, V., Musumeci, R., Ricucci, R. and Torrioni, P.M. (2015) *Becoming Adult in Hard Times: Current and Future Issues on Job Insecurity and Autonomy*, Turin: Accademia University Press.

Barbieri, P. (2009) 'Flexible employment and inequality in Europe', *European Sociological Review*, 25(5): 621–28.

Barbieri, P., Cutuli, G. and Passaretta, G. (2016) 'Institutions and the school-to-work transition: disentangling the role of the macro-institutional context', *Socio-Economic Review*, 16(1): 161–83.

Bertolini, S., Deliyann-Kouimtzi, V., Bolzoni, M. and Ghislieri, C. (eds) (2018) *Labour Market Insecurity and Social Exclusion: Qualitative Comparative Results in Nine Countries*. EXCEPT Working Papers, WP No. 53, Tallinn: Tallinn University, Available from: https://www.except-project.eu/working-papers/

Bertolini, S., Hofäcker, D. and Torrioni, P. (2018) 'The impact of labour market flexibilisation on the first transition to adult life in different welfare states: does contractual stability matter?', *Studies of Transition States and Societies*, 10(3): 28–50.

Billari, F. (2004) 'Becoming adult in Europe: a macro(/micro)-demographic perspective', *Demographic Research*, 3(2): 15–44.

Blossfeld, H.P., Hofäcker, D. and Bertolini, S. (eds) (2011) *Youth on Globalised Labour Markets: Rising Uncertainty and its Effects on Early Development and Family Lives in Europe*, Opladen: Verlag Barbara Budrich.

Blossfeld, H.P., Klijzing, E., Mills, M. and Kurz, K. (eds) (2005) *Globalization, Uncertainty and Youth in Society*, London: Routledge.

Blossfeld, H.P., Buchholz, S., Bukodi, E. and Kurz, K. (eds) (2008) *Young Workers, Globalization and the Labor Market*, Cheltenham: Edward Elgar Publishing.

Boyatzis, R.E. (1998) *Transforming Qualitative Information. Thematic Analysis and Code Development*, Thousand Oaks: Sage.

Braun, V. and Clarke, V. (2006) 'Using thematic analysis in psychology', *Qualitative Research in Psychology*, 3(2): 77–101.

Breen, R. (2005) 'Explaining cross-national variation in youth unemployment: market and institutional factors', *European Sociological Review*, 21(2): 125–34.

Bryan, M.L. and Jenkins, S.P. (2016) 'Multilevel modelling of country effects: a cautionary tale', *European Sociological Review*, 32(1): 3–22.

Buchmann, M.C. and Kriesi, I. (2011) 'Transition to adulthood in Europe', *Annual Review of Sociology*, 37(1): 481–503.

Caliendo, M. and Schmidl, R. (2016) 'Youth unemployment and active labor market policies in Europe', *IZA Journal of Labor Policy*, 5(1): 1–30.

Chisholm, L. and Deliyianni-Kouimtzi, V. (2014) 'Introduction', in L. Chisholm and V. Deliyianni-Kouimtzi (eds) *Changing Landscapes for Childhood and Youth in Europe*, Newcastle upon Tyne: Cambridge Scholars Publishing, pp xiv–xxix.

Choudhry, M.T., Marelli, E. and Signorelli, M. (2012) 'Youth unemployment rate and impact of financial crises', *International Journal of Manpower*, 33(1): 76–95.

Corijn, M. and Klijzing, E. (eds) (2001) *Transitions to Adulthood in Europe*, Dordrecht: Kluwer Academic Publishers.

De Witte, H. (2010) 'Job insecurity and psychological well-being: review of the literature and exploration of some unresolved issues', *European Journal of Work and Organizational Psychology*, 8(2): 155–77.

Diener, E. (2009) 'Subjective well-being', in E. Diener (ed) *The Science of Well-Being*, Dordrecht: Springer, pp 11–58.

Dietrich, H. (2013) 'Youth unemployment in the period 2001–2010 and the European crisis: looking at the empirical evidence', *Transfer: European Review of Labour and Research*, 19(3): 305–24.

Dvoulety, O., Lukeš, M. and Vancea, M. (2020) 'Individual-level and family background determinants of young adults' unemployment in Europe', *Empirica*, 47(2): 389–409.

Ebbinghaus, B. (2005) 'When less is more', *International Sociology*, 20(2): 133–52.

Eichhorst, W. and Rinne, U. (2017) *The European Youth Guarantee: A Preliminary Assessment and Broader Conceptual Implications*. IZA Policy Paper No. 128, Bonn: Institute of Labor Economics (IZA).

Elder, G.H., Johnson, M.K. and Crosnoe, R. (2004) 'The emergence and development of life course theory', in J.T. Mortimer and M.J. Shanahan (eds) *Handbook of the Life Course*, New York: Kluwer Academic/Plenum Publishers, pp 3–19.

Emmenegger, P., Kvist, J. and Skaaning, S.E. (2013) 'Making the most of configurational comparative analysis: an assessment of QCA applications in comparative welfare-state research', *Political Research Quarterly*, 66(1): 185–90.

Escudero, V. and Mourelo, E.L. (2017) *The European Youth Guarantee: A Systematic Review of its Implementation Across Countries*. International Labour Office Research Department Working Paper No. 21. Geneva: International Labour Office.

Esping-Andersen, G. (1990) *The Three Worlds of Welfare Capitalism*, Princeton: Polity Press.

Eurofound (ed) (2012) *NEETs - Young People Not in Employment, Education or Training: Characteristics, Costs and Policy Responses in Europe*, Luxembourg: Publications Office of the European Union.

European Commission (2010a) *Youth on the Move: An initiative to Unleash the Potential of Young People to Achieve Smart, Sustainable and Inclusive Growth in the European Union*, Brussels: European Commission.

European Commission (2010b) *Combating Poverty and Social Exclusion: A Statistical Portrait of the European Union 2010*, Brussels: Publications Office of the European Union.

European Commission (2011) *Moving Youth into Employment*, Brussels: European Commission.

European Commission (2016) *Investing in Europe's Youth*, Brussels: European Commission.

Eurostat (2020) 'When are they ready to leave the nest?' 12 August, Available from: https://ec.europa.eu/eurostat/web/products-eurostat-news/-/EDN-20200812-1.

Gallie, D. and Paugam, S. (eds) (2000) *Welfare Regimes and the Experience of Unemployment in Europe*, Oxford: Oxford University Press.

Gallie, D., Paugam, S. and Jacobs, S. (2003) 'Unemployment, poverty and social isolation: is there a vicious circle of social exclusion?', *European Societies*, 5(1): 1–32.

Gangl, M. (2002) 'Changing labour markets and early career outcomes: labour market entry in Europe over the past decade', *Work, Employment and Society*, 16(1): 67–90.

Gebel, M. and Giesecke, J. (2016) 'Does deregulation help? The impact of employment protection reforms on youths' unemployment and temporary employment risks in Europe', *European Sociological Review*, 32(4): 486–500.

Grunow, D. and Evertsson, M. (eds) (2016) *Couples' Transitions to Parenthood: Analysing Gender and Work in Europe*, Cheltenham: Edward Elgar Publishing.

Högberg, B., Strandh, M. and Baranowska-Rataj, A. (2019a) 'Transitions from temporary employment to permanent employment among young adults: the role of labour law and education systems', *Journal of Sociology*, 55(4): 689–707.

Högberg, B., Voßemer, J., Gebel, M. and Strandh, M. (2019b) 'Unemployment, well-being, and the moderating role of education policies: a multilevel study', *International Journal of Comparative Sociology*, 60(4): 269–91.

Hora, O., Horáková, M. and Sirovátka, T. (2019) 'Diversity of youth policy regimes and early job insecurity: towards an integrated approach', in B. Hvinden, C. Hyggen, M.A. Schoyen and T. Sirovátka (eds) *Youth Unemployment and Job Insecurity in Europe: Problems, Risk Factors and Policies*, Cheltenham/Northampton: Edward Elgar Publishing, pp 138–57.

Hur, S. (2018) 'The lost generation of the Great Recession', *Review of Economic Dynamics*, 30: 179–202.

Hvinden, B., Hyggen, C. and Schoyen, M.A. (2019a) *Youth Unemployment and Job Insecurity in Europe: Problems, Risk Factors and Policies*, Cheltenham: Edward Elgar Publishing.

Hvinden, B., O'Reilly, J. and Schoyen, M.A. (2019b) *Negotiating Early Job Insecurity: Well-Being, Scarring and Resilience of European Youth*, Cheltenham/Northampton: Edward Elgar Publishing.

Jylhä, M. (2009) 'What is self-rated health and why does it predict mortality? Towards a unified conceptual model', *Social Science and Medicine*, 69(3): 307–16.

Kalleberg, A.L. (2009) 'Precarious work, insecure workers: employment relations in transition', *American Sociological Review*, 74(1): 1–22.

Karamessini, M., Symeonaki, M., Stamatopoulou, G. and Parsanoglou, D. (2019) 'Mapping early job insecurity impacts of the crisis in Europe', in B. Hvinden, C. Hyggen, M.A. Schoyen and T. Sirovátka (eds) *Youth Unemployment and Job Insecurity in Europe. Problems, Risk Factors and Policies*, Cheltenham/Northampton: Edward Elgar Publishing, pp 24–44.

Kieselbach, T., Heeringen, K., Rosa, M., Lemkow, L., Sokou, K. and Starrin, B. (eds) (2001) *Living on the Edge: An Empirical Analysis on Long-Term Youth Unemployment and Social Exclusion in Europe*, Wiesbaden: VS Verlag für Sozialwissenschaften.

Kogan, I., Noelke, C. and Gebel, M. (eds) (2011) *Making the Transition: Education and Labor Market Entry in Central and Eastern Europe*, Stanford: Stanford University Press.

Kraaykamp, G., Cemalcilar, Z. and Tosun, J. (2019) 'Transmission of work attitudes and values: comparisons, consequences, and implications', *Annals of the American Academy of Political and Social Science*, 682(1): 8–24.

Lahusen, C., Schulz, N. and Graziano, P.R. (2013) 'Promoting social Europe? The development of European youth unemployment policies', *International Journal of Social Welfare*, 22(3): 300–9.

De Lange, M., Gesthuizen, M. and Wolbers, M.H.J. (2014) 'Youth labour market integration across Europe: the impact of cyclical, structural, and institutional characteristics', *European Societies*, 16(2): 194–212.

Leisering, L. (2003) 'Government and the life course', in J.T. Mortimer and M.J. Shanahan (eds) *Handbook of the Life Course*, New York: Kluwer, pp 205–25.

Marques, P. and Hörisch, F. (2020) 'Understanding massive youth unemployment during the EU sovereign debt crisis: a configurational study', *Comparative European Politics*, 18(2): 233–55.

Mayer, K.U. (2004) 'Whose Lives? How history, societies and institutions define and shape life courses', *Research in Human Development*, 1(3): 161–87.

Mayer, K.U. (2009) 'New directions in life course research', *Annual Review of Sociology*, 35: 413–33.

Müller, W. and Gangl, M. (eds) (2003) *Transitions from Education to Work in Europe. The Integration of Youth into EU Labour Markets*, Oxford: Oxford University Press.

Nolan, B. and Whelan, C.T. (1996) *Resources, Deprivation and Poverty*, Oxford; New York: Oxford University Press/Clarendon Press.

O'Rand, A.M. (2009) 'Cumulative processes in the life course', in G.H. Elder and J.Z. Giele (eds) *The Craft of Life Course Research*, New York: Guilford Press, pp 121–40.

O'Reilly, J., Eichhorst, W., Gábos, A., Hadjivassiliou, K., Lain, D., Leschke, J., McGuinness, S., Kureková, M.L., Nazio, T., Ortlieb, R., Russell, H. and Villa, P. (2015) 'Five characteristics of youth unemployment in Europe: flexibility, education, migration, family legacies, and EU policy', *SAGE Open*, 5(1): 1–19.

O'Reilly, J., Leschke, J., Ortlieb, R., Seeleib-Kaiser, M. and Villa, P. (eds) (2019a) *Youth Labor in Transition: Inequalities, Mobility, and Policies in Europe*, Oxford: Oxford University Press.

O'Reilly, J., Moyart, C., Nazio, T. and Smith, M. (eds) (2019b) *Youth Employment: The STYLE Handbook*, Bristol: Policy Press.

Papadopoulos, T. and Roumpakis, A. (2013) 'Familistic welfare capitalism in crisis: social reproduction and anti-social policy in Greece', *Journal of International and Comparative Social Policy*, 29(3): 204–24.

Passaretta, G. and Wolbers, M.H.J. (2019) 'Temporary employment at labour market entry in Europe: labour market dualism, transitions to secure employment and upward mobility', *Economic and Industrial Democracy*, 40(2): 382–408.

Rokicka, M., Unt, M., Täht, K. and Nizalova, O. (2018) 'Youth labour market in Central and Eastern Europe', in M.A. Malo and A. Moreno Mínguez (eds) *European Youth Labour Markets: Problems and Policies*, Cham: Springer, pp 61–78.

Saar, E., Unt, M. and Kogan, I. (2008) 'Transition from educational system to labour market in the European Union: a comparison between new and old members', *International Journal of Comparative Sociology*, 49(1): 31–59.

Sen, A. (1983) 'Poor, relatively speaking', *Oxford Economic Papers*, 35(2): 153–69.

Shore, J. and Tosun, J. (2019) 'Assessing youth labour market services: young people's perceptions and evaluations of service delivery in Germany', *Public Policy and Administration*, 34(1): 22–41.

Shavit, Y. and Müller, W. (eds) (1998) *From School to Work: A Comparative Study of Educational Qualifications and Occupational Destinations*, Oxford: Clarendon Press.

Stasiowski, J. and Kłobuszewska, M. (2018) 'Does the context matter? Labour market characteristics and job satisfaction among young European adults working on temporary contracts', *Studies of Transition States and Societies*, 10(3): 51–67.

Täht, K., Xanthopoulou, D., Figgou, L., Kostouli, M. and Unt, M. (2020) 'The role of unemployment and job insecurity for the well-being of young Europeans: social inequality as a macro-level moderator', *Journal of Happiness Studies*, 21(7): 2355–75.

Tosun, J., Unt, M. and Wadensjö, E. (2017) 'Youth-oriented active labour market policies: explaining policy effort in the Nordic and the Baltic States', *Social Policy & Administration*, 51(4): 598–616.

Tosun, J., Treib, O. and De Francesco, F. (2019a) 'The impact of the European Youth Guarantee on active labour market policies: a convergence analysis', *International Journal of Manpower*, 33(1): 76–95.

Tosun, J., Pauknerová, D. and Kittel, B. (eds) (2021) *Intergenerational Transmission and Economic Self-Sufficiency*, Basingstoke: Palgrave Macmillan.

Tosun, J., Arco-Tirado, J.L., Caserta, M., Cemalcilar, Z., Freitag, M., Hörisch, F., Jensen, C., Kittel, B., Littvay, L., Lukeš, M., Maloney, W.A., Mühlböck, M., Rainsford, E., Rapp, C., Schuck, B., Shore, J., Steiber, N., Sümer, N., Tsakloglou, P., Vancea, M. and Vegetti, F. (2019b) 'Perceived economic self-sufficiency: a country- and generation-comparative approach', *European Political Science*, 18(3): 510–31.

Unt, M. and Täht, K. (2020) 'Does early career unemployment at the peak of a recession leave economic scars? Evidence from Estonia', *The Annals of the American Academy of Political and Social Science*, 688(1): 246–57.

Walther A. (2006) 'Regimes of youth transitions: choice, flexibility and security in young people's experiences across different European contexts', *Young Nordic Journal of Youth Research*, 14(2): 119–39.

PART I

Labour market insecurity and youth well-being and health

2

Effects of unemployment and insecure jobs on youth well-being in Europe: economic development and business cycle fluctuations

Olena Nizalova, Gintare Malisauskaite, Despoina Xanthopoulou, Katerina Gousia, and Christina Athanasiades

Introduction

In terms of its societal impact, the global financial crisis of 2008 was considered to be the most significant crisis since the Great Depression in 1929 (Rollero and Tartaglia, 2009), and it is often referred to as the Great Recession. Ever since, Europeans, and particularly young Europeans, have been facing a threatening work situation because unemployment rates have increased substantially in most European countries (Chung et al, 2012; Eurostat, 2014). At the same time, temporary employment has followed suit, albeit at a lower speed, but affecting mostly young people.[1,2] Empirical evidence suggests that unemployment and job insecurity have detrimental effects on individuals' well-being, and not only in the general population (for reviews see Sverke et al, 2002; De Witte, 2005; Cheng and Chan, 2008; see McKee-Ryan et al, 2005, for a meta-analysis) but also among young people (see Voßemer and Eunicke, 2015). Hence, it is important to investigate the outcomes of unfavourable labour market conditions for young people in Europe, because employment opportunities mark young individuals' transition to adulthood (Bynner and Parsons, 2002). Any attempt to fully understand the conditions under which young people facing unemployment and job insecurity are particularly vulnerable must also account for the role of macrolevel moderators, given the large variations in social policies and economic growth observed across the different European countries (Voßemer et al, 2018).

Although it is plausible to think that the strength of the individual-level effects of unemployment and job insecurity on well-being may vary between poorer and richer countries, few studies have looked at potential cross-country differences and the role of macrolevel moderators in understanding this relationship (for example Eichhorn, 2013; Wulfgramm, 2014). Most of these studies focused on the moderating role of labour market policies or the countries' economic conditions, often measuring either GDP per capita or the country-level unemployment rate (UR). However, these two measures may have a completely different meaning when examined as moderators, and they should not be viewed as being interchangeable.

First, GDP and UR do not substitute each other, because some countries often experience jobless growth, whereas others may experience a decrease in UR due to a concerted effort by the government without any increase in GDP per capita. Second, conceptually, GDP and UR underline different phenomena. Thus, when they are investigated simultaneously, different mechanisms are being discerned and tested. GDP per capita reflects the level of resources per citizen available in the country such as employment-related (for example, unemployment benefits) or health-related (including health expenditure) resources. The present analysis focuses on GDP as an overall measure that captures all kinds of societal support and the capacity of the government to provide such support. In this way, it captures the broader context in contrast to previous empirical attempts that looked at specific policy measures (Voßemer et al, 2018). Based on conservation of resources (COR) theory (Hobfoll, 1989), it is argued that higher levels of GDP may buffer the detrimental effects on well-being of unemployment and job insecurity, because in countries with a higher GDP, people have access to more resources when they face difficult times – irrespective of that country's UR.

When the level of resources (as measured by the GDP) is held constant, there are two potential mechanisms to consider regarding the moderating role of UR. On the one hand, based on the principle of social comparison or the norm (see Clark, 2003), unemployment is likely to hurt less when there are more unemployed people around, because it is attributed externally and not to one's own, personal failure. On the other hand, from the standard economics perspective, higher UR means fewer prospects of finding a job for those currently unemployed – hence, strengthening the unfavourable effect of own unemployment. In reality though, both mechanisms are likely to be in place, and one can determine only empirically which of the two effects prevails.

The current analysis investigates the moderating role of both GDP per capita and UR simultaneously as moderators of the relationship between unemployment/job insecurity and well-being. This attempts to distinguish the economic (that is, resource) effect from the social norm effect. The GDP per capita is expected to represent mostly an economic resource. Even though the UR is likely to combine both economic and social norm considerations, this study expects that the effect of UR will mainly capture the social norm effect when simultaneously controlling for GDP.

Furthermore, the study also distinguishes between the moderating role of long-term trajectories and business cycle fluctuations, given their different nature with respect to the formation of individual expectations. Macroeconomics has long been preoccupied with the separation of long-term trends in key indicators from short-term business cycle fluctuations. There are two reasons to think that such a separation is relevant when analysing the moderating effect of macroeconomic conditions on the relationship between employment status and well-being. If one considers the resource availability argument (Hobfoll, 1989), the underlying reason for the separation of the long-term trend from the business cycle fluctuation lies within the state budgeting process. The budget is set annually, based on historic information and future spending forecasts. Therefore, it is more likely that short-term fluctuations will send a weaker signal to individuals with regards to resource availability compared to that from the long-term GDP trajectory. A similar mechanism is likely to be in place with regards to UR: a long-term unemployment trajectory should send a stronger signal to individuals with regards to social comparison than the business cycle fluctuation.

Theory and hypotheses

According to relative deprivation theory (Crosby, 1984), the bigger the discrepancy between the outcomes people achieve and the outcomes to which they feel entitled, the greater their feelings of relative deprivation. It has been argued that this experienced relative deprivation results in decreases in well-being (Fryer, 1998). Hence, people are likely to feel deprived when they feel that they are entitled to have a job (and the income resulting from it) that corresponds to their human capital (for example, education, experience, skills), but they are either unemployed or hold an insecure job that does not match their expectations. This feeling of deprivation may explain why unemployment and job insecurity relate to impaired well-being

(Sverke et al, 2002; De Witte, 2005; Cheng and Chan, 2008; Norton et al, 2018).

Nevertheless, the relationship between unemployment and both job insecurity and well-being is also subject to boundary conditions. For instance, on the individual level, social contacts have been found to buffer unfavourable outcomes of unemployment on well-being, because unemployed people who had more social contacts were better off than those with fewer contacts (Kilpatrick and Trew, 1985). Moreover, with higher (vs lower) levels of work-role centrality (that is, the degree to which work is central to one's life), unemployed individuals were found to experience lower levels of well-being, whereas supportive social relations, available financial resources, and an everyday routine helped unemployed people feel better (McKee-Ryan et al, 2005). The present study argues that country characteristics on the macrolevel, and specifically a country's GDP and UR, may also moderate the relationship between labour market status and well-being.

In line with Paul and Moser's (2009) meta-analysis revealing that the negative effects of unemployment on health were weaker in countries with higher (vs lower) GDP, the present study argues that unemployment and job insecurity will be less detrimental for individuals' well-being in countries that are financially better off. COR theory (Hobfoll, 1989) helps to explain the moderating role of a country's economic situation (GDP) on the relationship between unemployment/job insecurity and well-being. This theory posits that individuals strive to preserve and protect their resources and acquire additional resources to address threats in the environment. Thus, resources are important not only for their instrumental value but also for their value in helping individuals cope with stress, prevent well-being impairments, and feel better. Hobfoll (1989, 2002) recognises four types of resource: objects (such as a house or a car), conditions (for example, employment), personal characteristics (such as self-efficacy), and energies (including money). Considering that resources can be found on different levels of analysis (the individual or the societal level), the economic situation of a country can be operationalised as an energy resource on the societal level.

A central assumption of COR theory (Hobfoll, 1989, 2002) is that the availability of resources buffers the negative consequences of the threatening or demanding conditions that individuals face. Put differently, when resources are available, individuals may use them to deal with threats in their environment and thereby prevent reductions in their well-being. In countries that flourish economically (that is, are characterised by higher [vs lower] levels of GDP), unemployed individuals or those having an insecure job will have access to an adequate pool of societal resources (for example, unemployment benefits, better welfare system, better health care availability, and so on). Resource availability on the country level will help them deal more effectively with the demanding condition (that is, unemployment/job insecurity) they are facing and feel less threatened by it, thereby preventing a decline in well-being. In contrast, in countries with lower levels of GDP, the detrimental effects of unemployment and job insecurity on well-being will be stronger, because unemployed individuals or individuals with insecure jobs will have fewer available resources to deal with their precarious work situation. In line with this discussion, it is hypothesised that the positive relationship between unemployment/job insecurity and impaired well-being (unhappiness, dissatisfaction) will be weaker in countries with higher GDP than in countries with lower GDP (Hypothesis 1).

Relative deprivation theory (Crosby, 1984) assumes that people feel entitled to certain outcomes or conditions (for instance, having a job). However, the entitlement to certain outcomes is determined not only by individual beliefs but also by social comparisons that form individuals' social identities. According to social identity theory (Tajfel and Turner, 1986), individuals choose to belong to groups that project a positive identity to them when compared to an out group. In this context, people in insecure labour market positions will experience a decline in well-being mainly when they compare themselves to those employed with secure jobs. This is because upward social comparisons or comparisons with others who are better off result in lower self-regard (Tesser et al, 1988). However, irrespective of GDP levels, in countries where UR is higher, people in insecure labour market positions are likely to change their comparison group in order to protect their self-evaluation and self-regard. In this context, unemployed people and people experiencing high job insecurity are more likely to compare themselves with others who are in a similar labour market situation (that is, unemployed people or people with insecure jobs) and thus protect themselves from decreasing well-being.

This suggestion is also in line with attribution theory (Fiske and Taylor, 1991) which illustrates how individuals gather information from the environment to explain specific events. People in unfavourable employment conditions (unemployed or in insecure jobs) are more likely to assign the cause of their condition to the environment that is outside of their control (external attribution), and not to internal aspects such as their personal characteristics (for example, lack of skills) or motives (too lazy to look for a job or a better job). This is more likely to happen in countries with a higher UR in which it is common to be unemployed or have an insecure job, thereby making external attribution more plausible. When the cause of one's position in the labour market is attributed externally and not internally, the negative effects of unemployment and job insecurity on well-being will be less severe. In contrast, people who are unemployed or have insecure jobs in a country in which UR is low (where relatively few people are unemployed or have insecure jobs) are more likely to attribute their condition to themselves (internal attribution) and, thus, the effects on their well-being will be particularly unfavourable.

There is evidence showing that in more deprived environments characterised by higher URs, the impact of individual unemployment on well-being is weaker (Clark, 2003; Shields et al, 2009). However, it should also be noted that more recent evidence from Oesch and Lipps (2013) showed no support for the moderating role of UR on the link between individual unemployment and well-being in Germany and Switzerland. Moreover, in a study of the 28 OECD countries in the period 1999–2009, Stavrova et al (2011) found support for the moderating role of the norm effect but only for societal injunctive norms (what a society approves or disapproves of) but not for descriptive norms (the national level of unemployment). However, these latter studies did not account for the full period of the financial crisis in which the impact of descriptive norms in the form of a country's level of unemployment may have become more prominent for individuals. Thus, on the basis of this analysis, it is hypothesised that the positive relationship between unemployment/job insecurity and impaired well-being (unhappiness, dissatisfaction) will be weaker in countries with a higher UR than in countries with a lower UR (Hypothesis 2).

Finally, it is important to consider that a country's current economic position can consist of two components: a permanent or long-term economic trajectory and transitory business cycle fluctuations. In this respect, a country on a positive long-term economic trajectory may have more resources to buffer the negative effects of individual unemployment, irrespective of whether it is currently experiencing a downturn due to business cycle fluctuations. Likewise, a country on a negative long-term economic trajectory that experiences a sudden economic boom may not make this resource available to buffer the effect of individual unemployment/job insecurity due to the transitory nature of this increase in resources. Moreover, if the increase in unemployment is due to a business cycle fluctuation in an otherwise low UR country, it may be less likely to moderate the effect of individual unemployment on well-being.

From a psychological perspective, it could be argued that individual attitudes are more likely to be affected when individuals are exposed to a message that is more persuasive (Crano and Prislin, 2006). In this context, a change (a message) is more likely to persuade individuals and alter how they view the economic development of their country and how they react to it if it is systemic and develops into a long-term trajectory. For instance, in countries that are worse off economically but experience an unexpected positive change, this change is more likely to make people optimistic when it translates into a long-lasting positive trend. In that sense, an individual's well-being in response to their own unemployment and job insecurity will be less sensitive to business cycle fluctuations than to their country's position on its long-term trajectory. Thus, the hypothesis is that the long-term economic trajectory will have a stronger moderating effect on the positive relationship between unemployment/job insecurity and impaired well-being than business cycle fluctuations — that is, deviations in macrolevel UR and GDP from their respective long-term trends (Hypothesis 3).

A number of studies have concluded that men and women differ in how they experience unemployment, with unemployed women suffering fewer negative consequences mainly because of other complementary roles they are expected to fulfil inside the family (Paul and Moser, 2009). Connell (1991, 1995) has argued that work is primarily essential for the identity of men in order for them to successfully accomplish their role as 'breadwinners', to achieve independence, and to participate in social and public life. However, some scholars have questioned these differences between genders (Russell and Barbieri, 2000; Isaksson et al, 2004), arguing that women's experiences of unemployment have not been studied adequately. Moreover, other scholars have argued that the previous reasoning reflects traditional ideologies regarding gender roles and ignores the significant socio-economic changes in women's participation in the labour market as well as the heterogeneity of the female experience (for example, women's differences with respect to education, social class, and marital status) (Russell and Barbieri, 2000). Because previous studies have been inconclusive regarding the role of gender in how unemployment and job insecurity affect individual well-being, the present study accounts for gender differences when testing hypotheses in an attempt to shed light on previous non-systematic findings. This responds to calls (for example, Russell and Barbieri, 2000) stressing the need to link women's unemployment to macrolevel conditions (such as a country's welfare state) in order to better elucidate possible sources of gender gaps.

Method

Microdata

The study employed data from the European Social Survey (ESS). The ESS is carried out every two years and examines a range of issues such as employment, income, education, housing, family, health, work–life balance, life satisfaction, and other attitudes and behaviours. The present study used data from 35 countries covering all available waves (2002–14) and focused on young people only (aged 15–29). It ran separate regressions for males and females.

Microlevel variables

Unhappiness was measured by reversing participants' responses on a one-item happiness scale ('How happy are you, taking all things together?'). Participants rated this item on an 11-point scale ranging from 1 (*very unhappy*) to 11 (*very happy*). After reversing responses, high scores indicate high levels of unhappiness.

Dissatisfaction with life was measured by reversing participants' responses to a one-item, overall life satisfaction scale ('How satisfied are you currently with your life, in general?'). Participants rated this item on an 11-point scale ranging from 1 (*very dissatisfied*) to 11 (*very satisfied*). After reversing responses, high scores are indicative of high levels of dissatisfaction.

Employment status was measured by means of self-reports on an indicator variable distinguishing between those employed (0) and those unemployed (1).

Job insecurity indicated respondents' job contract type; more specifically, people were asked whether their job was permanent or temporary (permanent vs limited contract). Temporary contract workers were considered as having an insecure job.

Control variables. In all specifications, the study controlled for participants' age (in years) and age squared, secondary or tertiary education completion, and indicators for being married/living with partner or being separated/divorced. It also controlled for other labour market indicators with a list of dummy variables: being discouraged from work, being in education, being retired, doing housework, or labour market status identified as 'other'. Income (measured in deciles) was also included as a control variable to ensure that any potential negative effect observed in well-being outcomes is net of the individual income effect. If after controlling for income, the effects of unemployment or insecure employment were still to be observed, this would indicate that their impact goes beyond individual financial inconvenience, and thereby helps to explain the route to possible stigma related to these experiences. Due to a change in the survey design from income being expressed as a 12-category variable relevant to each country and its currency (between 2002 and 2006) to it being expressed in deciles in euros (between 2008 and 2014), income deciles for the years 2002–06 were imputed using uniform random values.[3] Furthermore, all specifications account for yearly fixed effects.

Macrolevel moderators

Economic situation. The economic situation on the country level was measured by two indicators: the country's UR and the level of country's GDP (at purchasing power parity, per capita, in thousands of 2011 international dollars, natural log of). Both were demeaned to allow a meaningful interpretation of the main effects in the specifications with interactions (Wooldridge, 2016). Data regarding the countries' UR for the years 1998–2014 is the share of unemployed (according to the International Labour Organization (ILO) measure[4]) in the total labour force (World Bank, 2016a). The per capita GDP includes all final goods and services produced within a country in a given year at their purchasing power parity value (PPP), divided by the average population of the same year (World Bank, 2016b).

Strategy for the analysis

Hypothesised effects were tested across ages and genders by constructing two different model specifications. The models were run using the whole available sample (2002–14 in 35 countries) of young individuals (15–29 years old) as mixed-effects multilevel regressions with three levels: individuals (Level 1) nested in years (Level 2), and nested in countries (Level 3) separately by gender.

Model 1:

$$Y_{itj} = \beta_0 + LM_{itj}\beta_1 + LM_{itj} \star Macro_{tj}\beta_2 + Macro_{tj}\beta_3 \\ + I_{itj}\beta_4 + X_{itj}b_X + T_t b_T + c_j + u_{tj} + \epsilon_{ijt}$$

Model 2:

$$Y_{itj} = \beta_0 + LM_{itj}\beta_1 + LM_{itj} \star MacroII_{tj}\beta_2 + MacroII_{tj}\beta_3 \\ + I_{itj}\beta_4 + X_{itj}b_X + T_t b_T + c_j + u_{tj} + \epsilon_{ijt}$$

where Y_{itj} is the dependent variable (variables representing well-being: unhappiness or dissatisfaction with life) of young person i in year t in country j. LM_{itj} is a vector of dummy variables indicating types of labour market status that includes the variables of interest: being unemployed, in an insecure job, and controls for other labour market statuses. The study was particularly interested in the effects of unemployment and job insecurity and their interactions with macrolevel moderators. The difference between Model 1 and Model 2 is how macrolevel moderators are defined. $Macro_{tj}$ stands for a vector of macrolevel moderators: demeaned natural log of GDP level per capita in PPP values and demeaned country-level UR. $MacroII_{tj}$ stands for country-level GDP trend and residual term along with country-level UR trend and residual term. All trend and residual measures were also demeaned following the procedure described in Wooldridge (2010). I_{itj} stands for individual level of income. X_{itj} is a vector of individual level controls, c_j, u_{tj} and ϵ_{ijt} correspond to different level error terms. All regressions were run separately by gender.

Economic trend (MacroII). To separate the nature of the signal individuals receive from the macroeconomic indicators into anticipated and unanticipated parts, both UR and GDP were decomposed using two different filtering methods: (a) linear filtering with first-order polynomial only, which separates time-series data into trend and cyclical components (Burns and Mitchell, 1946); and (b) the Hodrick–Prescott filter, which additionally allows for the smoothed-curve representation of the trend (compared to the linear trend in (a)). This is achieved through modifying parameters to adjust for the trend sensitivity to short-term fluctuations (Hodrick and Prescott, 1997). Comparing both ways of constructing the trend works as a sensitivity analysis, because it allows an investigation of whether the method of operationalising the trend introduces any significant differences in the results. The linear and Hodrick–Prescott filtered (Hodrick–Prescott [HP] procedure described in Baum, 2004) trends of UR and GDP growth and their residuals were derived separately for each country using macroeconomic data for the years 1996–2014. The acquired values were merged with the rest of the ESS data, and only 2002–14 data were used due to ESS availability. The natural log of a country's GDP per capita levels at PPP values and actual unemployment rates were used to derive trends and residuals over time.

When considering the main effects as points of reference, it should be acknowledged that one has to be careful regarding the magnitude of the estimated main effects of unemployment and job insecurity. These main effects are likely to be subject to possible endogeneity – a possibility that unhappier individuals or those who are more dissatisfied with life will be more likely to end up in unemployment or an insecure job. However, the literature has now shown that the causal mechanism is present in this relationship, albeit at a somewhat smaller magnitude (Kassenboehmer and Haisken-DeNew, 2009). However, with regard to the main effects of per capita GDP and the UR and their interactions with individual unemployment and job insecurity, it is plausible to think that these macrolevel effects are exogenous to individual decisions, and, hence, the coefficient estimates on the interaction terms will be consistent (Nizalova and Murtazashvili, 2016).

Results

Summary statistics for both individual and macroeconomic variables for male and female samples are presented in Table 2.1.

Hypotheses 1 and 2 were tested simultaneously for each dependent variable. Hypothesis 3 was tested in a separate analysis. Table 2.2 presents results for Model 1 (Hypotheses 1 and 2) and Table 2.3 presents results for Model 2 (Hypothesis 3). Each table compares outcomes for males and females on both unhappiness and dissatisfaction with life. As expected, being unemployed or having an insecure job was found to significantly increase youth unhappiness and life dissatisfaction relative to being employed in a secure job (Table 2.2). In countries with average GDP and UR, the effect of unemployment was stronger than that of job insecurity for both genders and both measures of well-being (unhappiness: 0.656 vs 0.053 for males and 0.385 vs 0.097 for females; life dissatisfaction: 0.904 vs 0.083 for males and 0.659 vs 0.109 for females[5]). Both effects, and particularly the effect of unemployment, were larger for life dissatisfaction than for unhappiness. Results also suggested that unemployment had a considerably larger effect on young men than insecure employment, whereas the difference between the two effects was much smaller for young women.

In Model 1 (Table 2.2), an increase in GDP level was associated with lower unhappiness and life dissatisfaction for the employed men and women (the reference group) in a statistically significant way. However, the economic significance of the effect was quite low – 1 per cent increase in GDP per capita was associated with a 0.008-point decrease on an 11-point unhappiness scale for employed men and 0.009 for employed women. The corresponding effects on life dissatisfaction were 0.013 and 0.012 respectively. Higher UR related significantly to increased unhappiness and dissatisfaction with life: a 1 per cent increase in UR was associated with a 0.030-point increase in unhappiness for

Table 2.1: Descriptive statistics for the samples (by gender)

	Males		Females	
	Mean	SD	Mean	SD
Dependent variables:				
Unhappiness	3.505	1.802	3.460	1.854
Life dissatisfaction	3.761	2.092	3.782	2.104
Explanatory variables:				
Macro variables:				
GDP level (ln)	10.395	0.416	10.360	0.433
Unemployment rate	8.093	3.883	8.196	3.837
Macro II variables:				
GDP level (trend-lin)	10.374	0.433	10.347	0.437
GDP level (res-lin)	0.012	0.051	0.012	0.052
Macro unemployment (trend-lin)	8.173	3.251	8.281	3.219
Macro unemployment (res-lin)	−0.08	2.234	−0.085	2.230
GDP level (trend-hp)	10.385	0.420	10.348	0.437
GDP level (res-hp)	0.011	0.047	0.011	0.048
Macro unemployment (trend-hp)	8.152	3.241	8.260	3.210
Macro unemployment (res-hp)	−0.059	2.100	−0.064	2.101
LM status of interest:				
Unemployed	0.069	0.254	0.056	0.23
Insecure employment	0.265	0.441	0.274	0.446
Other variables:				
Discouraged from work	0.023	0.149	0.021	0.145
In education	0.335	0.472	0.334	0.472
Retired	0.002	0.042	0.001	0.037
Housework	0.008	0.087	0.132	0.339
Other LM status	0.031	0.173	0.027	0.162
Income	5.627	2.874	5.299	2.858
Age	23.033	4.074	23.222	04.042
Age squared	547.130	184.370	555.580	183.690
Secondary education	0.713	0.452	0.645	0.479
Tertiary education	0.244	0.429	0.306	0.461
Married	0.192	0.394	0.297	0.457
Divorced	0.011	0.105	0.025	0.156

Table 2.1: Descriptive statistics for the samples (by gender) (continued)

	Males		Females	
	Mean	SD	Mean	SD
Year 2004	0.140	0.347	0.142	0.349
Year 2006	0.123	0.329	0.122	0.327
Year 2008	0.176	0.381	0.181	0.385
Year 2010	0.157	0.363	0.160	0.366
Year 2012	0.168	0.374	0.171	0.377
Year 2014	0.093	0.291	0.086	0.281
No. of observations	18,375		19,211	

Notes: ln – natural logarithm; LM – Labour Market; trend-lin – trend term of linear filtering; res-lin – residual term of linear filtering; trend-hp – trend term of Hodrick-Prescott filtering procedure; res-hp – residual term of Hodrick-Prescott filtering procedure.

employed men and a 0.034-point increase in unhappiness for employed women. Similar effects are observed for life dissatisfaction.

With respect to the moderating effects, when controlling for UR, GDP was found to be a statistically significant moderator of the positive relationship between unemployment and both unhappiness and life dissatisfaction for women, of insecure employment and unhappiness for women, and of the relationship between unemployment and life dissatisfaction for men. Whereas GDP was found to exacerbate the positive effect of unemployment on both unhappiness and dissatisfaction with life (which goes against Hypothesis 1), it reduced the positive effect of job insecurity (which supports Hypothesis 1) – albeit the latter effect was statistically significant only for unhappiness in both men and women and for life dissatisfaction in women. In terms of magnitude, a 1 per cent increase in GDP per capita increased the effect of being unemployed on life dissatisfaction for men by 0.005 points (0.452/100), which is about 0.05 per cent of the main effect of individual unemployment (Column 2). For women, it was a 0.004-point effect for both unhappiness (0.409/100) and life dissatisfaction (0.449/100), which corresponds to respectively 1.3 per cent and 0.8 per cent of the main effect. The moderating effects were larger in relative terms for job insecurity. For example, for men, a 1 per cent increase in GDP was associated with a reduction in the effect of an insecure job on life dissatisfaction by 0.002 points (-0.183/100), which constitutes 4 per cent of the main effect. UR had a statistically significant moderating effect only on the relationship between insecure employment and unhappiness for both genders. Results showed that the relationship

Table 2.2: Effect of micro- and macroindicators and their interactions on young male and female well-being (Model 1)

	Male		Female	
	Unhappiness	Dissatisfaction with life	Unhappiness	Dissatisfaction with life
	(1)	(2)	(3)	(4)
Income	−0.067**	−0.087**	−0.078**	−0.094**
	(0.005)	(0.005)	(0.005)	(0.005)
Unemployed	0.656**	0.904**	0.385**	0.659**
	(0.054)	(0.062)	(0.060)	(0.068)
Insecure job	0.053+	0.083*	0.097**	0.109**
	(0.030)	(0.034)	(0.030)	(0.034)
GDP level (ln, d-mean.)	−0.836**	−1.313**	−0.857**	−1.222**
	(0.130)	(0.164)	(0.150)	(0.175)
*Unemployed	0.193	0.452**	0.409**	0.449**
	(0.125)	(0.142)	(0.152)	(0.170)
*Insecure job	−0.183*	−0.149	−0.255**	−0.155
	(0.092)	(0.104)	(0.092)	(0.103)
Macr. unempl. (d-mean.)	0.030**	0.026*	0.034**	0.032**
	(0.010)	(0.012)	(0.010)	(0.012)
*Unemployed	0.016	0.021	0.005	0.024
	(0.013)	(0.015)	(0.015)	(0.017)
*Insecure job	−0.023**	−0.007	−0.026**	−0.011
	(0.009)	(0.010)	(0.009)	(0.010)
N (Individuals)	18,375		19,211	
N (Years)	155		155	
N (Countries)	35		35	

Notes: Significance levels: ** $p < 1\%$, * $p < 5\%$, + $p < 10\%$. ln – natural logarithm; LM – Labour Market. Rows with covariates preceeding by star correspond to the interaction term of the this covariate with the macro-level covariate above.

between job insecurity and unhappiness was reversed for those living in countries with higher levels of unemployment, which is in line with Hypothesis 2.

Although the moderating effects of macroeconomic indicators were relatively small at the margin, many of them were statistically significant when evaluated at the average values of these indicators. Hence, the effects were explored across the whole spectrum of possible values of the macroeconomic variables in graphical form. Figures 2.1 (results for males) and 2.2 (results for females) show graphs based on simulations of the effects of being unemployed or in an insecure job (evaluated with a 95 per cent confidence interval), allowing for either GDP or UR to vary while holding all other variables constant at the average values. The upper two rows in Figures 2.1 and 2.2 show results for unhappiness; the lower two rows, for life dissatisfaction. The first graph in each row presents the predicted levels of each well-being indicator for those employed, unemployed, and in insecure employment varying by the GDP or UR measured as the deviation from the mean. The second graph in each row presents how the difference in unhappiness or life dissatisfaction of those unemployed and in insecure jobs varies by GDP/UR (again in terms of deviation from the mean) from those employed in secure positions. This is effectively a marginal effect of being unemployed or in insecure employment evaluated at different levels of macrovariables. The moderating effects of GDP are presented in odd rows; those of UR are presented in even rows.

The graphs show that the overall levels of unhappiness/life dissatisfaction decrease with higher GDP and lower UR for all three groups. However, they decrease at a lower rate for the unemployed than for the other two groups. With regards to moderating effects, the findings are the following: (a) holding UR constant, GDP exacerbates the positive relationship between unemployment and both unhappiness and dissatisfaction with life for men and women; (b) holding GDP constant, UR has a weaker, but still exacerbating effect on the relationship between unemployment and well-being (virtually flat curves for the unemployed with intersecting confidence intervals); (c) although the effect of job insecurity on well-being is much smaller, where there is an effect, it is mitigated by GDP (in accordance with Hypothesis 1) and UR (in accordance with Hypothesis 2). Overall, the evidence regarding the moderating effects supports Hypothesis 1 and Hypothesis 2 with regards to job insecurity but not unemployment.

With regard to Hypothesis 3, Model 2 decomposes GDP and UR into long-term trends and shocks (or business cycle fluctuations) using either linear trend or Hodrick–Prescott filters (linear: odd columns; Hodrick–Prescott: even columns, in Table 2.3). The results using both methods were quite similar. A higher GDP trend was found to significantly reduce the unhappiness and life dissatisfaction of employed youth. These effects were comparable to those obtained for the level values of these measures in Model 1. An unexpected increase in a country's GDP level had a significant negative effect on

Figure 2.1: Moderating effects of macroeconomic indicators on well-being in men

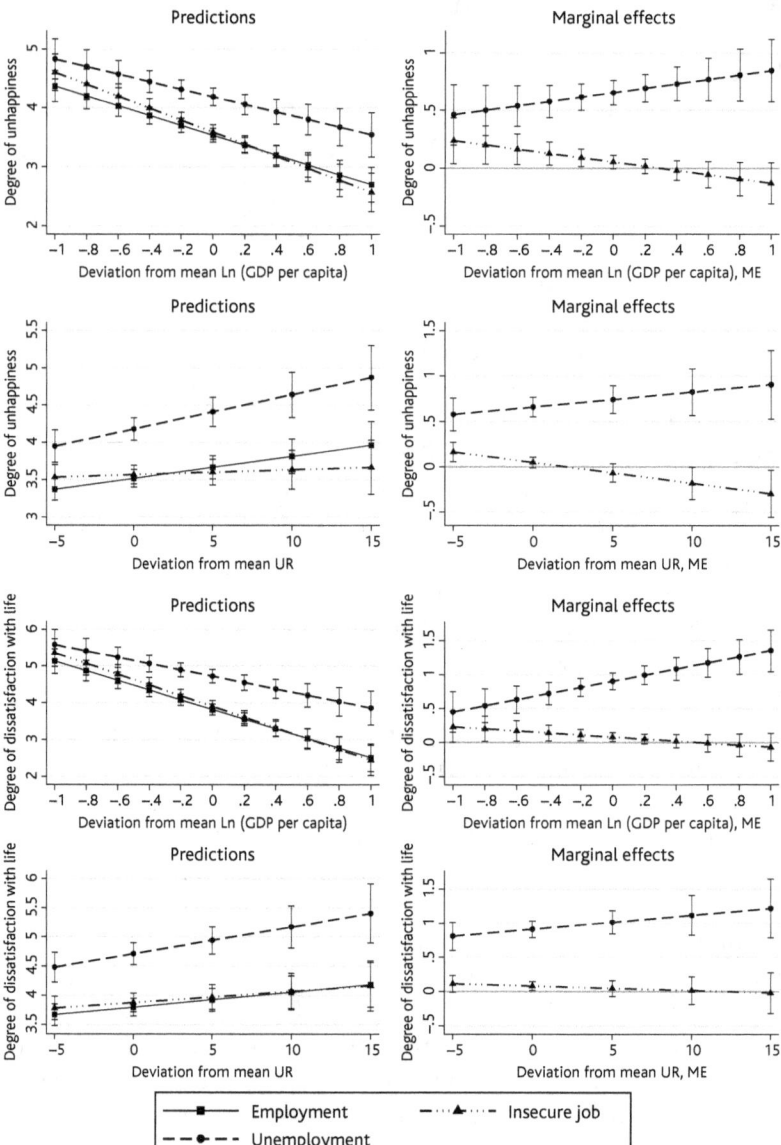

Figure 2.2: Moderating effects of macroeconomic indicators on well-being in women

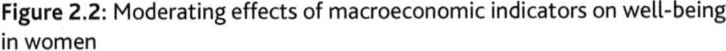

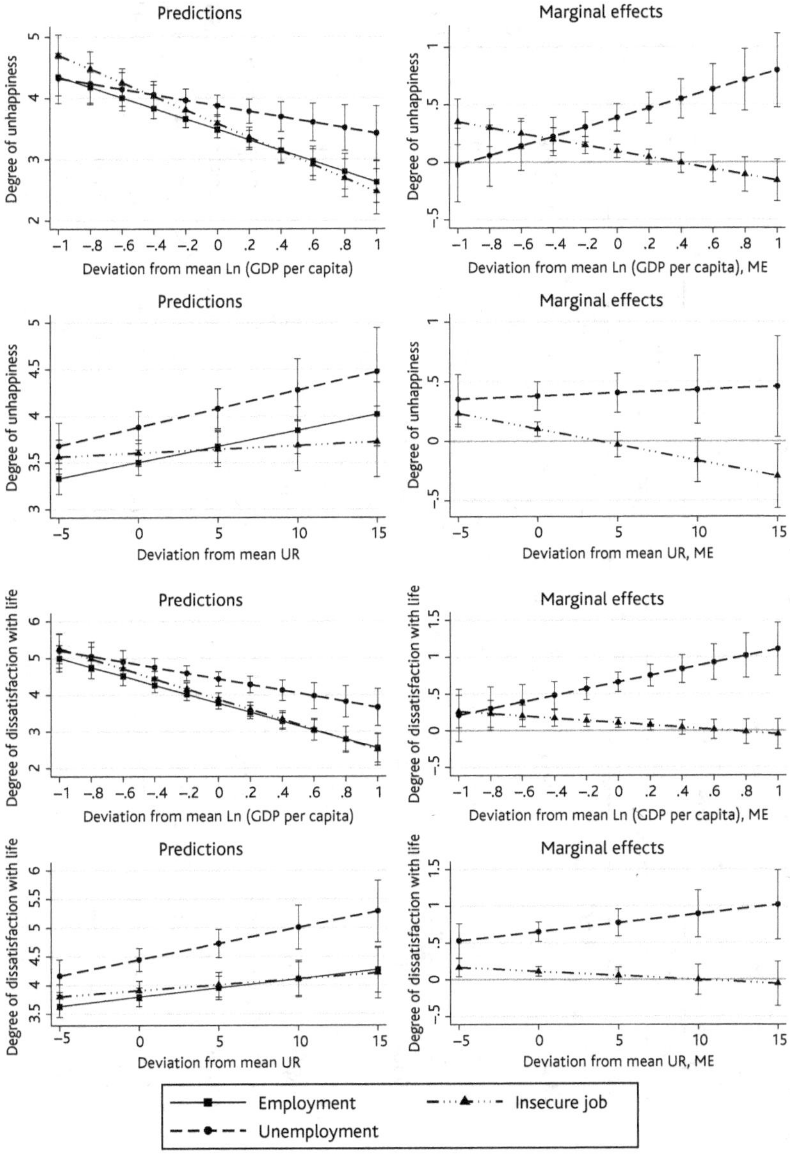

Table 2.3: Effect of micro- and macroindicators and their interactions on young male and female well-being (Model 2)

	Male				Female			
	Unhappiness		Life dissatisfaction		Unhappiness		Life dissatisfaction	
	Lin	HP	Lin	HP	Lin	HP	Lin	HP
	(1)	(2)	(3)	(4)	(5)	(6)	(7)	(8)
Income	-0.067**	-0.067**	-0.087**	-0.087**	-0.077**	-0.077**	-0.094**	-0.094**
	(0.005)	(0.005)	(0.005)	(0.005)	(0.005)	(0.005)	(0.005)	(0.005)
Unemployed	0.663**	0.663**	0.908**	0.907**	0.393**	0.394**	0.683**	0.685**
	(0.054)	(0.054)	(0.062)	(0.062)	(0.061)	(0.061)	(0.068)	(0.068)
Insecure job	0.053+	0.053+	0.082*	0.082*	0.098**	0.098**	0.110**	0.111**
	(0.030)	(0.030)	(0.034)	(0.034)	(0.030)	(0.030)	(0.034)	(0.034)
GDP level (trend)	-0.885**	-0.894**	-1.314**	-1.327**	-0.876**	-0.878**	-1.266**	-1.265**
	(0.132)	(0.132)	(0.173)	(0.172)	(0.155)	(0.155)	(0.182)	(0.182)
*Unemployed	0.189	0.185	0.473**	0.466**	0.305*	0.296+	0.392*	0.381*
	(0.129)	(0.130)	(0.147)	(0.148)	(0.155)	(0.155)	(0.173)	(0.173)
*Insecure job	-0.179+	-0.178+	-0.090	-0.085	-0.263**	-0.261**	-0.157	-0.155
	(0.095)	(0.095)	(0.108)	(0.109)	(0.096)	(0.096)	(0.108)	(0.108)
GDP level (res)	-0.472	-0.328	-0.762	-0.589	-1.249	-1.254	-2.261*	-2.294+
	(0.893)	(0.956)	(1.056)	(1.134)	(0.944)	(1.012)	(1.110)	(1.193)
*Unemployed	1.971	2.079	2.614+	2.605	-1.855	-2.258	2.360	2.418
	(1.384)	(1.516)	(1.577)	(1.727)	(1.570)	(1.725)	(1.756)	(1.929)

Table 2.3: Effect of micro- and macroindicators and their interactions on young male and female well-being (Model 2) (continued)

*Insecure job	-0.669	-0.745	0.489	0.598	-0.473	-0.520	-0.617	-0.589
	(0.814)	(0.893)	(0.928)	(1.019)	(0.821)	(0.901)	(0.920)	(1.010)
Macr. unem. (trend)	0.015	0.013	0.029	0.025	0.026	0.026	0.016	0.017
	(0.016)	(0.016)	(0.021)	(0.020)	(0.018)	(0.018)	(0.022)	(0.021)
*Unemployed	0.001	-0.000	0.012	0.011	-0.032+	-0.035+	-0.009	-0.014
	(0.017)	(0.017)	(0.019)	(0.019)	(0.019)	(0.019)	(0.021)	(0.021)
*Insecure job	-0.019+	-0.018+	0.009	0.010	-0.027*	-0.027*	-0.009	-0.009
	(0.011)	(0.011)	(0.012)	(0.012)	(0.011)	(0.011)	(0.012)	(0.012)
Macr. unem. (res)	0.040*	0.045**	0.033+	0.036+	0.023	0.024	0.020	0.019
	(0.016)	(0.017)	(0.019)	(0.020)	(0.018)	(0.019)	(0.022)	(0.022)
*Unemployed	0.066*	0.071*	0.064+	0.067+	0.034	0.040	0.108**	0.121**
	(0.029)	(0.031)	(0.033)	(0.036)	(0.032)	(0.034)	(0.036)	(0.038)
*Insecure job	-0.037*	-0.039*	-0.021	-0.024	-0.026	-0.027	-0.019	-0.019
	(0.017)	(0.018)	(0.020)	(0.021)	(0.018)	(0.019)	(0.020)	(0.021)
N (Individuals)	18,375				19,211			
N (Years)	155				155			
N (Countries)	35				35			

Notes: Lin = linear, HP = Hodrick-Prescott. Significance levels: ** – <1%, * – <5%, + – < 10%. ln – natural logarithm; LM – Labour Market; trend-lin – trend term of linear filtering; res-lin – residual term of linear filtering; trend-hp – trend term of Hodrick-Prescott filtering procedure; res-hp – residual term of Hodrick-Prescott filtering procedure. Rows with covariates preceeding by star correspond to the interaction term of the this covariate with the macro-level covariate above.

life dissatisfaction only in young employed females. The situation is reversed for UR: the long-term trend had no effect on the well-being of employed youth, whereas the unexpected increase in UR was found to increase both unhappiness and life dissatisfaction in employed men, but not in employed women.

The findings related to job insecurity are similar to the main analysis and more in line with Hypothesis 3 (if the effects are statistically significant). None of the macrovariables had a statistically significant moderating effect with respect to life dissatisfaction in men. However, there were significant moderating effects of GDP (UR) trends, but not residuals, for unhappiness for men in insecure employment and for both measures of well-being for women in insecure employment, albeit they are small in magnitude.

Discussion

The aim of the current empirical analysis was to understand under which specific conditions unemployment and job insecurity are particularly damaging for the well-being of young Europeans. To this end, the ESS dataset was used to investigate whether specific macrolevel factors, and particularly the country's economic situation (that is the country's UR and GDP), moderate the individual-level effect of unemployment and job insecurity on two well-being indicators: unhappiness and life dissatisfaction. An advantage of the current analysis is that it also investigated trends and business cycle fluctuations in the macrolevel moderators and how these determine the effects of labour market conditions on well-being. Furthermore, it accounted for potential differences in gender in the examined effects. The implications of the main study findings will now be discussed.

Main effects

In line with relative deprivation theory (Crosby, 1984) and previous empirical evidence (Sverke et al, 2002; De Witte, 2005; Cheng and Chan, 2008), unemployment and job insecurity were found to relate positively to unhappiness and life dissatisfaction in countries with average GDP and UR, even when controlling for one's individual income. When people feel that they are qualified to have a job or a better (that is, more secure) job but do not have one, they feel deprived, and this has negative consequences for their well-being (Harari et al, 2017) making them more unhappy and less satisfied with their lives.

Interestingly, the present analyses shed light on potential gender differences regarding the impact of unemployment and job insecurity on youth well-being. Results revealed that being unemployed is more detrimental for the well-being of males, whereas having an insecure job is more detrimental for the well-being of females. The former finding is in line with the traditional views regarding gender roles that assign a 'breadwinner' role to men (Connell, 1991, 1995). Accordingly, when men are considered responsible for earning, they experience impairments to their well-being when they do not have the means (employment) to satisfy their role. However, results also revealed that being in an insecure job position is more detrimental for the well-being of women than that of men.

Turning to the main effects of the macrolevel indicators on individuals' well-being, results showed that a higher GDP expressed either in level values or as trends and shocks related to better well-being outcomes (lower unhappiness and life dissatisfaction). These results support the assumption based on COR theory (Hobfoll, 1989) that country-level GDP can be viewed as an energy resource at the societal, macrolevel of analysis. When this resource is available, well-being is enhanced. Also, the well-being of young employed Europeans is worse when they live in countries with higher UR, possibly because they may be less likely to find a job that is in line with their skills and qualifications resulting in higher relative deprivation (Crosby, 1984).

Moderating effects

When it comes to the moderating effects of GDP, based on COR theory (Hobfoll, 1989), the positive relationship between unemployment/job insecurity and impaired well-being (unhappiness, job dissatisfaction) was expected to be weaker in countries with higher (vs lower) GDP. Higher GDP implies availability of societal resources, which could, according to COR theory, be used by individuals to deal more effectively with threatening conditions (unemployment or job insecurity). The analyses revealed some significant interaction effects, but not all were in line with expectations. Unexpectedly, GDP was found to exacerbate the positive effect of unemployment on life dissatisfaction (for both genders) and on unhappiness (for females). However, we found that GDP mitigated the effect of an insecure job on unhappiness for both genders. These results suggest that Hypothesis 1 holds for those with insecure employment but not for those who are unemployed. Availability of economic resources at the country level does not help individuals when they are excluded from the labour market, but it does help them when they have an insecure job. This could mean that there are other resources at play (for example, psychological support) that may matter more for unemployed individuals. However, these were not investigated in the present analysis.

Regarding Hypothesis 2, based on social identity theory (Tajfel and Turner, 1986), those unemployed or with insecure jobs living in a country with high unemployment rates were expected to be more likely to compare themselves with those in unfavourable labour market conditions (unemployed people or people with insecure jobs) and that this would prevent reductions in well-being. In other words, the positive relationship between unemployment/job insecurity and life dissatisfaction/unhappiness was expected to be weaker in countries with higher unemployment rates. Results partially confirmed this hypothesis for insecure employment, but not for unemployment.

To explain these findings, it is important to consider the role of relative comparisons. Clark et al (2008) found that happiness relates negatively to others' income and to own past income. In the context investigated here, it is conceivable that in times when many people in a country experience unfavourable working conditions (high UR), the negative effect of job insecurity on well-being may be mitigated by relative comparisons. Namely, and in line with attribution theory (Fiske and Taylor, 1991), individuals with insecure jobs are more likely to compare themselves with others who also experience high levels of insecurity, and to attribute their situation to the external environment. In contrast, when everyone has a job, having an insecure job may be taken as being a failure or being lazy (Furnham, 1982). Under such conditions, those working in insecure jobs are more likely to be affected negatively. When many people are affected by unemployment or a (growing) bad economic situation, having an insecure job may be as good as having a secure one. This is in line with Da Costa and Dias (2014) who suggested that ever since the start of the financial crisis, there is an increasing tendency to attribute individuals' (economic) failure to external societal forces rather than their own characteristics (internal attribution). Attributing one's unfavourable job situation to the environment protects ones self-worth and self-efficacy, which consequently prevents health and well-being impairment (Schwarzer et al, 1997). However, the same argument does not apply to the effect of unemployment on well-being. The present findings suggest that the financial worry related to the availability of jobs has a stronger effect than that of social comparison in the case of a higher macro unemployment rate. Unexpectedly, unemployment proved to have a stronger positive effect on impaired well-being at higher GDP levels. Potentially, this can be explained by relative deprivation theory rather than by the standard economic considerations of availability of resources.

An important contribution of this study is that it also investigated the role of long-term economic trajectories and business cycle fluctuations as moderators of the relationship between labour market status and youth well-being. It hypothesised that long-term economic trajectories (in GDP and UR) would have stronger moderating effects on the positive relationship between unfavourable labour market conditions and impaired well-being than business cycle fluctuations (sudden and abrupt changes in GDP and UR). It argued that a country on a positive long-term economic trajectory may have more resources to buffer the negative effects of individual unemployment irrespective of whether it is currently experiencing a downturn due to business cycle fluctuations. In a similar vein, a country on a negative long-term economic trajectory that experiences a sudden economic boom may not make this resource available to buffer the effect of individual unemployment/job insecurity due to the transitory nature of this increase in resources.

The evidence regarding the moderating role of long-term GDP and UR trajectories and business cycle fluctuations was rather mixed. A higher GDP trend, but not the residual, significantly reduced both unhappiness and life dissatisfaction for employed young men. For women, the same was true for unhappiness, but in the case of life dissatisfaction, the GDP residual also had an effect on the employed. Findings were different for UR. In the case of UR, the sudden increase was more relevant in increasing young employed men's unhappiness, whereas the long-term trend did not seem to have an effect. In the case of life dissatisfaction, both components of UR were found to have a similar effect on employed men. With regards to the moderating effects, both the long-term trajectory and the residual of GDP exacerbated the positive relationship between unemployment and both measures of impaired well-being for men and life dissatisfaction for women. In the case of female unhappiness, the two components worked in the opposite direction: whereas the long-term GDP trend exacerbated the effect of unemployment, the GDP residual actually mitigated it. For the UR, the findings were similar for both men and women – the long-term trend component had a small effect on the relationship between unemployment and life dissatisfaction and unhappiness for men, but the unexpected increase in UR dramatically exacerbated these effects.

In conclusion, this chapter has provided new findings on the moderating effects of macrolevel conditions under which unemployment and insecure labour market positions affect the well-being of young Europeans. Results showed that the economic situation of a country affects the strength of the relationship between unemployment/job insecurity and health/well-being. These results provide insights not only for theory development but also for developing policies aiming to protect the well-being of young Europeans.

Notes

[1] https://ec.europa.eu/eurostat/web/products-eurostat-news/-/WDN-20180813-1
[2] https://ec.europa.eu/eurostat/web/products-eurostat-news/-/DDN-20170502-1
[3] For an explanation of the method, see: http://www.talkstats.com/threads/european-social-survey-income-variable.44664/
[4] http://ww2.prospects.ac.uk/cms/ShowPage/Home_page/Main_Menu___News_and_information/Graduate_Market_Trends/Definitions_of_International_Labour_Organisation_measures/p!edXbLa
[5] All reported differences were statistically significant on the 1% level.

References

Baum, C.F. (2004) 'HPRESCOTT: Stata module to implement Hodrick–Prescott filter for timeseries data', *Statistical Software Components* S447001, Boston: Boston College Department of Economics.

Burns, A.F. and Mitchell, W.C. (1946) 'Effects of trend adjustment on cyclical measures', in A.F. Burns and W.C. Mitchell (eds) *Measuring Business Cycles*, Cambridge: National Bureau of Economic Research, pp 270–309.

Bynner, J. and Parsons, S. (2002) 'Social exclusion and the transition from school to work: the case of young people not in education, employment, or training (NEET)', *Journal of Vocational Behavior*, 60(2): 289–309.

Cheng, G. and Chan, D.K.-S. (2008) 'Who suffers more from job insecurity? A meta-analytic review', *Applied Psychology: An International Review*, 57(2): 272–303.

Chung, H., Bekker, S. and Houwing, H. (2012) 'Young people and the post-recession labour market in the context of Europe 2020', *Transfer: European Review of Labour and Research*, 18(3): 301–17.

Clark, A. (2003) 'Unemployment as a social norm: psychological evidence from panel data', *Journal of Labor Economy*, 21(2): 323–51.

Clark, A.E., Frijters, P. and Shields, M.A. (2008) 'Relative income, happiness and utility: an explanation for the Easterlin paradox and other puzzles', *Journal of Economic Literature*, 46(1): 95–144.

Connell, R.W. (1991) 'Live fast and die young: the construction of masculinity among young working-class men on the margin of the labour market', *Australia and New Zealand Journal of Sociology*, 27(2): 141–71.

Connell, R.W. (1995) *Masculinities*, Cambridge: Polity Press.

Crano, W.D. and Prislin, R. (2006) 'Attitudes and persuasion', *Annual Review of Psychology*, 57(1): 345–74.

Crosby, F. (1984) 'Relative deprivation in organizational settings', *Research in Organizational Behavior*, 6: 51–93.

Da Costa, L.P. and Dias, J.G. (2014) 'Perceptions of poverty attributions in Europe: a multilevel mixture model approach', *Quality and Quantity*, 48: 1409–19.

De Witte, H. (2005) 'Job insecurity: review of the international literature on definitions, prevalence, antecedents and consequences', *SA Journal of Industrial Psychology*, 31(4): 1–6.

Eichhorn, J. (2013) 'Unemployment needs context: how societal differences between countries moderate the loss in life satisfaction for the unemployed', *Journal of Happiness Studies*, 14(6): 1657–80.

Eurostat (2014) 'Archive: impact of the economic crisis on unemployment', Available from: http://ec.europa.eu/eurostat/statistics-explained/index.php/Archive:Impact_of_the_economic_crisis_on_unemployment

Fiske, S.T. and Taylor, S.E. (1991) *Social Cognition* (2nd edn), New York: McGraw-Hill.

Fryer, D. (1998) 'Labour market disadvantage, deprivation and mental health', in P.J.D. Drenth, H. Thierry and C.J. de Wolff (eds) *Handbook of Work and Organizational Psychology*, Vol. 2, Hove: Psychology Press, pp 215–27.

Furnham, A. (1982) 'Explanations for unemployment in Britain', *European Journal of Social Psychology*, 12(4): 335–52.

Harari, M.B., Manapragada, A. and Viswesvaran, C. (2017) 'Who thinks they're a big fish in a small pond and why does it matter? A meta-analysis of perceived overqualification', *Journal of Vocational Behavior*, 102: 28–47.

Hobfoll, S.E. (1989) 'Conservation of resources: a new attempt at conceptualizing stress', *American Psychologist*, 44(3): 513–24.

Hobfoll, S.E. (2002) 'Social and psychological resources and adaptation', *Review of General Psychology*, 6(4): 307–24.

Hodrick, R. and Prescott, E.C. (1997) 'Postwar U.S. business cycles: an empirical investigation', *Journal of Money Credit and Banking*, 29(1): 1–16.

Isaksson, K., Johansson, G., Bellaagh, K. and Sjoberg, A. (2004) 'Work values among the unemployed: changes over time and some gender differences', *Scandinavian Journal of Psychology*, 45(3): 207–14.

Kassenboehmer, S. and Haisken-DeNew, J. (2009) 'You're fired! The causal negative effect of entry unemployment on life satisfaction', *The Economic Journal*, 119(536): 448–62.

Kilpatrick, R. and Trew, K. (1985) 'Life-styles and psychological well-being among unemployed men in Northern Ireland', *Journal of Occupational Psychology*, 58: 207–16.

McKee-Ryan, F.M., Song, Z., Wanberg, C.R. and Kinicki, A.J. (2005) 'Psychological and physical well-being during unemployment: a meta-analytic study', *Journal of Applied Psychology*, 90(1): 53–76.

Nizalova, O. and Murtazashvili, I. (2016) 'Exogenous treatment and endogenous factors: vanishing of omitted variable bias on the interaction term', *Journal of Econometric Methods*, 5(1): 71–78.

Norton, E.C., Nizalova, O. and Murtazashvili, I. (2018) 'Does past unemployment experience explain the transition happiness gap?', *Journal of Comparative Economics*, 46(3): 736–53.

Oesch, D. and Lipps, O. (2013) 'Does unemployment hurt less if there is more of it around? A panel analysis of life satisfaction in Germany and Switzerland', *European Sociological Review*, 29(5): 955–67.

Paul, K.I. and Moser, K. (2009) 'Unemployment impairs mental health: meta-analyses', *Journal of Vocational Behavior*, 74(3): 264–82.

Rollero, C. and Tartaglia, S. (2009) 'Preserving life satisfaction during the economic crisis: what factors can help?', *Psicologia Politica*, 39: 75–87.

Russell, H. and Barbieri, P. (2000) 'Gender and the experience of unemployment', in D. Gallie and S. Paugam (eds) *Welfare Regimes and the Experience of Unemployment in Europe*, Oxford: Oxford University Press, pp 307–33.

Schwarzer, R., Bäßler, J., Kwiatek, P., Schröder, K. and Zhang, J.X. (1997) 'The assessment of optimistic self-beliefs: comparison of the German, Spanish, and Chinese versions of the general self-efficacy scale', *Applied Psychology: An International Review*, 46(1): 69–88.

Shields, M., Price, W.S. and Wooden, M. (2009) 'Life satisfaction and the economic and social characteristics of neighbourhoods', *Journal of Population Economy*, 22(2): 421–43.

Stavrova, O., Schlösser, T. and Fetchenhauer, D. (2011) 'Are the unemployed equally unhappy all around the world? The role of the social norms to work and welfare state provision in 28 OECD countries', *Journal of Economic Psychology*, 32(1): 159–71.

Sverke, M., Hellgren, J. and Naswall, K. (2002) 'No security: a meta-analysis and review of job insecurity and its consequences', *Journal of Occupational Health Psychology*, 7(3): 242–64.

Tajfel, H. and Turner, J.C. (1986) 'The social identity theory of intergroup behavior', in S. Worchel and L.W. Austin (eds) *Psychology of Intergroup Relations*, Chicago: Nelson-Hall, pp 33–48.

Tesser, A., Millar, M. and Moore, J. (1988) 'Some affective consequences of social comparison and reflection processes: the pain and pleasure of being close', *Journal of Personality and Social Psychology*, 54(1): 49–61.

Voßemer, J. and Eunicke, N. (2015) *The Impact of Labor Market Exclusion and Job Insecurity on Health and Well-Being Among Youth: A Literature Review*. EXCEPT Working Papers, WP No. 2, Tallinn: Tallinn University, Available from: http://www.except-project.eu/working-papers/

Voßemer, J., Gebel, M., Täht, K., Unt, M., Högberg, B. and Strandh, M. (2018) 'The effects of unemployment and insecure jobs on well-being and health: the moderating role of labor market policies', *Social Indicators Research*, 138(3): 1229–57.

World Bank (2016a) *Unemployment* [indicator], Available from: http://data.worldbank.org/in dicator/SL.UEM.TOTL.ZS

World Bank (2016b) *GDP, PPP* [indicator], Available from: http://data.worldbank.org/indicator/NY.GDP.MKTP.PP.CD

Wooldridge, J.M. (2010) *Econometric Analysis of Cross Section and Panel Data* (2nd edn), Cambridge; London: MIT Press Books, The MIT Press.

Wooldridge, J.M. (2016) *Introductory Econometrics: A Modern Approach* (6th edn), Mason: South-Western.

Wulfgramm, M. (2014) 'Life satisfaction effects of unemployment in Europe: the moderating influence of labour market policy', *Journal of European Social Policy*, 24(3): 258–72.

3

Health effects of unemployment in couples: does becoming unemployed affect a young partner's health?

Anna Baranowska-Rataj and Mattias Strandh

Introduction

Losing a job has been shown to cause stress and anxiety and lead to deteriorating physical health (Brand, 2015). Young people are particularly vulnerable to the changes in labour market conditions (Müller and Gangl, 2003; Bell and Blanchflower, 2011). Compared to people in the prime age group, they have fewer financial and social resources that can be mobilised to deal with the stress resulting from unemployment. Hence, the impact of unemployment on health in this group is of particular concern.

A large body of research has scrutinised changes in health and well-being among people who lose their jobs (for literature reviews, see McKee-Ryan et al, 2005; Paul and Moser, 2009; Voßemer and Eunicke, 2015; Wanberg, 2012). However, job losses may have consequences for not only those individuals who become unemployed but also their family members (Brand, 2015; Maitoza, 2019). The idea that the consequences of one household member becoming unemployed resonate within the whole family was already proposed in Komarovsky's (1940) classic study in the United States following the Great Depression. That seminal study took the perspective of a traditional family and focused on the authority relations of the man in his role as husband and father. However, changing gender relationships in the public and the private spheres have irreversibly altered power relations within

  This study has received funding from the European Research Council (ERC) under the European Union's Horizon 2020 research and innovation programme under grant agreement No. 802631.

modern families – one manifestation being the substantial increase in dual-earner households (Goldscheider et al, 2015). Therefore, the consequences of unemployment are relevant for both partners within a couple, and not just for its male representative.

This chapter examines the impact of transition to unemployment on self-rated health in young people's partners. Previous research has indicated that this group is the most vulnerable with respect to the magnitude of unemployment effects. Young people are at high risk of unemployment, are least established in the labour market, and, in many welfare state contexts, they lack access to welfare state benefits while at the same time, they do not have savings that could cushion reductions in household income (Blossfeld et al, 2011). In addition, this chapter looks at differences in the effects of unemployment on partners' health across European societies. It relates the magnitude of the impact of male and female partners' unemployment to the social norms determining the degree to which doing paid work is valued, as well as whose work – men's or women's – is valued relatively more highly. Specifically, it considers the role of the so-called work obligation (also known as work ethic) as a factor that may alter the impact of partners' unemployment on individual health. It also tests whether male partners' unemployment matters more in those societies in which social norms support the primacy of a breadwinner role, and whether female partners' unemployment is relatively more harmful in egalitarian societies.

The study is guided by theories on within-family diffusion of the health effects of adverse life course events such as transition to unemployment. These theories are used to explain how distress spreads between the professional and private lives of individuals and the channels through which it may also affect the health of other family members. This also adds to the rather scarce empirical evidence on the effects of partners' unemployment on health. The study also uses longitudinal methods and microdata from European Union Statistics on Income and Living Conditions (EU-SILC) survey. Unlike many surveys, EU-SILC provides information about both partners within a couple. This can be used to explore the wider impact of unemployment on the health of partners. The longitudinal dimension of the data provides an opportunity to control for pre-existing differences in health conditions. In addition, the methods used here reduce the possible bias resulting from unobserved heterogeneity. Finally, as EU-SILC includes data from 30 countries, the chapter examines the heterogeneity of effects of partners' unemployment across societies.

The effects of unemployment on health

Involvement in paid work has multiple functions for human health and well-being (Jahoda, 1981; Warr, 1987; Strandh, 2000). Employment is the key source of income, especially among young people. Income is necessary for satisfying physical needs and it gives the feeling of having control over one's life as well as making it possible to set private plans for the future. In addition, employment provides individuals with time structure, social contacts, and opportunities to develop skills as well as social status and identity. Being deprived of these benefits can be especially harmful for youth, because in the early stages of the life course, attaining economic stability and self-sufficiency are important markers of the transition to adulthood (Danziger and Ratner, 2010). Indeed, a large body of empirical research confirms that unemployment has negative effects on health, both in the general population and among youth (Voßemer and Eunicke, 2015).

Previous research on the health effects of unemployment has examined these effects by focusing on individuals who lose their jobs. However, it is necessary to consider family members of the unemployed and their health outcomes in order to advance understanding of the impact of labour market careers on health (Brand, 2015). The economic need for employment, central to understanding the effects of unemployment on individual health, should be equally valid for the family. Although economic deprivation and strain have been found to be associated with poorer family relations (Voydanoff, 1990; Conger et al, 1990), the effects of unemployment on marital instability cannot be explained solely by related reductions in income (Charles and Stephens, 2004). This suggests that there are non-monetary channels by which unemployment impacts on family members' health and well-being.

Previous research has often pictured other family members, and especially partners, as a buffer that absorbs the effects of negative life course events, but it has devoted relatively little attention to identifying the processes that channel this influence in relation to job loss and unemployment (Howe et al, 2004; Tattarini et al, 2018). Studies in psychology document so-called spillover effects – that is, the spread of emotions across different life domains. This transmission may concern not only positive but also negative emotions such as stress and strain. After distress spills over from the work-related to the home-related domain, it may cross over to closely related persons and especially to partners (Bakker et al, 2009). The crossover effects may result from sharing the partner's emotional state (Bakker and Demerouti, 2013). In addition, unemployment of one of the partners may lead to behaviours that place a burden on other family members, and this may, in turn, become a stressor for them, with negative consequences for their health (Rook et al, 1991).

Both monetary and non-monetary factors that are potential mediators of the impact of unemployment on a partner's well-being lead to the prediction that a partner of a jobless individual may experience more health problems compared to a partner of an employed individual. However, the magnitude of this effect may vary across societal contexts for reasons outlined later.

Societies differ substantially in the degree to which paid work is valued and not working is stigmatised, and there is also substantial heterogeneity in terms of social norms related to the division of paid work within couples. In some countries, it is believed that paid work is a moral duty of each individual. The so-called work obligation (or work ethic) refers to the moral embeddedness of work. This concept differs substantively from work-related individual motives or preferences about work (Niles, 1999; Furnham, 1982). Previous research has shown that the detrimental impact of unemployment on health and well-being tends be larger in contexts with a stronger work obligation, because of the stronger social stigma attached to being without a job (Stam et al, 2016). Following the same logic, one could argue that a partner's unemployment may be more harmful in such contexts.

Women's and men's work are not valued equally and not doing paid work is not stigmatised in all societies. As Paul and Moser (2009) frame it: 'masculine identity is intricately linked to having a job in Western societies and is severely threatened by unemployment'. Indeed, a number of empirical studies show that men are substantially more distressed by unemployment than women (Paul and Moser, 2009), although there is no consensus that these results are universal across all societal contexts (McKee-Ryan et al, 2005). Strandh et al (2013) have shown that the divergent findings regarding individual effects of unemployment may fit a contextual pattern in which gendered effects of unemployment on health may be stronger in societies with more traditional gender-role attitudes. At the same time, the health effects of unemployment may be expected to be similar for men and women in egalitarian societies. This argument can be transposed to explain the differences in the gendered impact of partners' unemployment across societies. Less detrimental effects of male partners' unemployment and relatively stronger effects of female partners' unemployment may be expected in countries that do not ascribe primacy to the male breadwinner role.

So far, few studies on the effects of unemployment on partners' health have employed longitudinal data and used methods that reduce the bias related to the selectivity of unemployed individuals with respect to pre-existing health differences. One study that overcame these shortcomings was carried out in Germany by Marcus (2013), who observed larger negative effects on mental health when male partners experienced job losses than when job losses were experienced by female partners. In a study using data from the UK, Mendolia (2014) has shown that when a husband loses a job, his wife's mental health deteriorates. Other studies on the consequences of partners' unemployment have focused on happiness or life satisfaction rather than on health (see for instance Nikolova and Ayhan, 2019). To the best of the authors' knowledge, except for the study by Baranowska-Rataj and Strandh (2020), there has been no research on partners' unemployment and health that takes a cross-country comparative perspective. Hence, the conclusions from previous research cannot be generalised to all European countries, and more evidence is needed on the societal conditions that moderate the effects of partners' job loss on individual health.

Research design

This study uses longitudinal methods that give an opportunity to disentangle the effects of partners' transition to unemployment on individual health from the impact of pre-existing individual health conditions. The first step uses random-effects models for descriptive purposes. The second step estimates correlated random-effects models in order to reduce the possible bias resulting from the unobserved heterogeneity among young people. Correlated random-effects models, also known as hybrid models, combine the high internal validity of fixed effects models with the high efficiency of random-effects models, leading to unbiased and equally precise estimates of the effects of interest (Bell and Jones, 2015).

Panel data are employed from the EU-SILC survey which covers 30 European countries over the period 2003–13. EU-SILC is a household survey providing information on both the labour market status and health of all adult family members living under the same roof. The latter is crucial from the point of view of the research questions on the health effects of unemployment within couples. Due to its longitudinal character, it is possible to control for baseline health conditions and other unobserved factors that may affect both labour market career dynamics and health. The sample includes people aged 18–30 years and their partners (if they have any).[1]

The key dependent variable is constructed on the basis of respondents' self-assessment of overall health at the time of the survey. Respondents rated their health using a 5-point scale ranging from 1 (*very good*) to 5 (*very bad*). Although self-assessed health may be subject to culture-related bias (Jürges, 2007), this measure has been shown to be a reliable indicator of health, because it correlates with subsequent deterioration of functional capabilities and with mortality across different social categories and contexts (Öm and Fredlund, 2001; Jylhä, 2009).

The key explanatory variables are the labour market status of individuals and their partners. To avoid excluding person observations of individuals who were unpartnered at some selected time points, partnership status was controlled. The labour market status variable distinguishes between employment, unemployment, and inactivity. The control variables in baseline models include age and educational attainment (elementary education [or less (ISCED 0–1)], lower secondary education [ISCED 2], upper secondary education [ISCED 3], post-secondary education [ISCED 4], and tertiary education [ISCED 5]). To control for pre-existing ill health and reduce the bias related to pre-selection of individuals with health problems into the group whose partners experience job separation, long-standing illness was controlled with a lag of one year.[2] Because both unemployment and health outcomes vary across welfare state regimes (Bambra, 2011; Bambra and Eikemo, 2008), fixed effects were included for the following groups of countries: (a) Nordic countries (Denmark, Finland, Iceland, Norway, and Sweden); (b) Western European countries (Austria, Belgium, France, Luxembourg, and the Netherlands); (c) the UK and Ireland (England, Scotland, Wales, Northern Ireland, and the Republic of Ireland); (d) Southern European countries (Greece, Portugal, Spain, and Italy); (e) post-socialist countries (Czech Republic, Hungary, Poland, Slovakia, Slovenia, Romania, Bulgaria, Estonia, Latvia, and Lithuania); and (f) a residual group of south-eastern European countries (Croatia, Cyprus, and Malta). Separate models were estimated for men and women.

The analysis of factors mediating the impact of unemployment on health between partners includes two potential mediators. First, information was used on the health status of the person who becomes unemployed. The second variable measuring the mediating impact of changes in household income is based on individual assessments of household financial difficulties (on a scale from 1 to 6, with higher scores indicating an ability to make ends meet very easily). Table 3.1 presents the distribution of all individual-level variables used in this analysis.

Table 3.1: Impact of individual and partner's unemployment on self-rated health among young men and women – results from panel data models

	Model 1 RE model, men		Model 2 Correlated RE model, men		Model 3 RE model, women		Model 4 Correlated RE model, women	
	Coef	SE	Coef	SE	Coef	SE	Coef	SE
Age	0.02***	(0.00)	0.02***	(0.00)	0.02***	(0.00)	0.02***	(0.00)
Education (ref. ISCED 2)								
ISCED0-1	0.01	(0.03)	0.00	(0.03)	0.05**	(0.02)	0.04*	(0.02)
ISCED3	−0.10***	(0.02)	−0.09***	(0.02)	−0.09***	(0.01)	−0.08***	(0.01)
ISCED4	−0.13***	(0.03)	−0.12***	(0.03)	−0.16***	(0.03)	−0.15***	(0.03)
ISCED5	−0.21***	(0.02)	−0.20***	(0.02)	−0.20***	(0.01)	−0.19***	(0.01)
LLSI*	0.35***	(0.02)	0.35***	(0.02)	0.37***	(0.01)	0.37***	(0.01)
Partnership status (ref. has a partner)								
No partner	0.04**	(0.02)	0.03*	(0.02)	0.02	(0.01)	0.01	(0.01)
Labour market status (ref: employment)								
Unemployment	0.10***	(0.02)	0.05**	(0.02)	0.07***	(0.01)	0.01	(0.02)
Inactivity	0.10***	(0.02)	0.09***	(0.03)	0.00	(0.01)	−0.02	(0.01)

Table 3.1: Impact of individual and partner's unemployment on self-rated health among young men and women – results from panel data models (continued)

	Model 1 RE model, men		Model 2 Correlated RE model, men		Model 3 RE model, women		Model 4 Correlated RE model, women	
	Coef	SE	Coef	SE	Coef	SE	Coef	SE
Partner's labour market status (ref. employment)								
Unemployment	0.04**	(0.02)	0.02	(0.02)	0.08***	(0.02)	0.05**	(0.02)
Inactivity	0.01	(0.01)	-0.01	(0.02)	0.02	(0.02)	-0.02	(0.03)
Country group (ref. Western European)								
Nordic	-0.02	(0.02)	-0.02	(0.02)	-0.01	(0.02)	-0.01	(0.02)
Anglo-Saxon	-0.06**	(0.03)	-0.06**	(0.03)	-0.03	(0.02)	-0.03	(0.02)
Southern	0.14***	(0.02)	0.13***	(0.02)	0.12***	(0.01)	0.11***	(0.01)
Post-socialist	0.14***	(0.01)	0.14***	(0.02)	0.14***	(0.01)	0.13***	(0.01)
South-Eastern**	-0.21***	(0.03)	-0.21***	(0.03)	-0.20***	(0.02)	-0.21***	(0.02)
Constant	1.05***	(0.06)	1.01***	(0.07)	1.31***	(0.05)	1.27***	(0.05)
N	17,209		17,209		28,114		28,114	

Notes: RE = random effects; SE = standard error.
Self-rated health ratings range from 1 (very good) to 5 (very bad).
* Limiting long-standing illness (LLSI), lagged values.
* $p < 0.10$, ** $p < 0.05$, *** $p < 0.01$.
Source: EU-SILC 2003–13

Table 3.2: Results for mediating role of reduced household income and partner's health

	Model 5 Correlated RE model, men		Model 6 Correlated RE model, women		Model 7 Correlated RE model, men		Model 8 Correlated RE model, women	
	Coef.	SE	Coef.	SE	Coef.	SE	Coef.	SE
Partner's labour market status (ref. employed)								
Unemployed	0.02	(0.03)	0.02	(0.02)	0.01	(0.02)	0.03	(0.02)
Inactive	0.00	(0.02)	−0.04	(0.03)	−0.02	(0.02)	−0.03	(0.03)
Mediators								
Partner's health	0.20***	(0.01)	0.17***	(0.01)				
Ability to make ends meet					−0.02***	(0.01)	−0.03***	(0.01)
Constant	0.82***	(0.07)	1.07***	(0.05)	1.29***	(0.07)	1.58***	(0.05)
N	14736		25170		17209		28114	

Notes: Control variables as in Table 3.1. RE = random-effects; SE = standard error. *p < 0.10. **p < 0.05. ***p < 0.01. Models 5 and 6 estimated only for partnered individuals; partnership status is excluded from the list of control variables in these models.
Source: EU-SILC 2003–13

The moderating role of work obligation was examined with a synthetic indicator developed on the basis of the European Values Survey (Stam, 2015). This indicator is composed of five items: 'To fully develop your talents, you need to have a job'; 'It is humiliating to receive money without having to work for it'; 'People who don't work turn lazy'; 'Work is a duty towards society'; and 'Work should always come first, even if it means less spare time'. These items reflect a secular functional approach to the concept of work (Jahoda, 1981). Higher scores indicate a strong work obligation.[3] To examine whether the effect of partners' unemployment differs across societies with diverging gender-role attitudes, a contextual variable was included to indicate the country-specific proportion of people who agree with the statement 'When jobs are scarce, men should have more right to a job than women' derived from the 2004 European Social Survey. This variable has been used in a number of previous studies to examine the antecedents and consequences of gender-role attitudes, because it measures social perception of the primacy of the male breadwinner role (Davis and Greenstein, 2009). The distribution of variables at the country level is provided in Table 3.2.

Table 3.3: Results for moderating factors: gender-role attitudes and work ethics

	Model 9 Correlated RE model, men		Model 10 Correlated RE model, women	
	Coef.	SE	Coef.	SE
Partnership status (ref. has a partner)				
No partner	0.00	(0.05)	−0.06	(0.04)
Partner's labour market status (ref. employment)				
Unemployment	0.00	(0.06)	−0.03	(0.06)
Inactivity	0.03	(0.04)	−0.11**	(0.05)
Gender-role attitudes	−0.20	(0.18)	−0.23	(0.21)
Interaction: Partner's labour market status × Gender-role attitudes				
No partner × Gender-role attitudes	0.00	(0.07)	−0.00	(0.10)
Partner's unemployment × Gender-role attitudes	−0.07	(0.08)	0.20*	(0.11)
Partner's inactivity × Gender-role attitudes	−0.00	(0.07)	−0.11	(0.09)
Work ethics	−0.17**	(0.09)	−0.28***	(0.10)
Interaction: Partner's labour market status × Work ethics				
No partner × Work ethics	0.05	(0.13)	0.11	(0.15)
Partner's unemployment × Work ethics	0.05	(0.08)	−0.07	(0.11)
Partner's inactivity × Work ethics	−0.09	(0.06)	0.31**	(0.13)
Constant	1.39***	(0.14)	1.69***	(0.15)
N	15,816		25,310	

Notes: Control variables as in Model 7 and 8 in Table 3.2. RE = random-effects; SE = standard error. *p < 0.10. **p < 0.05. ***p < 0.01. Gender-role attitudes: country-specific proportion of people who agree with the statement 'When jobs are scarce, men should have more right to a job than women' derived from the 2004 European Social Survey. Work ethics: an indicator developed by Stam et al (2013). Due to missing values in indicators of social norms, Croatia, Italy, and Malta were excluded from these analyses.
Source: EU-SILC 2003–13

Empirical results

For descriptive purposes, the first step estimated random-effects models that do not take the European diversity of social contexts explicitly into account. The results from these models which estimated separately for men and women are presented in Table 3.3 (Models 1 and 3). They show that the relationship between becoming unemployed and poorer self-rated health among both men and women is statistically significant. However, transition into inactivity is associated with a negative effect only among men. After controlling for unobserved heterogeneity among young people using correlated random-effects models (Models 2 and 4 in Table 3.3), the impact of both unemployment and inactivity weakens, remaining statistically significant in men but no longer playing a major role in women.

The results of these analyses also show the impact of partners' labour market status on self-rated health. Standard random-effects models (Models 1 and 3) indicate that individual unemployment is associated with scores indicating poorer health. The analyses reveal that it is not only the individual's but also the partner's unemployment that is associated with statistically significant poorer health among men and women. After controlling for unobserved heterogeneity within correlated random-effects models (Models 2 and 4 in Table 3.3), the impact of partners' unemployment weakens, remaining statistically significant among women, but having no effect among men. According to these results, women are not affected negatively by their own unemployment, but they do report poorer health if their husband is unemployed. The reverse is true for men. Partners' inactivity does not affect self-rated health among men or women.

The effects of control variables are stable across models and show hardly any gender differences. Age is associated with poorer self-rated health, whereas educational attainment is associated with more positive health outcomes. Limiting long-standing illness reported in the first wave of the survey is associated with substantially poorer health, which underscores the importance of controlling for baseline health in longitudinal analyses. Partnership status seems to play a positive role, but only for men's health. The analyses reveal health differences across welfare state regimes. Living in southern Europe and post-socialist countries is associated with a health disadvantage compared to western Europe or Nordic countries. Men living in Anglo-Saxon countries as well as in Croatia, Malta, and Cyprus tend to have better health, whereas among women, the same holds only for the south-eastern group of countries.

The theoretical framework indicates two specific mechanisms that lead to of the spread of health effects of unemployment among partners: reduction in household income and transmission of distress. Whereas a formal mediation analysis is beyond the scope of this chapter, it is possible to test whether income deprivation and partners' poor health are associated with worse individual health and also

Table 3.4: Sample structure – means and proportions

	Men		Women	
	Mean	SD	Mean	SD
Self-rated health	1.68	0.68	1.76	0.69
Age	27.12	2.64	26.79	2.76
ISCED0-1	5.3%		4.5%	
ISCED2	17.4%		15.5%	
ISCED3	50.9%		45.5%	
ISCED4	3.0%		3.4%	
ISCED5	23.4%		31.2%	
LLSI	12.0%		12.9%	
No partner	14.4%		10.5%	
Labour market status				
Employed	83.9%		60.3%	
Unemployed	9.2%		9.9%	
Inactive	6.9%		29.8%	
Partner's labour market status				
Employed	52.7%		76.1%	
Unemployed	8.6%		7.4%	
Inactive	24.3%		3.5%	
Nordic	16.3%		13.5%	
Anglo-Saxon	4.8%		5.0%	
Western	26.0%		25.6%	
Southern	13.3%		15.3%	
Post-socialist	35.9%		36.6%	
South-Eastern	3.6%		4.0%	
Mediators				
Partner's health	1.74	0.68	1.74	0.69
Ability to make ends meet	3.25	1.29	3.20	1.26

Note: SD = standard deviation.
Source: EU-SILC 2003–13

whether controlling for these variables reduces the effect of partner's unemployment on health. The results presented in Table 3.4 confirm all these expectations. An increased score in the scale indicating poor health of a partner is related to a rather substantial increase in individual reports of poor health. Controlling for partner's health eliminates the effect of partner's unemployment on individual health. The effects of a reduction in household income (measured on a scale from 1 to 6) seem to be much less strongly related to individual health, although they are statistically significant; and controlling for the household's ability to make ends meet also reduces the effect of partner's unemployment. In sum, it seems plausible to think that both mechanisms – a reduction in household income and the transmission of distress – may be at work, and both contribute to the impact of unemployment on health among partners.

The final analysis addresses the role of social norms that define the degree to which work is valued and not working is stigmatised and that specify whose work is valued more: that of male or female partners (Table 3.5). Results indicate that among men, partner's unemployment plays no role regardless of whether a society is conservative or egalitarian. Among women, the effect of partner's unemployment varies with gender-role attitudes – that is, conservative attitudes amplify the impact of partner's unemployment. However, gender-role attitudes themselves are not associated with self-rated health. Results show that societies with higher work ethics tend to have better self-rated health. At the same time, there is no interaction between partner's unemployment and work ethics, but there is an interaction between partner's inactivity and work ethics among women. It seems that in societies in which people believe that doing paid work is a moral duty, women who have a partner who is unemployed do not experience as much distress as those whose partner does not work and does not search for a job.

As a sensitivity analysis, work obligation was replaced with country-specific measures of an aggregate unemployment rate that has been used as a proxy for 'the social norm of unemployment' in previous research (Clark, 2003; Clark et al, 2010). This shows in which countries unemployment is not strongly stigmatised (see Table 3.6). This analysis shows a similar pattern: again, results indicated that among men, female partner's unemployment plays no role, regardless of whether a society is conservative or egalitarian, but gender-role attitudes do moderate the impact of partner's unemployment among women. Hence, these results also confirm that societal conservatism contributes to the transmission of health effects of unemployment from men to their female partners. The effects of the interaction between aggregate unemployment and partner's unemployment are also consistent with the theory-based expectations. An increase in the aggregate unemployment rate decreases the overall effect of partner's unemployment on women's health, indicating that in countries in which not having a job is more common

Table 3.5: Distribution of contextual variables across countries

Country	Gender-role attitudes	Work ethics	Unemployment rate	Sample size
Austria	21.6	3.7	5.1	1,560
Belgium	30.7	3.3	7.8	1,819
Bulgaria	33.2	4.1	9.0	1,264
Cyprus	40.0	4.0	9.8	1,059
Czechia	36.5	3.6	6.0	1,614
Denmark	8.3	3.5	5.5	549
Estonia	36.5	3.6	8.8	2,008
Greece	48.2	3.8	10.3	484
Spain	30.4	3.5	16.4	2,506
Finland	12.4	3.2	7.8	2,284
France	27.9	3.5	9.1	5,042
Croatia		3.4	16.2	138
Hungary	57.3	3.9	9.6	2,131
Ireland	12.8	3.5	11.3	542
Island	23.7		4.7	944
Italy		3.7	8.2	2,549
Lithuania	28.2	3.5	12.3	738
Luxembourg	25.0	3.6	4.8	2,226
Latvia	19.5	3.5	13.0	1,401
Malta		3.5	6.4	566
Netherlands	22.0	3.1	5.3	1,026
Norway	8.4	3.6	3.6	1,362
Poland	41.0	3.5	9.0	4,116
Portugal	38.9	3.9	13.4	1,059
Romania	35.0	3.9	6.1	791
Sweden	8.7	3.3	7.5	1,461
Slovenia	24.4	3.7	7.2	729
Slovakia	32.3	3.8	12.7	1,676
UK	25.3	3.3	7.1	1,679

Sources: Gender-role attitudes: European Social Survey 2004. Work ethics: Stam et al (2013). Unemployment rate: Eurostat. Sample size: EU-SILC 2003–13

Table 3.6: Results for moderating factors: gender-role attitudes and social norm of unemployment

	Men		Women	
	Coef.	SE	Coef.	SE
Partnership status (ref. has a partner)				
No partner	0.11**	(0.05)	0.05	(0.05)
Partner's labour market status (ref. employment)				
Unemployed	0.09	(0.07)	0.06	(0.07)
Inactive	0.01	(0.05)	0.00	(0.09)
Gender-role attitudes	−0.30*	(0.16)	−0.32*	(0.19)
Interaction: Partner's labour market status × Gender-role attitudes				
No partner × Gender-role attitudes	0.13	(0.11)	0.14	(0.10)
Partner's unemployment × Gender-role attitudes	0.03	(0.13)	0.16**	(0.08)
Partner's inactivity × Gender-role attitudes	−0.04	(0.06)	0.07	(0.07)
Unemployment rate	−0.01	(0.01)	−0.00	(0.01)
Interaction: Partner's labour market status × Unemployment rate:				
No partner × Unemployment rate	−0.01***	(0.01)	−0.02**	(0.01)
Unemployed partner × Unemployment rate	−0.01	(0.01)	−0.01**	(0.00)
Inactive partner × Unemployment rate	−0.00	(0.00)	−0.01	(0.01)
Macroeconomic shocks	−0.00	(0.01)	0.01	(0.01)
Interaction: Partner's labour market status × Macroeconomic shocks:				
No partner × Macroeconomic shocks	0.00	(0.01)	0.00	(0.00)
Unemployed partner × Macroeconomic shocks	0.01**	(0.00)	0.01	(0.01)
Inactive partner × Macroeconomic shocks	0.01**	(0.01)	−0.00	(0.01)
Constant	1.40***	(0.15)	1.61***	(0.15)
N	16,196		25,874	

Note: Control variables as in Table 3.1. SE = standard error. *p < 0.10. **p < 0.05. ***p < 0.01.
Source: EU-SILC 2003–13

Table 3.7: Results for additional analyses combining individual and partners' labour market status

	Men		Women	
	Coef.	SE	Coef.	SE
Partners' labour market status (ref. dual-earner household)				
Employed, no partner	0.04*	(0.02)	–0.02	(0.02)
Not employed, no partner	0.12***	(0.03)	0.02	(0.02)
Employed, partner not employed	0.00	(0.02)	–0.00	(0.03)
Not employed, partner employed	0.07**	(0.03)	–0.00	(0.01)
Both partners not employed	0.06**	(0.03)	0.04	(0.02)
Constant	1.03***	(0.06)	1.27***	(0.05)
N	17,226		28,141	

Note: Control variables as in Table 3.1. SE = standard error. *p < 0.10. **p < 0.05. ***p < 0.01.
Source: EU-SILC 2003–13

and less stigmatised, a male partner's unemployment is relatively less detrimental for women.

It could be argued that it is not only partner's unemployment but also the specific aspects of the division of paid work within a household that affect individual health and interact with social norms. For example, a male partner's unemployment could be seen as particularly difficult to accept and therefore detrimental for health if combined with a female partner's employment. Additional analyses examined this issue in more detail, but this required combining different groups of non-working partners because of the small number of observations in some specific categories (Table 3.7). Results show that for unemployed men, having a partner who does have a job is just as harmful as living in a jobless household. For women, living in a household with a partner who does not work does not seem to have any effect, most likely due to diverging effects of male partners' unemployment and inactivity.

Results could be also affected by idiosyncratic shocks such as the Great Recession. Therefore, additional analyses controlled for fixed effects of years, but introducing these control variables did not change the results (Table 3.8).

Discussion

This chapter adds to the literature on health effects of unemployment by showing that the negative effects of lack of jobs may go beyond

Table 3.8: Results for additional analyses using fixed effects for years of survey

	Men		Women	
	Coef.	SE	Coef.	SE
Partnership status (ref. has a partner)				
	0.03*	(0.02)	−0.03*	(0.02)
Partner's labour market status (ref. employment)				
Unemployed	0.05**	(0.02)	0.01	(0.02)
Inactive	0.09***	(0.03)	−0.02	(0.01)
Partner's labour market status (ref. employment)				
Unemployed	0.02	(0.02)	0.05**	(0.02)
Inactive	−0.01	(0.02)	−0.02	(0.03)
Fixed effects for years (ref. 2004)				
2005	0.03	(0.04)	0.10***	(0.03)
2006	0.03	(0.06)	0.08*	(0.04)
2007	0.07*	(0.04)	0.17***	(0.03)
2008	0.07	(0.04)	0.17***	(0.03)
2009	0.07	(0.04)	0.17***	(0.03)
2010	0.07	(0.05)	0.24***	(0.04)
2011	0.07	(0.04)	0.17***	(0.03)
2012	0.06	(0.04)	0.16***	(0.03)
2013	0.07*	(0.04)	0.19***	(0.03)
Constant	0.96***	(0.08)	1.09***	(0.06)
N	17,209		28,114	

Notes: Control variables as in Table 3.1. SE = standard error. *$p < 0.10$. **$p < 0.05$. ***$p < 0.01$.
Source: EU-SILC 2003–13

young people who became unemployed and also affect their partners (married or otherwise). The effects of a partner's transition into unemployment are stronger among women compared to men, implying that the impact of unemployment on health between partners is gendered. Results highlight the role of within-household social interactions and income pooling for health outcomes of young people who lose their jobs. The chapter also contributes to the literature discussing the moderating impact of cultural and structural conditions on the effects of unemployment on health. According to the present results, the degree to which the partner's unemployment is detrimental is conditional on the country-specific context. Young men's unemployment deteriorates their female partners' health most of all in conservative countries, with social norms supporting male breadwinner supremacy. These effects are also stronger in countries with stronger work ethics and lower in countries with high aggregate unemployment that serves as a proxy for the so-called social norm of unemployment.

The present study focuses on young people, because this social category has been shown to be most vulnerable to the macroeconomic shocks; and, at the same time, youth have few resources that could shield them from the effects of unemployment – whether their own or those of their partners. Nevertheless, it would be interesting to take a life course perspective and examine in a more systematic way how the magnitude of the spillover effects observed varies across different family members' life course stages. Because the available panel data cover up to four years for each individual, such an analysis could not be carried out here. However, future research using data stretching over a longer time span could examine this issue.

Although the analyses presented in this chapter pay a lot of attention to the moderating role of gender roles, this is done by examining the effect of partner's unemployment separately among women and among men and by analysing the interaction of these effects with country-level gender role attitudes. It would be interesting to take a more nuanced perspective on gender by considering the fact that men and women have different ideas about femininity and masculinity, different attitudes towards their own roles in their families, and different expectations towards partners (Springer et al, 2012). Moreover, given family diversity in modern societies, future research could consider the impact of partner's unemployment in the context of same-sex couples. However, these questions are beyond the scope of this chapter, because the available data do not provide detailed enough information to address them.

The results of this study are relevant for discussions about policies aiming to reduce the societal consequences of unemployment. Usually, introducing new policies is based on a careful assessment of costs and benefits. Much of the evaluation literature focuses on the benefits of policies supporting re-employment (Card et al, 2015) because high job finding rates reduce government expenses. Relatively less attention has been paid to the potential health benefits of policy support targeting people who are searching for jobs (for notable exceptions, see Wulfgramm, 2011; Saloniemi et al, 2014; Wulfgramm, 2011;

Wulfgramm, 2014; Voßemer et al, 2018) as well as implications for health expenditures (Biro and Elek, forthcoming). The current findings suggest that assessments of the benefits of programmes targeting the unemployed should not be restricted to the target persons of these policies but need to include their family members. In other words, the positive impact of programmes targeting the unemployed might be much larger overall than studies analysing individuals in isolation from their family members would imply. The call to pay attention to the benefits from policies that extend beyond the target group is in line with insights from previous studies that view welfare state support as a collective resource (Voßemer et al, 2018; Sjöberg, 2010; Baranowska-Rataj and Högberg, 2018).

Notes

[1] The sample includes all types of partnerships between married people and partners in consensual union (with or without a legal basis). Because the sample is restricted to young people, it did not condition on partner's age. In other words, information on partners' labour market status is included even if a partner is older than 30.

[2] By using a lagged variable, the analysis effectively uses panel data over the period 2004–14, because the first wave needs to be omitted from the analysis. Note that the control variable is different from the dependent variable (self-rated health), meaning we avoid conditioning on baseline outcome levels.

[3] Stam et al (2015) present evidence on the high reliability of these measures: their factor analysis shows that all items load on one factor with an eigenvalue of at least 1 in all countries with a Cronbach's alpha ranging from 0.58 to 0.79. In the present study, excluding countries with Cronbach's alpha lower than 0.65 does not change the results.

References

Bakker, A.B. and Demerouti, E. (2013) 'The spillover-crossover model', in J. G. Grzywacz and E. Demerouti (eds) *Current Issues in Work and Organizational Psychology: New Frontiers in Work and Family Research*, London: Psychology Press, pp 54–70.

Bakker, A.B., Westman, M., and van Emmerik, I.J.H. (2009) 'Advancements in crossover theory', *Journal of Managerial Psychology*, 24: 206–19.

Bambra, C. (2011) 'Health inequalities and welfare state regimes: theoretical insights on a public health "puzzle"', *Journal of Epidemiology and Community Health*, 65: 740–5.

Bambra, C. and Eikemo, T. (2008) 'Welfare state regimes, unemployment and health: a comparative study of the relationship between unemployment and self-reported health in 23 European countries', *Journal of Epidemiology and Community Health*, 63: 92–8.

Baranowska-Rataj, A. and Högberg, B. (2018) *Spillover Effects of Social Policies: Can the State Support for the Unemployed Affect Employees' Health and Wellbeing?* Report for Arena Ide, Stockholm, Available from: https://arenaide.se/rapporter/spillover-effects-social-policies/

Baranowska-Rataj, A. and Strandh, M. (2020) 'When things go wrong with you, it hurts me too: the effects of partner's employment status on health in comparative perspective', *Journal of European Social Policy*, 31: 1–18.

Bell, A. and Jones, K. (2015) 'Explaining fixed effects: random effects modeling of time-series cross-sectional and panel data', *Political Science Research and Methods*, 3: 133–53.

Bell, D.N. and Blanchflower, D.G. (2011) 'Young people and the Great Recession', *Oxford Review of Economic Policy*, 27: 241–67.

Biro, A. and Elek, P. (forthcoming) 'Job loss, disability insurance and health expenditure', *Labour Economics*, Available from: https://www.sciencedirect.com/science/article/pii/S0927537120300609

Blossfeld, H., Hofäcker, D. and Bertolini, S. (2011) *Youth on Globalised Labour Markets*, Opladen; Farmington Hills: Verlag Barbara Budrich.

Brand, J.E. (2015) 'The far-reaching impact of job loss and unemployment', *Annual Review of Sociology*, 41: 359–75.

Burström, B. and Fredlund, P. (2001) 'Self rated health: is it as good a predictor of subsequent mortality among adults in lower as well as in higher social classes?', *Journal of Epidemiology and Community Health*, 55: 836–40.

Card, D., Kluve, J. and Weber, A. (2015) 'What works? A meta analysis of recent active labor market program evaluations', *Journal of the European Economic Association*, 16(3): 894–931.

Charles, K.K. and Stephens, M. (2004) 'Job displacement, disability, and divorce', *Journal of Labor Economics*, 22: 489–522.

Clark, A., Knabe, A. and Rätzel, S. (2010) 'Boon or bane? Others' unemployment, well-being and job insecurity', *Labour Economics*, 17: 52–61.

Clark, A.E. (2003) 'Unemployment as a social norm: psychological evidence from panel data', *Journal of Labor Economics*, 21: 323–51.

Conger, R.D., Elder Jr., G.H., Lorenz, F.O., Conger, K.J., Simons, R.L., Whitbeck, L.B., Huck, S. and Melby, J.N. (1990) 'Linking economic hardship to marital quality and instability', *Journal of Marriage and the Family*, 52(3): 643–56.

Danziger, S. and Ratner, D. (2010) 'Labor market outcomes and the transition to adulthood', *The Future of Children*, 20: 133–58.

Davis, S.N. and Greenstein, T.N. (2009) 'Gender ideology: components, predictors, and consequences', *Annual Review of Sociology*, 35: 87–105.

Furnham, A. (1982) 'The Protestant work ethic and attitudes towards unemployment', *Journal of Occupational Psychology*, 55: 277–85.

Goldscheider, F., Bernhardt, E. and Lappegård, T. (2015) 'The gender revolution: a framework for understanding changing family and demographic behavior', *Population and Development Review*, 41: 207–39.

Howe, G.W., Levy, M.L. and Caplan, R.D. (2004) 'Job loss and depressive symptoms in couples: common stressors, stress transmission, or relationship disruption?', *Journal of Family Psychology*, 18: 639.

Jahoda, M. (1981) 'Work, employment, and unemployment: values, theories, and approaches in social research', *American Psychologist*, 36(2): 184–91.

Jürges, H. (2007) 'True health vs response styles: exploring cross-country differences in self-reported health', *Health Economics*, 16: 163–78.

Jylhä, M. (2009) 'What is self-rated health and why does it predict mortality? Towards a unified conceptual model', *Social Science & Medicine* 69: 307–16.

Komarovsky, M. (1940) *The Unemployed Man and His Family: The Effect of Unemployment Upon the Status of the Man in Fifty-Nine Families*, New York: Dryden Press.

Maitoza, R. (2019) 'Family challenges created by unemployment', *Journal of Family Social Work*, 22: 187–205.

Marcus, J. (2013) 'The effect of unemployment on the mental health of spouses: evidence from plant closures in Germany', *Journal of Health Economics*, 32: 546–58.

McKee-Ryan, F., Song, Z., Wanberg, C.R. and Kinicki, A.J. (2005) 'Psychological and physical well-being during unemployment: a meta-analytic study', *Journal of Applied Psychology*, 90: 53–76.

Mendolia, S. (2014) 'The impact of husband's job loss on partners' mental health', *Review of Economics of the Household*, 12: 277–94.

Muller, W. and Gangl, M. (2003) *Transitions from Education to Work in Europe: The Integration of Youth into EU Labour Markets*, Oxford: Oxford University Press.

Nikolova, M. and Ayhan, S.H. (2019) 'Your spouse is fired! How much do you care?' *Journal of Population Economics*, 32: 799–844.

Niles, F.S. (1999) 'Toward a cross-cultural understanding of work-related beliefs', *Human Relations*, 52: 855–67.

Paul, K.I. and Moser, K. (2009) 'Unemployment impairs mental health: meta-analyses', *Journal of Vocational Behavior*, 74: 264–82.

Rook, K., Dooley, D. and Catalano, R. (1991) 'Stress transmission: the effects of husbands' job stressors on the emotional health of their wives', *Journal of Marriage and the Family*, 53: 165–77.

Saloniemi, A., Romppainen, K., Strandh, M. and Virtanen, P. (2014) 'Training for the unemployed: differential effects in white- and blue-collar workers with respect to mental well-being', *Work, Employment and Society*, 28: 533–50.

Sjöberg, O. (2010) 'Social insurance as a collective resource: unemployment benefits, job insecurity and subjective well-being in a comparative perspective', *Social Forces*, 88: 1281–304.

Springer, K.W., Stellman, J.M. and Jordan-Young, R.M. (2012) 'Beyond a catalogue of differences: a theoretical frame and good practice guidelines for researching sex/gender in human health', *Social Science & Medicine*, 74: 1817–24.

Stam, K. (2015) *The Moral Duty to Work: A Cross-National and Longitudinal Study of the Causes and Consequences of Work Ethic Values in Contemporary Society*. PhD thesis, Department of Sociology, Tilburg: Tilburg University, Available from: https://research.tilburguniversity.edu/en/publications/the-moral-duty-to-work-a-cross-national-and-longitudinal-study-of

Stam, K., Verbakel, E. and de Graaf, P.M. (2013) 'Explaining variation in work ethic in Europe: religious heritage rather than modernisation, the welfare state and communism', *European Societies*, 15: 268–89.

Stam, K., Sieben, I., Verbakel, E. and de Graaf, P.M. (2016) 'Employment status and subjective well-being: the role of the social norm to work', *Work, Employment & Society*, 30: 309–33.

Strandh, M. (2000) 'Different exit routes from unemployment and their impact on mental well-being: the role of the economic situation and the predictability of the life course', *Work, Employment & Society*, 14: 459–79.

Strandh, M., Hammarström, A., Nilsson, K., Nordenmark, M. and Russel, H. (2013) 'Unemployment, gender and mental health: the role of the gender regime', *Sociology of Health & Illness*, 35: 649–65.

Tattarini, G., Grotti, R. and Scherer, S. (2018) 'The buffering role of the family in the relationship between job loss and self-perceived health: longitudinal results from Europe, 2004–2011', *Health & Place*, 52: 55–61.

Voßemer, J. and Eunicke, N. (2015) *The Impact of Labor Market Exclusion and Job Insecurity on Health and Well-Being Among Youth: A Literature Review*. EXCEPT Working Papers, WP 2, Tallinn: Tallinn University, Available from: http://www.except-project.eu/working-papers/

Voßemer, J., Gebel, M., Täht, K., Unt, M., Högberg, B. and Strandh, M. (2018) 'The effects of unemployment and insecure jobs on well-being and health: the moderating role of labor market policies', *Social Indicators Research*, 138: 1229–57.

Voydanoff, P. (1990) 'Economic distress and family relations: a review of the eighties', *Journal of Marriage and the Family*, 52(4): 1099–115.

Wanberg, C.R. (2012) 'The individual experience of unemployment', *Annual Review of Psychology*, 63: 369–96.

Warr, P. (1987) *Work, Unemployment, and Mental Health*: Oxford: Oxford University Press.

Wulfgramm, M. (2011) 'Can activating labour market policy offset the detrimental life satisfaction effect of unemployment?', *Socio-Economic Review*, 9(3): 477–501.

Wulfgramm, M. (2014) 'Life satisfaction effects of unemployment in Europe: The moderating influence of labour market policy', *Journal of European Social Policy*, 24(3): 258–72.

4

Multiple routes to youth well-being: a qualitative comparative analysis of buffers to the negative consequences of unemployment

Triin Lauri and Marge Unt

Introduction

Several societal changes such as increased global competition and the restructuring of national economies have hit young generations more severely than older cohorts (Blossfeld et al, 2008). Furthermore, in recent decades, youth transitions have become not only considerably prolonged but also de-standardised, leading scholars to characterise these as yo-yo transitions (Walther, 2006). The latter means that young people swing back and forth between different states such as educational programmes and work, and changes in one area may be accompanied by setbacks in others such as moving back into the parental home due to losing one's job (Stauber and Walther, 2006). The labour market situation for recent school leavers was further weakened by the 2008 economic crisis in the majority of European countries (except Germany) (Rokicka et al, 2015). At the same time, work is still considered to serve as a central component of identity as well as simply providing income, and unemployment can have devastating consequences for people's psychological well-being and their ability to relate to others (Gallie, 2013; see also Chapter 6 in this volume).

Furthermore, the last 20 years have seen major shifts in welfare state approaches to labour market policies emphasising the growing responsibility of people to make themselves 'employable' (de Graaf and Maier, 2017). Thus, from one perspective, there is more pressure on the unemployed; but at the same time, the risk of unemployment is increasing due to volatile labour markets. The new social investment state promises that youth will be taken more seriously in welfare state studies and policies (Otto et al, 2015). The most important functions of social investment policies are to create, mobilise, and preserve human capabilities (Hemerijck, 2015) in order to help people overcome difficult life events. Unemployment is one such difficult event, and it has been shown to have negative economic and social consequences for individuals (Gallie, 2013). Whereas the policy imperative is to 'make transitions pay' over the life cycle by providing 'active securities' or 'social bridges' across volatile transitions between jobs (Hemerijck, 2015), evidence has demonstrated that those who are already better off often benefit more from social investment measures (Cantillon, 2011; de Graaf and Maier, 2017). This questions some of the social investment state promises and makes younger generations especially vulnerable in the light of these policies because of their relative lack of wealth.

Although the volatility of labour markets and the de-standardisation of life courses are a pan-European phenomenon (Eurofound, 2014), there are important differences between countries in the ways they cope with these risks. This has led scholars to distinguish several youth regimes (Walther, 2006; Chevalier, 2016) inspired by the seminal welfare regime typology elaborated by Esping-Andersen (1990). Whereas classical welfare state studies have often focused on the consequences of poverty when assessing the potential of countries to de-commodify, it is clear that the consequences of unemployment encompass more than mere financial outcomes. Therefore, it is important to look at relationships between unemployment experience and subjective well-being which enable researchers to assess the perceptions of unemployed persons (Anderson and Hecht, 2015; Samuel and Hadjar, 2016). This study aims to explore how governments can make welfare-enhancing choices to increase youth well-being, especially for those who are most vulnerable. It understands well-being as a proxy for adaptation to the social environment. It uses life satisfaction to refer to long-term cognitive evaluation of life as a whole, and not happiness which is used mostly to describe momentary pleasant emotions (Eger and Maridal, 2015).

Whereas previous research generally agrees that unemployment has negative effects on an individual's well-being (see McKee-Ryan et al, 2005; Paul and Moser, 2009; Wanberg, 2012), in recent years, increasing attention has been paid to how and why the effects of unemployment on well-being vary in line with the arrangement of the welfare state and other contextual factors (Gallie and Paugam, 2000; Eichhorn, 2013, 2014; Oesch and Lipps 2013; Russell et al, 2013; Wulfgramm, 2014; Calvo et al, 2015; Voßemer et al, 2018). These studies have revealed that the loss of life satisfaction in the unemployed is often mitigated by more generous unemployment benefits (Wulfgramm, 2014; O'Campo et al, 2015; Voßemer et al, 2018). However, results on other types of policy such as activation measures are more ambiguous (Wulfgramm, 2014; Voßemer et al, 2018). Furthermore, besides policies, the nature of the family might have an effect on how youth experience unemployment (Gallie and Paugam, 2000). The extended family model – that is, the trend toward living for a longer period of time with parents and grandparents – tends to compensate for the negative consequences of unemployment on well-being in both financial and social terms. Additionally, research has indicated (Strandh et al, 2011; Gallie, 2013; Oesch and Lipps, 2013; Calvo et al, 2015) that the impact of personal unemployment might depend on the overall level of unemployment in a country. For instance, it could be more negative during times of high unemployment, because the prospects of re-employment are poorer and the increased insecurity translates into lower well-being (Strandh et al, 2011). On the other hand, higher aggregate unemployment may also be accompanied by lower negative effects of personal unemployment, because individuals can attribute their situation externally.

So far, some studies within the comparative literature on the welfare state (Gallie and Paugam, 2000; Walther, 2006; Chevalier, 2016) have addressed the variety of youth situations. The present study attempts to complement this comparative welfare literature on youth by extending the underlying model by both adding dimensions and encompassing a wider geographical coverage of European countries, and through approaching the model configurationally. The latter means that the study assumes that explanatory patterns work as packages, because, instead of having isolated effects, each attribute tends to empower or compensate each other attribute differently in different contexts. Furthermore, equifinality is assumed, meaning that there can be different routes or institutional packages to buffer the negative consequences of unemployment on well-being.

This chapter is organised as follows: first, it introduces the chosen explanatory framework, maps the empirical evidence so far, and derives configurational research hypotheses. Then, it proceeds by empirical analysis to estimate the outcome dimension – the effect of unemployment on well-being among young adults – and it introduces the operationalisation and calibration of the explanatory dimensions. Next, it investigates what combinations of contextual and institutional dimensions mitigate the negative effect of unemployment on well-being. Finally, it offers concluding remarks and implications for future research.

Analytical framework

When framing the research problem, the present study is influenced by Gallie and Paugam (2000) who conceptualise a country's ability to provide protection against misfortune in the labour market in a two-dimensional space: the unemployment welfare regime and models of family residence. Specifically, in line with their model, household support is assumed to have compensative abilities that mitigate the negative consequences of unemployment in certain contexts. Therefore, the experiences of unemployment should not be analysed homogeneously, but as phenomena that take place within particular contexts; because of this, they may have a different dynamic within each national context.

The first dimension – the unemployment welfare regime – is the nature and form of intervention, comprised mostly of different types of passive and active labour market instruments or policies (hereinafter PLMPs and ALMPs). For instance, it is plausible to assume that the well-being of the unemployed will vary in line with unemployment benefits. There are at least two mechanisms that explain the alleviating effect of PLMPs: the first is tied directly to resources and financial hardship and the second to reduced stigmatisation for material deprivation (overview in O'Campo et al, 2015; see Wulfgramm, 2014; Voßemer et al, 2018). Furthermore, the duration of unemployment is probably associated with the extent of and arrangements for ALMPs to assist the unemployed in their job search.

In this analysis, aspects of unemployment welfare regimes are called *institutional factors*. Gallie and Paugam (2000) distinguish between four types of employment welfare regime: universalistic Nordic countries, employment-centred continental European countries, liberal Anglo-Saxon countries, and subprotective Southern European countries. These types are operationalised on the basis of three measures: (a) level and duration of financial compensation; (b) degree of coverage, meaning the extent to which people receive benefits to compensate for being out of work, including both insurance-based and means-tested benefits; and (c) the extent of ALMPs. According to Gallie and Paugam (2000), two of these four regimes perform better in terms of alleviating the negative effects of unemployment on well-being: the subprotective and universalistic regimes. However, their routes to positive outcomes differ. Whereas in universalistic regimes, the welfare state's protective nature tends to be the explanatory factor, in southern countries, it is apparently support from the household and the family residence model that is crucial. Concerning the latter, Gallie and Paugam (2000) identify three models of family residence: an extended dependence model, a model of relative intergenerational autonomy, and a model of advanced intergenerational autonomy. Because the family residence dynamic is not determined entirely by the social protection regime, it is important to distinguish between these aspects when analysing the consequences of unemployment for well-being. Thus, according to this labour market policy and family model nexus, the welfare regime type is conceptualised as a system of public regulation concerned with assuring the protection of individuals and maintaining social cohesion by intervening in the economic, domestic, and community spheres through both legal measures and resource distribution (Gallie and Paugam, 2000: 3). This study follows this recommendation when determining the key explanatory conditions included in the analyses and adding family residential model as one of the *contextual* moderators of well-being in the unemployed.

Hypothesis 1: The functional equivalency hypothesis. There are two functionally equivalent combinations of conditions (routes) associated with a small negative effect of unemployment on well-being. These are:

$$\text{Universalistic route: PG} \star \text{PC} \star \text{AP} \star \text{fa} \rightarrow \text{LS; and}$$
$$\text{Subprotective route: pg} \star \text{pc} \star \text{ap} \star \text{FA} \rightarrow \text{LS}^1$$

The universalistic route to life satisfaction (LS) combines high benefit generosity (PG) and coverage (PC), as well as the capacitive criteria of active labour market policy (AP) and a low share of young persons living with their family (fa). Countries following this route are the ones with universalistic (unemployment) welfare regimes and advanced intergenerational autonomy. The subprotective route combines low levels in all institutional factors included in our analysis (pg, pc, ap) and a high level of young people living with parents (FA).

Empirical evidence on the moderating role of ALMP on well-being is ambiguous (Wulfgramm, 2014; Voßemer et al, 2018). Whereas Wulfgramm (2014) finds positive moderating or no moderating effects in ALMP expenditure, Voßemer et al (2018) find negative associations. One potential reason for these mixed findings is the challenge of measuring ALMP and its various substantial cross-national differences – not only in extent but also in overall orientation. Thus, ALMPs have different designs and targets. One broad distinction is whether they are oriented more towards training or re-employment (Bonoli, 2010; Nelson, 2013; Martin, 2015). For instance, Chevalier (2016) distinguishes between encompassing and selective youth economic citizenship, with the former emphasising the enhancement of human capital as the main role of ALMPs and the latter aiming to lower labour costs associated with hiring workers. Bonoli (2012) similarly emphasises that the effects of different ALMP instruments differ between contexts and economic cycles depending on whether they are more protection-, investment-, or recommodification-oriented. In some cases, measures that are described as 'active' do not really have the objective of increasing the likelihood of labour market (re-)entry. This type of ALMP, sometimes referred to as 'parking' (Bonoli, 2012), consists of work experience programmes in the public or non-profit sector, but also some training, typically in the form of shorter courses that have very little impact on chances of finding a job. Given this mixed evidence and the previous discussion of the different orientations of ALMPs, it is assumed here that for ALMPs to have capacitive effects (AP), they should meet either generosity (AG) or investment criteria (AI), i.e. AP = AG + AI.

Hypothesis 2: ALMP hypothesis. It is either the generosity of ALMP (AG) or the human capital investment orientation of ALMP (AI) that will be decisive in releasing potential capacitating effects of these policies on alleviation of the loss of well-being in the unemployed.

$$\text{Capacitating route: } AG + AI \rightarrow LS$$

In addition to institutional factors, the degree of social integration and concomitant well-being of the unemployed depends on *contextual factors*. High aggregate unemployment may increase the negative effect of personal unemployment, because people perceive lower chances of re-employment. However, it might also operate differently: if personal unemployment is attributed internally ('personal failure') and the social work norm is strong, unemployment might be easier to tolerate if there are many other unemployed people (Strandh et al, 2011; Oesch and Lipps, 2013; Wulfgramm, 2014). Therefore, in addition to the family residential model, the study includes the overall level of unemployment in a country as the second contextual moderator, because stigmatisation can be expected to be lower in countries that have higher aggregate unemployment. However, this association is expected to hold only in the case of the extended family model, because in regimes with advanced intergenerational autonomy, the importance of employability is related more strongly to self-fulfilment, and a period of unemployment still runs counter to the normative framework of appropriate behaviour. In other words, it is assumed that in more individualistic countries in which social investment policies are more developed (Bouget et al, 2015), these arrangements have established 'new' norms that appear to define the role of an active, responsible, and 'able' employee and citizen for everybody (de Graaf and Maier, 2017).

Hypothesis 3: UE hypothesis. The higher the overall level of unemployment in a country, the lower the related stigmatisation and the loss of well-being. However, this connection holds only in the case of the extended family model.

$$\text{Less stigmatisation route: UE} * \text{FA} \rightarrow \text{LS}$$

Method, data, and empirical analyses

Method

According to the hypotheses, the interplay between institutional and contextual factors is expected to be associated with the positive outcome – that is, a low negative effect of unemployment on well-being. This association will be explored with qualitative comparative analysis (QCA), arguably the most suitable method to reveal complex relationships in terms of conjuncturality, equifinality, and asymmetry (Ragin, 2008; Schneider and Wageman, 2012) and especially relevant in comparative welfare regime analyses (Emmenegger et al, 2013; Brzinsky-Fay, 2017). The mathematical basis of QCA is Boolean algebra and set theory instead of probability theory and linear algebra (Ragin, 1987).

QCA technique explores set relations in terms of necessity and sufficiency. A condition X is necessary ($\leftarrow$) for an outcome Y if X is also given whenever Y is given. X is sufficient ($\rightarrow$) for Y if Y also occurs whenever X occurs (Thomann and Maggetti, 2017). For the sufficiency analysis truth table alghorithm is used (Ragin, 1987). Truth table consists all logically possible configurations, its link with outcome and each cases' belonging into those configurations.

The main parameters of fit for QCA are consistency and coverage. Consistency indicates the strength of the theoretical argument[2] – that is, how consistently do the countries that combine a particular institutional and contextual policy mix (X) also display the effect of unemployment on well-being (Y). The meaning of coverage is similar to the 'variance explained' in regression analysis, and indicates the share of outcome (Y) explained by a particular combination of institutional and contextual conditions (X).[3] These two parameters tend to be negatively associated: the stricter the consistency threshold, the fewer the cases that can be explained, and vice versa. In addition to consistency and coverage, the proportional reduction in inconsistency (PRI) is also reported. This measures the degree to which a certain combination of conditions is a subset of the outcome, but also its negation. The analysis is conducted with the R packages (collections of functions and data sets developed by the community) QCA (Duşa and Thiem, 2014) and SetMethod (Quaranta, 2013).

In order to employ QCA, raw data are calibrated into membership scores (fuzzy scale data). This *calibration* process entails choosing three qualitative anchors for each outcome and condition included in the analysis: fully in (1), fully out (0), and the crossover point (0.50) when cases are not clearly in or out of the set. These thresholds were chosen based on an inspection of the data, because theoretically, there were no good justifications to be adopted. A method based on log odds[4] was used for the calibration procedure. The threshold for sufficiency was set at 0.75[5] and relied on a 'complex solution', meaning that it did not take logical reminders – theoretical configurations not covered empirically – into account when minimising the solution. Robustness tests were also employed to assess the sensitivity of our results. This approach follows Skaaning (2011) and focuses, first, on the choice of consistency thresholds in sufficiency analyses and, second, on the calibration thresholds in converting the raw outcome into set-membership values when employing robustness tests.

Measurement and calibration of outcome: the effect of unemployment on well-being

Well-being is defined according to the psychological literature on subjective well-being (Diener et al, 1999). This study follows the tradition of most quantitative studies on well-being and operationalises it with a single-item measure (Voßemer and Eunicke, 2015). In particular, life satisfaction measures reflect the cognitive component of individuals' well-being, meaning how people judge their life as a whole (Diener et al, 2013. Such global life satisfaction measures have been shown to be valid, reliable, and sensitive to change, making them appropriate for this analysis (Diener et al, 2013). Specifically, microdata from the European Union Statistics on Income and Living Conditions (EU-SILC) 2013 were used to operationalise the effect of unemployment on life satisfaction as the outcome dimension. Almost all European Union countries were included in the analysis except for Croatia, Cyprus, Luxembourg, and Malta for which there was no available information for all institutional and contextual factors.

In order to analyse the effect of unemployment on life satisfaction for youth, the sample was restricted to young persons aged between 16 and 29 years. The key variables of interest were employment status and life satisfaction. The dependent variable, life satisfaction, was based on the following question: 'All things considered, how satisfied are you with your life as a whole nowadays?' with answers on an 11-point scale ranging from 0 (*extremely dissatisfied*) to 10 (*extremely satisfied*). The life satisfaction measure was standardised for the analysis.

The key independent variable of interest was employment status. Respondents' self-defined status was used to differentiate between those who are in dependent employment and those who are unemployed. The employed included all workers having a job, regardless of their contract (temporary or permanent) or their working hours (part-time or full-time). 'Unemployment' was based on a self-defined status and considered whether the person has actively looked for a job in the last four weeks.

The analyses to estimate the effect of unemployment on life satisfaction also controlled for a number of variables that are assumed to affect the risk of unemployment as well as young people's well-being. Moreover, controlling for these variables makes the size of the effects more comparable across countries. Other than socio-demographics such as gender, age, and migration background, the study also adjusted for individuals' education level (defined as ISCED 0–2, ISCED 3–4, and ISCED 5–6) and years since leaving education.

Estimated effects of unemployment on life satisfaction for EU countries are shown in Figure 4.1, and these are used as the source to operationalise the outcome dimension using a design greatly influenced by Schneider and Makzin (2014). In line with previous studies (Wulfgramm, 2014, Voßemer et al, 2018), one can clearly see that the experience of unemployment reduces overall satisfaction with life among youth. However, the effect of unemployment on life satisfaction varies substantially across countries (between -0.35 and -1.07). In particular, the smallest negative effect is found in Slovenia (SI), but also in countries such as Belgium (BE), Finland (FI), Greece (EL), Ireland (IE), Poland (PL), Portugal (PT), Spain (ES), and Sweden (SE). At the same time, the effect is largest in the Czech Republic (CZ), Denmark (DK), Lithuania (LT), the Netherlands (NL), Slovakia (SK), and the United Kingdom (UK). The remaining nine countries – Austria (AT), Bulgaria (BG), Estonia (EE), France (FR), Germany (DE), Hungary (HU), Italy (IT), Latvia (LV), and Romania (RO), fall somewhere in between, making up 'hard-to-decide' cases in terms of outcome.

These data were prepared for configurational comparison by calibrating them. Based on the chosen crossover point (-0.7), there were 9 out of 24 cases with a positive outcome – Austria, Belgium, Finland, France, Denmark, Ireland, Germany, the Netherlands, and Sweden (see Appendix for fuzzy membership scores of each country). However, because the results did not suggest clear qualitative differences in terms of belonging to 'positive' or 'negative' outcome sets (for example, at

Figure 4.1: Estimated effect of unemployment on life satisfaction

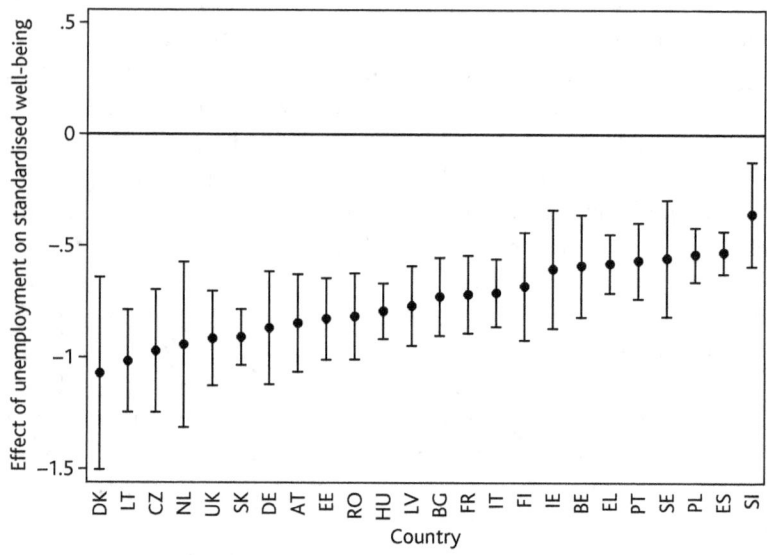

Source: EU-SILC 2013

the chosen crossover point, Finland and Italy were relatively similar), sensitivity tests were conducted with different thresholds to test the robustness of the results in terms of the chosen threshold. These results are reported in the discussion section (details are available upon request).

Measurement and calibration of explanatory dimensions

Five *institutional* and *contextual* factors were used to explain the buffering of the effect of unemployment on youth well-being (Table 4.1 provides an overview).

Two first indicators aim to capture the generosity and coverage of passive labour market policies. In operationalising the *generosity of PLMP* (PG), one of the main variables in previous analyses exploring the potential factors that might mitigate the negative effects of unemployment on life satisfaction has been the level and duration of financial compensation. The generosity of unemployment benefits has also shown the most robust results, because it has the capacity to provide a financial buffer and minimise stigmatisation. However, there are problems in finding the most valid indicators. Taking only replacement rates into account misses an important aspect, because there is also substantial variation in the duration of benefits. One alternative would be to use per capita expenditure indicators on PLMPs, because this may

Table 4.1: Dimensions included in the configurational comparison

	Label	Set	Operationalisation	Min	Max	Mean	Calibration thresholds	Source
Outcome	LS	Small effect of unemployment on well-being	Controlled difference in life satisfaction between employed and unemployed persons	−1.07	−0.36	−0.75	−0.4; −0.7; −1	EU-Silc 2013
Institutional factors	PG	Generosity of PLMP	PLMP_generosity (replacement*duration in fully paid weeks)	7.79	115.17	41.98	93; 50; 12.5	Own calculations based on qualitative reports2; Eurostat 2013
	PC	Coverage of PLMP	LMP beneficiaries per 100 persons wanting to work; Category 8	8.30	104.10	36.48	90; 45; 12	Eurostat 2013
	AP = AG + AI AG	Generosity of ALMP	(exp. per persons wanting to work)	33	7 085	1 940	5,000; 2,000; 200	Unt and Jeliazkova 2018
	AI	Investment orientedness of ALMP	(the share of expenditures in Cat. 2 above average)	1.10	3.18	2.24	2.8; 2; 1.5	Eurostat 2013
Contextual factors	FA	Extended family model	(the share of young persons living with family)	2.50	57.10	29.40	50; 30; 5	Eurostat 2013
	UE	High share of unemployment		5.20	27.50	11.11	18; 10; 6	Eurostat 2013

also include information on coverage. However, expenditure-based measures do not capture the design of unemployment benefit systems. Therefore, Eurostat Qualitative Reports of Labour Market Policy Statistics (Category 8, Out-of-work income maintenance and support, subcategory unemployment insurance) for European countries were used to construct a benefit generosity index that makes it possible to capture both replacement rates and benefit duration (average worker, maximum duration).[6] For instance, when calculating Austria's PG, nine months of maximum duration of unemployment insurance were first converted into weeks (9 × 4.33 = 38.97) and then multiplied by 55 (38.97 ×0.55 = 21.43), the replacement rate of that benefit, giving 21.43 – that is, 21 fully paid weeks. Thus, the PG index is a hypothetical benefit in which the replacement and duration indicators have been converted into fully paid weeks (see Table 4.2 for raw and calibrated data of all countries included in the analysis). Admittedly, this measure of PG might still have some limitations, because it delivers identical values for low, but long benefits and high, but short benefits – two scenarios that are quite different in terms of substance. However, this limitation is rather theoretical for the present data, because countries with the lowest replacement rates (Greece, Malta, Poland, and the UK) also have relatively short durations.

Next, Figure 4.2 shows how the explanatory dimensions relate to well-being. The PG varies quite substantially across Europe, with the lowest in the UK (7.79) and highest in Belgium (115.17). Fifty weeks was chosen for the crossover point, which is equivalent to almost one fully paid year. A substantial gap (30 fully paid weeks) is visible between countries with benefits above 64 (Spain) and below 34 (Sweden) fully paid weeks. According to the chosen criterion, seven countries have positive membership (more than 0.5) in the 'generosity of unemployment benefits' (PG) set that also includes Portugal and Spain. This is in contrast with Gallie and Paugam (2000), who classify Southern European countries as being subprotective regimes offering only limited support. Based on the present operationalisation and calibration, this continues to hold only for Greece and Italy.[7] Figure 4.2 additionally reveals that both the employment-centred continental and universal regimes – those usually considered to show relatively high levels of generosity – are rather diverse based on the present operationalisation, with Belgium, Denmark, Finland, and France being among the more generous while excluding Austria, Germany, and Sweden. This diversity might be one of the retrenchment consequences of the 2008 economic crisis (Kersbergen et al, 2015).

Table 4.2: Dimensions included in the analysis: raw and calibrated data

Operationalisation	Effect of unemployment on well-being		PLMP_generosity (replacement*duration in fully paid weeks)		PLMP_beneficiaries: LMP beneficiaries per 100 persons wanting to work_cat8		ALMP_generosity: LMP expenditure per person wanting to work (in PPS)		ALMP_investment orientedness: the share of training (cat 2) is above EU average (0.16)		Capacitive ALMP	Share of young persons (25–34) living with parents		Unemployment rate; general	
Source	EU-SILC 2013		Eurostat 2013, authors' calculations		Eurostat 2013		Unt and Jeliazkova 2018		Eurostat 2013		AP = AG + AI	Eurostat 2013		Eurostat 2013	
Calibration	−0.4, −0.7, −1		93; 50; 12.5		90; 45; 12		200; 2 000; 5 000					50; 30; 5		18; 10; 6	
Countries	LS	LS_cal	PG	PG_cal	PC	PC_cal	AG	AG_cal	AI	AI_cal	AP	FA	FA_cal	UE	UE_cal
AT	−0.85	0.19	21.43	0.09	39.8	0.38	2 697	0.67	0.47	1	1	22.6	0.29	5.4	0.03
BE	−0.59	0.75	115.17	0.99	104.1	0.98	7 085	0.99	0.16	1	1	17.9	0.19	8.4	0.23
BG	−0.73	0.43	31.18	0.18	15.4	0.06	158	0.04	0.01	0	0.04	50.5	0.96	13	0.75
CZ	−0.97	0.06	12.29	0.05	22.7	0.12	693	0.1	0.02	0	0.1	33.2	0.62	7	0.1
DE	−0.87	0.16	31.18	0.18	66.3	0.81	2 355	0.59	0.22	1	1	16.8	0.17	5.2	0.03
DK	−1.07	0.02	93.53	0.95	39.1	0.37	6 606	0.99	0.38	1	1	2.5	0.04	7	0.1
EE	−0.83	0.22	22.25	0.1	16.7	0.07	237	0.05	0.11	0	0.05	21.1	0.26	8.6	0.26
EL	−0.58	0.77	20.78	0.09	13.2	0.05	600	0.09	0.10	0	0.09	52.6	0.97	27.5	1
ES	−0.53	0.85	64.95	0.74	36.4	0.31	1 199	0.21	0.12	0	0.21	37.4	0.75	26.1	1
FI	−0.68	0.55	74.69	0.85	62.7	0.76	3 382	0.8	0.48	1	1	4.3	0.04	8.2	0.21

(continued)

Table 4.2: Dimensions included in the analysis: raw and calibrated data (continued)

Operationalisation	Effect of unemployment on well-being		PLMP_generosity (replacement * duration in fully paid weeks)		PLMP_beneficiaries: LMP beneficiaries per 100 persons wanting to work_cat8		ALMP_generosity: LMP expenditure per person wanting to work (in PPS)		ALMP_investment orientedness: the share of training (cat 2) is above EU average (0.16)	Capacitive ALMP	Share of young persons (25–34) living with parents		Unemployment rate; general	
FR	-0.72	0.46	68.59	0.79	70.5	0.85	3 279	0.78	0.38	1	1	11.9	0.1	10.3	0.53
HU	-0.79	0.29	23.38	0.11	29.8	0.2	671	0.1	0.00	0	0.1	42.7	0.87	10.2	0.52
IE	-0.60	0.73	25.98	0.13	91.4	0.96	2 511	0.63	0.37	1	1	19.4	0.22	13.1	0.76
IT	-0.71	0.48	19.92	0.08	20.7	0.1	784	0.12	0.15	0	0.12	48.1	0.94	12.1	0.69
LT	-1.02	0.04	23.38	0.11	14.3	0.06	302	0.06	0.04	0	0.06	31.1	0.54	11.8	0.66
LV	-0.77	0.34	22.42	0.1	13.6	0.05	321	0.06	0.12	0	0.06	32.3	0.59	11.9	0.67
NL	-0.94	0.08	67.13	0.77	68.9	0.83	4 398	0.92	0.09	0	0.92	10.5	0.09	7.3	0.12
PL	-0.54	0.84	15.59	0.06	8.5	0.03	607	0.09	0.02	0	0.09	43.5	0.88	10.3	0.53
PT	-0.56	0.79	67.55	0.77	33.3	0.26	956	0.15	0.30	1	1	45	0.9	16.4	0.92
RO	-0.82	0.24	31.18	0.18	12.1	0.05	33	0.04	0.00	0	0.04	43.5	0.88	7.1	0.1
SE	-0.55	0.81	34.21	0.22	40.2	0.39	3 832	0.86	0.13	0	0.86	4.3	0.04	8	0.18
SI	-0.36	0.97	24.70	0.12	17.1	0.07	779	0.12	0.05	0	0.12	43	0.88	10.1	0.51
SK	-0.91	0.11	12.99	0.05	8.3	0.03	485	0.07	0.00	0	0.07	57.1	0.98	14.2	0.83
UK	-0.91	0.1	7.79	0.03	30.4	0.21	600	0.09	0.02	0	0.09	13.8	0.13	7.5	0.13

The *high share of beneficiaries of unemployment benefits* (PC) is the second condition reflecting differences in coverage in countries' PLMPs. The degree of beneficiaries of unemployment benefits is operationalised on the basis of Eurostat, and measures the proportion of the beneficiaries of labour market policy support (regular support – that is percentage of LMP participants per 100 people wanting to work, Category 8[8] to include only out-of-work, support-related intervention). PC also varies substantially across European welfare states (Figure 4.2, upper-right panel) and is lowest in Slovakia (approximately 8 out of 100 persons looking for work receive benefits) and highest in Belgium[9] (104.1). Literature on welfare and/or employment regimes often distinguishes between Bismarckian and Beveridgian types of benefits (Bonoli, 1997; Kuitto, 2016), the former being generous but contribution-based (i.e. covering only those with solid employment profiles), the latter offering universal coverage. Gallie and Paugam (2000) extend this distinction to four types of coverage: (a) universal regimes – comprehensive; (b) employment-centred – variable; (c) liberal/minimal – incomplete; and (d) subprotective – very incomplete. Whereas these classifications are helpful in terms of analytical distinctions, they do not give any guidance on empirical equivalences. Therefore, 45 was chosen as the crossover point here to distinguish between high- and low-coverage (PC) countries because of the substantial gap between 40.2 (Sweden) and 62.7 (Finland). This means that countries in which at least 45 out of 100 people wanting to work receive benefits are considered to have a positive membership (more than 0.5) in PC. These are Belgium, Finland, France, Germany, Ireland, and the Netherlands.[10]

The *capacity of ALMPs* (AP) is the third condition for describing the employment policies of welfare regimes. According to the present analytical framework, in order to belong to the capacitive ALMP (AP) set, a country must be one of the generous ALMP (AG) or investment-oriented ALMP countries (AI) – in Boolean terms: AP = AG + AI. AG was operationalised as the expenditure per person wanting to work measured in purchasing power standards (PPS). AI was operationalised as the share of expenditure in training-related instruments,[11] coding countries above the EU28 average as investment-oriented and those below as not investment-oriented. Figure 4.2 shows these two alternative measurements of ALMP measurements by country. It shows that AG varies strongly across Europe, and is lowest in Romania (33 PPS per person wanting to work) and highest in Belgium (7,085 PPS). Although there is an extensive and growing literature on the potential reasons for government increases in ALMP expenditure (Vis,

Figure 4.2: Outcome dimension (LS), explanatory conditions and chosen crossover points

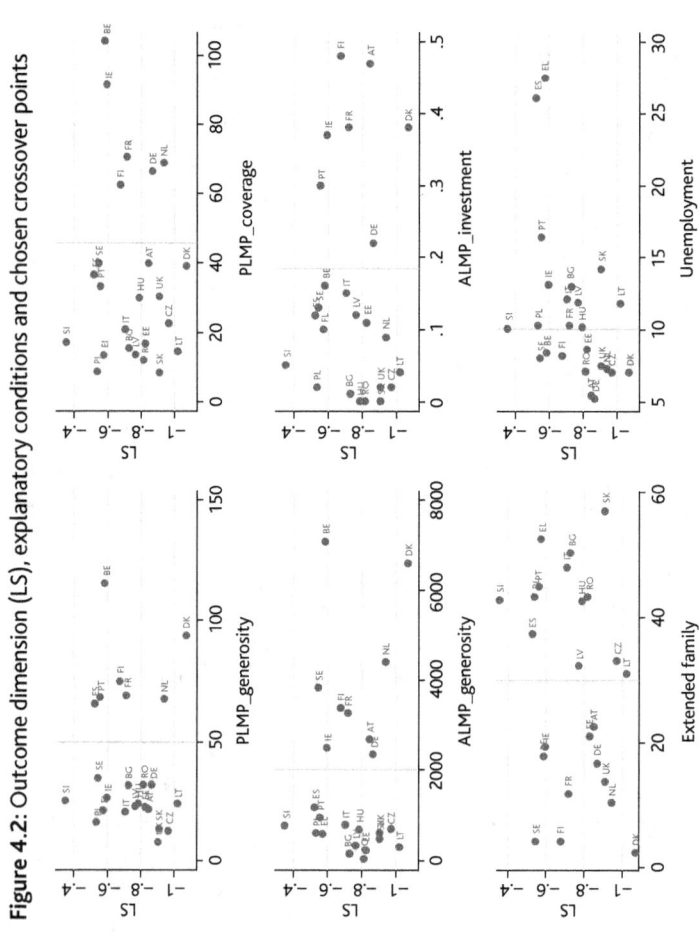

Sources: Outcome LS – EU-SILC, explanatory conditions – Eurostat 2013 (excl. ALMP_generosity for which per capita measures were available only from 2011)

2011; Gingrich and Ansell, 2015; Häusermann and Palier, 2017) and also on the design of ALMP in different countries (Bonoli, 2010; Nelson, 2013; Martin, 2015), these do not give normative guidance on satisfactory ALMP expenditure levels that could justify the present choice for calibration thresholds. Therefore, 2,000 PPS was chosen for the crossover due to the extensive gap between Germany (2,355 PPS) and Spain (1,199 PPS). Accordingly, there were nine countries with positive membership (more than 0.5) in the AG set, including all Nordic countries, as well as all countries in Gallie and Paugam's (2000) employment-centred model and Ireland. Looking at the investment orientation of ALMP (AI), six out of nine countries were the same as in AG with the addition of Portugal. The following dichotomous measure was used for AI: 1 if the share of expenditures in Category 2 (training) was above the average (0.16); and 0 if it was below (see Table 4.2 for raw and calibrated data).

Contextual factors were captured by two conditions. A country's family residence model was measured by the *share of young persons living with their families* (FA). Comparing the proportion of adult children aged 25 to 34 years living with their parents, it is evident that the process of defamilialisation is far more advanced in Northern than in Southern Europe – an aspect already highlighted by Gallie and Paugam (2000). However, as shown in Figure 4.2 (lower-left panel), patterns in Eastern and Central European countries are much less clear. FA varies substantially across Europe, being lowest in Denmark (2.5) and highest in Slovakia (57.1). For the crossover point, 30 per cent was chosen, because there are clearly distinguishable groups above and below the interval between 25 and 34 per cent. According to this calibration, there are 13 countries with positive membership (more than 0.5) in the FA set, including all Southern European countries, but also several Central and Eastern European countries. Also, in contrast to Gallie and Paugam (2000), Ireland is not in the 'extended dependence' set according to the present data and calibrations. Family residence was used here as a proxy for intergenerational support, yet the operationalisation has its limitations because it does not capture all forms of possible support such cash transfers.

In addition, *the level of aggregate unemployment* (UE) in a country was included as another important contextual aspect moderating the negative consequences of unemployment on well-being. Data on countries' unemployment rates (UE) were taken from Eurostat (2013), measuring the unemployment rate of the active population. UE varies between 5.2 and 27.5 per cent (see Figure 4.2) and is lowest in DE (5.2 per cent) and highest in EL (27.5 per cent). The crossover threshold was set at 10 per cent. When these countries are considered, there are 13 examples of 'high unemployment rate' countries. However, there are many borderline cases (SI: 10.1 per cent, HU: 10.2 per cent, FR: 10.3 per cent, and PL: 10.3 per cent).

Configurational analysis: identifying routes to well-being

The study explores the combinations of institutional and contextual factors that are potentially sufficient for relative well-being in the unemployed, defined as a small drop in life satisfaction compared to working youth.[12]

The sample of 24 countries selected in this analysis is represented in 11 of the 32 (2^5) logically possible combinations (configurations or routes). Table 4.3 (truth table) maps these routes and the countries that follow them (that is, belong to that particular configuration). Whereas consistencies are high – that is, the strength of many routes mapped in predicting positive outcome is high – there are two problems: one of idiosyncrasy – many routes are followed by only one country; and one of contradicting routes – some routes are followed by both positive and negative outcome countries (the former countries are highlighted in bold).

Next, the truth table was minimised[13] to remove potentially redundant configurations and allow the exploration of more generalisable patterns. The minimisation process reveals three routes which buffer negative consequences of unemployment (Table 4.4).

The first route comprising institutional and contextual factors labelled **covered support** (PC ★ AP ★ fa ★ UE), which is associated with lower negative effects of unemployment on well-being, combines a high share of PLMP beneficiaries, capacitive ALMP, a low share of young people living together with their families, and a high share of unemployment. Ireland and France follow the covered support route. Thus, in this particular context (fa ★ UE), it is coverage in combination with capacitive ALMP and not the generosity of PLMP that are necessary components in routes which mitigate the well-being of the unemployed in these countries.

The second route, called **extended family support** (PG ★ pc ★ FA ★ UE), which is associated with lower negative effects of unemployment on well-being, combines generous PLMP with limited coverage of PLMP, an extended family model, and a high level of unemployment. Typical cases for this route are Portugal and Spain. In light of the hypothesis, this route is the most similar to the subprotective route described and formulated earlier; however, compared to Gallie and Paugam's (2000) model and the first hypothesis derived from it,

Table 4.3: Truth table: empirical linkages between countries' combinations of institutional and contextual characteristics and outcomes

Generosity of PLMP	Coverage of PLMP	Capacitive ALMP	Extended family model	Level of unemploy-ment	Life satisfaction	n	Consistency	PRI	Cases
PG	PC	AP	FA	UE	OUT				
1	0	1	1	1	1	1	0.97	0.93	Portugal
1	0	0	1	1	1	1	0.97	0.90	Spain
0	1	1	0	1	1	1	0.94	0.78	Ireland
1	1	1	0	1	1	1	0.92	0.32	France
0	0	1	0	0	0	2	0.78	0.44	Austria, **Sweden**
1	0	1	0	0	0	1	0.71	0.14	Denmark
1	1	1	0	0	0	3	0.70	0.34	**Belgium, Finland**, Netherlands
0	1	1	0	0	0	1	0.67	0.18	Germany
0	0	0	1	1	0	9	0.64	0.38	Bulgaria, **Greece**, Hungary, Italy, Lithuania, Latvia, **Poland**, Slovenia, Slovakia
0	0	0	1	0	0	5	0.63	0.30	Czech Republic, Romania
0	0	0	0	0	0	2	0.46	0.05	Estonia, UK

Notes: Countries in bold are those with positive outcomes – that is, membership scores higher than 0.5 in LS. Consistency and PRI scores above 0.75 are highlighted in bold (Schneider and Wagemann, 2010). PRI is the measure expressing the degree to which one and the same row is a subset of the outcome, but also its negation – the smaller it is, the more this is the case.

Table 4.4: Sufficient routes to outcomes

	Covered support	Extended family support	Capacitive support
	Route 1	Route 2	Route 3
Generous PLMP (PG)		•	○
High share of beneficiaries of PLMP (PC)	•	○	○
Capacitive impact of ALMP (AP)	•		•
Extended family model (FA)	○	•	○
High share of general unemployment (UE)	•	•	○
Consistency	0.91	0.97	0.78
PRI	0.67	0.92	0.44
Raw coverage	0.29	0.29	0.22
Unique coverage	0.12	0.15	0.1
Cases	**Ireland**	**Spain**	**Austria**
	France	**Portugal**	**Sweden**
Solution consistency	0.86		
Solution PRI	0.71		
Solution coverage	0.52		

Notes: • - condition present; ○ - condition absent; Countries highlighted in bold are those with positive outcomes – that is, membership scores higher than 0.5 in LS.

generous PLMP is a necessary additional component of this route if it is to meet the sufficiency criteria. Furthermore, the analysis reveals several southern European countries that do not meet the generous benefit criteria (Greece, Italy).

The third route, **capacitating support** (pg * pc * AP * fa * ue), indicates that in the context of high intergenerational autonomy (a low level of young persons living with the family), only the presence of capacitive ALMP is sufficient for the higher well-being of the unemployed, as long as the general level of unemployment is not high. This route, exemplified by Austria and Sweden, is in line with the second hypothesis that countries with positive membership scores in AP will be more successful in buffering the negative effect of unemployment. However, it is important to emphasise that 'outside' of this particular contextual combination (high intergenerational autonomy and low unemployment), the sufficiency of AP is not revealed.

The third, 'less stigmatised' hypothesis – the claim that countries with extended family models and high levels of unemployment will be associated with less negative consequences for well-being – could not be confirmed empirically. More specifically, as indicated by the extended family route, this mechanism only seems to work in combination with generous PLMP (PG * FA * UE).

To conclude, whereas the three-route solution is quite solid in terms of consistency, coverage is moderately low – solution coverage 0.52 – indicating that it is able to explain approximately half of the cases. Because many positive outcome cases belong in the same configurations as negative outcome cases – in particular, Greece, Poland, and Slovenia – the model there seems to be missing some additional explanation for their routes to vulnerable youth well-being. Furthermore, because the definition of positive outcome depends on the calibration threshold, the sensitivity of the results was subjected to robustness tests. These focused on different thresholds for consistency of sufficiency and crossover points for outcomes (details available upon request).

In terms of the choice of consistency thresholds for sufficiency, the initial analysis (consistency for sufficiency at 0.75) was augmented with analyses using 0.8 and 0.7. Whereas easing the consistency threshold to 0.7 does not change the result, setting it at a stricter level of 0.8 leaves only two sufficient routes: covered and extended family support. In other words, increasing the strictness of consistency increases the strength of theoretical arguments for covered and extended family support, but countries that follow the capacitating route, such as Austria and Sweden, lose in empirical relevance and drop out of sufficient routes.

The next step was to test whether results still hold after relaxing the selection criteria for 'successful' countries at the crossover from -0.7 to -0.8.[14] This step adds five positive outcome cases (Bulgaria, France, Hungary, Italy, and Latvia) to the analysis. The biggest change is in the empirical relevance of the results, because, in addition to the initial three routes, an additional route emerges and the coverage becomes 0.86. Figure 4.3 depicts the main differences in results compared to the original analysis (while retaining the same consistency criteria of 0.75 for both).

The cases in the upper right-hand corner (surrounded by the circle) are those that can be explained – that is, those with positive membership in both the outcome set and (one of the) solution(s). It can be seen that whereas in the left-hand panel (the initial analysis), there are only

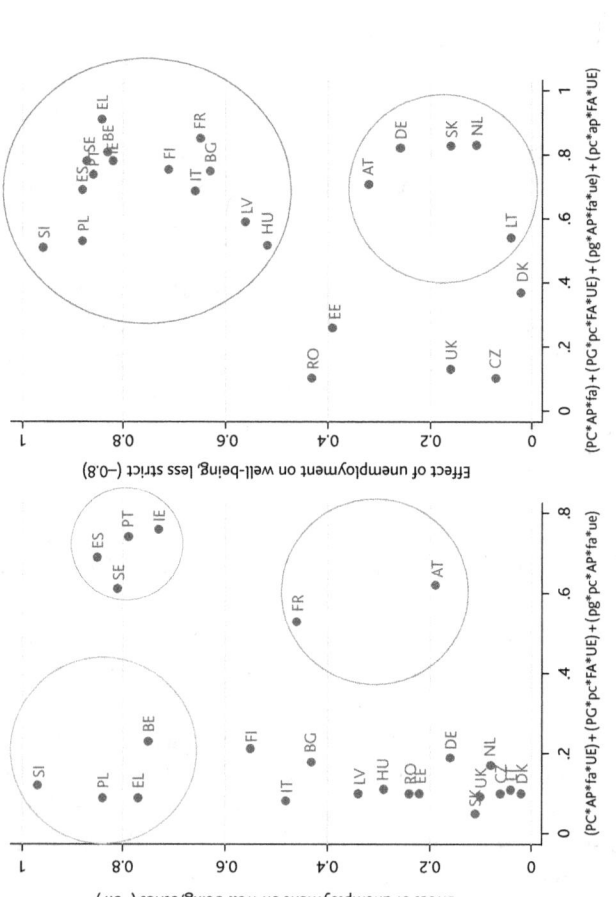

Figure 4.3: Sufficient routes to two alternatively calibrated outcomes and cases that can be explained by these

Notes: Left panel: strict calibration of outcome (crossover at −0.7; 9 positive outcome cases). Right panel: less strict calibration (crossover −0.8; 14 positive outcome cases). Upper right circle – explained cases; upper left circle – cases that have positive outcome but cannot be explained; lower right circle – cases in contradictory routes.
Source: Author's own

four cases, in the right-hand panel (ex post analysis), there are 13. The additional route that emerges depends only on contextual buffers to alleviate the loss of well-being in the unemployed. This route, pc ★ ap ★ FA ★ UE, which has moderately satisfactory consistency (0.75) but very good coverage (0.48), is exemplified by 10 countries: Belgium, Greece, Hungary, Italy, Latvia, Lithuania, Poland, Slovenia, Slovakia, and Spain. Whereas all three initial routes also survive this sensitivity test, the covered support route changes. More specifically, compared to its original format (PC ★ AP ★ fa ★ UE), the UE component becomes redundant in the covered route and the empirical relevance increases, because France and Ireland are joined by four other countries: Belgium, Finland, Germany, and the Netherlands. This also means that easing the calibration threshold of the outcome eliminated the problem of 'unexplained' cases – that is, the countries in the upper left-hand corner with a high value in outcome dimensions, which are not explained by any routes. However, the countries in the lower right-hand corner Figure 4.3 (within the circle) – those with high membership in one of the routes but no outcome – are still contradictory.

Conclusions

This study aimed to investigate the interplay of institutional and contextual aspects of labour market policies in mitigating the negative effects of unemployment on the well-being of young people. The research design was based on a configurational comparison, because it was assumed that combinations of different explanatory dimensions form distinct packages. The specification of the model was influenced primarily by Gallie and Paugam (2000), who combined employment regimes and family models as sources of alternative explanations for the well-being of the unemployed. However, their model was amended to take into account labour market conditions using the aggregate unemployment rate and applying this analytical framework across Europe. The explanatory model used here consisted of five dimensions: three institutional (the generosity and coverage of passive labour market policy and capacitive impact of active labour market policy) and two contextual (the share of unemployment and the prevalence of extended family model).

First, by using comparative microdata and applying multiple linear regression models, it explained the differences on the outcome dimension – the effect of unemployment on life satisfaction – for a wide range of European countries. The result was that even after controlling for several aspects such as education and age, the loss of life satisfaction among the unemployed still varied across countries. Furthermore, countries that do well have diverse welfare regime backgrounds. Second, it investigated whether there are distinguishable configurations of institutional and contextual factors that perform better in buffering the negative consequences of unemployment. The hypothesis was that there are four such configurations: first, the universal route, emphasising the strong presence of active and passive labour market policies; second, the subprotective route, which relies on extended family support; third, the capacitating route, emphasising the importance of activation measures; and fourth, the unemployment route, which relies on the extended family in the context of high unemployment rates that help to reduce the stigmatisation related to labour market exclusion. Based on the analyses and the subsequent robustness check, two functionally equivalent routes turned out to be the most robust: first, the covered route that combines both PLMP and ALMP in buffering the negative consequences of unemployment; and second, the extended family route in which generous PLMP combined with the extended family residential model facilitates a positive outcome. Whereas the policy design of the covered route is analogous to Gallie and Paugam's (2000) universal route, the mix of countries that exemplify it are mainly from continental rather than Nordic Europe (except Finland). At the same time, the extended family route provides an important addition to the suggested subprotective route as strong PLMP is a necessary component in it.

Moreover, results showed that the situation has turned out to be much more diverse than suggested by Gallie and Paugam (2000). Nordic countries in particular are much more diverse than expected, especially in terms of labour market-policy-related solutions, an aspect that is probably partly explained by recent retrenchment policies such as cuts in unemployment benefits (Arndt, 2017). Furthermore, the difference between Gallie and Paugam's (2000) universalistic and subprotective approaches is less clear, and even in Southern European countries, the importance of generous PLMP in addition to the extended family model (labelled extended family support in the present analysis) has been revealed. Thus, contrary to expectations, the family's ability to buffer negative consequences of unemployment is less clear.

In light of the existing understanding of the negative consequences of unemployment for youth well-being and its institutional buffers, and in accordance with many other studies (Wulfgramm, 2014; O'Campo et al, 2015; Voßemer et al, 2018), the present study did confirm that PLMP (in terms of either coverage or generosity) is an important and indeed a necessary component in both covered and extended family support. Assuming the contextual dependency of some buffers as theorised by Gallie and Paugam (2000) and the reported vagueness of the effect of ALMP (Wulfgramm, 2014; Voßemer et al, 2018), the study showed that ALMP and the extended family tend to compensate for each other. In other words, the capacitive potential of ALMP holds only in the context of advanced intergenerational autonomy and relatively low unemployment, whereas in the context of high overall unemployment, extended family support compensates for the lack of ALMP. QCA is especially well-suited to revealing these types of macrolevel conjunctural associations in comparative welfare policy studies (Emmenegger et al, 2013). At the same time, the sensitivity analysis revealed that political choices that rely on capacitive ALMP at the expense of PLMP do not robustly mitigate the loss in well-being in unemployed youth, indicating the importance of combined investment and compensation-oriented policies in youth regimes. This indicates a need for caution regarding the effectiveness of retrenchment policies that cut back compensation-oriented policies and shift the focus (solely) towards activation measures.

Finally, once the calibration threshold for the outcome is eased and a slightly larger drop in unemployed youth well-being is still considered a positive outcome, an additional route emerges that relies only on contextual moderators (UE hypothesis). Thus, by relaxing the threshold and also considering countries that show moderately negative effects of unemployment on well-being to be successful, families still act as crucial social and financial shock absorbers in several countries facing high unemployment, and they still succeed even without accompanying labour market policies. It is also worth noting that this additional route explains almost half of the cases.

In conclusion, this study has contributed to the literature on comparative welfare policies by investigating whether potential buffers provided by combinations of institutional and contextual factors mitigate the negative effect of unemployment on well-being. However, there are specific limitations to this study. First, the sample size is a challenge for the number of dimensions included in the analyses, and it leaves many logical reminders and few empirical relevancies for different configurations. Second, despite the eagerness to investigate countries' approaches to the well-being of unemployed youth, the operationalisation of policies oriented explicitly towards youth is difficult for most aggregate labour market policy instruments available in Eurostat. Finally, the outcome variable is currently controlled for compositional effects across countries, but is not sensitive to between-group differences on the country level. The study aimed foremost to apply Gallie and Paugam's (2000) model to a wider range of countries using QCA as a more flexible and system-oriented approach compared to the variable-oriented quantitative approach. Therefore, it did not test whether the explanatory dimensions might act differently for different subgroups,[15] although how institutional packages 'work' inside the countries for different groups with different educational resources is a highly relevant question, for example. Addressing this question would also make it possible to test the next set of vital questions: are more resourceful young people (in terms of education) more likely to benefit from active labour market measures alone, or is the combined approach of PLMPs and ALMPs also the most beneficial for them? Which configurations are the best for buffering well-being in unemployed young people with a low level of education?

Notes

1. In the formula, '*' denotes operator 'and', '+' denotes operator 'or', and arrows show sufficient (→) relationships between configuration and outcome.
2. Consistency of Sufficiency = SUM (X AND Y) / SUM X – that is, the sum of all conjunctions of particular X and Y (minimum rule), divided by the sum of Xs.
3. Coverage of Sufficiency = SUM (X AND Y) / SUM Y.
4. There are two predominant approaches to calibrating the interval scale data: (a) log-odds based and (b) regression based. In the former, four main steps are distinguishable: (i) select three thresholds (fully in, fully out, and crossover), (ii) calculate the deviations of raw scores from the crossover (x crossover) of each case, (iii) translate the crossover-centred data into the metric of log odds (see Ragin, 2008: 87), and (iv) transform log odds into membership scores: degree of membership = exp(log odds)/(1+exp(log odds)).
5. This decision means that only those configurations that are associated with a positive outcome with the consistency of 0.75 or higher are included in the calculations of solutions.
6. Because some simplifying assumptions have been made throughout this process of calculating the average generosity index, to avoid the risk of misinterpretations, OECD country chapters in the Benefits and Wages catalogue (www.oecd.org/els/social/workincentives) and Wulfgramm (2014) were used for comparison and robustness checks (details can be obtained from authors).
7. Alternative ways of operationalising PG would be one explanation for this contradictory finding. However, based on expenditure (share of Category 8: out-of-work income maintenance and support, in labour market policy [LMP] statistics in Eurostat, of GDP), the most regularly used indicator of 'welfare stateness' (Kuitto, 2016: 64), the result differs only slightly – ES, IT, and PT are all relatively high spenders, whereas EL is low (Eurostat, 2013).
8. LMP interventions in Eurostat are classified as follows: (1) LMP services (Category 1); (2) LMP measures; (3) Training (Category 2); (4) Employment incentives; (5) Sheltered and supported employment and rehabilitation; (6) Direct job creation; (7) Start-up incentives; (8) LMP supports (Out-of-work income maintenance and support; and (9) Early retirement.

9. The unit of observation in the LMP database is the LMP intervention, and data on participants are collected for each intervention, each of which is classified by the type of action. When gathering participants for each intervention in a category, there is an implicit assumption that each intervention (the unit of observation) is mutually exclusive, and that a person can participate in only one intervention at a time (Eurostat, 2013: Labour market statistics explained). However, it is also possible for double-counting to occur. For example, in Category 8 as used in this study, there could be a supplementary allowance that is used to top up unemployment benefit payments. In this case, participants could be double-counted, explaining, for instance, the percentage being above 100 in the case of BE.
10. Considering the validity of capturing the notion of coverage, using an alternative indicator was considered – that in the Social Insurance Entitlements Dataset – but PC from Eurostat was chosen instead to take into account both unemployment assistance and insurance-related benefits, because due to short employment spells, young cohorts are relatively more dependent on the former, making it more relevant in assessing their well-being.
11. Category 2 in Eurostat LMP statistics.
12. It is a common standard of QCA to start with a necessity analysis and follow this with a sufficiency analysis (Schneider and Wagemann, 2012) as in the present study. However, because none of the conditions included met the necessity criteria, all conditions were included in the sufficiency analysis. The latter makes up the so-called truth table.
13. The minimisation is based on the Quine–McCluskey algorithm.
14. An additional robustness check was made at crossover point -0.75, which adds three positive cases: Italy, France and Bulgaria.
15. Because leaving the parental home can be considered as one of the crucial steps towards adulthood, an additional analysis by residential status was performed. However, the life satisfaction of young unemployed people did not differ by residential status. The non-significant effect is driven by small sample sizes, but might also suggest that although prolonged co-residence with parents is a proxy for overall familialism on the macrolevel, different mechanisms leading towards higher life satisfaction are at play on the microlevel.

References

Anderson, C.J. and Hecht, J.D. (2015) 'Happiness and the welfare state: decommodification and the political economy of subjective well-being', in P. Beramendi, S. Häusermann, H. Kitschelt and H. Kriesi (eds) *The Politics of Advanced Capitalism*, Cambridge: Cambridge University Press, pp 357–80.

Arndt, C. (2017) 'Public policy-making and risk profiles: Scandinavian centre-right governments after the turn of the millennium', *European Political Science Review*, 9(4): 495–518.

Blossfeld, H.P., Buchholz, S., Bukodi, E. and Kurz, K. (eds) (2008) *Young Workers, Globalization and the Labour Market: Comparing Early Working Life in Eleven Countries*, Cheltenham; Northampton: Edward Elgar Publishing.

Bonoli, G. (1997) 'Classifying welfare states: a two-dimension approach', *Journal of Social Policy*, 26(3): 351–72.

Bonoli, G. (2010) 'The political economy of active labour-market policy', *Politics and Society*, 38(4): 435–57.

Bonoli, G. (2012) 'Active labour market policy and social investment: a changing relationship', in N. Morel, B. Palier and J. Palme (eds) *Towards a Social Investment Welfare State? Ideas, Policies and Challenges*, Bristol: Policy Press, pp 181–204.

Bouget, D., Frazer, H., Marlier, E., Sabato, S. and Vanhercke, B. (2015) *Social Investment in Europe: A Study of National Policies*, Luxembourg: Publications Office of the European Union.

Brzinsky-Fay, C. (2017) 'The interplay of educational and labour market institutions and links to relative youth unemployment', *Journal of European Social Policy*, 27(4): 346–59.

Calvo, E., Mair, C.A. and Sarkisian, N. (2015) 'Individual troubles, shared troubles: the multiplicative effect of individual and country-level unemployment on life satisfaction in 95 nations (1981–2009)', *Social Forces*, 93(4): 1625–53.

Cantillon, B. (2011) 'The paradox of the social investment state: growth, employment and poverty in the Lisbon era', *Journal of European Social Policy*, 21(5): 432–49.

Chevalier, T. (2016) 'Varieties of youth welfare citizenship: towards a two-dimension typology', *Journal of European Social Policy*, 26(1): 3–19.

De Graaf, W. and Maier, R. (2017) 'The welfare state and the life course: examining the interrelationship between welfare arrangements and inequality dynamics', *Social Policy and Administration*, 51(1): 40–55.

Diener, E., Inglehart, R. and Tay, L. (2013) 'Theory and validity of life satisfaction scales', *Social Indicators Research*, 112(3): 497–527.

Diener, E., Suh, E.M., Lucas, R.E. and Smith, H.L. (1999) 'Subjective well-being: three decades of progress', *Psychological Bulletin*, 125: 276–302.

Duşa, A. and Thiem, A. (2014) *QCA: A Package for Qualitative Comparative Analysis, R Package Version 1.1-4*, Available from: http://cran.r-project.org/package=QCA

Eger, R.J. and Maridal, J.H. (2015) 'A statistical meta-analysis of the wellbeing literature', *International Journal of Wellbeing*, 5(2): 45–74.

Eichhorn, J. (2013) 'Unemployment needs context: how societal differences between countries moderate the loss in life satisfaction for the unemployed', *Journal of Happiness Studies*, 14(6): 1657–80.

Eichhorn, J. (2014) 'The (non-)effect of unemployment benefits: variations in the effect of unemployment on life satisfaction between EU countries', *Social Indicators Research*, 119(1): 389–404.

Emmenegger, P., Kvist, J. and Skaaning, S.E. (2013) 'Making the most of configurational comparative analysis: an assessment of QCA applications in comparative welfare-state research', *Political Research Quarterly*, 66(1): 185–90.

Esping-Andersen, G. (1990) *The Three Worlds of Welfare Capitalism*, Princeton: Princeton University Press.

Eurofound (2014) *Social Situation of Young People in Europe*, Luxembourg: Publications Office of the European Union.

Eurostat (2013) *Labour Market Policy Statistics: Methodology 2013*, Luxembourg: Publications Office of the European Union.

Gallie, D. (2013) 'Economic crisis, the quality of work, and social integration: issues and context', in D. Gallie (ed) *Economic Crisis, Quality of Work, and Social Integration: The European Experience*, Oxford: Oxford University Press, pp 1–29.

Gallie, D. and Paugam, S. (2000) 'The experience of unemployment in Europe: the debate', in D. Gallie (ed) *Employment Regimes and the Quality of Work*, Oxford: Oxford University Press, pp 1–22.

Gingrich, J. and Ansell, B. (2015) 'The dynamics of social investment: human capital, activation and care', in P. Beramendi, S. Häusermann, H. Kitschelt and H. Kriesi (eds) *The Politics of Advanced Capitalism*, New York: Cambridge University Press, pp 282–304.

Hemerijck, A. (2015) 'The quiet paradigm revolution of social investment', *Social Politics*, 22(2): 242–56.

Häusermann, S. and Palier, B. (2017) 'The politics of social investment: policy legacies and class coalitions', in A. Hemerijck (ed) *The Uses of Social Investment*, Oxford: Oxford University Press, pp 339–48.

Kersbergen, K., Vis, B. and Hemerijck, A. (2015) 'The great recession and welfare state reform: is retrenchment really the only game left in town?', *Social Policy and Administration*, 48(7): 883–904.

Kuitto, K. (2016) *Post-Communist Welfare States in European Context: Patterns of Welfare Policies in Central and Eastern Europe*, Cheltenham; Northampton: Edward Elgar Publishing.

Martin, J.P. (2015) 'Activation and active labour market policies in OECD countries: stylised facts and evidence on their effectiveness', *IZA Journal of Labor Policy*, 4(4): 1–29.

McKee-Ryan, F., Song, Z., Wanberg, C.R. and Kinicki, A.J. (2005) 'Psychological and physical well-being during unemployment: a meta-analytic study', *The Journal of Applied Psychology*, 90(1): 53–76.

Nelson, M. (2013) 'Making markets with active labor market policies: the influence of political parties, welfare state regimes, and economic change on spending on different types of policies', *European Political Science Review*, 5(2): 255–77.

O'Campo, P., Molnar, A., Ng, E., Renahy, E., Mitchell, C., Shankardass, K., St John, A., Bambra, C. and Muntaner, C. (2015) 'Social welfare matters: a realist review of when, how, and why unemployment insurance impacts poverty and health', *Social Science and Medicine*, 132: 88–94.

Oesch, D. and Lipps, O. (2013) 'Does unemployment hurt less if there is more of it around? A panel analysis of life satisfaction in Germany and Switzerland', *European Sociological Review*, 29(5): 955–67.

Otto, H.U., Atzmüller, R., Berthet, T., Bifulco, L., Bonvin, J.-M., Chiappero, E., Egdell, V., Halleroed, B., Kjeldsen, C.C., Kwiek, M., Schröer, R., Vero, J. and Zielenska, M. (eds) (2015) *Facing Trajectories from School to Work: Towards a Capability-Friendly Youth Policy in Europe*, New York: Springer.

Paul, K.I. and Moser, K. (2009) 'Unemployment impairs mental health: meta-analyses', *Journal of Vocational Behavior*, 74(3): 264–82.

Quaranta, M. (2013) 'SetMethods: a package companion to "set-theoretic methods for the social sciences"', *R Package Version 1.0*, Available from: http://cran.rproject.org/package=SetMethods

Ragin, C.C. (1987) *The Comparative Method: Moving Beyond Qualitative and Quantitative Strategies*, Berkeley: University of California Press.

Ragin, C. (2008) *Redesigning Social Inquiry: Fuzzy Sets and Beyond*, Chicago: University of Chicago Press.

Rokicka, M. (ed), Kłobuszewska, M., Palczyńska, M., Shapoval, N. and Stasiowski, J. (2015) *Composition and Cumulative Disadvantage of Youth Across Europe*. EXCEPT Working Papers, WP No. 1, Tallinn: Tallinn University, Available from: https://www.except-project.eu/working-papers/.

Russell, H., Watson, D. and McGinnity, F. (2013) 'Unemployment and subjective well-being', in D. Gallie (ed) *Economic Crisis, Quality of Work, and Social Integration: The European Experience*, Oxford: Oxford University Press, pp 229–55.

Samuel, R. and Hadjar, A. (2016) 'How welfare-state regimes shape subjective well-being across Europe', *Social Indicators Research*, 129(2): 565–87.

Schneider, C.Q. and Makszin, K. (2014) 'Forms of welfare capitalism and education-based participatory inequality', *Socio-Economic Review*, 12(2): 437–62.

Schneider, C.Q. and Wagemann, C. (2010) 'Standards of good practice in qualitative comparative analysis (QCA) and fuzzy-sets', *Comparative Sociology*, 9(3): 1–22.

Schneider, C.Q. and Wagemann, C. (2012) *Set-Theoretic Methods for the Social Sciences: A Guide to Qualitative Comparative Analysis*, Cambridge: Cambridge University Press.

Stauber, B. and Walther, A. (2006) 'De-standardised pathways to adulthood: European perspectives on informal learning in informal networks', *Revista de Sociología*, (79): 241–62, Available from: https://papers.uab.cat/article/view/v79-stauber-walther/pdf-en

Skaaning, S.E. (2011) 'Assessing the robustness of crisp-set and fuzzy-set QCA results', *Sociological Methods & Research*, 40(2): 391–408.

Strandh, M., Novo, M. and Hammarström, A. (2011) 'Mental health among the unemployed and the unemployment rate in the municipality', *European Journal of Public Health*, 21(6): 799–805.

Thomann, E. and Maggetti, M. (2020) 'Designing research with Qualitative Comparative Analysis (QCA): approaches, challenges, and tools', *Sociological Methods & Research*, 49(2): 356–86.

Unt, M. and Jeliazkova, M. (eds) (2018) *Database of Youth Policies and Legislation on Youth Inclusion*. EXCEPT Working Papers, WP No. 54, Tallinn: Tallinn University, Available from: https://www.except-project.eu/working-papers/.

Vis, B. (2011) 'Under which conditions does spending on active labor market policies increase? An fsQCA analysis of 53 governments between 1985 and 2003', *European Political Science Review*, 3(2): 229–52.

Voßemer, J. and Eunicke, N. (2015) *The Impact of Labor Market Exclusion and Job Insecurity on Health and Well-Being Among Youth – a Literature Review*. EXCEPT Working Papers, WP No. 2, Tallinn: Tallinn University, Available from: https://www.except-project.eu/working-papers/.

Voßemer, J., Gebel, M., Täht, K., Unt, M., Högberg, B. and Strandh, M. (2018) 'The effects of unemployment and insecure jobs on well-being and health: the moderating role of labor market policies', *Social Indicators Research*, 138(3): 1229–57.

Walther, A. (2006) 'Regimes of youth transitions: choice, flexibility and security in young people's experiences across different European contexts' *Young*, 14(2): 119–39.

Wanberg, C.R. (2012) 'The individual experience of unemployment', *Annual Review of Psychology*, 63: 369–96.

Wulfgramm, M. (2014) 'Life satisfaction effects of unemployment in Europe: The moderating influence of labour market policy', *Journal of European Social Policy*, 24(3): 258–72.

5

Experiencing unemployment and job insecurity in two European countries: German and Italian young people's well-being and coping strategies

Christoph Schlee, Rosy Musumeci, and Chiara Ghislieri

Introduction

Although young people throughout Europe are increasingly experiencing labour market uncertainties (Müller and Gangl, 2003) and unemployment, there are marked differences between countries (Eurofound, 2012; Eurostat, 2018a, 2018b). Italy, with one of the highest youth unemployment rates in the EU (34.7 per cent in 2017), and Germany with the lowest (6.8 per cent) (Eurostat, 2018a, 2018b), present a strong contrast regarding the labour market situation of young people. Previous studies focusing on the multidimensional concept of job insecurity (Van Vuuren, 1990; Näswall and De Witte, 2003) have shown that in young people in particular, unemployment can have a negative impact on individual subjective well-being and mental health (Paul and Moser, 2009).

In general, there is a growing diffusion of 'insecure' jobs among youth in Europe (Baranowska and Gebel, 2010). In national and local labour markets that are especially poor in opportunities for young people, this phenomenon has an important negative impact on subjective well-being (Kieselbach, 2000; De Witte et al, 2016; Giunchi et al, 2016). Subjective well-being covers both cognitive (life satisfaction) and affective (personal feelings) elements (Diener et al, 1999).

Although many studies confirm the relationship between job insecurity or unemployment and well-being, the dynamics underlying it are not fully understood. Only a few studies have tackled this topic from a qualitative standpoint by highlighting the dynamics and the subjective processes operating in this relationship (for example,

Blustein et al, 2013) and comparing samples from countries in terms of the labour market and the welfare system. To date, there is also a lack of literature exploring the coping strategies – that is, cognitive and behavioural attempts to counter external and internal stress in a problem-oriented or emotional way (Lazarus and Folkman, 1984) – that young people put in place to reduce the negative effects of job insecurity or unemployment on well-being (Richter et al, 2013). The aim of this chapter is to improve understanding of how young people perceive their insecure work situations and how they deal with any negative impact on well-being on the individual level.

Based on a qualitative approach, this study investigates individual perceptions of well-being and the associated coping strategies of young people in Italy and Germany. It focuses on similarities and differences between these contexts in order to enrich knowledge of the relationship between unemployment and well-being in these two countries.

In sum, it addresses the following research questions: how do young people in Italy and Germany perceive their subjective well-being while experiencing objective job insecurity and unemployment? How do they deal with their situation in terms of well-being? Are there similarities or differences in coping strategies between young people from Italy and Germany and how can they be explained?

Well-being and labour market insecurity

Well-being – more specifically, subjective well-being – is a multidimensional concept that includes a physical component (health) and a psychological component. The psychological component, in turn, can be differentiated in terms of life satisfaction (cognitive) (Diener et al, 1999), and prevalent affective experience (emotional), (Warr, 1990). Psychological well-being can be general, domain-related, or related to spillover effects between life domains (Grebner et al, 2005).

This chapter considers unemployment and job insecurity together. Job insecurity is defined as a multidimensional concept (Van Vuuren, 1990) with objective and subjective dimensions (Näswall and De Witte, 2003). Job insecurity means uncertainty about the future (De Witte, 2005) and about the continuation of the job as such (Greenhalgh and Rosenblatt, 1984). Unemployment (among youth) means not being employed, but this chapter also considers persons who are not in education, employment or training (NEET) in this context. For more detailed definitions of the concepts, see Chapter 1 of this book.

Notwithstanding many quantitative results confirming the link between objective and subjective job insecurity and well-being, the mechanisms underlying this relationship are not completely understood. Employment has a manifest and latent function (Jahoda, 1981; Van Hoye and Lootens, 2013): the manifest function is related to financial benefits; the latent function, to the fact that a job provides structure in personal life. A job also provides the possibility of taking an active role in life and reaching personal and collective goals. Considering Jahoda's latent deprivation model, job insecurity and unemployment may lead to a decrease of well-being via the fear of not having sufficient income to live adequately in the present (and to project the future), but also through the loss of opportunity to be effective in a collective situation and to structure time in one's life (Paul and Moser, 2009).

In addition, social identity theory (Tajfel and Turner, 1979) may help in understanding the process: identity issues are particularly relevant in the current fragmented and discontinuous world (Albert et al, 2000; Piccoli et al, 2017).

The link between job insecurity or unemployment and well-being may also be understood using transactional stress theory (Lazarus and Folkman, 1984). In this frame, job insecurity is considered as a stressor (Wang et al, 2015): individuals who are threatened with a possible stressor undertake a primary appraisal to assess whether it is a risk to personal well-being, and a secondary appraisal to evaluate resources and strategies to cope with it. When a job is perceived as being at risk, it is most likely interpreted as a threat, because employment is important for the individual's personal, social, and economic life.

To face a stressor, people activate different strategies. Following Lazarus and Folkman's (1984) definition, coping strategies are cognitive and behavioural efforts that people use to face external and/ or internal stressing demands, and they can be distinguished as being either problem-focused (aimed at addressing the problem directly) or emotion-focused (aimed at dealing with feelings associated with the stressor). In some cases, people use avoidance strategies such as denial and escape from the situation (Carver et al, 1989).

Job insecurity also makes it hard to activate helpful coping strategies because the source of job insecurity is undefined: in fact, job insecurity is classified as a rather uncontrollable threat and is linked to a feeling of powerlessness (Greenhalgh and Rosenblatt, 1984).

Moreover, coping strategies to address the symptoms of precarious working condition (for example, health problems) can be located not only on the micro or individual level, but also on the macro and meso social levels. There are, for example, macrocontextual strategies related to actively seeking support from public institutions and the state, and mesolevel coping strategies that are related to actively seeking support from family and social networks (Fullin, 2004).

Following the literature on stress and coping, the effectiveness of problem-focused coping and emotion-focused coping depends on whether or not the source of perceived stress is clear (Folkman et al, 1979; Pinquart and Silbereisen, 2008): problem-focused coping is more effective with an identified source of stress, whereas emotion-focused coping seems to be a better choice if the source of stress is unclear (Armstrong-Stassen, 2005). However, research results on coping as a moderator in the relationship between job insecurity and well-being are contradictory (Richter, 2011). There is no consensus about which coping strategies may be more effective in dealing with job insecurity and in reducing negative consequences for well-being. This may also depend on the fact that studies have mainly considered general coping strategies and not specific ones.

Few studies describe and analyse the specific coping strategies used to face job insecurity (for example, Bagnara and Bargigli, 2009; Heuven et al, 2009; Blustein et al, 2013) and to buffer negative consequences on well-being. Heuven et al (2009) highlighted that some interviewees actively looked for another job as a coping strategy in response to job insecurity, whereas other respondents were more stressed and unable to start an active job search due to psychological problems. Blustein et al (2013) found that behaviours oriented towards improving employability limit the negative consequences of unemployment (for example, training and education, networking) on well-being.

Institutional context

Italy and Germany show extreme contrasts in terms of youth unemployment (those aged 15 to 24). Italy had a youth unemployment rate of 34.7 per cent in 2017, whereas Germany had a rate of 6.8 per cent. Within the European Union (EU-28), the average was 16.8 per cent (Eurostat, 2018a, 2018b). Italy and Germany have been differently affected by the economic crisis of 2008. Starting from two radically different educational systems (Reyneri, 2017), poor career prospects remain present even for university graduates in Italy (Rokicka et al, 2015), whereas in Germany, young people often see their insecure situation as being only temporary (for example, Schlee, 2018). Institutions and traditions seem to be very important when it comes to explaining the big inequalities within Europe (Dietrich and Möller, 2016). Labour market policies seem to be crucial for the individual experience of unemployment (Voßemer et al, 2017). For example, the generosity of unemployment benefits has a positive effect on the perceived well-being of those affected (Boarini et al, 2013). Germany, as a conservative welfare state, and Italy, as a Southern European state, differ in political measures and programmes in various fields. Compared to Italy, Germany has stronger state support through, for example, unemployment benefits and targeted policies for young people, whereas Italy has few active labour market policies (ALMPs) and no income support for young people without labour market experience (Bertolini and Torrioni, 2018). In Italy, family support seems to be more important for young people during periods of job insecurity and unemployment (see Chapter 10 in this volume). Due to these differences, the present study investigates young people's subjective well-being during unemployment or job insecurity, and how they deal with potential occurring limitations and insecurities in the two country contexts.

Data and methodology

The analysis is based on the full set of interviews from Germany and Italy that were conducted within the EXCEPT project (see Bertolini et al, 2018a). An overview of the general methodology can be found in Chapter 1 in this volume. Several socio-demographic criteria were considered in the sampling process. The sample consists of 90 young people (40 German and 50 Italian cases) aged 18–30 years who were mostly unemployed, NEET, and temporary workers, with different levels of education. Furthermore, they show differences in terms of migrant background and involvement in policy measures. The sample was balanced for gender. The Italian interviews were conducted in Turin in the north and Catania in the south, and the German interviews in different federal states: Bavaria, Baden-Württemberg, Hamburg, North Rhine-Westphalia, Saxony, and Saxony-Anhalt (Bertolini et al, 2018b; Schlee, 2018).

A qualitative approach was chosen to examine the perceptions, individual situations, and experiences of youth from a subjective point of view. Thematic analysis (Braun and Clarke, 2006) was used to discover patterns in subjective meanings. The research questions were explored with reference to several categories including perception of the current situation, well-being, and possible risk factors for well-being, and coping strategies such as how (limited) well-being can be improved. This referred to existing theories and research by investigating well-being in different dimensions (emotion-focused; problem-focused) and including the levels of coping strategies to be found (micro, meso, macro) as sub-categories. In addition, inductive sub-categories (data driven) were formed to respond flexibly to emerging phenomena in order to allow for an open analysis approach. Overall, the study applied a combination of a semantic approach focusing on explicit meanings of the data, and a latent approach going beyond what had been said (Braun and Clarke, 2006). A further step elaborated the similarities and differences between the two countries in terms of the developed themes.

Findings

Labour market insecurity and well-being: subjective perceptions and risk factors

This section presents the interconnections between job insecurity or unemployment and well-being by reporting on the individual perceptions of well-being in objectively insecure labour market situations and on existing risk factors for well-being that emerged among the German and Italian interviewees during the analysis.

Joblessness leaves a profound mark on the lives of the interviewees in Italy: in many interviews, the *sense of malaise* reported, often bordering on experiences of *depressive moods*, has to do with being *disheartened*, with living with the deep *disappointment* engendered by the impossibility of finding a job. Unemployment means staying at home, not meeting people, and lack of participation in a community of work. Work is generally considered by some interviewees to be a possible source of well-being, a tool with which to construct identity: "it is the engine of life" (Paolo, M, 23, LE, TE, IT).[1] Moreover, several interviewees stress the importance of having a job that is compatible with the rest of one's life and that will also make it possible to have adequate space for family and private life.

Across the German interviews, it is also clear that work, especially the income it brings, plays an important role in perceptions of individual well-being. Inter alia, interviewees mentioned basic needs (for example, shelter, food), having a feeling of (financial) security, having something to do, and being autonomous. If one or more of these essentials is missing, well-being is limited depending on individual life situations and attitudes. Then, at least a sense of *unease or malaise* appears, too.

Moreover, *pessimistic thinking* often emerged from the interviews in both countries. In the cases of Tamara and Mara, the main theme is a *sense of hopelessness*: repeated failure in attempts to find a new job lead to negative thoughts about the future including *despair* and *pessimism*: "My worry is that I'll have no future" (Mara, F, 30, ME,

U, IT); "Sadness. So many times, I want to cry because I do not feel fulfilled and independent" (Tamara, F, 23, ME, NEET, IT). Marc (M, 24, LE, U, DE) also wants to be independent, but due to his unemployment, he is reliant on others' support, which makes him *feel sad* and creates a *feeling of inferiority*. In addition, *concerns, fear, and desperation* due to deprivation and poor future prospects resulting from current unemployment appear in some German interviews too:

> 'I'm worried about a lot of things at the moment [pause] I'm afraid of the future. I'm afraid that I can't find a job. I'm afraid that I can't find a flat and pay for it. I'm afraid that I can't cope with the whole situation. The whole situation is making me crazy.' (Tom, M, 20, ME, NEET, DE)

In particular, those who experience unemployment for several years often have *strong fears about the future*. They show strong signs of *stress* and *strain*, in many cases due to financial deprivation. Reported poor prospects for labour market integration seem to be particularly evident among young people with a low level of education or without vocational training or an apprenticeship.

Additionally, for some parents, especially single mothers, strong negative impacts on their own well-being appear as *worries and fears about their own children and their ability to care for them*. Lena (F, 21, ME, U, DE) describes the uncertain financial situation caused by her own unemployment and additionally perceives hurdles to finding a job as a single mother.

Elsewhere in the Italian cases, it is isolation, the lack of activities to signal the passing hours of the day, that emerges from Tommaso's narrative. He describes the shift from thinking that he has a great deal of free time to experiencing this 'free' time as *empty* and *frustrating*:

> 'I have lots of free time, too much free time, that's what I would change [pause] the first few months you say "Yes, that's fine, that's great" [pause] After two weeks of getting up at 11, you feel that you no longer want that [pause] The days are all the same.' (M, 22, ME, U, IT)

A change in the perception of the situation also became apparent for Tina (F, 18, LE, TE, DE) and Maria (F, 27, HE, TE, DE). Some young people who had left or finished school or apprenticeships, or graduated from university, initially accepted unemployment as a normal part of transition into the labour market and they even enjoyed the free time it offered. However, as time went on, feelings of *discomfort, malaise,* and *strain* intensified and became *feelings of uncertainty, fear of the future,* and *despair.*

In the German interviews, these feelings seem to be strongly related to a perception of *stigmatisation* (Goffman, 1986) as a result of being unemployed and/or receiving unemployment benefits (especially over an extended period). Despite the positive effect of financial support, an emerging *feeling of financial security,* some of the young interviewees felt a *psychological burden* due to stigmatisation:

'When you get to know someone for the first time ... you first have to say, "Yes, I'm unemployed" [grows quiet] so it's always been "But why? Are you lazy?" or stigmatised, something like that. You always get put into a category like that.' (Katrin, F, 27, LE, U, DE)

Sometimes these negative feelings appear together with a *lack of sense of belonging* to society and a *lack of identity* as well as a stressful feeling of *being dependent on institutions and society*: "Well, I do feel a little like an antisocial loser" (Laura, F, 25, LE, U, DE). In contrast, the Italian interviewees show no such perceptions.

Some Germans such as Klaus (M, 29, ME, U, DE) and Anna (F, 21, LE, U, DE) are *ashamed* that they are not financially independent because they receive unemployment benefits or informal financial support from their friends and family. Hence, they are not in compliance with the norm, whereas in Italy, more young people are unemployed and the unemployed are not generally viewed as outsiders.

In some German interviews, *experiencing poor treatment* (for example, condescending behaviour, lack of support in job search) from employees of the federal employment agency seems to be a factor in poor well-being during unemployment. In addition, some report being sanctioned financially (reduced unemployment benefits) by the agency. This causes a feeling of *incomprehension, unfair treatment,* and *being left alone.* This often results in *despair* and even greater *financial insecurity.*

To an even greater extent than German participants, many Italians also reveal a feeling that they do not receive enough institutional support to face up to the labour market and its challenges. This is linked to a feeling of *dissatisfaction* and the perception that living in a country such as Italy, especially southern Italy, is in itself a risk factor. The dominant metaphor is that of a challenge, a fight, a clash. Simply put, young people feel that they have to *fend for themselves*, find and create opportunities for themselves:

> 'In Italy, I think growing up is almost a test of courage! [laughs] because you feel right up against adversity: difficulty in finding work, people impeding you in finding work in every way because ... they are afraid that you will also steal their job because maybe they have the same difficulties as you. That is, becoming an adult in Italy is ugly!' (Aurelio, M, 22, ME, TE, IT)

Furthermore, in a few German cases, precarious employment, poor working conditions, and part-time or short-term contracts emerged as negative influences on individual well-being. This occurs especially when young people work for temporary employment agencies, and therefore *feel uncertain* due to the impossibility of planning their future. However, in some German and Italian cases such as Franco (M, 30, HE, NCJ, IT), even when a job contract is not secure, work is a source of well-being in itself: this is the case when the work performed is considered meaningful, corresponds to individual interests, and permits self-expression. In the German interviews, this is especially true when the work gives interviewees a degree of financial independence.

Besides the negative effects caused by unemployment or job insecurity, other risk factors for subjective well-being emerged. Although they are not the focus of this chapter, they play an important role in how young people perceive their situation. Physical and psychological limitations such as health problems, being the victim of an accident, poor working conditions, or family conflict are examples of other influences that came to light during the analysis and are important when interpreting individual cases.

This brief description of some young people's perceptions of labour market uncertainty in Italy and Germany and how they relate to their own well-being showed similarities as well as differences. Some other German respondents did not perceive their situation as uncertain (see also Beelmann et al, 2001; Rogge, 2013), largely because of their own coping strategies and protective factors in their lives.

Coping strategies for well-being

This section reports on the main coping strategies adopted by Italian and German interviewees to manage or improve the situations and difficulties arising with regard to their well-being. Here, coping strategies means strategies the interviewees use or activate to *face the symptoms of their precarious working conditions* or to *change their employment prospects and conditions*. Where appropriate, this section also reports on the repercussions of adopting certain strategies on the well-being of individual interviewees. Coping strategies are differentiated in terms of the level – micro, meso or macro – on which they operate and the chapter is structured in these terms. The perceived insecurities emerge diversely and with varying intensity. Accordingly, the coping strategies also vary.

Microlevel coping strategies

Microlevel coping strategies for well-being are the behaviours, cognitive mechanisms, and emotional strategies used by the individual. This section starts by highlighting strategies to *deal with job insecurity and unemployment that have consequences for individual well-being*. In Germany, *seeking jobs or vocational training* on the internet or in newspapers is a common strategy. In addition, job applications are used in different ways to escape immediately insecure life situations or to avoid the risk of a negative impact of unemployment (for example, through financial deprivation, stigmatisation). There are successes in some cases such as Finn (M, 18, LE, U, DE) who got an opportunity to do an internship and acquire work experience (and some money). However, when young people experience prolonged failure with this strategy, it can have a considerable impact on their well-being and can exacerbate the negative effect of unemployment or job insecurity leading to desperation and hopelessness. In the Italian cases, *job search through submitting* CVs is an 'active' coping strategy, but it can also generate malaise or frustration and result in the avoidance of job search.

In the German cases, it is apparent that some young people try *to enhance their employability* or *gain labour market experience* by improving their own education by, inter alia, returning to school (and graduating) and/or the use of internships, in some cases as part of labour market programmes (ALMPs). They are aware of the importance of having a school certificate as a positive signal to employers: "That always looks good, if you have grades or certificates" (Sven, M, 25, LE, U, DE).

In addition, some, like Sven again, *lower or change their aspirations,* as a result of their experiences. They agree to work part-time and/or for temporary employment agencies, sometimes under worse working conditions (low payment, small dismissal protection, and limited chance of being further employed or permanently employed) in order to avoid strong financial deprivations or to try and gain a foothold in the labour market. This strategy seems similar to the concept of adaptive preferences (Elster, 1983).

Other interviewees from Italy, especially from the south, seek to *'escape'* *the psychic malaise* associated with the impossibility of finding fulfilment in work in one's own country by planning to *emigrate*. On the one hand, this is described as necessary for realisation as a person and to live happily; on the other hand, it is not devoid of emotional costs: "I would not like to leave Sicily because it is my home, my place but what can I do? [Bitterly] It's spirit of survival!" (Gaia, F, 24, ME, U, IT). In the German interviews, in contrast, emigration does not seem to be an issue. Most interviewees are aware of the generally good employment opportunities in Germany and opportunities for integration into the labour market (compared to other countries). Only a few such as Klaus (M, 29, ME, U, DE) consider moving abroad, but they are still sceptical as to whether this will actually improve their situation. Moreover, they could currently claim unemployment benefits to ensure a minimum level of security, if necessary.

The interviews offer further examples of microlevel coping strategies used by young people to *reduce or minimise existing negative experiences or to improve individual well-being*. Some interviewees use *leisure time activities* available to them as a way of coping emotionally with the working situation; this can simply mean going to the restaurant as in Erika's case (F, 29, LE, U, IT).

Another strategy observed in the German interviews is to avoid stress and find some harmony by *lowering one's expectations and needs* as well as *living economically*, which is often necessary due to reduced financial resources during periods of unemployment. This often goes hand in hand with *accepting the current situation*, in particular for the long-term unemployed with lower secondary education (that is, without vocational training): "Meanwhile I just accepted it … I actually see more chances for success at my age, if I just take these jobs as an unskilled worker and try to gain a foothold from there" (Marc, M, 24, LE, U, DE).

In other Italian cases, the effort to find personal gratification that the work setting is unable to provide is not made 'within' one's own job and current employment situation but 'outside' the workplace. This means trying to reduce the stress associated with precarious employment situations or joblessness by *commitment to their own interests and hobbies*; a coping strategy that allows them to maintain, as far as possible, a certain detachment from the source of their own malaise. Concita (F, 23, ME, U, IT) says that she pushes herself to experience the artistic dimension of life including photography; Pedro (M, 21, ME, PE, IT), for his part, music; Andrea (M, 24, ME, TE, IT) engages in sport; Margherita (F, 24, ME, U, IT) dedicates time to her favourite hobby of dancing. Some German interviewees also use and focus on other areas such as hobbies as a distraction from the negative consequences of job insecurity on well-being. However, some mention financial limitations and how these get in the way of exercising their hobbies, and this, in turn, can negatively affect their well-being. Klaus (M, 29, ME, U, DE), for example, leaves his apartment only for important appointments, because he no longer has enough money to go partying or meeting friends.

In many cases in both countries, a subsequent *falling back on the present* or a *suppressing* of their own current insecure situations and possible consequences that may arise in the future emerge: "I just push away what might be in a few months" (Katrin, F, 27, LE, U, DE). For the majority of Italians in the sample, negative influences seem to be offset by the *preservation of a gaze towards future horizons* in which one 'dreams' of achieving a (stable) relationship in a couple, the formation of a family of one's own, having children, and a house. Thinking, in short, that sooner or later, one will manage to reach that horizon, nursing that hope, is a coping strategy against the associated anxiety and disquiet – at times declared explicitly, at other times, only hinted at.

Comparable to repression, a few people use *criminal activities* or *drug use* in an attempt to escape their insecure situation with its accompanying stress and anxiety. Klaus, for example, dealt and consumed drugs not only to overcome financial deprivation but also to cope with anxiety: "Back then I was dealing drugs and I was also consuming drugs to escape this nightmare and that is how I basically paid my bills" (Klaus, M, 29, ME, U, DE). Later he regretted these actions. In the Italian cases, drug use does not occur as a response to concerns or fears, but in some cases, the use of tranquillisers and medicines is mentioned.

Another strategy is *to think positively into the future* and *to believe in oneself*, especially in one's own skills and opportunities in terms of labour market success based on one's own qualification. This is strongly associated with *optimism*. It is particularly true for German interviewees with a university degree and good prospects for the future. They see their insecure situation as being only temporary. In addition, interviewees who have completed their training or improved their health situation as well as those who are doing internships or have been invited to job interviews such as Simon (M, 25, LE, U, DE) are optimistic, and this prevents severe discomfort. As far as protective factors are concerned, on a microlevel, the Italian interviewees also cite personal aspects, subjective attitudes such as *optimism*, and *positive thinking*. Optimism and well-being seem to be linked in a virtuous circle: the interviewees presenting situations of greater well-being are also those who describe themselves as being more positive and optimistic about the future: "I'm an optimist ... I'll be able to deal with job insecurity" (Carlo, M, 26, LE, TE, IT). Alongside *optimism*, *being proactive* and *self-determination* are considered to be personal resources that sustain well-being because, underlying these, there is a desire to build a satisfactory life situation.

To protect himself from the negative effects on his well-being of a precarious employment situation, Franco (M, 30, HE, TE, IT) endeavours to give value to and to appreciate the expressive and relational aspects of his job; he claims to find satisfaction in jobs that are in line with his own interests and downplays the instrumental aspects (contractual stability and income) by activating, it would seem, a strategy of *cognitive dissonance or of 'compensation'*, or even of '*adaptation*'. Franco describes himself, moreover, as being quite 'relaxed' because he enjoys some self-esteem and considers himself confident about his future employment situation.

In other cases still, it is the thought of *sharing a common employment situation and common risks (even for health) with the young generation* to which one belongs that serves as a microlevel coping strategy to control the malaise emotionally and mentally and avoid the risks of developing serious forms of malaise due to insecurity and lack of work. This makes them feel less bad about their situation. Ester (F, 26, ME, NCJ, IT) thinks that she shares this discomfort with many of her peers and feels that she does not want to end up like many young people who develop full-blown psychological conditions. Therefore, she tries to shake herself up so as not to fall victim to panic attacks and medication. Some of the German interviewees also *gloss over* or try to *normalise* their situation. This is often combined with *optimism*, especially by those who have a good education (for instance, vocational training) and therefore generally good future prospects on the labour market. Fabian, who is on the verge of another period of unemployment, defines his insecure situation as a normal and temporary part in anyone's life and therefore looks into the future relaxed:

> 'So I see it really laid-back since nowadays it's simply a fact that sometimes people are unemployed. I'm not embarrassed about ... I'll find something again during the winter.' (Fabian, M, 22, ME, TE, DE)

However, as already mentioned, being unemployed and receiving unemployment benefits can create a feeling of stigmatisation. Some additionally experience stress and burden because they are unable to care for themselves and therefore have to accept help from other people or the state. In order to ward off negative influences, several, such as Katrin (F, 27, LE, U, DE), say to themselves that the situation has come about through no fault of their own; or they convince themselves that they are not dependent on other individuals, but rather on the state. In this context, some additionally highlight that it is simply their right as citizens to receive this form of support (for example Maja, F, 24, ME, U, DE).

Mesolevel coping strategies

When focusing on the mesolevel, we can highlight that the majority of German interviewees use their individual *social network* – that is, family, partner, friends, and other important people in young people's lives, in other words, their social capital (Bourdieu, 1983) – to enhance individual well-being or to avoid or mitigate the negative impact on it. This *informal support* appears in the form of *advice* and *assistance during job searches or the application process* as well as in *establishing contact with employers*. Its success depends largely on a variety of factors, including the 'quality' of the individual's social network and related resources. Nevertheless, it became clear that youth who have the possibility of receiving informal support often show a better sense of well-being than those without. This seems to be a protective factor and can lead to some relief (of stress).

The family's (and other people's) support appears useful, on the one hand, to cope with labour market insecurities. On the other hand, in the form of *emotional support*, against negative consequences for well-being caused by unemployment or improve the perception of the current life situation by helping to feel (re)integrated into the social environment and not feel left alone or excluded: "Well, they (parents) were really motivational because they kept saying that everything is just normal" (Julia, F, 27, HE, U, DE).

Strongly related to this emotional support, other young people meet friends or pursue their hobbies in order to have a positive feeling and *escape* from the sense of burden: "Whenever I am outside and meet my friends, then mainly just to escape everything for about an hour or two. To think about something else" (Marc, M, 24, LE, U, DE).

In addition, *material support* via their own social network was also evident, especially from the family of origin, partners, and close friends.

This support, such as giving not only shelter, being able to live together, and financial help but also emotional support, proved to be extremely important for improving or maintaining one's own well-being during labour market insecurities. Thea reports about the importance of sharing the rental costs: "I'd be helpless without my friend … If I had to pay the apartment on my own, then [pause] I wouldn't have a chance at all with my salary" (Thea, F, 21, LE, TE, DE).

In Italy, the family of origin – and, in certain cases, also uncles and aunts, grandparents, or peers such as cousins – appears to be the most significant source of *emotional* and *psychological support* for the interviewees. Mara, for example, is looking for a job and is depressed. Her family's emotional support is so important to her that it stops her from even considering the idea of emigrating to find work: "I have no desire to go abroad, because my family is here" (F, 29, ME, U, IT).

Likewise, Renata (F, 22, ME, U, IT), who describes herself as an energetic and optimistic woman, turns to her family of origin for considerable support (economic and emotional). There is where she finds the motivation and encouragement to carry on without becoming depressed by the difficulties encountered in the labour market. Thanks to strong and significant protection, she is still well integrated within the environment in which she lives. Many interviewees state that they have recourse to, and greatly appreciate, the emotional support of their families of origin. However, some consider this to be basically insufficient to contain the malaise associated with their employment situation, albeit they acknowledge that this support impacts positively on their well-being and mental stability. Camilla (F, 23, ME, NCJ, IT) lives with her family and is satisfied, but she strongly desires to leave her parents' house and move in with her current boyfriend. However, her working conditions do not allow this.

In some cases, despite appreciation of the family support, this is considered to be definitively ineffective when it comes to coping with the real cause of their own malaise: the absence of a job. For example, Franco says:

'My mum [pause] I mean, she tries to help me, to support me [pause] but for the way I am, these are words that don't work with me. You feel like a loser, useless [pause] It's bad … the thing that would make the situation less complicated, it's a job.' (Franco, M, 29, HE, NCJ, IT)

In certain cases, it is friends (or boyfriends/girlfriends) above all who are a source of emotional and psychological support. Carlo (M, 25,

LE, TE, IT), highlights the fundamentally positive role of the relational dimension: it is the social dimension and solidarity in participation and volunteering that seem important. It is the human relationships with friends and co-workers that seem to give meaning to his existence.

Among those interviewees who do not seem to experience their situations of job insecurity with anxiety and malaise, Franco, for example, states that this is because he receives considerable financial and emotional support from his family as well as from his informal social network of friends: "I feel lucky because I have an enormous group of friends, I have my family, I have so many things" (Franco, M, 30, HE, TE, IT).

Other interviewees utilise different *channels and relations* to cope with the malaise and the sense of dissatisfaction with their own employment circumstances. Tamara (F, 23, ME, U, IT) attends church together with her family and is able to derive some comfort and peace of mind from it. In other cases, work, even if informal, provides an opportunity for personal expression, and despite the frustration experienced, represents an instrument of well-being.

In both countries, it can be seen that social relationships, especially the family, play an important and often crucial role in directly addressing job insecurity and unemployment as well as in increasing well-being through emotional or financial support. In the Italian cases, support from the nuclear family seems to be used to a greater extent than in the German cases, where due to the greater availability of formal support the family often serves simply as a source of emotional support (for example, providing advice) and help in financial emergencies.

Macrolevel coping strategies

Macrocontextual strategies refers to actively *seeking support* from public institutions and the state to improve or manage impaired well-being associated with young people's labour market situation. In the German cases (for example, Sven, M, 25, LE, U, DE), *attending programmes and measures* (ALMP) can be a useful way *to improve skills* (catch up on school certificates) and to gain *work experience* in order to finally improve employability and prospects for the future. Sometimes it is possible to get a foot in the door of some firms for apprenticeships or gain employment through internships; or it offers a means of establishing structure in daily life through clear tasks. Simon, who improved his situation, now has better job prospects and improved well-being: "Well yes, it just brought me ahead. Definitely. It brought a little [pause] yes [pause] structure to my life. Encouraged me" (Simon, M, 25, LE, U, DE).

However, young people perceive policy programmes and measures very differently. Certain measures are obligatory in Germany if young people want to claim financial support. This can cause stress and appear as an additional burden. Moreover, some are not satisfied with labour market integration measures because these were often not tailored to individual needs and therefore are considered unsuccessful and useless: "I think participating in courses about 'how to clean my workplace' or 'how to use the ten-finger writing system' is stupid. I think these courses are useless" (Tom, M, 22, ME, NEET, DE). However, regarding the Italian cases, for example, Gaia turned to the Garanzia Giovani [youth guarantee scheme] and views the experience positively. She states:

> 'I was depressed. … it saved me because I found myself with a job, a role, employment. It was positive. It's been the only positive thing that has happened to me [laughs].' (Gaia, F, 24, ME, U, IT)

Whereas many interviewees in the Italian sample appreciate the opportunities afforded by macrolevel strategies in helping them cope with their own malaise and focus on improving their employment situations and employability through policy and institutional channels, many interviewees declare that they do not trust politicians and institutions to improve their situation. Several of these young people state that they are not completely convinced that the institutions are interested in doing anything practical to help young people.

Another important protective factor that appears repeatedly in the German interviews is the use of *passive income support policies*, especially unemployment benefits (*Arbeitslosengeld*, unemployment insurance; *Arbeitslosengeld II*, means-tested welfare payments). With this support, difficult financial bottlenecks caused by unemployment can often be absorbed and well-being can be strengthened, or, in some cases, negative influences can be averted: "Without it [Arbeitslosengeld II], I'd probably live under a bridge. I am really thankful for that … I wouldn't know what to do with two children and no job" (Simon, M, 25, LE, U, DE). Others like Jana (F, 28, ME, PE, DE) do not worry about future unemployment because they would be entitled to receive unemployment benefits. However, perceptions of the sufficiency of the amount vary across the interviews, and this, in turn, can have a negative effect on well-being if there is a feeling of financial deprivation. In Italy, the insurance income protection system does not provide unemployment benefit for first job seekers, so the majority of young people in the sample affected by labour market uncertainties were not entitled to any formal support.

However, as already mentioned, dependency on and interaction with the federal employment agency in Germany can have a negative impact on well-being. The agency's actions (such as financial sanctions) are sometimes perceived as obstacles or the reason for the deterioration of their own situations. In general, a lack of entitlement to formal support may also occur, mostly for young people under 25 years of age and still living in their parents' household.

Another strategy related to well-being is the support received from *social workers or the social work institutions* as well as other *(health) institutions* that provide emotional support and useful advice. Kerstin (F, 23, LE, U, DE), who has been suffering from mental health issues such as anxiety states and depression, uses professional help in the form of therapies.

The interviews showed that some young people try to overcome labour market uncertainties directly or reduce the negative impact on well-being; their strategies have led to success and they have been able to achieve better future prospects as well as establish structure and meaning in their daily lives. However, despite similarities in the strategies adopted by young people, there are large differences between Germany and Italy, in particular the stronger formal support structures and measures available in the former.

Conclusions

The aim of this study was to examine young people's perceptions of unemployment and job insecurity in Italy and Germany as well as the coping strategies they use to maintain well-being. Due to a lack of research on this topic, the aim was to better understand how the potentially negative effects on individual well-being indicated in previous research (Kieselbach, 2000; Voßemer and Eunicke, 2015; De Witte et al, 2016) are managed within the framework of the two different country contexts. The study applied a qualitative approach to 90 semi-structured interviews with young people experiencing unemployment or job insecurity in Germany and Italy conducted as part of the EXCEPT project (Bertolini et al, 2018a).

In summary, results on the individual perceptions of the situation of young people are consistent with previous research indicating a general tendency towards negative effects on individual well-being (for example dissatisfaction, malaise, worries, and anxiety). In this respect, the meanings of work and the functions it entails (Jahoda, 1981) play an important role. However, the cognitive and affective aspects of these negative effects vary between cases, not only within but also between the two countries (Warr, 1990; Diener et al, 1999).

As other research in Germany has also indicated (Grimmer, 2016), young unemployed adults can perceive their situation negatively due to stigmatisation. Norms can be one possible explanation for this, because only a small percentage of youth are unemployed, thereby suggesting that if you cannot find a job, it is your fault. In Italy with its high unemployment figures, in contrast, the situation is seen more as a 'generational fact' because it applies to so many young people. The young share a common condition and this 'mitigates' the negative consequences on well-being, at least in terms of any stigmatisation. Nevertheless, uncertainties are often present that are sometimes more obvious than in the German cases where the state provides stronger formal (financial) protection (unemployment benefits) which can reduce the negative impact on well-being in some cases.

Overall, however, the impact on subjective well-being in both countries seems to depend strongly on individual coping strategies. In both country samples, the microlevel reveals that many young people use the same or similar strategies (see also Lazarus and Folkman, 1984) in their respective contexts, such as optimistic thinking and ignoring or whitewashing the current insecure situation in order to avoid a (potentially) negative influence on their own well-being (emotion-focused); or searching for jobs and writing applications to counter uncertainties such as financial limitations or a lack of meaning, self-identification, and tasks (problem-focused). However, the context appears to play a decisive role. Compared to many Italians, German participants seem to have better prospects for their future, although they are in the same insecure labour market situation, because of the opportunities available to them through school-leaving qualifications or (vocational) training (still to be acquired or already existing). The German dual vocational education and training system, plays a decisive role in this respect (see also Blossfeld and Stockmann, 1998/1999): in contrast to Italy, many young people in Germany with fixed-term contracts are doing an apprenticeship or are at the point of transition into the labour market. There is a strong probability that, over time, this will become permanent employment. In many Italian cases, in contrast, this seems to be more of a general problem of the labour market situation. As a result, they often compare themselves with like-minded people to feel better about their situation (emotional coping).

On the mesolevel, it was obvious that the family and other social relations are very important. As a recurring pattern in many German cases, they use this resource as a protective factor or a help (financially, when no formal support is available or it is insufficient), sometimes for advice, and for emotional support. In Italy, on the other hand, the nuclear family seems to be a permanent and strongly present support in many areas and on different levels (see also Chapter 10 in this volume). One explanation for these differences is cultural: there is stronger attachment to the family in Italy, and stronger state support in Germany.

When focusing on coping with macrolevel strategies, there were several German cases in which formal support in the form of unemployment benefits or ALMPs can provide some form of security or lead to the development of better prospects for the future. On the one hand, this improves well-being or prevents stronger negative feelings that would otherwise arise from existing financial disadvantages. On the other hand, additional negative effects on young people's well-being emerge due to stigma associated with unemployment or dependency on state benefits. This also becomes clear when the support and counselling services offered by the employment agencies are perceived as insufficient (see also Shore and Tosun, 2017). In many Italian cases, there seems to be a general distrust of the state, with the state seeming to contribute to improvements in only a few cases. Overall sources of coping can also have a negative impact on well-being and sometimes exacerbate the situation, with family conflicts tending to be portrayed in Italy, and perceived problematic interactions (for example sanctions, condescending treatment, lack of support) from the Federal Employment Agency in Germany.

Across the interviews, the majority of German cases reveal that informal and formal support are used in combination, whereas in Italy, there seems to be a much stronger reference to family support. All in all, it proved to be important to focus strongly on individuals and see how intensively they apply which strategies and which combinations of strategies. It was often difficult to distinguish between tackling poor well-being and the job insecurity/unemployment which often led to it. Generally, various strategies emerged in a latent or undifferentiated way during the analysis. Behaviours and actions can be used for specific or multiple purposes, and that makes it difficult to examine and distinguish them. Here, a qualitative approach proved advantageous, because it addressed the subjective perspective and individual strategies that could be elaborated from an analysis of narratives and the respective context – that is, the personal background and life situation of participants.

However, despite all its advantages, it is naturally also important to consider the limitations of a qualitative research design. These particularly involve the generalisability of results. Nonetheless, the study could make valid statements about the situation of young people and provide important insights into their subjective experiences of their insecure situation, what influence this has on their well-being, and the coping strategies they apply in Italy and Germany. These reveal the particularly strong role of the institutional setting, the labour market situation, and social policies.

Note

[1] The information in brackets represent pseudonym, sex, age, level of education, employment status, and country of the interviewee. For explanation of the abbreviations, see Chapter 1.

References

Albert, S., Ashforth, B.E. and Dutton, J.E. (2000) 'Introduction to special topic forum – organizational identity and identification: charting new waters and building new bridges', *Academy of Management Review*, 25(1): 13–17.

Armstrong-Stassen, M. (2005) 'Coping with downsizing: a comparison of executive-level and middle managers', *International Journal of Stress Management*, 12(2): 117–41.

Bagnara, S. and Bargigli, L. (2009) 'Job insecurity and successful re-employment: examples from Italy', in T. Kieselbach, S. Bagnara, H. De Witte, L. Lemkow, and W. Schaufeli (eds) *Coping with Occupational Transitions: An Empirical Study with Employees Facing Job Loss in Five European Countries*, Wiesbaden: VS Verlag für Sozialwissenschaften, pp 225–78.

Baranowska, A. and Gebel, M. (2010) 'The determinants of youth temporary employment in the enlarged Europe: do labour market institutions matter?', *European Societies*, 12(3): 367–90.

Beelmann, G., Kieselbach, T. and Traiser, U. (2001) 'Jugendarbeitslosigkeit und soziale Ausgrenzung: ergebnisse einer qualitativen Analyse in Ost- und Westdeutschland', in J. Zempel, J. Bacher, and K. Moser (eds) *Erwerbslosigkeit*, Wiesbaden: VS Verlag für Sozialwissenschaften, pp 133–48.

Bertolini, S. and Torrioni, P. (2018) 'Institutional aspects of EXCEPT countries' in S. Bertolini, K. Deliyanni-Kouimtzi, M. Bolzoni, C. Ghislieri, V. Goglio, S. Martino, A. Meo, V. Moiso, R. Musumeci, R. Ricucci, P.M. Torrioni, C. Athanasiades, L. Figgou, A. Flouli, M. Kostouli, and M.N. Sourvinou (eds) *Labour Market Insecurity and Social Exclusion: Qualitative Comparative Results in Nine Countries*. EXCEPT Working Papers, WP No. 53, Tallinn: Tallinn University, pp 35–48, Available from: https://www.except-project.eu/working-papers/

Bertolini, S., Bolzoni, M., Moiso, V. and Musumeci, R. (2018a) *The Comparative Qualitative Research Methodology of the EXCEPT Project*. EXCEPT Working Papers, WP No. 56, Tallinn: Tallinn University, Available from: https://www.except-project.eu/working-papers/

Bertolini, S., Moiso, V. and Musumeci, R. (eds) (2018b) *Young Adults in Insecure Labour Market Positions in Italy – the Results from a Qualitative Study*. EXCEPT Working Papers, WP No. 18. Tallinn: Tallinn University, Available from: https://www.except-project.eu/working-papers/

Blossfeld, H.P. and Stockmann, R. (1998/1999) 'The German dual system in comparative perspective', *International Journal of Sociology*, 28(4): 3–28.

Blustein, D.L., Kozan, S. and Connors-Kellgren, A. (2013) 'Unemployment and underemployment: a narrative analysis about loss', *Journal of Vocational Behavior*, 82(3): 256–65.

Boarini, R., Comola, M., De Keulenaer, F., Manchin, R. and Smith, C. (2013) 'Can governments boost people's sense of well-being? The impact of selected labour market and health policies on life satisfaction', *Social Indicators Research*, 114(1): 105–20.

Bourdieu, P. (1983) 'Ökonomisches Kapital, kulturelles Kapital, soziales Kapital', in R. Kreckel (ed) *Soziale Ungleichheiten*, Göttingen: Schwartz, pp 183–98.

Braun, V. and Clarke, V. (2006) 'Using thematic analysis in psychology', *Qualitative Research in Psychology*, 3(2): 77–101.

Carver, C.S., Scheier, M.F. and Weintraub, J.K., (1989) 'Assessing coping strategies: a theoretically based approach' *Journal of Personality and Social Psychology*, 56(2): 267–83.

De Witte, H. (2005) 'Job insecurity: review of the international literature on definitions, prevalence, antecedents and consequences', *South African Journal of Industrial Psychology*, 31(4): 1–6.

De Witte, H., Pienaar, J. and De Cuyper, N. (2016) 'Review of 30 years of longitudinal studies on the association between job insecurity and health and well-being: is there causal evidence?', *Australian Psychologist*, 51(1): 18–31.

Diener, E., Suh, M., Lucas, R.E. and Smith, H. (1999) 'Subjective well-being: three decades of progress', *Psychological Bulletin*, 125(2): 276–302.

Dietrich, H., and Möller, J. (2016) 'Youth unemployment in Europe – business cycle and institutional effects', *International Economics and Economic Policy*, 13(1): 5–25.

Elster, J. (1983) *Sour Grapes: Studies in the Subversion of Rationality*, Cambridge: Cambridge University Press.

Eurofound (2012) *NEETs. Young People Not in Employment, Education or Training. Characteristics, Costs and Policy Responses in Europe*, Dublin: European Foundation for the Improvement of Living and Working Conditions.

Eurostat (2018a) 'Statistical yearbook: 2018 edition', Available from: https://ec.europa.eu/eurostat/statistics-explained/index.php/Eurostat_regional_yearbook

Eurostat (2018b) 'Unemployment statistics', Available from: https://ec.europa.eu/eurostat/statistics-explained/index.php?title=Unemployment_statistics#Youth_unemployment

Folkman, S., Schaefer, C. and Lazarus, R.S. (1979) 'Cognitive processes as mediators of stress and coping', in V. Hamilton and D.M. Warburton (eds) *Human Stress and Cognition: An Information-Processing Approach*, London: Wiley, pp 265–98.

Fullin, G. (2004) *Vivere l'instabilità del lavoro*, Bologna: Il Mulino.

Giunchi, M., Emanuel, F., Chambel, M.J. and Ghislieri, C. (2016) 'Job insecurity, workload and job exhaustion in temporary agency workers (TAWs): gender differences', *Career Development International*, 21(1): 3–18.

Goffman, E. (1986) *Stigma: Notes on the Management of Spoiled Identity*, New York: Simon & Schuster.

Grebner, S., Semmer, N.K. and Elfering, A. (2005) 'Working conditions and three types of well-being: a longitudinal study with self-report and rating data', *Journal of Occupational Health Psychology*, 10(1): 31–43.

Greenhalgh, L., and Rosenblatt, Z. (1984) 'Job insecurity: toward conceptual clarity', *The Academy of Management Review*, 9(3): 438–48.

Grimmer, B. (2016) 'Being long-term unemployed in Germany: social contacts, finances and stigma', in C. Lahusen and M. Giugni (eds) *Experiencing Long-Term Unemployment in Europe: Youth on the Edge*, London: Palgrave Macmillan, pp 39–69.

Heuven, E., Schaufeli, W., and Bakker, A.B. (2009) 'Job insecurity and successful re-employment: examples from the Netherlands', in T. Kieselbach, S. Bagnara, H. De Witte, L. Lemkow, and W. Schaufeli (eds) *Coping with Occupational Transitions: An Empirical Study with Employees Facing Job Loss in Five European Countries*, Wiesbaden: VS Verlag für Sozialwissenschaften, pp 169–223.

Jahoda, M. (1981) 'Work, employment, and unemployment: values, theories, and approaches in social research', *The American Psychologist*, 36(2): 184–91.

Kieselbach, T. (ed) (2000) *Youth Unemployment and Health: A Comparison of Six European Countries*. Psychology of Social Inequality, Vol. 9, Wiesbaden: VS Verlag für Sozialwissenschaften.

Lazarus, R.S. and Folkman, S. (1984) *Stress, Appraisal, and Coping*, New York: Springer.

Müller, W. and Gangl, M. (2003) *Transitions from Education to Work in Europe: The Integration of Youth into EU Labour Markets*, Oxford: Oxford University Press.

Näswall, K. and De Witte, H. (2003) 'Who feels insecure in Europe? Predicting job insecurity from background variables', *Economic and Industrial Democracy*, 24(2): 189–215.

Paul, K.L. and Moser, K. (2009) 'Unemployment impairs mental health: meta-analyses', *Journal of Vocational Behavior*, 74(3): 264–82.

Piccoli, B., Callea, A., Urbini, F., Chirumbolo, A., Ingusci, E. and De Witte, H. (2017) 'Job insecurity and performance: the mediating role of organizational identification', *Personnel Review*, 46(8): 1508–22.

Pinquart, M. and Silbereisen, R.K. (2008) 'Coping with increased uncertainty in the field of work and family life', *International Journal of Stress Management*, 15(3): 209–21.

Reyneri, E. (2017) *Introduzione alla Sociologia del Mercato del Lavoro*, Bologna: Il Mulino.

Richter, A. (2011) *Job Insecurity and Its Consequences: Investigating Moderators, Mediators and Gender*, Stockholm: Stockholm University.

Richter, A., Näswall, K., Bernhard-Oettel, C. and Sverke, M. (2013) 'Job insecurity and well-being: the moderating role of job dependence', *European Journal of Work and Organizational Psychology*, 23(6): 816–29.

Rogge, B. (2013) *Wie uns Arbeitslosigkeit unter die Haut geht: Identitätsprozess und psychische Gesundheit bei Statuswechseln*, Konstanz: UVK Verlagsgesellschaft.

Rokicka, M., Kłobuszewska, M., Palczyńska, M., Shapoval, N. and Stasiowski, J. (2015) *Composition and Cumulative Disadvantage of Youth across Europe*. EXCEPT Working Papers, WP No. 1, Tallinn: Tallinn University, Available from: https://www.except-project.eu/working-papers/

Schlee, C. (2018) *Young Adults in Insecure Labour Market Positions in Germany – The Results from a Qualitative Study*. EXCEPT Working Papers, WP No. 19, Tallinn: Tallinn University, Available from: https://www.except-project.eu/working-papers/

Shore, J. and Tosun, J. (2017) 'Assessing youth labour market services: young people's perceptions and evaluations of service delivery in Germany', *Public Policy and Administration*, 34(1): 22–41.

Tajfel, T.R. and Turner, J.C. (1979) 'An integrative theory of intergroup conflict', in W.G. Austin and S. Worchel (eds) *The Social Psychology of Intergroup Relations*, Monterey: Brooks-Cole, pp 33–47.

Van Hoye, G. and Lootens, H. (2013) 'Coping with unemployment: personality, role demands, and time structure', *Journal of Vocational Behavior*, 82(2): 85–95.

Van Vuuren, T. (1990) *Met Ontslag Bedreigd. Werknemers in Onzekerheid Over Hun Arbeidsplaats bij Veranderingen in de Organisatie*, Amsterdam: VU-uitgeverij.

Voßemer, J. and Eunicke, N. (2015) *The Impact of Labour Market Exclusion and Job Insecurity on Health and Well-Being Among Youth: A Literature Review*. EXCEPT Working Papers, WP No. 2, Tallinn: Tallinn University, Available from: https://www.except-project.eu/working-papers/

Voßemer, J., Gebel, M., Täht, K., Unt, M., Högberg, B. and Strandh, M. (2017) 'The effects of unemployment and insecure jobs on well-being and health: the moderating role of labor market policies', *Social Indicators Research*, 138(3): 1229–57.

Wang, H.J., Lu, C.Q. and Siu, O.L. (2015) 'Job insecurity and job performance: the moderating role of organizational justice and the mediating role of work engagement', *Journal of Applied Psychology*, 100(4): 1249–58.

Warr, P.B. (1990) 'Decision latitude, job demands and employee well being', *Work Stress*, 4(4): 285–94.

PART II

Labour market insecurity and youth autonomy

6

Meanings of work in the narratives of Italian, Estonian, and Polish young people who experience labour market insecurity

Eve-Liis Roosmaa, Epp Reiska, Jędrzej Stasiowski, Sonia Bertolini, and Paola Maria Torrioni

Introduction

Ever since the mid-19th century, paid work has held a central role in modern societies, not only in securing social inclusion and integration but also in constructing individual and social identities (Albano and Parisi, 2017).[1] This chapter focuses on the ways in which youth in different national contexts construct the meaning of work and the expectations towards work that are embedded in their personal labour market experiences. Qualitative interviews are analysed from Italy, Estonia, and Poland – different countries that share some cultural and institutional characteristics. All three countries belong to Western culture, yet Estonia and Poland share a post-socialist past, whereas Poland and Italy are Catholic countries, and are thus more likely to hold certain traditional views, all which might shape the meanings of work.

According to the European Values Study (EVS) 2008, work is *very* important in one's life for about 64 per cent of respondents in Italy, 56 per cent in Poland, and 46 per cent in Estonia. There are some age variations. In Poland and Estonia, young people (aged 15 to 29 years) indicate that the level of significance of work in their lives is similar to the country average; but for youth in Italy, work is somewhat less significant (57 per cent) compared to the Italian average. Hence, quantitative data suggest that work holds a different position in young people's lives in these three countries.

The aim of this chapter is to study whether and how meanings given to work differ for youth in Italy, Poland, and Estonia by analysing qualitative semi-structured interviews. To some extent, interviewees have faced or are still facing labour market insecurities (for example, unemployment and low salary as well as part-time, temporary, or non-contractual jobs). Thus, the way they construct the meanings of work is likely to be shaped not only by cultural and structural conditions but also by their specific labour market experiences. Therefore, this study investigates whether different country contexts reveal differences or similarities in constructing meanings of work depending on young people's experience of the labour market.

As described in the following section, a vast body of research is based on quantitative analysis. Hence, the study presented here gives valuable qualitative insight into understanding how work-related meanings are constructed, presented, and interpreted by youth in their personal narratives, with a focus on three country cases.

The conceptual framework and the classification of the meanings of work stems from the work of Jahoda (1981, 1982), Warr (1987, 2007), and Albano and Parisi (2017). These all deal with the classification of work characteristics or functions to represent the different meanings or values attached to them.

Theoretical considerations

Many empirical value studies deal with attitudes and values in relation to work because of the importance of work not only as a primary source of income or economic security but also as a basis for other phenomena of social life such as social participation, social status, identity, consumption patterns, health, and family life (Roe and Ester, 1999).

Since Rosenberg's (1957) study of young people's occupational choices, much attention has been paid to the value assigned to various aspects of work. Moreover, research on work-related attitudes and work or occupation selection criteria has been fostered since the 1980s, when the EVS, a large-scale, cross-national, and longitudinal survey on basic human values, was established.

This chapter focuses on meanings of work, but first also the concept of values should be defined, although these are not complete synonyms. Both meanings and values concern the *importance* or the worth of something for someone; one could say that if something – for instance, a certain aspect of work – is meaningful, then it holds importance or value. Although the respective literature reveals numerous definitions of values (Allport, 1955; Rokeach, 1973; Hofstede, 1980), there is, nonetheless, a consensus about the core of the concept. According to social psychologists, values are cognitive structures that guide human conduct by influencing the processes by which people represent and evaluate themselves and the world (Allport, 1955; Hofstede, 1980). Values are relatively stable over time; they concern ideas and beliefs related to individuals' main goals of life and the achievement of these goals in ways that they consider to be 'right'. Furthermore, values are ordered in terms of their relative importance and they therefore form a system of priorities (Schwartz, 1994; Smith and Schwartz, 1997).

Hofstede (1980) assumed that work values can be interpreted as the extent to which people attach importance to various job characteristics, aspects, or, in Jahoda's (1981) terminology (see following paragraph), functions. Thus, by analysing functions of work that appear in youth narratives, one can touch upon more general values or meanings of work. The following introduces three classifications of work characteristics that are summarised and systematised in Table 6.1.

Jahoda, an Austrian psychologist, was interested in the value and meanings of work in a modern industrial society. She supported her empirical work with Merton's paradigm of functional analysis that led her to distinguish between *manifest*, 'deliberately intended', and *latent*, 'unintended by-products of purposeful action', functions of employment (Jahoda, 1981). She assumed that 'earning a living' is a main manifest function of work, and codified latent functions of work as follows. First, work gives a time structure to the day – lack of it might be devastating for an individual (feeling bored, wasting time, and so on) (Jahoda, 1982: 24). Second, employment gives numerous opportunities for social contacts and shared experience with people 'outside the nuclear family'. Third, it provides an opportunity to strive towards 'goals and purposes that transcend their own' – a sense of a collective purpose: being useful to other people. Fourth, it 'defines aspects of personal status and identity', and, lastly, it 'enforces activity'.

Jahoda used her model to explain the lower level of well-being of unemployed people who were deprived of all or some of these functions. She stated that latent functions of employment help understanding of 'motivation to work that goes beyond earning a living' and give necessary 'ties to reality' that are essential for human well-being. Nonetheless, employment itself might also bring negative psychological consequences, and Jahoda also admits that there might be other latent functions of employment or that they might be covered by other social institutions besides work (Jahoda, 1981).

Jahoda's theory has been applied in numerous studies on well-being and work. Some of these question the significance of certain latent functions (Paul and Batinic, 2010) or discuss their relative importance (Waters and Moore, 2002), but the overall model has proved to be a useful theoretical framework (see also Hoare and Machin, 2006).

Table 6.1: Summary of concepts regarding meanings of work

Manifest (deliberately intended)	Latent (unintended by-products)		
	Intrinsic *Features within job tasks themselves (related to inner motivation; what gives quiet satisfaction; the value it has 'in itself')*		Extrinsic *Attributes external to job tasks (work as instrument; what one can get out of work, tangible work characteristics)*
Earning a living/ Availability of money/ Good pay Career outlook/ Good job security	Jahoda	Albano and Parisi*	Jahoda	Warr	Albano and Parisi
	Opportunities for social contact and shared experience	Meeting people	Gives a time structure to the day	*Externally generated goals*	To have time off at the weekends Generous holidays
	Opportunity to strive towards 'goals and purposes that transcend their own'	A job in which you feel you can achieve something A useful job for society	Enforces activity	*Externally generated goals*	
	Defines aspects of personal identity	A job that meets one's abilities An opportunity to use initiative	Defines aspects of personal status	Valued social position	
	Warr	A job that is interesting		Environmental clarity Supportive supervision *Equity: fairness of employment relationship* Physical security of job environment	Not too much pressure
	Opportunity for interpersonal contact				
	Externally generated goals Equity: morality in an employer's relationship with society				
	Opportunity for skill use Opportunity for control				
	Variety				

Notes: Italics indicate meanings of work that appear in more than one cell.
* Albano and Parisi's (2017) classification of work-related aspects is based on the EVS using items that have been included in the questionnaire over several survey waves

Source: Jahoda, 1981; 1982; Warr, 1987; 2007; Albano and Parisi, 2017; authors' own interpretations

Warr (1987), from a psychological standpoint, described nine main characteristics of the environment in employment that are also applicable in unemployment (or retirement). An insufficient level of these features would define a bad job. Warr stressed that several job characteristics do not have a linear relationship with a good job and thus with individual well-being or happiness. The following six features contribute to individual happiness to a limited extent: (a) *opportunity for control* over activities and events; (b) *opportunity for skill use* and development; (c) *externally generated goals* (obligations and targets deriving from multiple roles); (d) *variety* in job requirements; (e) *environmental clarity* (transparency of other people and systems); and (f) *opportunity for interpersonal contact*. Too much or too little of each of these job characteristics may bring about undesirable levels of psychological stress. Linearly related to well-being are the following job features: (g) *availability of money*; (h) *physical security* at the workplace; and (i) *valued social position* (such as status in society, task significance, meaningfulness, contribution to the community, wider society).

Warr (2007) introduced another three job characteristics that are specifically relevant for employment: (j) *supportive supervision*; (k) *career outlook* (security of employment, availability of extended tenure, promotion, and so on); and (l) equity (for example, fairness in employment relationship, no discrimination, morality in an employer's relationship with society).

Warr's nine-component framework builds on Jahoda's theorising in that her *contacts with people outside family* and *personal status and identity* appear as the environmental features *contact with others* and *valued social position* (Warr, 2007: 90). Jahoda's other three latent functions are subsumed here within *externally generated goals*, and Warr has added other environmental characteristics. This extension is consistent with Jahoda's observation, because she states that there are other latent by-products in addition to five broad latent categories (1981: 189).

Albano and Parisi (2017) presented analyses of a quantitative longitudinal dataset – the EVS 1981–2008/9 – covering a period that is long enough to be able to detect changes in individuals' value systems. The authors used one of the most common dichotomous classifications of work-related values: intrinsic versus extrinsic (Kalleberg, 1977; Ros et al, 1999). *Intrinsic* values or meanings are related mostly to inner motivation and self-realisation but also to the social aspects of work: a job that is interesting, in which you feel you can achieve something, an opportunity to use initiative, a job that matches one's abilities, a useful job for society, or meeting people. In contrast, *extrinsic* meanings represent instrumental aspects of work: good pay, good job security, not too much pressure, to have time off at the weekends, and generous holidays. Based on their analysis of five European countries, Albano and Parisi (2017) concluded that work values remain stable over time between cohorts, demonstrating the specific character of work values acquired in a given cultural climate.

Regarding Italy, Albano and Parisi (2017: 72) found that the importance assigned to good pay alongside job security did not change over the period 1981–2009, but that each separate aspect of work increased in its significance. Nonetheless, in the latter part of this period (1999–2009), the importance of all work characteristics declined (social aspects somewhat more than intrinsic and extrinsic).

Based on the EVS, but focusing on Central and Eastern European (CEE) countries, Borgulya and Hahn (2013) found a rather stable value system during the period 1999–2009. Nevertheless, extrinsic aspects of work increased: in particular, good hours and generous holidays gained in importance. There was also a moderate increase in the importance of intrinsic work orientations such as a wish to have an interesting or responsible job and to achieve something. However, they found that usefulness for society had decreased in its importance.

Value studies broadly agree that people in industrialised countries, or countries with a similar level of development, have relatively similar work values (Mortimer and Lorence, 1995). The nature of the work is shaped by both the wider social structure and the different management styles and organisational cultures in enterprises. It is considered that although there might be differences between countries in work values, their nature and the factors that shape them are similar.

Research on work values often assumes that youth value paid work less than older generations because of their insecure labour market position or their post-materialist values (Hagström and Gamberale, 1995; Hult and Svallfors, 2002; see also Inglehart, 1971). Indeed, a study from the 1990s showed an increase in intrinsic work values among youth due to post-materialist values (Hagström and Gamberale, 1995). However, research indicates that unemployed young adults do value work and prefer full-time jobs (Hult and Svallfors, 2002). Based on 11 European countries, Rainsford et al (2019) found that among youth, overqualification is associated with higher levels of extrinsic work values; and in the case of a somewhat older group of younger adults (closer to 35 years of age), unemployment has a negative effect on intrinsic values. Thus, young people are not a homogeneous group in relation to how unemployment and low quality work conditions shape their work values.

In terms of Jahoda's (1982) distinction between manifest and latent work functions, a study of six European countries indicated that youth value both – that is, not only salary but also regular and meaningful activity, social contacts, status, identity, and personal development (Bergqvist and Eriksson, 2015). Hence, studies show that extrinsic and intrinsic work values or manifest and latent work functions do not contradict each other, but rather coexist together to form a specific individual value pattern (Gesthuizen and Verbakel, 2011).

Institutional context

One could ask how the institutional context shapes the meanings of work that are based on values and are probably related more to the cultural context. However, as pointed out by Jahoda (1981), other institutions have the potential to fulfil the functions of work. Therefore, the institutional context frames the experiences of youth, either by helping or not helping to cover some functions of work; and by doing so, it shapes the meanings of work.

The three countries analysed represent different ideal-typical welfare state regimes in terms of Esping-Andersen's (1990) well-known typology. According to the extensions of the classical tripolar typology, Italy represents the Southern European welfare state (Ferrera, 1996; Bonoli, 1997), whereas post-socialist Central and Eastern European (CEE) countries are often either excluded or classified as one homogeneous group. Over the last decade, the CEE countries have received more attention, and variation among them has been recognised. Hence, Estonia and Poland are mostly classified as different types of welfare state regimes: Estonia as a former USSR type and Poland as a post-communist European type (Fenger, 2007), whereas according to Aspalter et al (2009), the Polish welfare state has evolved into the continental European type. Extensions of the varieties of capitalism literature (Hall and Soskice, 2001; Ebbinghaus and Manow, 2003) classify Estonia as a neoliberal type (weak welfare state with radically liberalised markets) and Poland as an embedded neoliberal type (more socially inclusive, less market-radical compared to Estonia) (Bohle and Greskovits, 2007). The following section provides a more detailed overview of the institutional characteristics relevant to the present analysis.

Providing sufficient income

In case of unemployed youth, Estonia differs from Poland and Italy because in the latter two, youth looking for their first job are not entitled to unemployment benefits. However, in Estonia, the amount of unemployment allowance is insufficient to replace the income from paid employment (about one third of the minimum wage in 2016 when interviews were conducted), and higher unemployment insurance benefit depends on tenure, and is, therefore, often out of reach for young people (Reiska et al, 2018).

Youth entering the labour market who are either unemployed or earning low wages could be entitled to income support. In this respect, young people find themselves in different situations. In Italy, there is no national and universal minimum income insurance or individual insurance (Bertolini et al, 2018a). In Estonia, low level support exists, but access to it is restricted based on the total income divided per household member (youth living with parents are often not eligible) (Reiska et al, 2018). In Poland, the general scheme of last resort with additional categorical benefits covers most people in need of support (Bertolini et al, 2018a): social assistance benefits are granted to those whose income is below a certain threshold, and there are different types of additional allowances.

Providing meaningful activity and social contact

Although there is no question that meaningful activity can be found outside of the institutional framework in, for example, volunteering, hobbies, and so forth (Jahoda, 1981), active labour market policies (ALMPs) can also cater for these needs. In Italy, the ALMPs targeted at youth are few, whereas in Poland and Estonia, there are some specific measures, and their importance has increased (Bertolini et al, 2018a). Based on the investment in ALMPs targeted at all unemployed, Bertolini et al (2018a: 26) stated that Italy is characterised by a low level of investment, whereas Poland and Estonia have recently started spending more.

Career outlook and job security

Job security as well as possibilities of career advancement depend on the country context. In terms of labour market regulation, Italy and Poland have a similar system with a highly segmented labour market and large differences between highly regulated protected and weakly regulated unprotected contract types. In Estonia, there is low segmentation in the labour market and limited use of temporary or part-time contracts (Bertolini et al, 2018a). The percentage of temporary contracts makes these country differences evident: in Estonia, only 11.2 per cent of youth have temporary contracts, whereas the share of youth working on temporary contracts is 48.6 per cent in Italy and 64.4 per cent in Poland

Table 6.2: Characterisation of national context (2015)

	Unemployment rate (%)		NEET rate	Part-time employment (%)			Temporary contracts	
	Under 25 years	25–74 years		15–24 years	15–64 years	Involuntary part-time employment (age 15–24)	15–24 years	15–64 years
Italy	10.6	6.1	21.3	29.5	9.5	8.8	11.2	3.1
Estonia	5.5	4.1	10.8	22.8	18.3	83.7*	48.6	10.8
Poland	6.8	4.2	11.0	14.1	6.8	25.6	64.4	22.2
EU avg.	8.4	5.6	12.0	32.3	19.6	28.0	40.3	11.9

Note: *Data for the group aged 15–24 years is not available for Estonia, so data is provided for the 15–29 age group instead.
Source: Eurostat, 2018

(Table 6.2). However, the low labour market regulation in Estonia also makes it easier to dismiss employees with permanent contracts (Bertolini et al, 2018a). In the 15 to 24 years age group, part-time employment is most widespread in Italy (29.5 per cent), but what is more important, for 83.7 per cent of Italian youth, the decision to work part-time is involuntary. In Estonia and Poland in contrast, where the share of youth working part-time is lower, this is mostly voluntary (Table 6.2).

Possibilities of finding a job and career advancement also depend on the level of unemployment. In 2015,[2] youth unemployment was highest in Italy (10.6 per cent), whereas in Estonia and Poland, it was below the EU average. Moreover, the NEET rate was highest in Italy (about 20 per cent) compared to close to 10 per cent in Estonia and Poland (Table 6.2).

Research questions

The contextual information provided previously suggests that both differences and similarities can be expected when comparing the meanings youth give to work in the three countries. Hence, the question here is what are the differences and similarities between the meanings of work and the expectations towards work constructed in the narratives of youth in different contexts?

Data and methodology

The empirical material consists of 143 interviews with youth aged 18 to 30 years who are in an insecure labour market situation, conducted

Table 6.3: Sample description

	Education			Employment status			
	Low (ISCED 0–2)	Medium (ISCED 3–4)	High (ISCED 5–6)	Unemployed	Temporary work	Permanent work	NEET
Italy ($n = 50$)	12	26	12	21	17	6	6
Estonia ($n = 53$)	23	21	9	37	10	4	2
Poland ($n = 40$)	7	21	12	18	19	3	0

Note: In many cases, interviewees who defined themselves as unemployed had some non-contractual work experience.

in Estonia, Italy, and Poland from the end of 2015 to November 2016. All country samples are well balanced in terms of gender and age. In terms of education, the sampling target was set at reaching youth with low and medium levels of education, because these are the groups facing more difficulties on the labour market. The interviewees' employment status reflects the situation of youth in the national labour market described in the previous section (see Table 6.3).

The methodology used in this article draws on the framework adapted in the EXCEPT project (Bertolini et al, 2018b). In the first phase, interview data were analysed using thematic analysis that involves searching through a dataset for repeated patterns of work meanings (Boyatzis, 1998; Braun and Clarke, 2006; Grunow and Evertsson, 2016) as described in Table 6.1. Additional meanings emerging from data were added. The second phase consisted of comparing the coded qualitative information across the three countries and observing how different or similar meanings of work emerge in the interviews with young people. The comparison between these data corpuses was carried out using thematic network analysis (Attride-Stirling, 2001). Analysis of specific themes (the manifest and latent meanings of work) was conducted by taking the themes deriving from country analysis and assembling them into similar, coherent categories. Decisions about how to group themes and categories were made based on the content, and, where appropriate, on theoretical grounds. These groupings compose the thematic networks.

Findings

Drawing on Merton's paradigm of functional analysis, manifest, 'deliberately intended' functions of employment could be differentiated from latent, 'unintended' functions. The analysis is structured based on Table 6.1 which summarises the conceptual framework, starting with the description of manifest functions of work followed by intrinsic and extrinsic latent functions of work.

Manifest functions of work

Following Jahoda (1981), earning a living is the main manifest function of work. Warr (1987) added job security and career outlook to this category. These theoretical considerations are reflected in the narratives of interviewees.

In all three countries, work was most often defined through its basic manifest, extrinsic function: *source of financial resources*. Interviewees often stressed that the crucial aspect of work is an adequate income. However, youth were not overly demanding – they defined good pay as one that is sufficient to allow them to manage everyday expenses. The emphasis interviewees placed on aspects of their experience varied slightly by country. For example, in Estonia, the relative importance of good pay seems to be greater for those who are unemployed such as Marju, who has done some service sector jobs for the past three years without being offered a stable job:

> 'Well, main role is making money, that's what it means. One must work to earn as much as possible, the better life you have. [pause] At the moment, looking for example, at customer services, then a desk-job, working with people, from 9 to 5, so that Saturdays-Sundays would be free.' (Marju, F, 28, LE, U, EE)

A similar pattern was observed in Poland: unemployed people were more prone to focus on the manifest functions of employment. It might be hypothesised that this attitude was a direct consequence of unemployment: if they have no job, youth lower their expectations towards work. For example, Paweł finished basic vocational school, but did not manage to find a job in his field – car mechanics. Instead, he worked informally as a waiter. With low and unstable income, he was forced to live with his parents – in this situation, the only short-term priority was to earn more.

> 'My work was supposed to be something that I really like doing and it should bring me some money, but it comes out that now I'm just looking for some work to get some money.' (Paweł, M, 20, ME, U, PL)

Within the Polish sample, lower educated youth tend to focus even more on the instrumental aspect of a job, whereas the better educated mention it among intrinsic meanings of work. For example, Zenek (M, 24, LE, NCJ, PL) focuses only on earning money "to live, pay the bills, everything". In contrast, Ewa, a representative of the better educated, puts the financial dimension first, but also mentions several intrinsic values: a job giving the opportunity for social contacts or work as a source of satisfaction:

> 'So, for me, work is mainly about the salary plus some kind of fun because you spend time with people and satisfaction, something like this, let's say.' (Ewa, F, 30, HE, TE, PL)

In Estonia, some interviewees seemed to value salary somewhat less if it meant they could do a *job they like* or a job that is related to their field of studies, whereas working only for money was associated with something involuntary. This is well illustrated by Tauri from a small Estonian town in which job opportunities are scarce; his ideal job would be as a car mechanic:

> 'If I worked in the field I have studied, then well. [pause] When I would receive more or less, let's say, normal, above minimum wage, then you just work like that. You can work even like that. ... Yes, these are two different things. When you like the job, then you go to work, you can stay longer and do it and this is good and you will get more money. [pause] But when it is only, that you need to do it. [pause] That you need to earn money to live, then you are there against your own will actually. These are two different things.' (Tauri, M, 22, LE, U, EE)

Youth who were underemployed or had dull, uninteresting jobs often focused on the financial aspects of work. One of the strategies executed in such situations was transposition: while claiming that their work is only there to provide money for a living, they mentioned other life domains in which they satisfy their needs (such as hobbies, family). For example, Magda, from a city where there is a high demand for jobs that do not require higher education, had impressive work experience, but many of the jobs available were below her qualifications. She described her job in terms of a source of money necessary to pursue her passions:

'For me, to work is to be able to realise my dreams later on. I don't work for the work itself, it's just to be able to do something afterwards. It's just to earn some money. And then, possibly I could do what I like.' (Magda, F, 28, HE, NCJ, PL)

It is obvious that any type of work is associated with a given social role: a professional status. However, in the case of youth, job and related salary might be regarded not only as a source of income but also as an indicator of public *recognition*, equitable treatment, and a sign of one's achievements. These are, again, latent functions of a job that are closely related to its main manifest function. For example, the recognition and dignity that work gives is very important for Helena, a mother raising three children who therefore has practically no work experience and has never applied for a job:

'When you are just at home and you get the childcare allowance and the social services pay your bills. It is like, well, money for nothing. But I think if you do something and get money for it, it feels better [laughs] I think so.' (Helena, F, 24, LE, U, childcare leave, EE)

In Poland and Italy, interviewees' statements about work were strongly related to *autonomy*. They associated work with the possibility of living independent lives. Being able to provide for yourself was recognised as a proof of adulthood, a sign of an identity as a grown-up person. For instance, this is evident in the case of Mara. At the time of the interview, she had been unemployed for four months and was struggling to find a job. Absence of work, the consequent lack of money, and the inactivity are at the centre of her story. She strongly connects the meaning of work with autonomy:

'[work means] Independence. Really, it's really the word that comes [pause] to do what I want, how I want, when I want, a future, to have a future. Because at the moment I don't see it, meaning that at home with my parents I cannot see it. A future as an independent person. [pause] Being a kept person, for now, it's not nice to say so, but [pause] if don't have any help, now, from what I read, they will give some money, to those who turn 18. And those who have turned 18 for quite some time already? What should they do?' (Mara, F, 29, LE, U, IT)

A very similar pattern could be recognised in Joanna's story. She perceived a job with an adequate income as a ticket for leaving the parental home:

R: The lack of money was really bothering me. A lot. This financial independence. You had to ask for everything, right? Even though I had everything that I needed from my parents, but I wanted to have more, and I wanted to manage it by myself.
I: You just wanted to move out to take up some job?
R: Actually yes, to have my own money. (Joanna, F, 27, ME, NCJ, PL)

Obviously, work provides the necessary funds to rent a flat and cover everyday expenses. However, the same manifest function has an important symbolic and latent dimension. Labour income serves as a way to demonstrate independence from parents, it is symbolic confirmation of becoming an adult, or it is simply the minimal condition to be met to leave the parental home or start one's own family and live an independent, serious life. These patterns were visible in Italy and Poland, but less evident in Estonia. The explanation might be that Polish and Italian youth encounter more structural (such as availability of housing) or cultural barriers when leaving the parental home than their Estonian counterparts.[3]

Important issues related to income were *stability* and *predictability*. Estonian and Polish youth defined job security in various ways: for those who work unofficially, it means that the salary is paid as agreed. For others, it is having a (permanent) contract or the prospect of stable employment in the future. In Poland, temporary contracts are so common among young people that they are not perceived as a problem. This is understandable considering the very good performance of the labour market: a high level of temporary contracts is cushioned by a relatively low level of youth unemployment. Thus, for Polish interviewees, subjective job insecurity mattered more than the type of contract.[4]

According to Italian interviews, as for the previous generation, the idea of a permanent job is very persistent among young people, despite the drastic changes in the labour market: temporary work is widespread among the young, but unlike in Poland, it is combined with a high level of youth unemployment. Some young Italians see their future as very traditional – for example, having a child conditional on getting a permanent contract. Giulia (F, 26, LE, PE, IT) luckily got her permanent contract and is now making her plans: in the next five years, she wants to have her first child, buy a car, and buy a house.

In sum, despite all these differences, the majority of interviewees agree that earning money is the fundamental aspect of any job. However, those who did not point to any other important aspects were in the minority: usually, different meanings and dimensions of work overlap in their statements. A good example is Reena's definition of work – she lists many aspects of work and mentions salary only as the last one:

> 'Where I feel that I am needed, useful, that my work is a lot of help, that I can do it and I feel that I want to go to work. Wake up with this feeling. And, of course [pause] the physical conditions should be good, not these bad conditions for example light. Such elementary things. So, there would be lots of light and comfortable to work. There are no problems with temperature and such things. And, of course, people also, who you work with, they support each other and [pause] comfortable working environment. … Well and also the salary.' (Reena, F, 27, HE, U, EE)

The following section examines other work aspects that are important for the interviewees.

Latent functions of work

As stated previously, the narratives of youth most often combine several latent and manifest functions when describing the meaning of work. This section seeks to distinguish the two types of latent function – intrinsic and extrinsic – in the stories of young people.

Latent intrinsic aspects of work

Starting with latent intrinsic aspects, the most pronounced in all the countries is the wish to have an *interesting job*. As Michalina from Poland puts it, she does not want to be forced to do something she does not like. Tauri from Estonia, quoted in the previous section, also sees working only for money as doing something involuntary:

> 'For me, a job should be something that I really want to do. I can't imagine to be forced to work, to do something that I don't like, wake up every day with a pain that I need to go to work.' (Michalina, F, 26, ME, NCJ, PL)

Connected with the idea of an interesting job, youth in all three countries emphasise *self-development* or *using one's skills and abilities*. For instance, for Polish youth, a job was often perceived as a path towards self-development and self-fulfilment, the manifest function of earning a living being mentioned along with these latent functions:

> 'Well, a job for me is a chance to grow, to gain new skills, and let's say, building my own character, some positive traits. ... but also just to earn money, to have something to afford living, pursuing my hobbies, outside of work.' (Anna, F, 27, HE, U, PL)

Likewise, in the narratives of employed Italian young people, the meaning of work is connected to *self-fulfilment*; and often, the desire to start working is linked with the wish to gain experience, whatever the contractual conditions may be. As in the Polish case mentioned previously, for Veronica, self-realisation is combined with the manifest function of earning a living.

> 'Well, [work] means from the most basic things, such as earning money to survive, basically to reach a goal, something, I mean, something I studied for, I worked for, for years, and at the same time ... the image, for me, of work, that I would like it to be, but maybe it's not, it is a work that would give me a personal satisfaction [pause] not just work to purely survive, but a job that gives me satisfaction, that makes me [pause] happy. Even if I don't know whether in real life [pause] I know that now it's something quite utopian, but [pause] I hope that this would be, this will be the work.' (Veronica, F, 26, HE, U, IT)

In Estonian interviews, self-development and using one's skills were also mentioned quite often, but more by young people who had acquired some professional qualifications or had work experience, as in the case of Miina who has a bachelor's degree and, in addition to shorter term work experiences, has worked for about a year as a consultant:

> 'Work is [pause] I don't know, for me it's like applying some of my skills, in this sense it's not like some of my specific skills but maybe something that I know how to do or my general set of skills for something that would generate some kind of [pause] For me also voluntary work is work, especially when I was younger, but now, because everything costs money [laughs] then also this [money] is important.' (Miina, F, 24, HE, U, EE)

Going beyond self-development and skill use, interviewees in all countries mention that work provides an opportunity to *take the initiative* and *achieve something, make a difference*; but compared to previously described functions, the latter appears less in young people' narratives. There are some interviewees, for example Ott, who deem this to be very important. He has switched jobs several times because of the lack of influence he sees himself having in the company.

> 'I am a different kind of person. I can't keep my opinion to myself. I work in some place for a month and then already I go to the manager and make my proposals [about how to organise work better]. And if he takes these into account or not, I don't care very much, that someone who has been working there for ten years doing the same job and let's say they are offended by it or whatever. ... When I feel, that I am not needed, the work doesn't motivate me anymore. That's it.' (Ott, M, 28, HE, U, EE)

Another very frequently mentioned theme in the interviews from all three countries is the importance of *job climate* and the *relationship with colleagues*. Karolina and Agata from Poland explain that friendly colleagues provide an opportunity for communication and improve the work environment.

> 'I was lucky because I have really nice people in my room, they are warm, I like working there. ... [Work is] something cool. I mean, money is important as well, but I'm not coming here for the salary. For me it's more about just to go out, not to stay at home. ... I had nothing to do at home, so I preferred to go to work, as a kind of entertainment, to spend some time with people. (Karolina, F, 21, LE, TE, PL)

> 'Good job [pause] I would like to work in a team, in a team of young people, and I would like it to be creative, so I could create something, not just recreating others' work.' (Agata, F, 27, HE, U, PL)

The importance of friendly colleagues or being able to discuss decisions with someone is also clearly underlined by Estonian youth. Elisabet, who has been at home with children for several years and misses communication, hopes to establish friendships.

> 'Working conditions, working environment or a team [colleagues] could be friendly, understanding. Nobody wants, I don't know,

some kind of an arrogant manager, right. And also, I certainly like such things like if the team goes to some places together or have some events with families and such kind of things. That employers could be humane, right. These are all rather logical [self-evident] things.' (Elisabet, F, 25, LE, U, EE)

In some cases, good relationships with colleagues and sharing knowledge (informal learning) can compensate for other shortcomings of working life. For example, Carlo from Italy says that the relationships compensate even for the salary being paid late:

'the cool thing is the relationships, which also compensate for the fact of getting your salary late. ... The aspect that I like most about my job is its humanity, that is personal enrichment, sharing, relationships [pause] that is, the sharing of knowledge.' (Carlo, M, 25, ME, TE, IT)

In all three countries, some interviewees mentioned the importance of the job being *useful for other people* or *society* in general; yet, this is not a widespread narrative. Michalina (F, 26, ME, NCJ, PL) from Poland and Antonio (19, M, ME, TE, IT) from Italy both stress that working for them means helping others; and in Michalina's words, "putting someone's good above yours, it's about sacrificing". Brigitta adds that the values of the workplace should be in accordance with her values, a meaning of work that could be associated with Warr's (2007) *equity* in terms of morality in an employer's relationship with society.

'The environment is important for me, that I feel what I do is good and it does good to the people, I wouldn't like to work in a restaurant where I don't like the food or what I feel isn't healthy or is somehow bad for the people. ... So the idea and the mission should be right, and the people there [pause] and actually the salary is also important.' (Brigitta, F, 24, HE, NCJ, EE)

Latent extrinsic aspects of work

Compared to other functions of work described previously, latent extrinsic aspects were mentioned less frequently. However, the *time-structuring* effect of work and *security* in terms of a contract or receiving the agreed salary were mentioned in all three countries.

Youth in all countries see that work gives *structure to one's day* and provides *meaningful activity*. Kevin (M, 24, LE, NCJ, EE) says he does not want to be idle; doing something gives him self-confidence. Konrad describes how he was getting frustrated while unemployed – having a job was necessary to help organise his day and provide clear goals:

> 'If I can do something, I'm happy, if not, I'm starting to be nervous. When I am supposed to do something and nobody wants to tell me how to do it, it's no good.' (Konrad, M, 23, ME, U, PL)

Mohammed makes a comparison between a person who goes to work and a "boy", describing the structure of the day for each of the two as follows (I = Interviewer, R = Respondent).

> I: Ok [pause] you mean it also gives you a certain structure, way of life?
> R: Yes, you wake up in the morning, you go to work, in the afternoon you come back home, you do what you have to do, in the evening you may go out for a coffee or something like that, then you come home at night and you go to sleep. Instead, as a boy [pause] you go out in the morning, come back in the evening, and that's all. (Mohammed, M, 19, LE, U, IT)

In addition, the *financial security* provided by work was mentioned in all countries, although with some variations in meaning. In Italy, youth have long-term financial security in mind: despite changes in the labour market, the idea that you can plan your life only if you have a permanent contract persists.

> 'So, I'm afraid I'll spend all my life in precarious jobs without any security or economic stability – and economic stability gives psychological stability. If you don't have the first you don't have the second, you're always in a state of anxiety because you don't know how the month is going to end, if you have debts you don't know what's going to happen, and if something unexpected happens ... unfortunately I can see that money is very important, it's extremely difficult to go into society without it [pause] even on the level of friendship. It's hard to be friends, it's hard to find a girl'. (Andrea, M, 24, ME, TE, IT).

Polish youth also strive for stability in working life. This is marked by a permanent contract that would give them above all a psychological or mental sense of security. Lukasz puts the security aspect over the potential salary and would even be ready to work for a minimum wage if the contract was permanent.

> 'For me it's always a family – in the first place, so I would like to have a stable job, I would like to have some kind of security, especially the psychological one. Not that I have one internship, then it finishes so maybe I'll find another one, or some job on the mandatory contract … just any job, maybe not a physical one, but more like an office job, that would give me some stability, even for the minimum wage, but stable, in which I can be certain that I'll get the salary every month, that I could take a loan, or buy something on an instalment plan. Just to have this psychological comfort.' (Łukasz, M, 29, HE, TE, PL)

Estonian youth talk about financial security in a short-term perspective (although for some, long-term plans were tied to this as well): a good job is one in which the salary is agreed in advance and paid on time. Mai, a single mother of two with very little work experience, describes what job security means for her: knowing what is expected of her, *environmental clarity* in Warr's (1987) terms, and the salary being paid as agreed.

> 'And that, for example, there is a certain salary. Secure job and solid salary. That, okay, I understand that work tasks sometimes change, and this is all that I can go with. But, for example, a certain solid sum, you know that you will receive it. That it does not depend on this if you are like, well I tend to do more work, if I go to work and they give me tasks to do and I get it done sooner that I'm supposed to.' (Mai, F, 29, LE, U, EE)

In addition, among Estonian youth, importance was given to a *stress-free working environment* defined by the interviewees as "not having someone on your back" or "checking up on you". The latter could be associated with *supportive supervision* (Warr, 2007). This is closely connected with having friendly colleagues who make a major contribution to creating a pleasant working environment.

> 'Definitely the colleagues. Well, it develops over time; you can't see it right away. So, let's say it's a nest of vipers [laughs], where they talk behind your back, saying you are taking their job coming here like that; I have been working here for 10 years and you come in and think you are someone [laughs]. Such attitudes, this

is stressful, then I think, I would leave this place crying. I am sensitive to such things.' (Tuuli, F, 29, ME, U, EE)

Some of the Estonian interviewees also mention the importance of *physical security* at work. For instance, Jaano, who worked in the wood industry, explains that although the salary is good, he would not take a job with harmful working conditions:

'Cleanliness for example, I went to *** [name of company]. This is a really big company, but the air inside was really awfully dusty. ... This is not good at all. My brother went to another company and there they had all these devices to suck [the dust]. Here they had nothing. ... Well yes, they offered good salary and stuff, but just the working conditions. It starts affecting your health, breathing in the sawdust and stuff, this is not good.' (Jaano, M, 27, LE, U, EE)

Conclusions

The aim of this chapter was to examine whether and how youth meanings of work differ in Italy, Poland, and Estonia. The study is based on semi-structured qualitative interviews, conducted with young people aged 18 to 30 years who share the experience of labour market insecurity (unemployment or a non-contractual, temporary, low paid, or part-time job). The analysis was structured around existing classifications of meanings and functions of work (Jahoda, 1981, 1982; Warr, 1987, 2007; Albano and Parisi, 2017) and distinguished three main categories of meanings: (a) manifest; (b) latent intrinsic; and (c) latent extrinsic.

Findings show that in the three countries analysed, the youth narratives regarding the meaning of work are largely similar. This is in accordance with value studies that maintain that due to the universality of the nature of the work, people in countries with similar levels of development will hold relatively similar work values (Mortimer and Lorence, 1995).

Rather obviously, work as a source of financial resources – that is, salary, earning a living, the *manifest function* in Jahoda's (1981) terms – is the most dominant meaning. In relation to labour market experience, the significance of salary appears to be greater for the unemployed or those with little or no work experience. This is in accordance with Inglehart's (1971) scarcity hypothesis, positing that the shift towards post-materialist values occurs after gaining material security. Results are also in line with Rainsford et al (2019) who found that among the somewhat older group of young people in Europe (closer to 35 years of age), unemployment had a negative effect on intrinsic values.

Most studies on the meanings or values of work are quantitative. Therefore, the current analysis offers a different perspective and enables one to observe how these meanings are constructed in youth narratives. Moreover, the interviews conducted make it possible not just to point to a hierarchy of various meanings of work (Schwartz, 1994; Smith and Schwartz, 1997), but to indicate how these meanings are intertwined and form particular configurations. Thus, almost all young people emphasise some other aspects of work in addition to salary, and sometimes salary is even mentioned last (see also Bergqvist and Eriksson, 2015). Moreover, there are also those who interpret working only for money as something involuntary. For some, the *latent intrinsic functions* of work, such as an interesting, self-fulfilling job or opportunities for social contacts, can compensate for receiving a lower salary. In the latter case, young people talk about the importance of good relations with colleagues and managers and the benefits of working in a team.

Qualitative data make it possible to reveal variations in the meanings of the same categories or concepts. Providing for oneself is seen not only as a source of income but also as being associated with dignity, self-worth, stability, and – especially in the case of Poland and Italy – autonomy and adulthood (the opportunity to move out of the parental household and start a family). Estonian youth do not emphasise the link between earning a salary and autonomy, because for the most part they already live separately[5] (although, in several cases, with support from the family). In addition, Italian youth highly value a job with a permanent contract, whereas for Polish youth, temporary contracts are not an issue. This is because temporary work is relatively common in both countries, but in Poland, it is combined with comparatively low youth unemployment. The importance of job security in the Italian case corresponds with previous quantitative studies (Albano and Parisi, 2017). In Estonia, however, temporary work is not widespread.

Regarding *latent intrinsic functions* of work, it appears that youth in all three countries highly value jobs that are interesting and offer self-fulfilment, development, and the use of one's skills. However, such meanings of work are more prevalent in the stories of young people with a higher level of education or work experience (see also Rainsford et al, 2019). A few interviews also support Jahoda's (1981) statement that some latent functions might be provided by social institutions or domains of life other than regular employment. Thus, those who do not have particularly interesting jobs or cannot fully apply their knowledge and skills admit that working means only earning a living; but, in turn, this enables them to satisfy latent functions such as doing something of personal interest outside working hours.

In all countries, youth value the opportunities for interpersonal contacts provided by work. They reflect on being motivated by working with others, having contact with people outside the family, discussing work-related matters, and sharing knowledge with colleagues. Sometimes, in the same context, meanings of *latent extrinsic aspects* are mentioned such as environmental clarity (knowing what one should do at work) or supportive supervision. Less apparent in youth interviews are intrinsic meanings of work associated with usefulness to society, taking the initiative, and making a difference (see also Borgulya and Hahn, 2013). Overall, *latent extrinsic aspects* of work are less prominent in youth narratives. Nonetheless, they do mention work as giving a time structure for the day as well as security. However, the concept of security is related more to financial and contractual aspects of work, whereas only Estonian interviewees also emphasise the physical security of the workplace.

Compared to previous studies, interviews with youth do not reveal new meanings of work. Nevertheless, they indicate interesting associations, interconnections, and sometimes substitutions between various meanings. In summary, youth narratives seem to confirm that individual well-being still depends on having a job (Albano and Parisi, 2017).

Qualitative studies do have their limitations, and the results presented here are not generalisable to all youth in Italy, Poland, or Estonia who have experience of labour market insecurities. However, these results deliver important subjective insights into specific youth experiences, backgrounds, and respective narratives related to the construction of work meanings.

Notes

[1] It is debatable whether work has a central role in today's advanced modern societies. There are two currents: one underlines that work is no longer central (Arendt, 1958; Rifkin, 1995); the other emphasises the centrality of work in structuring identity, time, and organisation of life (Gallino, 2000; Paugam and Russel, 2000). However, this question is beyond the scope of the current chapter.

[2] Data are provided for 2015 because the interviews took place in 2015 and 2016. Hence, these data best describe the context during the time when the interviewees were looking for a job.

[3] Several stories from Estonian interviewees revealed that they left the parental home early because they had poor relations with their parents or were kicked out. In

contrast, other interviewees described how their family helped them to purchase a place of their own or how relatives offered housing rent-free.
4   However, Polish youth probably would agree that having a permanent contract is necessary in certain situations: it significantly simplifies access to bank loans and protects future employment after childbirth (not necessarily the case with temporary contracts).
5   In 2016, the average age at which young Italians left the parental household was 30.1 years. In Poland, it was 28 years. In contrast, Estonian youth left their parental homes at the average age of 23.6 years (Eurostat, 2016). These differences might be rooted in either structural (availability of affordable housing for youth) or cultural barriers.

References

Albano, R. and Parisi, T. (2017) 'What's still important about work? A longitudinal and cross-country analysis of prevalent attitudes towards work during the last 40 years', *Well-Being at and through Work*, 9: 55–96.

Allport, G.W. (1955) *Becoming: Basic Considerations for a Psychology of Personality*, New Haven: Yale University Press.

Arendt, H. (1958) *The Human Condition*, Chicago: University of Chicago Press.

Aspalter, C., Jinsoo, K. and Sojeung, P. (2009) 'Analysing the welfare state in Poland, the Czech Republic, Hungary and Slovenia: an ideal-typical perspective', *Social Policy & Administration*, 43(2): 170–85.

Attride-Stirling, J. (2001) 'Thematic networks: an analytic tool for qualitative research', *Qualitative Research*, 1(3): 385–405.

Bergqvist, T. and Eriksson, B. (2015) 'Passion and exploitation among young adults with different labour market status in Europe', *Nordic Journal of Working Life Studies*, 5(2): 17–31.

Bertolini, S., Bolzoni, M., Moiso, V. and Musumeci, R. (2018b) *The Comparative Qualitative Research Methodology of the EXCEPT Project*. EXCEPT Working Papers, WP No. 56, Tallinn: Tallinn University, Available from: https://www.except-project.eu/working-papers/

Bertolini, S., Deliyanni-Kouimtzi, K., Bolzoni, M., Ghislieri, C., Goglio, V., Martino, S. Meo, A., Moiso, V., Musumeci, R., Ricucci, R., Torrioni, P. M., Athanasiades, C., Figgou, L., Flouli, A., Kostouli, M. and Sourvinou, M.-N. (2018a) *Labour Market Insecurity and Social Exclusion: Qualitative Comparative Results in Nine Countries*. EXCEPT Working Papers, WP No. 53, Tallinn: Tallinn University, Available from: https://www.except-project.eu/working-papers/

Bohle, D. and Greskovits, B. (2007) 'Neoliberalism, embedded neoliberalism, and neocorporatism: paths towards transnational capitalism in Central-Eastern Europe', *West European Politics*, 30(3): 443–66.

Bonoli, G. (1997) 'Classifying welfare states: a two dimensional approach', *Journal of Social Policy,* 26(3): 351–72.

Borgulya, A. and Hahn, J. (2013) 'Changes in the importance of work-related values in Central and Eastern Europe: Slovenia and Hungary against the trend?', *Journal of Arts and Humanities,* 2(10): 24–36.

Boyatzis, R.E. (1998) *Transforming Qualitative Information: Thematic Analysis and Code Development,* London: Sage.

Braun, V. and Clarke, V. (2006) 'Using thematic analysis in psychology', *Qualitative Research in Psychology,* 3(2): 77–101.

Ebbinghaus, B. and Manow, P. (2003) *Comparing Welfare Capitalism: Social Policy and Political Economy in Europe, Japan and the USA,* London: Routledge.

Esping-Andersen, G. (1990) *The Three Worlds of Welfare Capitalism,* Cambridge: Polity Press.

Eurostat (2016) 'Database', Available from: https://ec.europa.eu/eurostat

Eurostate (2018) 'Database', Available from: https://ec.europa.eu/eurostat

Fenger, M. (2007) 'Welfare regimes in Central and Eastern Europe: incorporating post-communist countries in a welfare regime typology', *Contemporary Issues and Ideas in Social Sciences,* 3(2): 1–30.

Ferrera, M. (1996) 'The "southern" model of welfare in social Europe', *Journal of European Social Policy,* 6(1): 17–37.

Gallino, L. (2000) 'L'idea di flessibilità sostenibile: prospettive e problemi in rapporto a differenti modi di lavorare', *Quaderni di sociologia,* 23: 111–28.

Gesthuizen, M. and Verbakel, E. (2011) 'Job preferences in Europe', *European Societies,* 13(5): 663–86.

Grunow, D. and Evertsson, M. (2016) *Couples' Transitions to Parenthood: Analysing Gender and Work in Europe,* Cheltenham: Edward Elgar Publishing.

Hagström, T. and Gamberale, F. (1995) 'Young people's work motivation and value orientation', *Journal of Adolescence,* 18(4): 475–90.

Hall, P.A. and Soskice, S. (2001) 'An introduction to varieties of capitalism', in P.A. Hall and D. Soskice (eds) *Varieties of Capitalism: The Institutional Foundations of Comparative Advantage,* Oxford: Oxford University Press, pp 1–68.

Hoare, P.N. and Machin, M.A. (2006) 'Maintaining wellbeing during unemployment', *Australian Journal of Career Development,* 15(1): 19–27.

Hofstede, G. (1980) *Culture's Consequences: International Differences in Work Related Values,* Beverly Hills: Sage Publications.

Hult, C. and Svallfors, S. (2002) 'Production regimes and work orientations: a comparison of six Western countries', *European Sociological Review*, 18(3): 315–31.

Inglehart, R. (1971) 'The silent revolution in Europe: intergenerational change in post-industrial societies', *American Political Science Review*, 65(4): 991–1017.

Jahoda, M. (1981) 'Work, employment, and unemployment: values, theories, and approaches in social research', *American Psychologist*, 36(2): 184–91.

Jahoda, M. (1982) *Employment and Unemployment: A Social-Psychological Analysis*, Cambridge: Cambridge University Press.

Kalleberg, A.L. (1977) 'Work values and job rewards: a theory of job satisfaction', *American Sociological Review*, 42(1): 124–43.

Mortimer, J.T. and Lorence, J. (1995) 'Social psychology of work', in K.S. Cook, G.A. Fine and J.S. House (eds) *Sociological Perspectives on Social Psychology*, Needham Heights: Allyn and Bacon, pp 497–523.

Paugam, S. and Russel, H. (2000) 'The effects of employment precarity and unemployment on social isolation', in D. Gallie and S. Paugam (eds) *Welfare Regimes and the Experience of Unemployment in Europe*, Oxford: Oxford University Press, pp 243–64.

Paul, K.I. and Batinic, B. (2010) 'The need for work: Jahoda's latent functions of employment in a representative sample of the German population', *Journal of Organizational Behavior*, 31(1): 45–64.

Rainsford, E., Maloney, W.A. and Popa, S.A. (2019) 'The effect of unemployment and low-quality work conditions on work values: exploring the experiences of young Europeans', *Annals of the American Academy of Political and Social Science*, 682(1): 172–85.

Reiska, E., Roosmaa, E.L., Oras, K. and Taru, M. (2018) *Young Adults in Insecure Labour Market Positions in Estonia – the Results from a Qualitative Study*. EXCEPT Working Papers, WP No. 23, Tallinn: Tallinn University, Available from: https://www.except-project.eu/working-papers/

Rifkin, J. (1995) *The End of Work*, New York: Penguin.

Roe, R.A. and Ester, P. (1999) 'Values and work: empirical findings and theoretical perspective', *Applied Psychology: An International Review*, 48(1): 1–21.

Rokeach, M. (1973) *The Nature of Human Values*, New York: Free Press.

Ros, M., Schwartz, S.H. and Surkiss, S. (1999) 'Basic individual values, work values, and the meaning of work', *Applied Psychology: An International Review*, 48(1): 49–71.

Rosenberg, M. (1957) *Occupations and Values*, New York: Free Press.

Schwartz, S.H. (1994) 'Are there universal aspects in the content and structure of values?', *Journal of Social Issues*, 50(4): 19–45.

Smith, P.B. and Schwartz, S.H. (1997) 'Values' in J.W. Berry, C. Kagitcibasi and M.H. Segall (eds) *Handbook of Cross-Cultural Psychology: Volume 3: Social Behaviour and Applications*, London: Allyn and Bacon, pp 77–118.

Warr, P.B. (1987) *Work, Unemployment and Mental Health*, Oxford: Clarendon Press.

Warr, P.B. (2007) *Work, Happiness, and Unhappiness*, Mahwah: Lawrence Erlbaum Associates.

Waters, L.E. and Moore, K.A. (2002) 'Reducing latent deprivation during unemployment: the role of meaningful leisure activity', *Journal of Occupational and Organizational Psychology*, 75(1): 15–32.

7
Housing autonomy of youth in Europe: do labour and housing policies matter?

Valentina Goglio and Sonia Bertolini

Introduction

Leaving one's home of origin is regarded as one of the key markers of the transition to adulthood (Shanahan, 2000; Corijn and Klijzing, 2001). Indeed, the individual life courses of youth are socially embedded in the macroinstitutional and structural as well as cultural context that defines the set of opportunities and constraints to which individual persons respond when making their life course decisions and transitions.

The factors that influence the means and timing of young people's housing autonomy in different institutional contexts are complex and interwoven. They include historical differences, social and cultural norms, institutional frameworks, and macrolevel economic factors such as the structure of labour markets and access to housing (Buchmann and Kriesi, 2011; Breen and Buchmann, 2016; Bertolini et al, 2019).

On the macrolevel, following Moreno (2012), comparative European research has shown the combined influence of the welfare regime on what some authors refer to as the transition regime (Walther, 2006), and of culture (Billari and Liefbroer, 2007; Giuliano, 2007; Goldscheider and Goldscheider, 1989, 1996; Surkyn and Lesthaeghe, 2004) on the diverse trends observed in the transition to adulthood in various European countries.

Macrolevel factors and labour market integration are not the only determinants of such a complex phenomenon as leaving one's home of origin and setting up one's own household. Indeed, there is a wide body of literature highlighting the role of other micro- and mesolevel determinants. Young people's opportunities and transition to adulthood are strongly influenced by the individual's original collocation in the class structure (MacDonald et al, 2005), resulting in specific mechanisms of transition for different social classes (Bernardi and Poggio, 2004; Barbera et al, 2010). Gender is another important determinant: in certain contexts, employment and the level of earnings may be more important for men who are expected to be breadwinners, and somewhat less important for women who may rely on their partners' income (Aassve et al, 2001). The combination of gender and social class has also shown how British working-class women left the parental home for reasons that were different from those of men; and in the United States, how young women of Southern European and Hispanic origin lowered their nest-leaving expectations (Goldscheider and Goldscheider, 1989). Moreover, the general process of expansion in education in recent decades (Schofer and Meyer, 2005) has had the effect of postponing entry into the labour market and subsequent stabilisation (Mortimer et al, 2005).

However, this chapter will focus on one of the main determinants of the decision to leave the parental home: the level of individual economic resources directly available to young adults (Ermisch, 1999; McElroy, 1985). In this respect, the situation in the labour market and the consequent availability of economic resources coming from the job are important in structuring the decision to leave the parental home (Blossfeld, 1995; Galland, 2001; Heinz, 2001; Mayer, 1997; Scherer, 2004; Schizzerotto, 2002). If young people experience difficulties in labour market integration and perceive their situation as unstable and insecure, they may be relatively less willing to make such a step (Aassve et al, 2001). There is a large body of evidence confirming the importance of employment and the level of earnings for opportunities to leave the parental home and for feeling autonomous among youth (Aassve et al, 2001; Buck and Scott, 1993; Iacovou, 2010; Mulder et al, 2002; Mulder and Clark, 2000; Nilsson and Strandh, 1999; Vitali, 2010).

According to these studies, having a job is a prerequisite for establishing one's own household especially among individuals who, for various reasons, cannot expect to receive financial support from family members (Jacob and Kleinert, 2008; Vitali, 2010). Exit from the parental home reduces opportunities to receive material and emotional support from the family of origin. This makes the negative consequences associated with the risk of losing employment much stronger for those who decide to establish their own home (Aassve et al, 2007; Parisi, 2008). Unemployed or inactive youth may have very limited opportunities to leave the parental home due to their lack of economic resources. But opportunities for housing independence vary widely, including among those young people who actually are involved in paid work. In particular, the attention of researchers has recently turned towards the role of stability of employment (Fernandes et al, 2008; Becker et al, 2010; Barbieri et al, 2014). Labour market positions with high degrees of economic uncertainty prevent youth from making blind long-term commitments (Oppenheimer et al, 1997; Mills and Blossfeld, 2003). Thus, irrespective of the level of income received by young adults, the expected variation in income may deter them from investing in household formation (Fernandes et al, 2008). Another important factor in this respect is that temporary jobs produce wage discounts, namely lower levels of income (due to lower bargaining power) and 'wage scars' through the employment history of individuals employed in temporary positions (for example, due to limited promotion opportunities) (Gebel, 2009). Yet, the role of employment and earnings varies across countries depending not only on the structure of the labour market and on the educational system (which may smooth the school-to-work transition) but also on the different welfare state regimes.

Previous studies have shown whether and to what degree labour market vulnerability affects decisions about leaving the parental home and forming a family; and they have indicated how this differs across countries and across different welfare state regimes (Aassve et al, 2002; Blossfeld et al, 2005; Müller and Gangl, 2003). Specific institutional configurations of the labour market and welfare state, as well as macrostructural conditions, are relevant explanations for country differences and for their impact on unemployed young people's decisions to leave home.

Country-specific institutional arrangements produce distinctive national responses to the global social processes (labour market flexibilisation and privatisation of social security), and different institutional settings are linked to different patterns of exposure to social risks (Bonoli, 2004; Rovny, 2014; Taylor-Gooby, 2004). Thus, for the purposes of this work, the focus is on institutional determinants, because national institutional backgrounds, and policies in particular, are expected to have a mediating effect on how young people's risks of labour market exclusion and job insecurity translate into risks of social exclusion (Mills and Blossfeld, 2003). In general, in countries that provide more generous support for youth, the impact of labour market weakness on housing autonomy is reduced. Nonetheless, it remains unclear what dimensions of the institutional setting may be most important when it comes to buffering labour market insecurity and fostering individual autonomy among young people.

Against this background, the intention is to study how macrolevel indicators can moderate the relationship between the individual labour market position and youth housing autonomy. In particular, the study focuses on labour market exclusion. This concept depicts a broad condition in which individuals are not integrated into the productive system, and this entails both the conditions of involuntary exclusion such as unemployment and voluntary conditions such as inactivity or being a student. This work narrows down the focus to the condition of unemployment alone (versus a situation of employment) but does not disaggregate the relationship between employment and housing autonomy further by distinguishing between permanent and temporary workers. This is because, although an important microlevel factor in the transition to housing autonomy, previous research using cross-sectional data has shown that the association between temporary employment and housing autonomy is weak and not significant for most EU28 countries (Baranowska-Rataj et al, 2016).

Youth autonomy has multiple definitions in the social sciences. Most of these are linked to the notion of becoming an adult in different aspects of life (Cicchelli, 2013). For instance, it involves the capacity to take steps towards independence from the parental household, the ability to create one's own universe, and the ability to govern one's own life through relevant choices. Housing autonomy, the condition in which young people live outside of the parental home, is a crucial step enabling other stages of the individual's life course. For this reason, the present chapter narrows the focus to housing autonomy alone. As far as macrolevel indicators are concerned, the focus is on two key macroindicators: employment protection legislation (EPL) and the amount of public investment in housing policies in the EU28 member states.

Indeed, a high level of employment protection can guarantee continuity of jobs and thus of income. However, for those who are excluded from the labour market, a high level of employment protection translates into increased difficulties of integration into the labour market. In the last few decades, many European countries partially deregulated the labour market by decreasing the restrictions on temporary work, often targeting this at young people (Baranowska and Gebel, 2010). However, doubts about the effectiveness of these reforms soon arose (Kahn, 2010; Noelke, 2016). As Gebel and Giesecke (2016) have shown, deregulating the use of temporary contracts increased the risk of temporary employment for young people, but did not reduce their risk of unemployment: for young men with a low level of education; it even increased it.

On the other hand, monetary transfers to support the costs of housing or policies that reduce the cost of housing itself decrease the economic burden of autonomous living that the individual has to bear. In particular, cash subsidies supporting rent have a positive effect on young adults' housing autonomy, especially for those with lower incomes who are exposed to income instability. Therefore, a lower cost of living can reduce the negative effect of the loss of income associated with job loss.

There is abundant literature on the direct effect of EPL on labour market opportunities for young people; however, the moderating role of this particular macrolevel factor on the relationship between the labour market and housing has yet to be investigated. Similarly, despite the growing literature on the problem of the affordability of homes on a family budget (particularly in the case of young people), there is a lack of studies that investigate the moderating role of state investment in housing policies.

This chapter is organised as follows. The next section frames the analyses in the existing literature, highlighting this study's innovative perspective. The following section describes the research design including the hypotheses, the data, and the method of analysis. This is followed by the research findings and some concluding observations.

Theoretical background

Countries differ significantly in the extent to which they provide security with respect to potential job loss and unemployment (Ebralidze, 2011; Gallie, 2007). Specific institutional configurations of the labour market and welfare state, as well as macrostructural conditions, are relevant explanations for differences between countries and the impact they have on the decision to leave home for unemployed young people.

Regulation and social policies are expected to filter the impact of increasing labour market exclusion and job insecurity for young people in different ways (Blossfeld et al, 2012; Mills and Blossfeld, 2003), and this can impact on their decisions about leaving their parental home (Bertolini, 2021a, 2021b, 2018).

This chapter uses a two-step multilevel model (Bryan and Jenkins, 2013) to analyse the moderating role of EPL and of housing policies on the relationship between unemployment and housing autonomy of youth. It, formulates two main hypotheses. The first predicts that a high level of EPL for permanent contracts will negatively moderate the relationship between unemployment and housing autonomy. This is because a high level of regulation decreases the risk of losing a job for those already employed (insiders); but, on the other hand, it may make it difficult for the unemployed (outsiders) to get into employment because employers tend not to hire outsiders when the costs of firing employees is high (Baranowska and Gebel, 2010).

The same hypothesis is used to test the moderating role of high EPL for temporary contracts on the relationship between unemployment and housing autonomy. The role of stricter regulation of temporary contracts, in particular restrictions on renewals, may be ambiguous: indeed, depending on the context, it may increase the chances of temporary workers ending up in unemployment (dead end) in labour markets with low mobility and in a situation of economic crisis, or ending up in permanent contracts (stepping stone effect) in efficient labour markets and a favourable economic situation. Because the time period covered by the analyses was characterised by unfavourable economic conditions, it is hypothesised that high EPL will have a negative moderating role on temporary contracts. Hence, stricter regulation of temporary contracts will make it harder for unemployed young people to get new jobs, even temporary ones, and thus harder for them to bear the costs of independent living due to lack of income.

The second hypothesis assumes that generous policies supporting the costs of independent living directly (with cash subsidies) or indirectly (with social housing policies) will positively moderate the association between unemployment and housing autonomy, thus reducing the negative effect of unemployment. This is because generous policies on housing help the individual to manage the costs of living autonomously even in the case of job loss. This lowers the pressure of housing costs for unemployed people who face reduced financial resources due to lack of employment income.

Because this chapter aims to address the role of the institutional setting and policies in association with labour market disadvantage and leaving the parental home, understanding the way labour protection is regulated is a good example of whether and how institutional regulation may play a role in moderating the relationship between individual labour market position and housing autonomy.

Indeed, many European countries have partially deregulated their labour markets by decreasing the restrictions on temporary work, and this is often targeted at youth (Baranowska and Gebel, 2010). However, doubts have been cast on the effectiveness of these reforms (Kahn, 2010; Noelke, 2016). As Gebel and Giesecke demonstrated (2016), deregulating the use of temporary contracts increased the risk of temporary employment for young people, but did not reduce the risk of unemployment. High levels of EPL regulation may make it difficult for temporary workers to get a permanent job, increasing the fear of subsequent unemployment. In addition, high levels of employment protection will increase temporary employment rates, because it will be more efficient for employers to hire temporary staff whose contracts expire after a certain date, thus avoiding potential firing costs. This has the potential to change the profile of people in employment toward a greater number of temporary employees who are less likely to be able to achieve housing autonomy (Baranowska and Gebel, 2010).

As far as the level of regulation for temporary contracts is concerned, empirical evidence has contested the theoretical assumption that a low level of regulation of temporary contracts would be associated with a higher rate of temporary employment (Nunziata and Staffolani, 2007 in Baranowska and Gebel, 2010). Although loose regulation of temporary employment may appear to provide further incentive for employers to lower the potential cost of ending contracts that already contain a defined end date, empirical research has shown that there is no association between EPL and the incidence of temporary contracts (Booth et al, 2002 in Baranowska and Gebel, 2010).

When investigating the role of institutional factors in the relationship between labour market conditions and housing autonomy, one significant indicator is the level of expenditure specifically identified by states to help citizens with the costs of housing. Indeed, monetary transfer to support the cost of housing or policies that reduce the cost of housing, reduce the economic burden on individuals of living autonomously. In particular, cash subsidies to support rent have a positive effect on housing autonomy for young adults, especially those on lower incomes who are exposed to income instability. Indeed, generous public spending on housing may lower the cost of living, and this is particularly relevant for unemployed people who, compared to their employed peers, experience lack of income. If affordable housing is provided and/or costs associated with renting are subsidised, even unemployed people can meet the cost of housing, which results at the macrolevel in a reduction of the negative effect of unemployment on the chances of living autonomously.

Based on the literature presented in this section, two main hypotheses are formulated for this study regarding the moderating effect of institutional factors on the relationship between labour market exclusion and housing autonomy.

Hypothesis 1: Employment protection legislation will play a moderating role in the relationship between unemployment and housing autonomy. A high level of EPL for permanent contracts

(EPL regular) will negatively moderate the relationship between unemployment and housing autonomy, in other words it will increase the negative effect of unemployment. A high level of EPL for temporary contracts (EPL temporary) is also expected to negatively moderate the relationship between unemployment and housing autonomy.

Hypothesis 2: Public policies supporting housing will play a moderating role in the relationship between unemployment and housing autonomy. Generous policies supporting housing autonomy either directly (through cash subsidies) or indirectly (through social housing policies) can positively moderate the association between unemployment and housing autonomy – that is, reduce the negative effect of unemployment.

Data and methods

The multilevel analyses presented here are based on individual cross-sectional data from the European Statistics on Income and Living Conditions (EU-SILC) survey for the year 2014. The database contains individual-level observations for 28 European countries that qualify the data as multilevel, with individuals at level one nested in countries at level two. The sample used for the individual-level regressions is made up of individuals aged 16 to 29 years who are employed or unemployed (inactives and students excluded).

The dependent variable, housing autonomy, refers to the residential circumstances of the individual: an individual is considered as having housing autonomy when she or he lives in a household not including her or his parents (variable equal to 1 if parents are not members of the household, equal to 0 otherwise).

The main independent variable is labour market exclusion, operationalised as a dichotomous variable equal to 1 if the self-reported economic status of the respondent is unemployed, equal to 0 if employed.

The logistic regressions also include a set of control variables such as age, gender, immigrant status, level of education, and area of residence (urban or rural). Finally, housing autonomy is strongly associated with the presence of a partner (Holdsworth and Morgan, 2005; Iacovou, 2010; Ruspini, 2015), because living with a partner may work as the main driver of the decision to live independently and may also work as a buffer in the case of labour market exclusion. As a result, the presence of a partner in the household is introduced as a further control.[1]

The macrolevel indicators used in the second-level regression are collected from official sources such as Eurostat and OECD. The

Employment Protection Legislation Index elaborated by OECD is used to test the moderating role of EPL separately for permanent and temporary contracts.

The moderating role of housing policies is tested with data on the amount of public expenditure on rent benefits (as a percentage of GDP) combined with the amount of general public expenditure on housing support (as a percentage of GDP) and public expenditure on housing and social exclusion recorded by Eurostat. All these measures indicate intervention by public authorities to help households meet the cost of housing, despite variations in implementation at the individual country level. The first measure refers to transfers granted by a public authority to tenants in order to help them with the costs of housing. The provision of the benefit is guaranteed for a limited period of time and access is conditional on meeting a qualifying criterion (means test) (Eurostat Glossary, 2018). The other two measures are part of the social protection framework that encompasses all interventions from public or private bodies intended to relieve households and individuals of the burden of a defined set of risks or needs (Eurostat Glossary, 2018) – in this case, housing risk, when housing and social exclusion are not classified elsewhere. For example, expenditure for housing benefits may refer to housing tenure in which the property is owned by a government authority and social housing benefit is given based on qualifying criteria based on income and employment. It may also refer to expenditure for housing and social exclusion not classified elsewhere. This refers to means-tested public schemes that also entitle individuals at risk of social exclusion, but are a residual category of need that differs from the other schemes (for example, old age, unemployment, disability). The macrolevel variables are summarised in Table 7.1.

As for the method, the study applies multilevel analyses using a two-step approach. As recently highlighted in the literature (Bryan and Jenkins, 2013, 2016), this method turns out to be particularly useful when the researcher has a dataset characterised by a relatively small number of macrolevel units but a relatively high number of observations within each group (countries).

The first step consists in estimating separate individual-level regressions between the dependent and independent variable for each country. Such a coefficient becomes the dependent variable in the second step which entails the estimation of the effect of the macrolevel variable (independent) on the coefficient of the individual-level relationship (dependent variable) through a linear regression model. The process requires an additional adjustment for standard errors that, in the case of the estimated dependent variable, tend to be biased and

Table 7.1: List of macrolevel indicators

Macrolevel indicator	Source
Employment protection legislation index – Strictness of employment protection (regular contracts) – Strictness of employment protection (temporary employment)	Indicators of Employment Protection, OECD (https://www.oecd.org/employment/emp/oecdindicatorsofemploymentprotection.htm)
Social protection benefits for housing – Rent benefits (means-tested) as percentage of gross domestic product (GDP) Expenditure as percentage of GDP – HOUSE Expenditure on housing and social exclusion not classified elsewhere	Eurostat Tables by benefits – housing function (https://ec.europa.eu/eurostat/web/products-datasets/product?code=spr_exp_fho)

estimated inconsistently due to the heteroscedasticity of the first-level sampling error in which variance differs across observations (Jusko, 2005; Lewis and Linzer, 2005).

In this case the country-level logistic regressions are estimated first with being residentially autonomous (not living with parents) as the dependent variable and the proxy for labour market exclusion (being unemployed) as the independent variable with controls included. Then, the average marginal effects are estimated that, in the second step, turn into the dependent variable of a linear regression model in which the independent variable is the macrolevel indicator of interest (public expenditure on rent benefits as a percentage of GDP). Finally, standard errors of this second regression are corrected in order to take into consideration the uncertainty coming from using an estimated dependent variable. The error term of the second step regression includes a first component due to the individual-level regression (heteroscedasticity due to variance in the sampling error across countries) and a second component that is the country-level error term. Thus, standard errors of the second step linear regression model are corrected by adding a weight that is computed as in Huber (2005) and Baranowska and Gebel (2008).

Results

This section presents the results emerging from the two-step multilevel regression for the moderating role of selected macrolevel factors on the association between labour market exclusion and housing autonomy.

Figure 7.1: Average marginal effect (AME) of being unemployed (vs employed) on housing autonomy

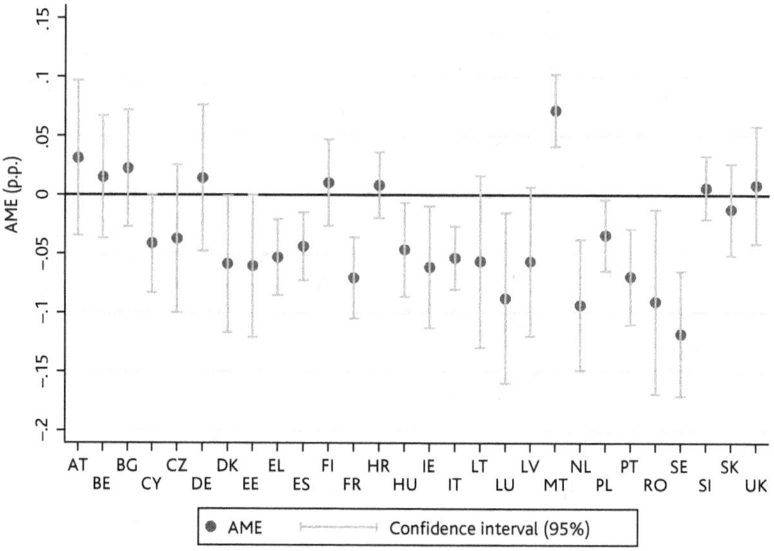

Source: Authors' own elaboration on EU-SILC UDB, 2014 – version 2 of August 2016

First, results are presented from the logistic regressions run on the individual level separately for each country. Figure 7.1 illustrates the average marginal effect of being unemployed (versus being employed) on autonomous living in all EU28 member states in the year 2014. The regressions show that in the majority of EU28 countries, being unemployed is associated negatively with autonomous living (compared to those who are employed). The association is substantial and statistically significant for half of the countries considered: in Denmark, Estonia, Greece, France, Ireland, Italy, Luxemburg, the Netherlands, Portugal, Romania, and Sweden, unemployed young people are between 5 and 10 percentage points less likely than employed people to live autonomously. This negative relationship is also observable in Cyprus, Hungary, Poland, and Spain, but with a lower gap (less than 5 percentage points) in the chances of living autonomously between the two groups. In contrast, Malta stands out as an outlier, indicating an advantage for unemployed people that might, however, be affected by the small sample size. The remaining countries show a non-significant relationship between unemployment and housing autonomy, with extremely low and non-significant coefficients.[2] As mentioned in the data section, the direct effect of the presence of a partner is associated positively with housing autonomy in line with previous studies. The indirect effect of a partner, as a control variable in the relationship between unemployment and housing autonomy, tends to reduce the negative association with unemployment, but generally does not reverse the direction of the relationship.

Given this overview of the relationship on the individual level (Step 1), the next step is to test whether some of the country variation can be explained by structural and institutional features.

One of the advantages of the two-step approach is that it provides a clear visualisation of the multilevel relationship between micro- and macrolevel variables in a simple scatterplot. Figures 7.2 and 7.3 plot the average marginal effects calculated on the individual level on the macrolevel indicators of interest for each hypothesis. The next section examines each of the hypotheses in detail.

Hypothesis 1: Employment Protection Legislation

The distributions of the macrolevel variables for the level of employment protection do not give a straightforward indication of the direction of the relationship with the variable of interest. A clear pattern does not emerge from the two panels in Figure 7.2: the negative effect

Figure 7.2: Indicators of employment protection legislation (EPL) and average marginal effect (AME) of being unemployed on housing autonomy

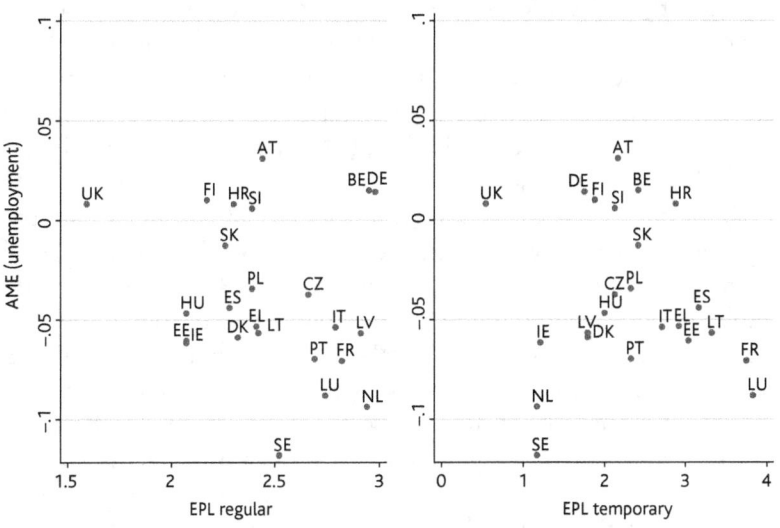

Source: Authors' own elaboration on EU-SILC UDB, 2014 and OECD data

of unemployment on housing autonomy is observable not only in a country with high employment regulation such as France, but also in a country such as Estonia that, on the contrary, is characterised by a lower level of regulation.

Yet, some internal trends can be spotted. For example, in countries with high EPL (>2.5 points) for regular employment such as France, the Netherlands, Portugal and Sweden, being unemployed is associated more negatively with housing autonomy than in other countries with less strict regulation. However, there are also countries with a high level of EPL regulation (Belgium and Germany) and a non-negative association. At the same time, the opposite trend – low regulation/non-negative association – is not observable except in the United Kingdom (UK). A quite substantial group of countries with intermediate values for EPL (2 to 2.5 points) shows a non-negative association between unemployment and housing autonomy (Austria, Finland, Hungary, the Slovak Republic, and Slovenia).

In the case of temporary contract regulations (right-hand panel of Figure 7.2), the distribution takes an inverted Y shape providing a non-univocal pattern. Indeed, there are countries with a high negative association between unemployment and housing autonomy with high levels of EPL and others with relatively low levels for temporary contracts (Ireland, the Netherlands, and Sweden on the one hand, and France, Luxemburg, and Lithuania on the other). Testing this type of association with a linear regression model in the second step (Table 7.2) reveals that the association between the macrolevel variables (both for permanent and temporary contracts) is negative but non-statistically significant (Models 1 and 5). This indicates that a statistically robust moderating effect of EPL for both regular and temporary contracts cannot be observed: the level of regulation of employment is not statistically associated with a decrease or increase in the (mostly negative) association between unemployment and housing autonomy occurring on the microlevel. However, as mentioned in the theoretical section, the decision to leave the parental home and live independently from the family of origin is a complex transition influenced by several factors that can also influence the labour market condition itself. As an example, the macroeconomic situation on the country level is one of the key factors that may play a role in the association between unemployment and housing autonomy: a negative macroeconomic situation (for example, proxied by a high unemployment rate or low GDP growth) may make the situation of unemployed people even worse, overruling the level of EPL. Therefore, these two main indicators of labour market and economy conditions are added as

Table 7.2: Second step regression for macrolevel indicators of EPL and the association between unemployment and housing autonomy; linear regression coefficients

	EPL for regular contracts				EPL for temporary contracts				No control for partner	
	(1)	(2)	(3)	(4)	(5)	(6)	(7)	(8)	(9)	(10)
EPL regular	−0.0326	−0.0357	−0.0358	−0.0389+					−0.0598**	
	(0.0230)	(0.0237)	(0.0235)	(0.0225)					(0.0270)	
EPL temporary					−0.00662	−0.00646	−0.00637	−0.00378		−0.00774
					(0.00954)	(0.00997)	(0.00992)	(0.00983)		(0.0120)
Youth unemployment rate (15–25)		−0.000362				−5.25e-05				
		(0.000789)				(0.000834)				
Total unemployment rate (15–74)			−0.000795				−0.000197			
			(0.00185)				(0.00198)			
GDP growth				−0.00757				−0.00608		
				(0.00504)				(0.00541)		
Constant	0.0376	0.0536	0.0534	0.0604	−0.0288	−0.0279	−0.0274	−0.0293	0.0612	−0.0685**
	(0.0577)	(0.0649)	(0.0643)	(0.0573)	(0.0230)	(0.0280)	(0.0285)	(0.0228)	(0.0669)	(0.0286)
Observations	24	24	24	24	24	24	24	24	24	24
R^2	0.084	0.100	0.101	0.180	0.021	0.021	0.022	0.076	0.183	0.019

Note: Standard errors in parentheses; *** $p < 0.01$, ** $p < 0.05$, + $p < 0.1$.
Source: Authors' own elaboration on EU-SILC UDB, 2014; OECD data and Eurostat data

control variables (Models 2 to 4 and 6 to 8). The estimates show that when controlling for the dynamism of the economy (namely, excluding the noise generated by the level of GDP growth), stricter regulation for regular contracts negatively moderates the association between unemployment and housing autonomy, further worsening the chances of housing autonomy for unemployed people. Indeed, estimates in Model 4 indicate that one unit increase in EPL for regular contracts intensifies the negative effect (as depicted by the average marginal effects in Figure 7.2) by almost 4 percentage points, and the relationship is significant within 90 per cent confidence intervals.

In addition, a sensitivity check was run without controlling for the presence of a partner (Models 9 and 10). The presence of a partner is a major predictor of housing autonomy and a confounder in the relationship between unemployment and housing autonomy. When removing this effect (that is, controlling for the presence of the partner), the net association between unemployment and housing autonomy decreases.

The models indicate that the (generally) negative association between unemployment and housing autonomy is further exacerbated when EPL for regular contracts is high (Model 4). When excluding the major confounder, the presence of a partner, and also the dynamics of the economy, the moderating effect of (stricter) regulation on a regular contract remains negative and is statistically significant.

Thus, Hypothesis 1 is partly verified, at least for the assumption of a negative moderating role of EPL for regular contracts when controlling for the dynamics of the economy. Where the labour market is divided into protected and non-protected segments (EPL for regular contracts is high), it becomes more difficult to find a new job for those who are outside, and the disadvantage of unemployed people in terms of housing autonomy is further exacerbated. A moderating role of EPL for temporary contracts, on the contrary, is slightly negative but the relationship is weak (less than 1 percentage point) and never statistically significant.

Hypothesis 2: Public expenditure on housing policies

This section repeats the same exercise using macrolevel indicators for public expenditure on housing policies. In this case, it is evident that no clear association can be observed for any of the three indicators (Figure 7.3). Indeed, in most countries, such benefits assume a very low level, and most of the dots are skewed to the left side of the graph near to zero. This is particularly the case for rent benefits (first panel

Figure 7.3: Indicators for expenditure on housing policies (rent benefits, housing benefits, housing and social exclusion benefits) and average marginal effect (AME) of being unemployed on housing autonomy

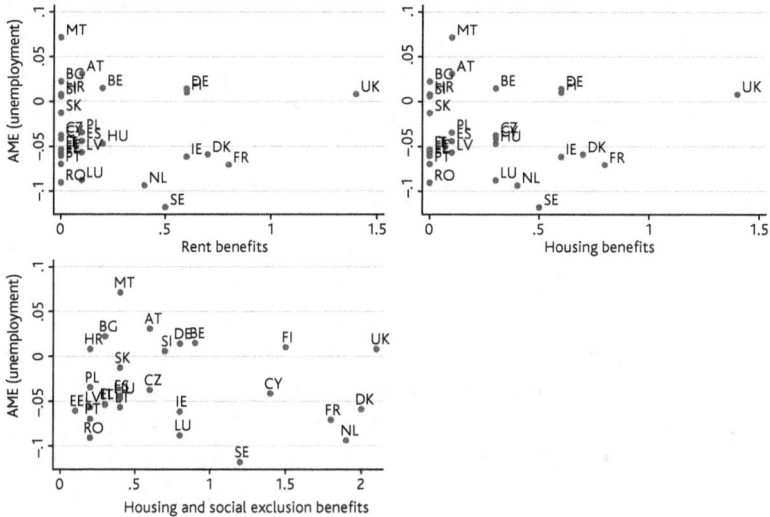

Source: Authors' own elaboration on EU-SILC UDB, 2014 and Eurostat data

in Figure 7.3) that are almost equal to zero (as a percentage of GDP) for most countries with the only exceptions being the UK, France, Denmark, Ireland, Finland, and Germany (and to a lesser extent the Netherlands and Sweden). However, for these countries, the relationship between unemployment and housing autonomy can also assume directly opposing outcomes: in Finland, Germany, and the UK, high expenditure in rent benefits (as a percentage of GDP) is associated with a neutral effect of unemployment on housing autonomy, whereas the association is negative for the other countries. A very similar pattern can be observed for housing benefits (second panel in Figure 7.3), with the same countries mentioned before in the same position, joined by a small group of countries – Cyprus, the Czech Republic, and Hungary – with a slightly negative effect of unemployment on housing autonomy (smaller than 5 percentage points). Again, most countries are skewed towards zero and no pattern can be identified.

As far as the indicator on expenditure for housing and social exclusion is concerned, a clear pattern is not observable. Nonetheless, two groups of countries seem to emerge (third panel in Figure 7.3). Indeed, no clear correlation can be spotted between level of expenditure and association between unemployment and housing autonomy. However, there is a group of countries on the right side of the graph that is characterised by relatively high levels of expenditure (greater than 1per cent of GDP). However, they show very different outcomes in terms of the effect of unemployment on housing autonomy.

There is a second group of countries characterised by a medium to low level of expenditure (between 0.5 per cent and 1 per cent of the GDP) that again show very different outcomes ranging from a negative, a null, or even a positive association between unemployment and housing autonomy.

However, it has to be considered that there may be a positive correlation between higher levels of expenditure for social exclusion policies and higher levels of poverty or social vulnerability in the country – in other words, the level of expenditure is not really high because policies are more developed, but because there is a high number of recipients due to diffuse social vulnerability. Such a situation may correlate negatively with unemployment, given that, in a situation of diffuse poverty and social vulnerability, such compensatory policies are not really able to tackle the dimension of housing autonomy, but can only satisfy basic needs. Hence, it emerges that the level of expenditure cannot play any moderating effect on the relationship between unemployment and housing autonomy.

In this respect, it would be interesting to further investigate the cases of Finland and the UK with more detailed qualitative data. These countries have a similar null association between unemployment and housing autonomy, but relatively high expenditure on rent and housing benefits. Moreover, Denmark, France, and the Netherlands also reveal a negative microlevel association and relatively high levels of public expenditure. For the remaining countries, the level of expenditure is extremely low, with the consequence that it cannot be expected to make any difference.

Second, as for other types of policies (for example, passive labour market policies), strict eligibility criteria may result in there being a very restricted number of people who can actually benefit from these measures. This may eventually exclude particular categories and result in subsidies being of a limited amount. For example, young people are generally excluded from social housing projects that tend to assign apartments to large families with dependent children, or they may be excluded because of fragmented and non-standard working careers that do not entitle them to access such benefits. Thus, from a macrolevel perspective, it is hard to grasp a possible moderating effect. This is also

Table 7.3: Second step regression for macrolevel indicators of housing policies and the association between unemployment and housing autonomy; linear regression coefficients

	Rent benefits	Housing benefits	Housing and social exclusion benefits
Expenditure on rent benefits	0.0122		
	(0.0248)		
Expenditure on housing benefits		0.0119	
		(0.0255)	
Expenditure on housing and social exclusion			−0.00201
			(0.0143)
Constant	−0.0451***	−0.0455***	−0.0407***
	(0.0106)	(0.0113)	(0.0139)
Observations	28	28	28
R^2	0.009	0.008	0.001

Note: Standard errors in parentheses. *** p<0.01, ** p<0.05, + p<0.1
Source: Authors' own elaboration on EU-SILC UDB, 2014 and Eurostat data

influenced by the way such policies are designed, often leaving out the category of interest: young people.

Indeed, the associations using linear regression models in the second step of the multilevel approach (Table 7.3) show that indicators of public expenditure on housing policies have a weak moderating effect (about 1 percentage point – not statistically significant) on labour market exclusion and youth housing autonomy.[3]

Conclusions

Leaving the parental home is a crucial transition in the process of becoming an adult. It is also a complex decision involving several dimensions on the micro-, meso-, and macrolevels. Individuals make their decisions based on economic circumstances, cultural aspects, and personal preferences. However, they are also influenced by macrolevel factors determined on the institutional level that may make the transition smoother (or harder).

This chapter focused on the latter aspect and tested whether and to what extent a particular set of macrolevel factors may moderate the association occurring on the microlevel between labour market (involuntary) exclusion and the housing autonomy of young people in Europe.

Economic factors are not the only predictor of housing autonomy. In several countries, the presence of a partner, for example, is another strong determinant of the probability of living independently from the family of origin. Nonetheless, the job situation is important in structuring life courses, and the availability of economic resources from paid labour is the main source of income particularly for young people, providing them with the means to bear the costs of independent living. Moreover, this is a domain in which empirical research can provide targeted policy suggestions, and in which policies may intervene more effectively than in other domains (for example, in the cultural sphere).

Using microlevel data from EU-SILC and macrolevel data from OECD and Eurostat, this study tested whether institutional configurations such as the level of EPL for regular and for temporary contracts, and the level of public expenditure in housing policies, may moderate (worsen or loosen) the microlevel association between unemployment and housing autonomy. The microlevel association tends to be negative in most of the EU28 countries considered, indicating that unemployed individuals have lower chances of living independently from the family of origin compared to their employed peers. Findings from multilevel models indicate that a clear-cut moderating effect is not observable for any of the two measures taken into consideration. But there are some important differences.

Indeed, as hypothesised, a negative moderating effect is observable depending on the level of protection of regular contracts. A high level of EPL for regular contracts negatively moderates (worsens the mostly negative) association between unemployment and housing autonomy, indicating that in segmented labour markets in which regular employment is protected and it is harder for unemployed young people to get a new job, the negative effect of lack of job on the chances of independent living is further exacerbated. However, no significant moderating role is observable in this respect for the level of protection of temporary contracts. As far as the relationship between unemployment and housing autonomy is concerned, different degrees of regulation of temporary contracts are not associated with regular patterns of decreasing or increasing chances of independent living for young unemployed people. This is consistent with the ambiguous role of EPL for temporary contracts, as highlighted in the literature, which is also tightly linked to the characteristics of the labour market. Indeed, restrictions in the use of temporary employment may on one hand lead to upward mobility to permanent jobs in efficient labour markets and under favourable economic conditions; on the other hand, however, they may lead to downward mobility and unemployment in conditions of low job mobility and an economic recession.

Similarly, the analyses show that public policies aimed at supporting housing do not significantly moderate the (negative) relationship between unemployment and housing autonomy for young people in Europe. Indeed, the level of public expenditure tends to be very low in many of the European countries considered. Its distribution divides into two main groups: on the one side, countries with very limited or even non-existent investment in housing policies; on the other side, a small group of countries with relatively generous spending (the UK, Denmark, Finland, France, Germany, Ireland, the Netherlands, and Sweden). Both groups however, show heterogeneous outcomes when the microlevel association between unemployment and housing autonomy is taken into consideration. In this respect, the two-step multilevel modelling becomes particularly informative insofar as it gives a clear picture of the ongoing trends and points to interesting cases that may be investigated further with qualitative data. As an example, further investigation of cases such as the UK and France (with relatively high expenditure) or Austria and Spain (with relatively low expenditure) but opposite outcomes on the microlevel, may provide interesting insights into the mechanisms behind the functioning of policies. Indeed, findings point to the importance of considering qualitative aspects such as the design of the policies, policy mechanisms, eligibility rules, and barriers to specific groups if one wants to fully grasp whether or not measures put into place to buffer microlevel events achieve their potential. Moreover, behind these aggregate data, other critical features may be at work such as the role of parental support (Ronald and Lennartz, 2018). Indeed, intergenerational support for housing (in the form of financial contributions or gifts, exchange, or housing inheritance) has emerged as an important alternative to (the lack of or underdeveloped) housing policies. Nonetheless, the growing role of family resources as a substitute for welfare for younger generations raises important issues of intergenerational equity and of widening social inequalities among the children of different families.

Notes
[1] Information about the partner represents an endogenous variable in the model that may create overcontrol bias because unemployment also affects chances on

the marriage/partner market. Therefore, findings with and without partner are compared in the results section.
2. In this respect, it has to be considered that with cross-sectional data, one cannot get rid of a reverse causation problem, because although one is able to observe the characteristics of individuals who are already out of parental home, the conditions under which these individuals took the decision to exit the parental home are not known.
3. The association remains non-significant after recoding expenditure variables into dichotomous variables, as a further check due to the very low levels of expenditure that characterise some countries reveals.

References

Aassve, A., Billari, F.C., Mazzuco, S. and Ongaro, F. (2002) 'Leaving home: a comparative analysis of ECHP data', *Journal of European Social Policy*, 12(4): 259–75.

Aassve, A., Davia, M.A., Iacovou, M. and Mazzuco, S. (2007) 'Does leaving home make you poor? Evidence from 13 European countries', *European Journal of Population / Revue Européenne de Démographie*, 23(3–4): 315–38.

Aassve, A., Billari, F.C. and Ongaro, F. (2001) 'The impact of income and employment status on leaving home: Evidence from the Italian ECHP sample', *Labour*, 15(3): 501–29.

Baranowska, A. and Gebel, M. (2008) *Temporary Employment in Central- and Eastern Europe: Individual Risk Patterns and Institutional Context*. Mannheimer Zentrum für Europäische Sozialforschung, Working Paper 106, Mannheim: Mannheimer Zentrum für Europäische Sozialforschung.

Baranowska, A. and Gebel, M. (2010) 'The determinants of youth temporary employment in the enlarged Europe: do labour market institutions matter?', *European Societies*, 12(3): 367–90.

Baranowska-Rataj, A., Bertolini, S., Bolzoni, M., Goglio, V., Martino, S., Meo, A., Moiso, V., et al (2016) *Report on the Impact of the Institutional Setting and Policies on the Autonomy of Youth in Insecure Labour Market Positions in EU-28 & Ukraine*. EXCEPT Working Papers, WP No. 9, Tallinn: Tallinn University, Available from: https://www.except-project.eu/working-papers/

Barbera, F., Negri, N. and Zanetti, M. (2010) 'Introduzione', in N. Negri and M. Filandri (eds), *Restare Di Ceto Medio*, Bologna: Il Mulino, pp 15–46.

Barbieri, P., Cutuli, G. and Scherer, S. (2014) 'Giovani e lavoro oggi: uno sguardo sociologico a una situazione a rischio', *Sociologia del Lavoro*, 136: 73–98.

Becker, S.O., Bentolila, S., Fernandes, A. and Ichino, A. (2010) 'Youth emancipation and perceived job insecurity of parents and children', *Journal of Population Economics*, 23(3): 1047–71.

Bernardi, F. and Poggio, T. (2004) 'Home ownership and social inequality in Italy', in K. Kurtz and H.P. Blossfeld (eds), *Home Ownership and Social Inequality in Comparative Perspective*, Stanford: Stanford University Press, pp 187–232.

Bertolini, S. (2018) *Giovani Senza Futuro? Insicurezza Lavorativa e Autonomia Nell'Italia di Oggi*, Roma: Carocci.

Bertolini, S. (2021a) *Flessibilmente Giovani: Percorsi Lavorativi e Transizione Alla Vita Adulta Nel Nuovo Mercato Del Lavoro*, Bologna: Il Mulino.

Bertolini, S. (2021b) 'La relazione tra flessibilizzazione del mercato del lavoro e formazione della famiglia: come si decide in condizioni di incertezza lavorativa', in M. Naldini, C. Solera and P.M. Torrioni (eds) *Corsi Di Vita, Generazioni e Mutamento Sociale*, Bologna: Il Mulino, pp 47–67.

Bertolini, S., Goglio, V., Moiso, V. and Torrioni, P.M. (2019) 'Leaving home in insecure conditions: the role of labour market policies and the housing market in Europe', *Studies of Transition States and Societies*, 10(3): 9–27.

Billari, F.C. and Liefbroer, A.C. (2007) 'Should I stay or should I go? The impact of age norms on leaving home', *Demography*, 44(1): 181–98.

Blossfeld, H.P. (ed) (1995) *The New Role of Women: Family Formation in Modern Societies*, Boulder: Westview Press.

Blossfeld, H.P., Buchholz, S., Hofäcker, D. and Bertolini, S. (2012) 'Selective flexibilization and deregulation of the labor market: the answer of Continental and Southern Europe', *Stato e Mercato*, 96(3): 363–90.

Blossfeld, H.P., Klijzing, E., Mills, M. and Kurtz, K. (eds) (2005) *Globalization, Uncertainty and Youth in Society*, London: Routledge.

Bonoli, G. (2004) 'New social risks and the politics of post-industrial social policies', in K. Armingeon and G. Bonoli (eds) *The Politics of Post-Industrial Welfare States: Adapting Post-War Social Policies to New Social Risks*, Abingdon: Routledge, pp 3–26.

Booth, A.L., Dolado, J.J. and Frank, J. (2002) 'Symposium on temporary work: introduction', *The Economic Journal*, 112(480): F181–F188.

Breen, R. and Buchmann, M. (2016) 'Institutional variation and the position of young people: a comparative perspective', *The Annals of the American Academy of Political and Social Science*, 580(1): 288–305.

Bryan, M.L. and Jenkins, S.P. (2013) *Regression Analysis of Country Effects Using Multilevel Data: A Cautionary Tale*, IZA Discussion Papers, No. 7583, Bonn: Institute of Labor Economics (IZA).

Bryan, M.L. and Jenkins, S.P. (2016) 'Multilevel modelling of country effects: a cautionary tale', *European Sociological Review*, 32(1): 3–22.

Buchmann, M.C. and Kriesi, I. (2011) 'Transition to adulthood in Europe', *Annual Review of Sociology*, 37(1): 481–503.

Buck, N. and Scott, J. (1993) 'She's leaving home: but why? An analysis of young people leaving the parental home', *Journal of Marriage and Family*, 55(4): 863–74.

Cicchelli, V. (2013) *L'autonomie Des Jeunes: Questions Politiques et Sociologiques Sur Les Mondes Étudiants*, Paris: La Documentation Française.

Corijn, M. and Klijzing, E. (eds) (2001) *Transitions to Adulthood in Europe*, Netherlands: Springer Netherlands.

Ebralidze, E. (2011) 'Labor market regulation and perceived job insecurities in the early career: do Danish employees worry less?', in H.P. Blossfeld, D. Hofäcker and S. Bertolini (eds) *Youth on Globalized Labour Markets*, Opladen, Farmington Hills: Verlag Barbara Budrich, pp 93–118.

Ermisch, J. (1999) 'Prices, parents, and young people's household formation', *Journal of Urban Economics*, 45(1): 47–71.

Eurostat (2018) 'Social protection (spr)', Glossary, Available from: https://ec.europa.eu/eurostat/cache/metadata/en/spr_esms.htm [Accessed 12 November 2018].

Fernandes, A., Becker, S.O., Bentolila, S. and Ichino, A. (2008) 'Income insecurity and youth emancipation: a theoretical approach', *The B.E. Journal of Economic Analysis & Policy*, 8(1): 1–42.

Galland, O. (2001) 'Precarietà e modi di entrare nella vita adulta', in C. Saraceno (ed) *Età e Corso Della Vita*, Bologna: Il Mulino.

Gallie, D. (2007) 'Welfare regimes, employment systems and job preference orientations', *European Sociological Review*, 23(3): 279–93.

Gebel, M. (2009) 'Fixed-term contracts at labour market entry in West Germany: implications for job search and first job quality', *European Sociological Review*, 25(6): 661–75.

Gebel, M. and Giesecke, J. (2016) 'Does deregulation help? The impact of employment protection reforms on youths' unemployment and temporary employment risks in Europe', *European Sociological Review*, 32(4): 486–500.

Giuliano, P. (2007) 'Living arrangements in Western Europe: does cultural origin matter?', *Journal of the European Economic Association*, 5(5): 927–52.

Goldscheider, F.K. and Goldscheider, C. (1989) 'Family structure and conflict: nest-leaving expectations of young adults and their parents', *Journal of Marriage and Family*, 51(1): 87–97.

Goldscheider, F.K. and Goldscheider, C. (1996) *Leaving Home Before Marriage: Ethnicity, Familism, and Generational Relationships* (reprinted edn), Madison: University of Wisconsin Press.

Heinz, W.R. (2001) 'Lavoro e corso di vita: prospettive di ricerca comparative', in C. Saraceno (ed), *Età e Corso Della Vita*, Bologna: Il Mulino, pp 335–55.

Holdsworth, C. and Morgan, D. (2005) *Transitions in Context: Leaving Home, Indpendence and Adulthood*, Maidenhead: Open University Press.

Huber, J.D. (2005) 'Institutional context, cognitive resources and party attachments across democracies', *Political Analysis*, 13(4): 365–86.

Iacovou, M. (2010) 'Leaving home: independence, togetherness and income', *Advances in Life Course Research*, 15(4): 147–60.

Jacob, M. and Kleinert, C. (2008) 'Does unemployment help or hinder becoming independent? The role of employment status for leaving the parental home', *European Sociological Review*, 24(2): 141–53.

Jusko, K.L. (2005) 'Applying a two-step strategy to the analysis of cross-national public opinion data', *Political Analysis*, 13(4): 327–44.

Kahn, L.M. (2010) 'Employment protection reforms, employment and the incidence of temporary jobs in Europe: 1996–2001', *Labour Economics*, 17(1): 1–15.

Lewis, J.B. and Linzer, D.A. (2005) 'Estimating regression models in which the dependent variable is based on estimates', *Political Analysis*, 13(4): 345–64.

MacDonald, R., Shildrick, T., Webster, C. and Simpson, D. (2005) 'Growing up in poor neighbourhoods: the significance of class and place in the extended transitions of "socially excluded" young adults', *Sociology*, 39(5): 873–91.

Mayer, U.K. (1997) 'Notes on a comparative political economy of life courses', in L. Mjoeset, F. Engelstad, G. Brochmann, R. Kalleberg and A. Leira (eds) *Comparative Social Research*, Greenwich: JAI Press, pp 203–26.

McElroy, M.B. (1985) 'The joint determination of household membership and market work: the case of young men', *Journal of Labor Economics*, 3(3): 293–316.

Mills, M. and Blossfeld, H.P. (2003) 'Globalization, uncertainty and changes in early life courses', *Zeitschrift Für Erziehungswissenschaft*, 6(2): 188–218.

Moreno, A. (2012) 'The transition to adulthood in Spain in a comparative perspective: the incidence of structural factors', *YOUNG*, 20(1): 19–48.

Mortimer, J.T., Oesterle, S. and Krüger, H. (2005) 'Age norms, institutional structures, and the timing of markers of transition to adulthood', *Advances in Life Course Research*, 9: 175–203.

Mulder, C.H. and Clark, W.A.V. (2000) 'Leaving home and leaving the state: evidence from the United States', *International Journal of Population Geography*, 6(6): 423–37.

Mulder, C.H., Clark, W.A.V. and Wagner, M. (2002) 'A comparative analysis of leaving home in the United States, the Netherlands and West Germany', *Demographic Research*, 7(17): 565–92.

Müller, W. and Gangl, M. (eds) (2003) *Transitions from Education to Work in Europe: The Integration of Youth into EU Labour Markets*, Oxford: Oxford University Press.

Nilsson, K. and Strandh, M. (1999) 'Nest leaving in Sweden: the importance of early educational and labor market careers', *Journal of Marriage and Family*, (61)4: 1068–79.

Noelke, C. (2016) 'Employment protection legislation and the youth labour market', *European Sociological Review*, 32(4): 471–85.

Nunziata, L. and Staffolani, S. (2007) 'Short-term contract regulations and dynamic labour demand: theory and evidence', *Scottish Journal of Political Economy*, 54(1): 72–104.

Oppenheimer, V.K., Kalmijn, M. and Lim, N. (1997) 'Men's career development and marriage timing during a period of rising inequality', *Demography*, 34(3): 311–30.

Parisi, L. (2008) 'Leaving home and the chances of being poor: the case of young people in Southern European countries', *Labour*, 22(1): 89–114.

Ronald, R. and Lennartz, C. (2018) 'Housing careers, intergenerational support and family relations', *Housing Studies*, 33(2): 147–59.

Rovny, A.E. (2014) 'The capacity of social policies to combat poverty among new social risk groups', *Journal of European Social Policy*, 24(5): 405–23.

Ruspini, E. (2015) 'Role and perceptions of women in contemporary Italy', in A. Mammone, E. Parini and G. Veltri (eds) *The Routledge Handbook of Contemporary Italy: History, Politics, Society*, London, New York: Routledge, pp 64–76.

Scherer, S. (2004) 'Family and Work, in Changequal Network: State of the Art Report', Available from: https://cordis.europa.eu/

Schizzerotto, A. (ed) (2002) *Vite Ineguali: Disuguaglianze e Corsi Di Vita Nell'Italia Contemporanea*, Bologna: Il Mulino.

Schofer, E. and Meyer, J.W. (2005) 'The worldwide expansion of higher education in the twentieth century', *American Sociological Review*, 70(6): 898–920.

Shanahan, M.J. (2000) 'Pathways to adulthood in changing societies: variability and mechanisms in life course perspective', *Annual Review of Sociology*, 26(1): 667–92.

Surkyn, J. and Lesthaeghe, R. (2004) 'Value orientations and the second demographic transition (SDT) in Northern, Western and Southern Europe: an update', *Demographic Research*, 3(3): 45–86.

Taylor-Gooby, P. (ed) (2004) *New Risks, New Welfare: The Transformation of the European Welfare State*, Oxford: Oxford University Press.

Vitali, A. (2010) 'Regional differences in young Spaniards' living arrangement decisions: a multilevel approach', *Advances in Life Course Research*, 15(2–3): 97–108.

Walther, A. (2006) 'Regimes of youth transitions: choice, flexibility and security in young people's experiences across different European contexts', *YOUNG*, 14(2): 119–39.

8

Is housing autonomy still a step towards adulthood in a time of job insecurity?

Sonia Bertolini, Rosy Musumeci, Christina Athanasiades, Anastasia Flouli, Lia Figgou, Vassiliki Deliyanni-Kouimtzi, Veneta Krasteva, Maria Jeliazkova, and Douhomir Minev

Introduction

This chapter focuses on how housing autonomy affects the transition to adulthood among youth in Italy, Greece, and Bulgaria. The three countries represent two different models of welfare regime: the Southern and the Eastern European regimes. However, in terms of economic situation and policies, especially for young people, they are quite similar. All three countries are also characterised by a collectivist culture, strong family relations that compensate for the fragmented and residual welfare systems, and highly valued social support networks that also include intergenerational ones. Furthermore, during the last decade, the inhabitants of all three countries have suffered serious problems in the economic sphere with very high rates of youth unemployment. In Greece, the financial crisis was particularly severe; in Bulgaria, there are high levels of emigration among young people.

These situations have seriously limited youth autonomy, emotionally, psychologically and financially, and especially for some groups of young people who depend heavily on their parents' economic status and capital.

In all three countries, young adults are late leavers – that is, they continue to live with their parents up to the age of 29, compared to youth from northern and central European countries who exit the parental home sooner. According to the literature (Chtouris et al, 2006), this lengthy period of living with the family of origin may delay the transition to a financially independent and socially integrated adult life. Questions about the way young people perceive this delay in the context of social and economic hardship, how they construct their adult identity, and which factors have the greatest influence on this process, remain unanswered.

Previous literature indicates, however, that housing autonomy is a crucial marker for the transition to adulthood (Sokou and Papantoniou, 2000; Baranowska et al, 2015). This chapter asks whether housing autonomy still represents a crucial step towards adulthood among youth in countries in which they suffer from economic recession and flexibilisation of the labour market, and in which young people leave home late either as couples (married) or after at least one of the partners (usually the male) has a secure job.

Although a number of quantitative studies point to the fact that flexibilisation of the labour market has postponed housing autonomy, there are no studies addressing these questions from a qualitative perspective that focus particularly on the voices and experiences of young people. This chapter addresses this issue.

State of the art

According to traditional theories of transition to adulthood, leaving the parental home is always considered a step towards becoming an adult. See Chapter 1 in this volume for a literature review. In this paragraph we focus on specific literature relating to the three countries that are the focus of this chapter: Italy, Greece, and Bulgaria. *Housing autonomy*, in particular, is considered important, because it is one of the explicit markers of the achievement of individual independence and the assumption of roles of responsibility. Furthermore, the way in which a young person leaves home is also important because of its interdependence with and consequences for other spheres of life with which it is strictly linked. For example, living independently is considered a step towards adulthood that is related to taking full responsibility for one's actions and being able to create an identity independent of that of one's parents. Leaving the parental home is also a transition that makes other key transitions to adulthood possible.

As mentioned before, leaving the parental home is traditionally considered an important step towards adulthood in Italy, Greece, and Bulgaria. However, young people in these countries traditionally leave the parental home later than youth in Northern and Central Europe, and usually after they have found a permanent job or have started a new family by getting married. For young people in Southern Europe, the main reason to leave the parental household has been 'to settle down' within a stable two-person relationship (Saraceno, 2001), preferably through marriage, rather than starting a period of experimentation with independent living that is the popular exiting model among young people in Northern Europe. Intergenerational support and family help are usually considered central to gaining housing autonomy in these countries (Ronald and Lennartz, 2018).

Bulgaria is one of the countries in which young people live with their parents until a later age than their peers in other EU countries. Young women leave home earlier than young men, but more often to move in with a partner than to live on their own. The reasons why Bulgarian youth continue to live with their parents are predominantly economic. The low labour incomes and high poverty rates mean that considering the idea of a home of one's own is not an option. Due to this situation, young people's short-term strategies are centred around meeting basic needs. The young people targeted in our research are in a vulnerable position and highly dependent on their parents who, as a rule, do not have much in the way of financial resources at their disposal. Thus, housing independence is becoming a marker of belonging to high-income status groups (for the young persons themselves and/or their parents). Additionally, many young people, according to other research (Mitev and Kovacheva, 2014), see living with their parents as the easiest solution. Taking this decision also reflects a cultural norm in Bulgarian society that parents should care for their children 'as long as they can' (Mitev and Kovacheva, 2014: 82). In Bulgaria, staying at home for a prolonged period is regarded by young people as being 'obvious' (European Commission, 2005: 88). Life in the parental home gives youth 'more freedom to choose their own lifestyle, even if in the family home, in addition to enjoying the financial and practical advantages of living with their parents' (Mitev and Kovacheva, 2014: 82).

Recently, however, as a result of the complexity of the labour market, transition to adult life has become an increasingly multifaceted process. The transition to a more autonomous and independent way of living appears to be a prolonged, diverse, or even at times reversible process (Mitchell, 2006). This makes adulthood a rather complex and less linear notion to define. Various studies have shown the existence of a variety of transition models that do not conform to a general standard and do not display a gradual linear movement, but have great heterogeneity (Mayer, 2001). Due to the reduction in their welfare and residential independence, the numbers of young people returning to their parental home after losing their jobs or after finishing their studies with their parents' financial assistance are growing constantly. Under these circumstances, cohabitation with the parental family reflects how contemporary labour market factors are strongly affecting family dynamics. This reality is further reinforced by the fact that traditional benchmarks such as marriage, becoming a parent, establishing a separate household, and obtaining employment are no longer perceived as prerequisites of an adult identity, but as personal preferences and choices (Furstenberg et al, 2004).

The social capital of young people in Greece consists basically of family, relatives, and friends. These completely replace the non-existent welfare state system. In other words, the Greek nuclear family has been traditionally the primary protective mechanism that supports young people both financially and emotionally for a lengthy period of time (Sokou and Papantoniou, 2000; Chtouris et al, 2006). When young people are also university students, this carefree period is prolonged; Greek society places such great value on higher education that parents do not expect their children to work while studying (Sokou, 1987). Instead, they believe that they should be able to provide everything for them without them having to depend on state resources or other external support.

The two patterns of family formation, which are found among European young people, come with different kinds of exchange and forms of support across families and kin, as well as different options available to young people, as suggested by Cavalli and Galland (1996). On the one hand, early exit from the parental household can be supported by cultural values, but also by a favourable labour and housing market as well as welfare state provisions. On the other hand, if the family is the main financial resource and the housing market is tight, it is more difficult for young people to leave the parental household when they are not yet established in the labour market. Furthermore, it is more expensive for their parents to help them to live on their own. In addition, if the family culture does not support educational strategies oriented towards early independence and autonomy, it is obvious that the transition to adulthood will take much longer.

Evidence from recent research has shown that job insecurity delays decisions regarding transition to adult life such as leaving the parental home (Blossfeld et al, 2005; Nazio, 2008; Bertolini, 2011; Blossfeld et al, 2011; Jansen, 2011; Reyneri, 2011; Bertolini et al, 2018). However, these studies are quantitative, and they do not explain the preferences or the mechanisms behind this postponement. Is it that housing autonomy is no longer central to the process of becoming an adult? Do young people still believe that housing autonomy is important, but find themselves forced to postpone it, with significant negative consequences for their well-being?

Institutional context

As mentioned in the introduction, the three countries in this analysis differ in terms of their welfare regime models – Southern and Eastern – but are quite similar in terms of their economic situation and policies, especially for young people.

Regarding young people's behaviours, they are similar in that young adults are late leavers compared to youth from Northern and Central European countries who exit the parental home at earlier ages (Chtouris et al, 2006).

This is especially true for Italy where exit from the parental home follows a 'latest-late model' (Billari, 2004). In fact, Italians leave the parental home on average when they are 30 years old (Eurostat). The proportion of young people aged 18–34 years still living with their parents in Italy in 2016 is 66 per cent (the average in Europe is 48 per cent). For men it is 72 per cent and for women, 60 per cent.

Similarly, according to Eurofound (2014), young Greeks leave the parental home at the age of 29, thus postponing their hopes of autonomy and independence (Marvakis et al, 2013). In detail, the age by which half of all young people in Greece have left the parental home was 31.5 for men and 26.3 for women in 2011 – that is, 5.2 and 3.0 years respectively above the EU28 average (Eurofound, 2014).

In addition, the family safety net, which used to be the primary source of income for unemployed youth in Greece, has recently come under great pressure because parents are also having to face unemployment and salary cuts. Therefore, it comes as no surprise that the poverty rate is now highest among couples living with their grown-up children (Matsaganis and Leventi, 2014). Also, according to Mudler and Clark (2002), there appears to be a positive association between parental income and the propensity to return home as well as between personal income and the likelihood of moving out of the parental home (Iacovou, 2010).

Regarding Bulgaria, data over the years indicate a continuous rise in the age at which young Bulgarians leave their parental home. Whereas in 2004, they left home at the age of 28.3 years, in 2016 this was 29.4 (the general EU average is 26.1 years). This is due to different factors. First, the socio-economic landscape has been characterised for more than 20 years by a high degree of poverty and social exclusion (40.4 per cent in 2016 according to Eurostat), poor quality of life, low quality of jobs on the labour market, and permanent and huge flows of internal and external migration. Although with fluctuation, this was also associated with a shortage of jobs in most of the years up to 2017. Recently, unemployment has decreased and a shortage of labour has been declared, although thousands of young people continue to be listed as not in education, employment, or training (NEET). Nevertheless, recent data again confirm that about 25 per cent of the young people living in the country still intend to leave it – most often due to the unsatisfactory quality of available jobs.

Second, data from population and housing censuses show that the proportion of Bulgarians owning their own homes is high and considerably higher than in other European countries (97.5 per cent in 2011). The number of homes has been increasing since 1965, and it is still continuing despite a slowdown since 1992. The parallel negative population growth leads to a discrepancy and a consequent decrease in the number of inhabitants per home. At the same time, the situation is quite different in big cities compared with smaller towns and villages. Overcrowded dwellings and poor condition of the housing stock are reported for those parts of the big cities in which vulnerable groups usually live. In contrast, in smaller settlements, houses are purposefully built to accommodate several generations. Therefore, they provide opportunities to live relatively independently. Indeed, many of these houses allow residential autonomy for families while living under the same roof (as Bulgarians say ironically: 'See another person who built a school for a house'). Hence, in many cases, it is not just a parents' home, but often a multifamily house ready to settle different families (regardless of whether the property belongs formally to the parents or, as in many cases, has already been transferred legally to the children).

Research questions

Starting from this theoretical background, this chapter will focus on:

1. What does housing autonomy mean for young people with respect to transition to adulthood?
2. Which factors do young people believe may interfere with housing autonomy?
3. What kind of coping strategies do young people use to achieve personal and/or housing autonomy, and how do young people cope with their need for independence if they still live with their parents, but feel deprived of housing autonomy?

Data and methodology

The empirical material analysed in this chapter is composed of 133 qualitative interviews conducted with young people as part of the EXCEPT project in Bulgaria (43), Greece (40), and Italy (50). Chapter 1 of this volume describes the process and the characteristics of the qualitative research.

Nineteen of the 40 interviewed young people in the Greek sample, 25 out of the 50 in the Italian sample, and 25 out of the 43 in the Bulgarian sample were aged 18 to 24 years; the others were aged 25 to 30 years.

Of the 40 young people in the Greek sample, 14 did not live in their parents' home, including those living with partners or roommates. Four of these were unemployed, two had temporary jobs, four had non-contractual jobs, and four were classified as NEET. In the Italian sample, 14 young people out of 50 lived independently (alone or in partnerships) at the time of the interview. Three of them were unemployed, one had a non-contractual job, and the rest (ten) were permanent or temporary workers. Among the Bulgarian interviewees, 15 young people out of 43 lived alone or in partnerships outside their parents' home. Five of them had secure jobs; six had temporary jobs; two were unemployed; one had a non-contractual job, and one was classified as NEET.

Table 8.1 shows that about a third of the Greek sample aged 18 to 24 years (7 out of 19) lived alone or in partnerships, the highest proportion of the three samples. At the opposite extreme, in the Italian sample, only a sixth of the young interviewees aged 18 to 24 years (4 out of 25) lived alone. Among the older interviewees aged 25 to 30 years, half of the Bulgarian sample lived alone (9 out of 18), whereas only one third of the Greeks (7 out of 21) lived independently, the lowest proportion among the three national samples.

In the group aged 25 to 30 years, two of the seven Greek young people living outside their parents' home were unemployed, one had a temporary job, three had non-contractual jobs, and one was NEET. In the group aged 18 to 24 years living outside their parents' home, one had a temporary job, two were unemployed, one had a non-contractual job, and three were NEET.

Table 8.1: Number of interviewees by age and housing status

	Italy	Greece	Bulgaria
18–24 years, living alone	4 (25)	7 (19)	6 (25)
18–24 years, living with parents	21 (25)	12 (19)	19 (25)
25–30 years, living alone	10 (25)	7 (21)	9 (18)
25–30 years, living with parents	15 (25)	14 (21)	9 (18)

Note: Total numbers in parentheses.

In the Bulgarian sample, in the group aged 25 to 30 years, four of the nine young people living outside their parents' home had secure jobs, three had temporary jobs, one had a non-contractual job, and one was unemployed. In the group aged 18– to 24 years, one of the six young people living outside their parents' home had a secure job, three had temporary jobs, one was unemployed, and one was NEET.

In the Italian sample, 16 people (10 women and 6 men) had a low risk of social exclusion. All but two of them were working (in temporary or permanent jobs, 2 had non-contractual jobs). One half of the Italian interviewees with a low risk of social exclusion lived with their parents; the other half lived alone. The majority were either partially (10) or totally (2) autonomous in economic terms.

Findings

Meanings of housing autonomy

In Italy, the majority of young people interviewed (Bertolini et al, 2018) had a general acceptance of the idea that, even as adults, children remain in the family because of traditional values and strong familial links. This was expressed particularly strongly by young people from the south of Italy, the Sicilian city of Catania.

At the same time, however, some interviewees considered it to be very important to become autonomous, especially as they grew older. Young people usually believed that moving out of the parental home implied starting a new family. This is undoubtedly a very traditional notion of the transition to adult life, particularly when compared to previous generations, but it still seemed to be present in Italy – at least as an ideal path:

> 'The fact that I still live with my [parents] I do not know, maybe in Sicily is a normal thing because only when I get married, I can go out from my parental home. This is something normal in Sicilian tradition [laughs] [pause] For now, I consider living with my parents to be a normal thing because all of my friends are living with their parents but also when someone is employed, she or he cannot go away from home because we are in Sicily and one cannot escape from the parental home.' (Concita, F, 23, ME, U, IT)

Bearing in mind that this traditional background is linked to the cultural and institutional context, the perception of centrality of housing autonomy in the process of becoming an adult varied widely in relation to the age, gender, and job situation of the interviewees.

For the interviewees in the younger age group, it seems that leaving the parental home is often not perceived as an urgent need, but rather as an idea that they translated into a more practical plan when engaged in a stable relationship. In some of these cases, the lack of housing autonomy created frustration. For example, Camilla (F, 22, ME, U, IT) referred to the frustration created by not having a (permanent) job and income, with the result that housing autonomy and the life that she would like to live (getting married soon to her current boyfriend, and having a house and some children) were not attainable. Camilla seemed to be stressed particularly by the length of time that achieving these goals might take; she was afraid of repeating the experience of her older sisters who had been engaged for a long time but were only able to marry after many years because of their lack of work. She would like to leave her parental home and live with or marry her boyfriend "right now".

In some cases, such an idea was considered to be a step that would take place sometime in the future under the right conditions (job/money). In other cases, they had simply not considered it yet.

On the other hand, it also seemed that the permanence of living in the parental home was, in some cases, taken for granted as the natural way of things for younger people regardless of their job situation: "I'm not old. It's not that I'm 30 and I'm still at home. I'm 22 and I'm forming and I'm trying to create my future, right?" (Renata, F, 22, ME, U, IT).

The group aged 25 to 30 years revealed a change in perspective. The desire to move out was usually expressed as being more urgent, whereas living in the parental home seemed to be something that required explanation and some motives. The transition to autonomous living was seen as a step towards adulthood, and expectations that it would actually take place became all the more relevant as time passed by. Therefore, the feeling of being unable to take this step, on the one hand, or the decision to postpone it despite a favourable juncture, on the other hand, seemed to need explanation and justification.

Older interviewees without a job described the issue in even more pressing terms. For them, moving out appeared to be a strongly desired, but painfully unattainable step:

I: What would make you decide to move out? What is lacking now?

R: The money, really, the money, I mean, I love them, there will be chances to see each other, but [pause] no, it's only the money, otherwise I would have been out already. Because at a certain point, you reach an age at which [pause] you really need to be by yourself [pause] or with someone else you choose to be with. (Mara, F, 29, ME, U, IT)

They had reached a certain age and a point in their lives at which they should live on their own in order to develop their personalities and become independent from their parents.

For young people in Greece, independent living appeared to be linked to the concept of autonomy. Most referred to their need to live alone, away from the parental home, so as to be able to act independently and shape their lives of their own accord. This rhetoric applied both to those who had already left the parental home as well as those who were still living with their parents. This can be seen in the following extracts:

I: I see [pause] and what made you leave the parental home?
R: It was my need for autonomy, my need to have my own space, to have my own life [pause] the truth is that my parents would interfere with my life because we were living together [pause] so I couldn't always be myself and do the things I liked because my parents wouldn't approve [pause] in general you don't feel [pause] that you have the chance to develop, the chance to do the things you like, to have interests [pause] you feel like you have to answer to your parents the way you did as a kid. So certainly, you don't feel like an adult, like a person who stands on her own feet and is an adult. (Labrini, F, 27, HE, U, living alone, EL)

According to the previous two extracts, leaving the parental home was associated with autonomy and adulthood. In their own words, independent living offers young people the opportunity to live their own lives and make decisions without being accountable to parents, which is the essence of becoming an adult.

Furthermore, young people in Greece realise that housing autonomy is important for personal development as well as for moving forward in life. They acknowledge the fact that parents will not always be around to take care of things. Therefore, they feel they should be able to stand on their own feet and take on responsibility for themselves and their expenses.

However, even when it comes to the young people who already live alone, the majority still depend on their parents for financial resources, either because they are unemployed and in search of work, or because their wages do not suffice to cover their expenses. Thus, as shown in the following extracts, their autonomy is considerably limited, highlighting the fact that spatial and independent living alone do not necessarily lead to full autonomy (either psychological or financial).

> I: Uh in general, is your money enough?
> R: Uh, not always. My parents help me, at least for the time being, because it hasn't been long since they left and since I've been on my own, so I still try to find my balances. Yes so, if things get hard I tell my dad and he sends me money, since he has a job and a good salary in England … on the other hand, I don't want to ask for money, I want to feel autonomous. Yes, if things get hard, I ask him [for money]. (Valeria, F, 24, ME, TE, living alone, EL)

On the other hand, young people who were still living with their parents during the interviews, despite their financial dependency, regarded themselves as autonomous and at least emotionally independent. In the following two extracts, Foteini and Spiros explain that they feel autonomous in a way, because they are able to take care of themselves or make decisions about their lives. Nevertheless, at the same time, they admit that their autonomy is limited due to financial dependency and co-living conditions that are dictated basically by the financial crisis and the limited opportunities for employment.

> 'I think I am 100 per cent (autonomous), meaning that if you leave me alone in a house, I know how to do everything, I am completely autonomous. But financially speaking, this pulls me back, it takes all my autonomy back, because I can't support myself, I don't have the money to do so, I can't find the money, no one gives me the chance to get the money, so this pulls me back.' (Foteini, F, 20, ME, U, living in parental home, EL)

Overall, what becomes obvious from the previous extracts is a competing association between financial/housing autonomy and the transition to adulthood. On the one hand, young people acknowledge the importance of being economically independent and living separately from parents in order to become adults; on the other hand, they feel at least partially autonomous and capable of taking independent decisions even though they continue to live with their parents due basically to external socio-economic conditions.

For most young Bulgarians, adulthood is tightly linked with the ability to make decisions about one's life and to take responsibility for the consequences of these decisions. Many of the young Bulgarians consider themselves to be autonomous, because they can decide for themselves even when they live in their parents' home. However, most of them (regardless of their housing position) share the view that at a certain point of time, all young individuals have to leave their parents' home. This idea is perceived more or less as a default option, an important part (but not the first one) of the transition from adolescence to adulthood. Young people consider the act of leaving their parents' home as a natural outcome of their transition from adolescence to adulthood. In other words, when they reach a certain age, it is time for them to move:

I: And actually, what did make you leave, to decide to live independently?
R: Well, I'm 26 and in my point of view, it is right for a young adult to have a place of their own, to live independently, and to move from parents, from everybody, because this is the right thing to do. You cannot stay at mommy and daddy's place all your life. (Biliana, F, 27, HE, TE, living alone, BG)

In general, the idea of housing autonomy is more often related to setting up one's own family and having children. Most of the interviewees consider that having their own family and children is an important prerequisite to thinking about housing autonomy. Of course, even in these cases, there is the possibility of living together with parents, especially when there is sufficient housing space.

Eva (F, 21, LE, NEET, BG) sees it as quite normal to live with her parents until she finds a husband, to whose home she will then move. She is a girl of Roma origin, without education and employment. Eva is happy with her situation. She thinks that she will leave her parents' home when she gets married, but not at all costs: "It is normal that we live with them [her parents]. We will stay with them until the time comes." Although living with them, she feels independent and shares the information that occasionally, when the others are out of money, she helps the family out with her savings.

However, for another group of young people, housing autonomy seems illogical, financially irrational, and not adequately responsive to family relations. Katya, who is living with her parents says: "And once I have home, I have my room, my space. So, this is just cohabitation, no, no interference. And my parents are extremely supportive. So, in any case, I don't see why I should leave" (F, 29, HE, TE, living in parental home, BG).

It could be said that some kind of psychological independence and economic autonomy (especially labour remuneration) is very important for the young people, whereas housing autonomy is not prioritised.

Prerequisites for housing autonomy in different institutional contexts

Even today, young people in Italy still consider having a stable job and economic autonomy to be a prerequisite for housing autonomy. It is relevant to stress here that housing autonomy is perceived ideally as a consequence of gaining economic autonomy and job stability, even if it is not at all clear how exactly they can achieve this. Lacking such knowledge seems to halt every decision. In addition, housing autonomy proves to be strictly linked to the idea of a secure income:

> I really want to go and live alone in Turin. I've never taken this step, because first, I have a brother who is ill and so we try to help him, and second, because I'm often away, and it is useless to pay rent if I'm gone, because I have no fixed income. (Anna, F, 27, HE, TE, IT)

Knowing that you will not be able to get any allowances should your income decrease, and understanding that parental support is linked to living under the same roof certainly appears to be driving all young people in Italy in Anna's direction. Indeed, there is little endorsement of the idea of moving to a place of their own while simultaneously asking for help from your parents and looking for work.

Similarly, according to the Greek interviewees, having a secure job is very important for young people to help them organise their lives, be independent, and make plans for the future. In the following two extracts, Alice, like other interviewees, insists that a stable job paying a standard amount of money every month is important for them in order to take the step towards independent living.

> R: The fact that I still can't support myself financially because, I still don't have a secure job [pause] and by secure, I mean

I: that every single month I would certainly get my salary no matter ... truly this is the only thing that holds me back.
I: So, if you were to get your money every month you would leave?
R: Yes, if I knew for certain that I would get the money, I would leave and rent my own apartment so as to start my own life, stand on my feet, and be autonomous and in a position to take care of my own finances. (Alice, F, 25, ME, U, living in parental home, EL)

The fact that a stable job with high earnings is a prerequisite for housing autonomy is also reflected in the experience of young people who used to live alone but were obliged to return to their parents' family home when they lost their jobs. For example, in the following extract, this situation is described by a young man who was obliged to move back in again with his parents, with negative consequences for his everyday life and well-being.

'Yes ... uh I can tell that this is an issue that [pause] of course it was hard for me at first, because basically I was living on my own for some time so, I got myself in a situation where I had to return back ... I stopped working from [pause] well it was a high earning job ... so, I had to go back home because. I had no savings [low voice].' (Nikos, M, 27, HE, NCJ, living in parental home, EL)

The Bulgarian National Youth Strategy (Ministry of Labour and Social Policy, 2011: 19–20) asserts that the main reason Bulgarian young people continue to live with their parents is the lack of financial means to rent or buy a home of their own. The extremely low wages, which barely cover basic needs, often mean that the salary or wage is the most important feature of a job, and they minimise their ambitions with regard to security, availability of a contract, future prospects, housing and living conditions. Most of the young people interviewed emphasise that the salary is the most important aspect of a job.

Anton (M, 24, HE, TE, living in parental home, BG) lives with his parents who are supporting him during his studies. He would like to move out of his parents' home, but he would not consider buying or renting. He regrets that his parents do not have another apartment. Otherwise, he would move out immediately. "Oh, yes. After all, I'm 24 and I want to be more independent. When I find a permanent and well-paid job, I will leave immediately." The only thing that stops him is that he has no steady income to cover all his costs.

He does not feel comfortable when he acknowledges that his parents help him financially.

Another factor that influences the decision to leave the parental home is the responsibility of taking care of elderly people. In several cases, the young interviewees feel an obligation to support and care for their parents and grandparents.

Vanio lives with his mother and grandmother, but he does not feel restricted by living with them and does not want to live anywhere else:

> 'I don't need another place. I feel good in our house. I can't leave my mother and grandmother alone. They can't do on their own [pause] Why be worried? Our house is 80 square metres, on two floors. I'm alone on the second floor [pause] I'm already a big man. I am not a child; I even feel like a head of the family [pause] Well, we mutually help each other [pause] [if we live together]?' (Vanio, M, 18, LE, NCJ, living in parental home, BG).

In some cases, the young people do not even think about living independently, not only because of the lack of income but also due to subjective feelings of fear of feeling isolated and a preference for living next to people with whom you have strong bonds of mutual help.

Coping strategies for housing autonomy in times of labour instability

In Italy, for those with a job, an added reason for continuing to live in the parental home was that they need either to save enough money to afford their own place before moving out or to ensure that they would be able to support themselves in the future.

When it comes to the mechanisms that link a weak attachment in the job market to postponing exiting the parental home, the interviews showed that attitudes have changed compared to those highlighted in previous research (Blossfeld et al, 2005). Indeed, job insecurity is likely to make it impossible for young people to make optimal life course decisions: the suspension of the decision appears to be the mechanism young people use to manage high insecurity and uncertainty. They tend to shift towards a short-term decision-making horizon because self-binding decisions become problematic.

In Italy, young people continue to believe that it is essential to have a stable job and a secure income before attaining housing autonomy and completing the process of reaching adulthood:

'And [pause] have a family [pause] Having a job, a steady job [emphasis] and a child [pause] also have some time to spend with the family. This is being [pause] adult, in quotes, to me.' (Dante, M, 19, LE, U, IT).

However, the institutional context in which they are embedded, which has scarcely invested in policies for youth, does not support young people to reach the steps of transition to adult life. In these situations, they are forced to make decisions under conditions of uncertainty in which the probabilities associated with one's career choices are unknown (Bertolini, 2011) and the probability to reach a stable job is very low. The interviews reveal how leaving one's family of origin today is no longer just postponed, as evidenced by some previous research conducted in Italy, but is pushed further and further into the future and mostly 'dreamed of' rather than actually planned. In fact, the interviewees have no clear idea of the intermediate steps they must take to achieve their goals, nor do they have any idea of the tools that this process would require.

Indeed, perhaps as a result of ever decreasing job opportunities due to the economic crisis, it appears that job insecurity in Italy prompts young people to consider only the immediate present or the foreseeable future (which – as already noted – is dreamed of rather than planned).

In this view, youth have to focus entirely on the present; consequently, autonomy is limited both in time and space. And that is exactly what prevents young people from making up their minds to leave their family of origin. For the present sample, being autonomous mostly means managing daily or short-term economic problems and decisions and being able to pay for their leisure-time expenses or a little more. Of course, this could also be due to the fact that it is difficult for economic reasons to leave the parental home, especially in countries in which institutional support and job policies are limited. It may be that young people are adapting to the constraints of their situation, readjusting their preferences downwards (Elster, 1999), and building a new rhetoric to justify their situation and hide the fact that they are the losers in globalisation.

Similarly, young people in Greece cannot count on the support of policies to leave the parental home. Instead, they rely almost exclusively on the financial support of their immediate family. This has always been a huge issue in Greece, because family seems to support young people in a variety of life dimensions and actually replaces state welfare services.

In their effort to move forward in life and make plans for the future, young people in Greece adopt a variety of strategies in order to save money and achieve their wishes. For example, in the following extract, Vaso explains that, for the time being, she is staying with her parents in order to save money and make a new start abroad.

> 'Meaning that, I know that this situation goes on because right now, financially it's to my advantage to keep on living with my parents for a couple more years and thus save money and be able to start anew abroad with more security uh [pause] despite trying something here and live alone here because I see no future.' (Vaso, F, 28, HE, TE, living at parental home, EL)

There are also a couple of interviewees who even postponed their independent living and remained in their parental home in order to save money and realise their plans for the future, such as to buy a house or to study abroad.

> 'Financially maybe I would have the means to, let's say to rent my own place, but I don't think that it would be necessary for the time being. Meaning that, to me it's a priority to save uh to save money. Maybe to buy at some point (a house), when things get better.' (Stavros, M, 28, HE, TE, living partially with parents, EL)

Another strategy with which to achieve independent living is to move away with somebody else (a partner, for instance) in order to share expenses and make ends meet.

> 'My boyfriend lives in a house [pause] in a house with his brother, the two of them, and their parents help them with the bills and all that [pause] uh and he suggested that when we will both be in a good place financially [pause] just stable not necessarily good … to rent a house the two of us and this is a prospect that I like [pause] it's very positive mainly because I think that I won't be able to do this on my own [pause] and a roommate helps a lot.' (Victoria, F, 27, HE, U, living in parental home, EL)

In Bulgaria, young people rely mainly on support from their parents in order to live outside the parental home. A number of interviewees pointed out that parents help their children financially even though they do not live with them. However, being able to provide support is highly dependent on the parents' own economic situation. As most of the respondents are socially excluded and this is often inherited from their parents, the capacity of these parents to sufficiently support their children is likely to be quite limited.

Some of the interviews show that life outside the parental home is only possible for young people if they share a dwelling and expenses with friends or a partner. Petar (M, 29, HE, PE, BG) has higher education and has worked in his specialty ever since he graduated (he is a psychologist). However, the salary he earns does not allow him to rent home of his own. That is why he lives with a roommate, with whom he shares the cost of the house. "If I had to live absolutely alone, to meet absolutely all the costs and bills, it would be practically impossible." He is convinced he could not support a family on the salary he earns.

Another strategy contemplated by some young people is to take a loan from a bank to buy a home. Several people mentioned this option, all of whom had partners and planned to pay back the loan together. Ekaterina (F, 24, HE, PE, BG) lives in her parents' home in Sofia together with her boyfriend, her brother, and her brother's girlfriend. They do not pay any rent and they share the expenses; thus, they manage to cope. Despite this, the situation is not satisfactory for her because she wants to live independently with her boyfriend. To deal with this situation, they plan to get a loan from a bank and buy their own flat. "Of course, I would be happier if I were alone with my boyfriend because I like to have personal space."

However, getting a housing loan is usually a wish, rather than a realistic option. The young respondents talked about this option, but almost none of them had pursued it. This is because of the huge economic risk involved which young people are not ready to take. It is all closely connected with young people's job situation. Ani (F, 24, HE, U, living in parental house, BG): "Absurd! In my current situation – there is no way! Without a decent job and taking into account the current level of salaries, and the prices [pause]. You must be very bold and rather stupid to get a mortgage."

One way young people cope with their need for independence when they live with their parents is to adjust their subjective feelings of autonomy to the available opportunities. As mentioned at the beginning, the idea that young people are autonomous when it comes to taking decisions for themselves and that they feel independent although they live with their parents is echoed in most of the interviews. One example of how some young Bulgarians accept their situation is the story of Sotir (M, 20, ME, U, living in parental home, BG). He lives with his girlfriend in his parents' home along with his sister and brother. Despite this, he feels that he is independent because he is already an adult and his parents cannot interfere in his decisions.

Sotir feels independent in his actions, although he is receiving financial support from his parents. For him, the financial support is accepted as something normal: parents should support their children. He believes that it is too early to be separated from his parents, especially now when there is no work and he cannot stand alone.

Conclusions

The transition process can have dissimilar paths, in which housing autonomy can be achieved along different modalities.

In Greece, as in Italy and Bulgaria, and in contrast to countries in the north of Europe, there is a general acceptance of the idea that even adult children remain in the family. However, some of the interviewees consider it very important to become autonomous.

In Italy, the process of transition to adulthood may take different pathways in which housing autonomy is constructed in different ways. One possible interpretation is that the diffusion of job insecurity does not allow young people to leave the parental home, and as a consequence, many young adults readjust their preferences (readjustment of preferences downwards, see Elster, 1999) and construct a new rhetoric to justify their situation, suggesting that leaving the parental home is not central.

Greek youth think that it is important to live alone in order to achieve independence. At the same time, however, they admit that financial hardship and job insecurity limit their housing autonomy. Therefore, they try to act as adults and take decisions/control over their lives even though they remain in their parental home.

In all three countries, young people usually believe that moving out of the parental home implies starting a new family. This is undoubtedly a very traditional notion of the transition to adult life, particularly when compared to previous generations, but it still seems to be present in these countries, at least as an ideal path.

Even if the desirable model in Bulgaria is the same, one difference appears to be that Bulgarian people tend to live with their parents even when they get married. This is linked to the economic background. Although young people in Bulgaria aspire to autonomy, they prioritise their well-being over housing autonomy, for example. This is linked to high fragmentation: young people in families with low economic status especially have to address many other and more basic needs before considering housing autonomy – particularly when living in the parents' home is possible. In summary, in Bulgaria, the analysis of interviews suggest that the transition to maturity and the drive toward autonomy are primarily focused on improving the individual economic situation – in particular, finding jobs with adequate pay –to meet daily needs rather than focusing attention on long-term planning. In many cases, this is not related directly to living in a separate home, especially when the relationships in the family are good, the structure of dwelling allows relative autonomy for different occupants, and the total available area and living space per person are adequate.

The comparison between the countries raises some interesting questions. First, even though the three countries have different welfare state systems, young people appear to have similar problems, and they seem to have access to similar policies and programmes. Are the Mediterranean and Eastern European welfare state systems similar with respect to youth policies?

In all three countries, family ties seem to be very strong, and they protect young people during the transition to adult life in terms of both housing and the economic situation. Whereas quantitative data show a postponement of housing autonomy in times of labour instability, the statements of young people reveal the diffusion of a new modality of becoming an adult. Looking at labour market conditions – low incomes in Bulgaria, long-term unemployment in Greece, labour market precarity in Italy, and the fact that young people in these countries generally have no access to unemployment insurance (because of the contributory system in all three countries) – extended cohabitation with parents becomes a normal step. In this regard, leaving the parental home is no longer considered an important step towards becoming an adult, or at least not the only way to become an adult in a time of economic constraints. It is possible to live in the parental home in the long-term as in Italy; live together but apart from parents, or return to the parental home if needed as in Greece; or form a family but still live in the same house as parents as in Bulgaria.

Autonomy seems possible inside the family in these countries. This result suggests a reflection about the consequences of this model transition into adulthood. This produces very strong links between generations and very limited territorial mobility. Does this have consequences in terms of limited capacity for autonomy among young people in a flexible labour market?

And what are the consequences in the case of a mismatch? A prerequisite of labour market flexibility is a high degree of territorial mobility. Can the labour market adjust to the mismatch suggested by these findings? And, finally, how far is this a model for a 'liquid society'?

References

Baranowska-Rataj, A., Bertolini, S., Ghislieri, C., Meo, A., Moiso, V., Musumeci, R., Ricucci, R. and Torrioni, P.M. (2015) *Becoming Adult in Hard Times: Current and Future Issues on Job Insecurity and Autonomy*, Turin: Accademia University Press.

Bertolini, S. (2011) 'The heterogeneity of the impact of labour market flexibilization on the transition to adult life in Italy: when do young people leave the nest?', in H.P. Blossfeld, D. Hofäcker and S. Bertolini (eds) *Youth on Globalised Labour Markets: Rising Uncertainty and its Effects on Early Employment and Family Lives in Europe*, Opladen, Farmington: Verlag Barbara Budrich Publishers, pp 163–87.

Bertolini, S., Deliyanni-Kouimtzi, K., Bolzoni, M., Ghislieri, C., Goglio, V., Martino, S., Meo, A., Moiso, V., Musumeci, R., Ricucci, R., Torrioni, P.M., Athanasiades, C., Figgou, L., Flouli, A., Kostouli, M. and Sourvinou, M.N. (eds) (2018) *Labour Market Insecurity and Social Exclusion: Qualitative Comparative Results in Nine Countries*. EXCEPT Working Papers, WP No. 53, Tallinn: Tallinn University, Available from: https://www.except-project.eu/working-papers/

Bertolini, S., Hofäcker, D. and Torrioni, P.M. (2018) 'Does contractual stability matter? The impact of labour market flexibilisation on the first transition to adult life in France, Germany and Italy', *Studies of Transition States and Societies*, 10(3): 28–50.

Billari, F. (2004) 'Becoming Adult in Europe: A Macro(/Micro)-Demographic Perspective', *Demographic Research Special Collections*, 3(2): 15–44.

Blossfeld, H.P., Klijzing, E., Mills, M. and Kurz, K. (eds) (2005) *Globalization, Uncertainty and Youth in Society*, London: Routledge.

Blossfeld, H.P., Hofacker, D. and Bertolini, S. (eds) (2011) *Youth on Globalised Labour Markets: Rising Uncertainty and its Effects on Early Employment and Family Lives in Europe*, Opladen, Farmington: Verlag Barbara Budrich Publishers.

Cavalli, A. and Galland, O. (eds) (1996) *Senza Fretta di Crescere. L'Ingresso Difficile Nella Vita Adulta*, Naples: Liguori.

Chtouris, S., Zissi, A., Papanis, E. and Rontos, K. (2006) 'The state of youth in contemporary Greece', *Young*, 14(4): 309–22.

Elster, J. (1999) *Alchemies of the Mind: Rationality and the Emotions*, Cambridge: Cambridge University Press.

Eurofound (2014) *Mapping Youth Transitions in Europe*, Luxembourg: Publications Office of the European Union.

European Commission (2005) *Families and Transitions in Europe (FATE)*, Luxembourg: Office for Official Publications of the European Communities.

Furstenberg, F.F., Kennedy, S., McLoyd, V.C., Rumbaut, R.G. and Settersten, R.A. (2004) 'Growing up is harder to do', *Contexts*, 3(3): 33–41.

Iacovou, M. (2010) 'Leaving home: independence, togetherness and income', *Advances in Life Course Research*, 15(4): 147–60.

Jansen, M. (2011) 'Employment insecurity and its repercussions on family formation: a theoretical framework', in H.P. Blossfeld, D. Hofäcker and S. Bertolini (eds) *Youth on Globalised Labour Markets: Rising Uncertainty and its Effects on Early Employment and Family Lives in Europe*, Opladen: Verlag Barbara Budrich, pp 39–68.

Marvakis, A., Anastasiadou, M., Petritsi, I. and Amagnostopoulou, T. (2013) 'Youth shows the way - but whither? Youth and extreme right in Greece', *FES-Athens*, 2 February 2014, Available from: http://www.fesathens.org/pages/ellinikos/drasis/enantia-stin-akrodexia.php

Matsaganis, M. and Leventi, C. (2014) 'The distributional impact of austerity and the recession in Southern Europe', *South European Society and Politics*, 19(3): 393–412.

Mayer, K.U. (2001) 'The paradox of global social change and national path dependencies: life course patterns in advanced societies', in A.E. Woodward and M. Kohli (eds) *Inclusions and Exclusions in European Societies*, London: Routledge, pp 89–110.

Mitchell, B.A. (2006) 'The boomerang age from childhood to adulthood: Emergent trends and issues for aging families', *Canadian Studies in Population*, 33(2): 155–78.

Mitev, P.E. and Kovacheva, S. (2014) *Young People in European Bulgaria: A Sociological Portrait 2014*, Sofia: Friedrich Ebert Foundation.

Mulder, C.H. and Clark, W.A. (2002) 'Leaving home for college and gaining independence', *Environment and Planning A: Economy and Space*, 34(6): 981–99.

Nazio, T. (2008) *Cohabitation, Family and Society*, London: Routledge.

Reyneri, E. (2011) *Sociologia del Mercato del Lavoro*, Bologna: Il Mulino.

Ronald, R. and Lennartz, C. (2018) 'Housing careers, intergenerational support and family relations', *Housing Studies*, 33(2): 147–59.

Saraceno, C. (ed) (2001) *Età e Corso Della Vita*, Bologna: Il Mulino.

Sokou, K. (1987) 'Unemployment in a developing country: the case of Greece', in D. Schwefel, P.G. Svensson and H. Zollner (eds) *Unemployment, Social Vulnerability and Health in Europe*, Berlin: Springer, pp 118–28.

Sokou, K. and Papantoniou, V. (2000) 'Youth unemployment and health in Greece', in T. Kieselbach (ed) *Youth Unemployment and Health*, Wiesbaden: Springer, pp 139–52.

9

Becoming economically autonomous: young people in Italy and Poland in a time of job insecurity

Antonella Meo, Valentina Moiso, Jędrzej Stasiowski, and Zofia Włodarczyk

Introduction

Previous research on young people has focused mainly on the attainment of housing autonomy as a key marker of their transition to adulthood by showing that it has major consequences for life course outcomes such as socio-economic status and well-being (Galland, 2000; Buchholz et al, 2009; Tosi, 2017). A growing body of literature has analysed the consequences of youth unemployment and job precariousness for their autonomy mainly in terms of postponing departure from the parental home and forming one's own family (Mills and Blossfeld, 2005; Liefbroer and Toulemon, 2010). In this framework, less attention has been paid to the economic dimension of young people's autonomy.

This chapter aims to fill this gap by providing empirical evidence on the crucial role of attaining economic autonomy in the contemporary transition to adulthood. Young people are increasingly affected by flexible forms of employment, face a higher risk of unemployment, and take longer to establish themselves in stable and continuous employment (Blossfeld et al, 2005; Baranowska and Gebel, 2010; Armano et al, 2017. This situation increases young people's difficulties in becoming economically autonomous, especially in countries with a more flexible and unregulated labour market in which institutional protection is also on a low level.

By investigating the economic dimension of autonomy, this chapter explores how labour market disadvantages affect youth perspectives on their economic security and how they define autonomy subjectively in light of their available resources. Specifically, the focus is on the *subjective* dimension of economic autonomy and on its links to both young people's self-representations and their perceptions of job insecurity in two different countries: Italy and Poland.

Theoretical considerations

In the sociology of youth, the transition perspective has provided the main framework for analysing autonomy (Galland, 1991; Bynner, 2005; Molgat, 2007; Manzoni, 2016). The youth period has been constructed as a stage of life between childhood and adulthood (Kelly, 2001). Whereas childhood is associated with physiological immaturity, emotional and economic dependence, and primary ties to parents and siblings, adulthood is framed in terms of psychological maturity, emotional and economic autonomy, and primary ties to an adult partner and children (Freeland, 1991). Traditionally, the so-called five main markers have defined the transition to adulthood as finishing formal education, entering the labour force, leaving the parental home, getting married, and becoming a parent (Galland, 1991; Hareven, 1994).

Against this background, research on the change in young people's transitions from youth to adulthood has stressed their ongoing destandardisation, individualisation, and fragmentation (Bruckner and Mayer, 2005; Elzinga and Liefbroer, 2007; Silva, 2012). Scholars analysing the effects of labour market flexibilisation and employment precariousness on youth life courses (Shanahan, 2000; Corijn and Klijzing, 2001) have shown how transitions are increasingly characterised by reversibility and uncertainty (Molgat, 2007). In particular, the transition from school to work has become more discontinuous and less uniform with the labour market options becoming more precarious. However, despite the relevance of youth economic autonomy to their transition to adulthood, there is little research on this issue.

Nevertheless, attaining economic autonomy has become a critical component of the contemporary transition to adult life (Lee and Mortimer, 2009). For many young people, just having a job does not mean attaining economic independence from their parents, and a job is increasingly insufficient to provide adequate economic resources to achieve personal aims and the adult status. As Manzoni (2016) has highlighted, independence from parents does not manifest to the same extent in the various life domains for all young people. For example, they may be residentially independent from their parents but economically dependent on them.

It is important to underline that the literature reveals no agreed or univocal definition of the economic autonomy concept. Some related terms, such as 'independence', 'self-sufficiency', 'self-reliance', or 'self-supporting', can be found. The notion of self-sufficiency became the embodiment of a poverty reduction policy (Hawkins, 2005). Some scholars have examined the role of family socialisation towards work in adolescence in fostering economic self-efficiency, and its subsequent influence on the transition to adulthood, status attainment, and financial independence in young adulthood (Lee and Mortimer, 2009). Other scholars are interested in how circumstances in childhood affect the development of independence in youth by investigating what determines their financial independence in terms of psychological factors such as economic self-efficacy, money management, and problem-solving abilities (Brougham et al, 2011). Individual economic factors such as young people's income and assets, work status, and educational attainment are positively associated with financial independence. Results indicate that family economic factors such as parental income, parental capital, and financial assistance decrease the level of young adults' financial independence (Xiao et al, 2014). Other studies have dealt with the concept of self-sufficiency as having enough resources to meet one's needs without public support, but criticised the vagueness of the concept and its interchangeability with the terms self-reliance and well-being (Hawkins, 2005). The lack of economic autonomy can be regarded as a vulnerability factor (Misztal, 2011). Having low economic autonomy mainly means to be dependent on either the family and/or the state for money transfers or material support – that is, for the latter, dependent on social policies (for example, unemployment benefits). Dependence on others constitutes a significant risk factor that considerably increases the probability of ending up in situations of social vulnerability. Vulnerability does not necessarily involve current material deprivation, but rather insecurity and exposure to risk (Chambers, 1989).

Given the paucity of research on the economic dimension of youth autonomy, this chapter aims to develop a new conceptual framework based on empirical findings that will analyse autonomy among young people from a wider perspective than the transition or the focus on the issue of independence from parents.

Research questions and aims

This chapter tries to answer the following questions. How do youth interviewees define economic autonomy? Do they see themselves as economically autonomous and to what extent? Are young people's subjective job insecurity and self-perceived economic autonomy linked? How does young people's subjective job insecurity affect their perception of the economic opportunities and constraints within which they have to act? How do they perceive their agency in relation to their ability to satisfy their personal needs, given the structural constraints resulting from their weak attachment to the labour market?

The subjective perspectives of Polish and Italian youth on their economic autonomy will be addressed along two main lines of analysis. First, the study will try to address the link between young people's occupational status and their self-perceived economic autonomy by looking at their insecure labour market position as the important structural factor constraining individual options and leeway. Both unemployment and insecure jobs can lead to detrimental economic consequences by hampering youth's achievement of economic independence. Job insecurity has become increasingly evident in European countries in recent years. The literature shows that what matters is also the perception of job insecurity and not only the objective job situation itself (Sverke et al, 2010; Ebralidze, 2011). This chapter will pay special attention to subjective job insecurity, by assuming that feelings of uncertainty about jobs are relevant in defining the opportunities and constraints within which individuals act, and will define their present and future economic needs along with their decisions, choices, and projects. Perceived job insecurity refers to worries about the continuation of their job and the fear of becoming unemployed and thereby losing their job and income (Hartley et al, 1991; Sverke et al, 2002). Moreover, job insecurity concerns the perceived difficulty in finding a first job or a new job after a period of unemployment. Individual evaluations of one's own economic position, as well as subjective definitions of autonomy and self-representations, are intimately intertwined and must be framed in the two national contexts considered here, which are characterised by different institutional settings, social protection systems, and models of solidarity in informal networks.

Second, the study will analyse the variability in self-perceptions of individual autonomy or feelings about becoming adult in terms of the relation between individual economic agency and structural factors. Economic autonomy is defined as the degree to which a person feels independent and self-governing in achieving their own financial goals. The chapter will adopt a bottom-up definition of economic autonomy and explore self-perceived economic autonomy by giving voice to the young people directly. At the same time, it will also investigate factors that affect these self-perceptions: young people's available economic resources, available social support, and their material or financial needs. Finally, it will take into consideration the interviewees' economic agency – the degree to which they decide how to use their individual economic resources themselves and feel themselves to be self-sustaining individuals. According to Walther (2006), in a context of de-standardised transitions to work, young people are required to take decisions that are more individual, and their subjectivities become increasingly important. Although the term *agency* has been defined in different ways (Bandura, 1989; Emirbayer and Mische, 1998), it has been used to refer to a sense of responsibility for one's life course, the belief that one is in control of one's decisions and is responsible for their outcomes (Côté and Levine, 2002; Schwartz et al, 2005). The agency–structure debate has been a perennial, and somewhat intractable, concern in sociology dating back to its founders (see Emirbayer and Mische, 1998). In this chapter, the relationship between economic autonomy and economic agency is considered as worthy of attention. Young people can perceive and speak about their economic agency in terms of different degrees of economic autonomy. Structural conditions, concerning young people's available financial resources and needs, the level and stability of their income, their past working paths, their current economic situation, their parents' economic and cultural capital, family relations, social norms and values, as well as labour market regulation and institutional settings, can be analysed in terms of the structure that restricts or enhances youth economic agency.

Data and method

The sample taken into account here is composed of 90 interviews conducted in Italy and Poland in the period December 2015–November 2016. All semi-structured interviews were recorded, fully transcribed, and analysed according to a shared and common analytical framework. Samples in both countries covered people aged 18 to 30, balanced by gender and level of education, who were atypical workers or unemployed.

The Italian sample consisted of 50 young people (25 men and 25 women); 25 were aged 18 to 24, whereas the other 25 were aged 25 to 30. Regarding their educational level, 26 out of 50 interviewees had a secondary level of education (ISCED 3, only one ISCED 4), 12 had a low level of education (ISCED 0–2), and 12 had tertiary education (ISCED 5–6). In terms of involvement in targeted policies, 27 interviewees had been involved in policy measures, but only one with a form of economic support, and 23 participants had not participated in any such measures.

The original Polish sample consisted of 40 young people, but due to the issue of comparability, we excluded individuals who belonged to the Polish risk group – people with disabilities. Thus, the final sample consisted of 34 individuals, including 16 females. During fieldwork, every second interviewee was living with her or his parents. As regards Polish interviewees' educational level, 21 per cent of interviewees in the sample had lower secondary education (ISCED 2), 50 per cent had finished upper secondary school (ISCED 3-4, two of these had post-secondary non-tertiary education – ISCED 4) and 29 per cent had tertiary education (ISCED 5-6). Half of the Polish sample consisted of people who were targeted by some active labour market policies (ALMPs) – as registered unemployed, they usually had experiences of participating in paid internships, career counselling, or training provided by the local labour offices. However, not a single person among our Polish and Italian interviewees had ever received unemployment benefits at the time of the interviews.

Institutional context

Conducting international comparative research demands a great deal of caution due to numerous contextual differences that might affect final conclusions. Obviously, the qualitative material gathered here comes from two completely different cultural settings. Nonetheless, Italy and Poland do share some cultural similarities. Both countries are described as Catholic, familistic, and collectivistic, with traditional gender-role ideologies (Yodanis, 2005). Polish youth, like Italian youth, tend to stay longer with their parents than the average European. In 2016, the average age of a young Pole leaving the parental household was 28 years; in Italy, it was 30. These numbers place young Poles closer to the Southern European nations than some of their closest neighbours (Eurostat, 2016).

Despite these cultural similarities, the patterns of the Polish economy and Polish labour market institutions are barely comparable to those in Italy. The economy and labour market institutions are among the most important structural factors affecting the individual life trajectories of young people who are starting their working careers. In this area, there are substantial differences between both countries.

In the classic Esping-Andersen typology, Italy is an example of a Southern European welfare state, whereas Poland is a post-socialist, non-liberal welfare state of the post-communist European type (Fenger, 2007). However, over the last decade, the Polish welfare state has evolved into the continental European (Christian Democratic) type

(Aspalter et al, 2009). This has brought the Polish welfare regime closer to the German, Austrian, or French models than the Mediterranean or Southern European models. Although young and precarious workers lack protection in both countries, the direction of recent reforms differ (Bertolini et al, 2018). Looking at ALMPs designed to decrease the length of periods of unemployment, Italy belongs to a group of countries with a low level of investment, whereas Poland has recently started to develop ALMPs directed specifically at youth. In Italy, few active policies are directed towards young people, and there is no national and universal minimum income insurance (Granaglia and Bolzoni, 2016). As regards family policies, there are few work–family measures and limited defamilisation (Saraceno, 2011). In Poland, the importance of active policies for young people is increasing – youth are prioritised as a risk group and targeted with ALMP measures, particularly internships co-financed by the state. Poland places increasing importance on family policies, particularly thanks to the introduction of the national programme 500+ that assigns monthly transfers for the second child in every Polish family (also for the first child in the poorest families). In contrast, Italy belongs to a group of countries in which, both before and after the 2008–09 economic crisis, support of families has remained at a very low level.

In 2013, the unemployment level for early school leavers in Italy was among the highest in the EU (37 per cent). In Poland, it was close to the European average (20 per cent). Similarly, in Poland, the percentage not in employment, education, or training (NEET) among recent school leavers was close to the European average in 2013 (nearly 30 per cent), whereas in Italy, it reached one of the highest levels in the whole EU (exceeding 50 per cent). Italy is ranked among those countries in which the negative effects of the 2008–09 economic crisis were the most significant. It is also a country with the most difficult labour market situation for recent school leavers aged 15 to 29 years (Bello and Cuzzocrea, 2018). Poland, on the other hand, did not experience harsh consequences of the global economic breakdown. In fact, there has been positive economic growth since 2007. Thus, according to the statistics, Polish youth are in a much better situation on the labour market than their Italian colleagues.

However, there are some institutional similarities between the two countries. The Italian labour market is highly regulated and segmented (Barbieri, 2011). In Poland, the labour market is also highly segmented, but it shows a medium level of regulation (Bogumil, 2015). Both countries are characterised by high shares of temporary workers (above 50 per cent, which gives them a leading position in the EU), particularly among youth who have just finished their education (Rokicka et al, 2015). Poland has one of the highest percentages of temporary workers among young employees. Whereas in 2017, the European average was 43.9 per cent, in Poland it was 68.2 per cent and in Italy 61.9 per cent (Eurostat, 2017). A gradual increase in the use of temporary contracts in Poland was driven by 'competitiveness strategies used by employers to minimise labour costs and the increasing weakness of the state' (Lewandowski and Magda, 2017: 149). As a consequence of direct labour market deregulation (Bertolini, 2011), temporary contracts are also popular in Italy.

The two countries involved in this analysis share some aspects of the labour market situation, but it is important to acknowledge that Polish and Italian youth act in completely different institutional settings.

Economic autonomy and job insecurity

Italian youth appear to remain in a more difficult situation on the labour market than their Polish colleagues. Their working trajectories are fragmented and disordered, characterised by various forms of precarious, underpaid, and unprotected work, and by multiple interruptions. They have experienced episodes of unpaid work, late payment, and broken promises of regularisation. These problems are particularly visible in the south of Italy. Costantino (M, 27, LE, TE, IT) shows an awareness of the problems of the labour market in southern Italy and the difficulties in achieving a stable job position because of a structural shortage of qualified job opportunities. His perception of being exposed to job insecurity is linked to his territorial background. Contextual constraints limit his chances of stable integration into the labour market. Edoardo (M, 30, HE, TE, IT) clearly expresses what emerges from the Italian interviewees in terms of worries about job insecurity and economic autonomy: "if the economy went well". Flexibility would offer more opportunity to gain experience, especially for young people with higher education, but also for those who are searching for employment. However, if the institutional context does not support the young people in changing jobs (lack of minimum income scheme and unemployment benefits), they can experience difficulties in finding another job on the labour market and worry about their existing job.

> 'This blessed permanent contract [pause] is not necessarily my goal, and I could exaggerate and say that it is not necessarily the goal of my generation in general. For some, it is a sense of

security, for others it is not. If the conditions were favourable, if the economy went well, there were more opportunities [pause] but what the hell, I've also had three-year contracts and then I had to change! But it is also true that at a certain point then [pause] you want some stability, so even just having a contract would suit me.' (Edoardo, M, 30, HE, TE, IT)

On the other hand, Polish youth, who have experiences of numerous fixed-term or informal jobs, are able to make their own choices thanks to the more favourable labour market conditions. However, the overall picture is more complex, because territorial disparities still play an important role in the Polish labour market. Polish youth living in bigger cities with low unemployment are less concerned about finding a new job. Hence, their unstable fixed-term or informal contracts are not usually accompanied by feelings of subjective insecurity – they are aware that they can always find something else. For example, Magda, living in a small town near the Polish–German border, is not concerned about her temporary contact. The relatively good situation in the local labour market gives her a strong sense of security:

'Because I know that I will always find some job. So, I don't have this pressure, that if I lose this current job, I won't make it, that I will be worried and who knows what else.' (Magda, F, 28, HE, NCJ, PL)

In contrast, youth living in rural areas and smaller towns with a worse situation in the labour market encounter greater problems in finding jobs and are more concerned about losing them. Michalina (F, 26, ME, NCJ, PL) and Adrianna (F, 22, HE, TE, PL) returned to the countryside after their studies to live with their parents. For them, finding a suitable job is barely possible in the local labour market.

In general, in both countries the main concerns of youth are the size and stability of their salaries. A low level of income significantly reduces young people's agency. Consequently, it negatively affects their self-perception as economically autonomous individuals. This point is raised by Carlo from Italy, one of the few interviewees who defines himself as economically autonomous. His dissatisfaction does not seem to be linked to the insecurity of his job, but rather to the low level of his salary.

'The five hours a day you put in at this place [fair trade shop and café] are not enough [pause] now I'm looking for another job, maybe I could go on a vacation the way I'd like to; if I ever do go on vacation, I just make it a longer weekend, going where I want to without having to be too careful about money.' (Carlo, M, 26, HE, TE, IT).

This type of dissatisfaction is also widespread among Italian interviewees who do not define themselves as fully autonomous:

'If I had a contract even in a supermarket, I would take it immediately. I'd continue with the tattoos, like now, but it makes me feel safer to have a fixed contract, I mean a salary. Like this, instead, you live one day to the next, if something comes in good, otherwise [laughs]. And I'm lucky because I still live at home with my parents … or if you wanna have a family, forget it!' (Ester, F, 26, ME, non-contractual and non-paid job, IT).

In Poland, low salaries combined with relatively high rents are a barrier to leaving the parental home:

'Most of all, I would like to have a kid, but not now, not in these times, right? It's just not doable, in general to afford a child, in my opinion. Too low income, too many expenses.' (Konrad, M, 23, ME, U, PL)

Low salaries are a major concern among Polish youth. They are also the reason for the existence of a vast group of partially autonomous youth described in the following paragraphs.

The present analysis assessed whether experiences of job insecurity affect young people's economic agency. Unstable income, feelings of uncertainty and fear of losing a job constrain the individual's freedom of choice. Therefore, young people who find themselves in such a position tend to postpone important life decisions and adopt a short-term perspective. In this sense, the concept of subjective job insecurity can help to explain differences in interviewees' perceptions of themselves as autonomous or not. Subjective job insecurity hampers youth economic autonomy. However, in both countries, worries about job loss, not finding a new job, or income insecurity are not related directly to the type of job contract. An illustrative example also comes from Monika who is one of the three interviewees with permanent job contracts – theoretically the most stable, perceived as a goal of young people's careers, and as a sign of a secure position in the labour market. Monika has worked hard and finally achieved a secure job in public administration. She is in a long-term relationship with her fiancé. However, she does not feel secure in her job, she does not feel fully autonomous, and she is postponing leaving her parental home:

> 'But here, it was actually because there were some rumours that they plan to liquidate the budget-administration teams. So, on the one hand, it's like a budget department, there is this contract for the indefinite period, but as I've said, in case of liquidation no contract will [pause] [local government] can just commission our tasks to the municipal council entity. There is an option that some employees would be transferred there, but it's hard to say what it would look like. So, for the moment it's quiet.' (Monika, F, 29, HE, PE, PL)

Many Polish young people working on fixed-term contracts do not perceive this as a source of uncertainty or insecurity. However, the type of contract is mentioned as an important issue for formal reasons, mainly by people who need it to gain access to certain financial services.

> I: Have you tried with such fixed-term contracts or fee-for-task agreements to buy something in instalments?
> R: It's just not an option. You won't get it from a bank, because I've tried it more than once, just for fun, to check whether it would work out but [pause] no way. You have to have the contract for at least one year. (Lech, M, 28, NCJ, PL)

Even when there are no universal regulations or laws restricting access to credit based on a job contract, the scoring models and risk assessment procedures used by financial institutions to evaluate their clients' financial credibility take the type of contract into account. Having a regular contract significantly increases the probability of getting any type of loan, especially in the case of a home mortgage. This objective dimension of job insecurity depends on the ways in which financial institutions treat various types of job contract. This *institutionalised* job insecurity imposes a structural constraint on youth economic agency and, by this means, it might negatively affect their perceptions of their own level of economic autonomy.

Subjective economic autonomy: agency and its constraints

Whereas quantitative studies make it possible to set the objective threshold of economic autonomy (earnings above a certain level, no risk of material deprivation, living apart from parents), the present analysis shows the fuzzy nature of this concept from a subjective point of view. Young people's perceptions of economic autonomy are shaped by individual assessments of the balance between available resources and personal needs or goals.

Despite the subjective nature of young people's evaluations regarding financial independence, it may be possible to construct an analytical continuum of young people's perceptions of their own economic autonomy. This would start with individuals who feel totally economically dependent on their relatives, pass through a large category of young people who do not feel fully autonomous (partially economically independent), and finish with a category of economically self-governing young people.

Looking at the interviewees' income in their periods of activity in Italy reveals that the amount is relatively small, ranging mostly from €400 to €1,000 per month. In most cases, therefore, the net income earned does not guarantee self-sufficiency. Moreover, most respondents (36 out of 50) live with their parents. Even those who are working define themselves as partially economically autonomous, because they have limited resources that do not allow them to leave home. In fact, for most, the family of origin is the major source of economic support. Only one of the Italian interviewees has access to institutional support but lives with, and depends on, his parents.

The Polish sample has a slightly different composition. Like the Italian group, most of the interviewees do not have sufficient income to fully support themselves, and they assess themselves as not fully economically autonomous (24 out of 34). There are references here to partial economic autonomy or dependency. Only 10 respondents consider themselves completely autonomous. Interestingly, the income declared by autonomous Polish youth (an average of 1860zł per month, roughly equivalent to about €432) does not differ significantly from those who see themselves as partially autonomous (1410zł per month, equivalent to circa €328). The average income of the non-autonomous group is much lower (310zł or about €72 per month).

At the extreme poles of the continuum of economic autonomy

In both countries, only a few respondents define themselves as fully independent from the economic point of view. However, the structural conditions within which they enact their economic agency seem to be very different. In fact, those who declare their full economic autonomy can be divided into two categories differing according to their levels of economic agency. The first is made up of interviewees who perceive themselves as fully economically independent and self-governing in achieving their own financial goals. They can turn to their parents for substantial financial help, but they are able to live apart from their parents without such help. However, this does not mean that they do not accept any form of external support. For example, Łukasz defines himself as economically autonomous; he is not dependent on his parents' financial help. He is living with his fiancée and daughter in a cheaply rented little flat. However, he can count on his family's support when it comes to babysitting his child or other domestic duties:

> 'We just live one block of flats further, so we have my parents just in front of us, parents in law next to us, and my brother lives nearby. So, we live separately, but we have this comfort, that there is always someone around to help us.' (Łukasz, M, 28, HE, TE, PL)

In contrast, the second category of autonomous individuals consists of youth who declare themselves to be economically independent, do not receive informal support from their parents or partner, but provide for themselves and/or their families with significant effort and many sacrifices. They have already left their parental homes, but their economic agency is limited by external factors: mainly low and unstable income combined with a lack of formal and informal support. For example, Marcel and his girlfriend live together in a small rented flat. They cannot count on considerable support from their parents. Their total income is 2,000 zł (about €465) after taxes, and this has to cover the expenses of two people. However, Marcel makes ends meet; he has no financial obligations and perceives himself as fully economically autonomous, but he is aware that they remain in a precarious situation:

> 'It is an OK life, I guess. Although the income I have with my girlfriend [pause] This level of income and the money we live on each month are totally unthinkable for most Poles [pause] but I don't think it's really so bad.' (Marcel, M, 28, ME, TE, PL)

His economic autonomy does not result in a wide range of possible life choices. The economic context and the inadequacy of institutional support do not provide them with the tools they need to foresee and build their future. In his interview, Carlo, who shares accommodation in Italy, presents himself as economically independent and content to live on the money he makes from his part-time job. He works as a salesman and part-time bartender at a fair-trade cafe run by a cooperative of which he is a member-worker.

> 'For me, the important thing is being able to pay rent, eat, and buy cigarettes without having to ask anybody for anything. If I achieve that amount, I am relieved for the bills and the rent. Then the rest, everything else is [pause] extra [pause] It's not that I'm a big spender, other than eating a sandwich when I'm out, or another beer [pause] eating dinner out, going to discos – zero, I also don't travel much, that is, I'll take a train, stay with friends who can host me.' (Carlo, M, 26, HE, TE, IT)

In both samples, few young interviewees define themselves as not being economically autonomous at all. The present research focuses on young adults who have already finished their education and usually have some sources of income other than pocket money from their parents. Young people who describe themselves as non-autonomous have no self-earned income. In Poland, such situations refer to interviewees who are completely financially dependent on their parents, relatives, or social benefits. The last case is quite unique and refers to two single mothers staying in a public shelter whose special status entitles them to allowances (Jowita, F, 28, ME, U, PL; Zuzia, F, 28, LE, U, PL). Both of them treat their social benefits as a normal source of income (Zuzia additionally receives alimony for her child), but they do not have any work and are completely dependent on the formal support they receive. The third case (Damian, M, 19, ME, U, PL), who is one of the youngest in the Polish sample, is still considering starting university, and thus he feels obliged to find any job to support himself. In Italy, especially in the south, cases of people who have no income and live off parental support are more common. Many are unemployed, work in the black economy, or are atypical workers who receive very low and intermittent income. Many belong to working-class or precariat families. When the family of origin is affected by deprivation and material hardship, the interviewees feel themselves to be a burden and feel obliged to help their parents. Lacking income as a result of unemployment, they are forced to live with their parents and give up housing autonomy. Economic dependence and poor living conditions can also compromise their perception of autonomy in terms of being able to make their own decisions, take on responsibility, and make choices. Youth who have left the parental home to attend university or enrol in other educational training programmes (that is, residentially autonomous individuals) also belong to this group. They have never had a stable job and have almost no experience in managing their own money. The link between autonomy and employment emerges as an important issue, in particular, among unemployed interviewees. A general agreement among them is that "if there is no work, there is no autonomy" (Erika, F, 29, LE, NEET, IT). In other words, to become economically autonomous you need an "income from work".

Partially economically autonomous youth

In both countries, the largest category revealed through the analysis is respondents who are in the middle of the continuum; youth who, due to an instable labour market situation or insufficient income, define themselves as partially economically autonomous. Looking at the five classic markers defining the transition to adulthood (Galland, 1991; Hareven, 1994), one might say that the interviewees who are partially economically autonomous are stuck somewhere between the stage of entering the labour market and the following stages of leaving the parental home or starting their own family. Their life situations are very different. They have some income from work or training, but it is insufficient and often discontinuous. This makes them dependent on informal social support. The latter varies a lot in form (financial, material, housing) and degree. Usually, the main source of support is parents or other relatives. They work on more or less regular temporary contracts, working informally, or receiving a small remuneration as part of a training scheme financed, in Poland, by the district labour office. Their income, compared to their needs, is not sufficient to move out of the parental home. Thus, they cannot think about themselves as being fully economically independent. Low income constrains their economic autonomy – they cannot view themselves as being fully autonomous; they cannot leave the parental home or start their own family:

> 'Now being independent has become my priority. Now I'm trying to do everything not to be dependent anymore. Because I just feel that, at this age, you already have some experience, and living with your family, in quite a small flat, it's just tiring and irritating. It's been five years that I'm with my girlfriend, and after such a time it would be cool to live together, the only problem is just a lack of funds.' (Damian, M, 23, ME, U, PL)

> 'Being autonomous simply means having the [pause] economic resources that allow you to support yourself, to have a home even

if paying rent, and [pause] to think of yourself and take care of yourself at the very least, at least for yourself.' (Franco, M, 30, HE, NCJ, IT)

However, interestingly, their evaluations of their level of economic autonomy are based on the universal need for youth to think about themselves as being, at least partly, independent individuals.

> 'With €500 per month, I could maintain my scooter, always considering that I did not have to help anybody else (living with his parents) and I only had myself to think of, right? However, I already had to think about motorcycle insurance, gasoline, my own stuff [pause] some gifts for my girlfriend based on my salary. Yes, I feel quite autonomous.' (Matteo, M, 28, ME, U, IT)

Even though they are unemployed or in temporary work with low pay, they often reframe their subjective definition of economic autonomy to fit their current life situation and sustain their perception of themselves as (partially) independent.

> 'In general, I'd say I'm at 90 per cent. Because I support myself financially, I do everything by myself, the washing machine, everything by myself. Sometimes, I ask my mum about the degrees for the wash, just to be a little [pause] and then my ADSL [internet connection] and my phone, my dad's paying for them, but the rest, petrol, insurance, rent, my dogs, I pay for it all. I do everything by myself and don't ask anyone for help, like ironing, washing, I do it all, I do my own shopping, I take the dogs out by myself, I've got no one to give me a hand. Yes, alright, sometimes they do it to help me.' (Emma, F, 19, ME, TE, IT)

The money at their disposal allows them to cover some of the everyday, short-term expenses: paying for the phone, going out with their friends, having a coffee or dinner in the city, paying for fuel for their cars, or contributing a little to the household budget. For example, Adrianna (F, 22, HE, TE) makes about 1,200 to 1,400 zł a month, of which 850 zł is internship remuneration, and the rest – a few hundred zlotys that varies from month to month – is extra money she makes cleaning or singing in a band. She spends the money on her needs, including car fuel, cosmetics, clothes, and, occasionally, lunch at work. Her parents cover accommodation and grocery expenses. She has no savings of her own, and rarely manages to put some money aside for the next month.

'Well, I seem to be independent, but only based on these internships, so I have some money on my own, but if I have to move out, pay for some room just by myself, I wouldn't be able to afford it. So, I'm not entirely independent. My parents always help me somehow, and I have a roof over my head and some food in the fridge.' (Adrianna, F, 22, HE, TE, PL)

Partially autonomous young people often stress their ability to cover personal or individual expenses. Despite living with their parents, both Italian and Polish youth stress that that they do not have to ask parents for money for every single need. Having their own, self-earned money provides them a space for executing their agency. Feelings of being an autonomous person involve, for many respondents, the possibility of acting independently in managing their income, keeping their expenses under control, and being able to also save a little money to cope with periods of unemployment. Thanks to this strategy, partially autonomous youth can build a perception of themselves as economically autonomous, adult individuals.

However, one noticeable difference between Polish and Italian youth is that the Italian participants stress the importance of doing domestic chores as a sign of independence and adulthood. This link between subjective economic autonomy and doing domestic chores emerges only among unemployed Italians. Etymologically speaking, the word 'economy' comes from the Greek οἶκος (oikos), 'house', and νόμος (nomos) 'law' (that is, what is right, what sets the rule), and originally indicated a way of conducting your household and managing its goods. For example, Luigi (M, 29, ME, NCJ, IT) defines managing everyday life not only through being able to provide for himself, but also through his ability to manage everyday chores (for example, washing, ironing). Another example comes from Mara:

'Me, I iron my stuff at home, just to say. It's really [pause] there are many things that let you become independent and adult. One of them is also to [pause] to be independent in the handling of your own stuff, no? To get by yourself, really [pause] at 100 per cent, to clean, to wash [pause] to iron [pause] everything. To make the bed by yourself, from time to time.' (Mara, F, 30, ME, U, IT)

Polish youth often state economic autonomy as a minimal condition for adulthood, but they never mention managing everyday duties in this context – it seems that they treat it as obvious that they do the domestic chores themselves. However, some of them mention that they feel obliged to contribute financially to their parents' household budget as long as they carry on living with them. For most Polish and Italian interviewees, it is crucial to emphasise at least one aspect of their autonomy and adulthood. As mentioned, the interviewees who still live with their parents tend to underline other aspects of their autonomy than independent living such as partial economic autonomy or psychological autonomy. For example, when asked about their understanding of adulthood, they stress ideas of psychological maturity or responsibility:

> 'Being an adult, I guess it's more about this financial aspect, and being mature, it's more spiritual. I would separate this because, talking about being mature, it's much broader [pause] being responsible for yourself, for your actions, for someone else, like in a family, et cetera. And being an adult, it's just about being able to afford oneself, once you have some job.' (Michalina, F, 26, ME, NCJ, PL)

> 'Becoming an adult means having self-awareness, to ask for help if necessary, not to do: ah I'm big, I'm adult now, I don't need to ask anyone for anything.' (Camilla, F, 23, ME, NCJ, IT)

Maturity is a concept that also emerges from the interviews collected in Italy, whereas responsibility towards others – partners or children – is scarcely present in the interviews with young Italians. The interviewees not only reconstruct the meanings of financial independence, but also adopt behavioural strategies that ensure the minimal level of their economic agency. The most common strategy involves limiting personal needs and cutting expenses deemed unnecessary such as holidays or leisure activities. They stress that they only buy goods in sales or else cheap items, avoid expensive shops, and look for free recreational activities.

> 'Obviously the first time I had money to myself [I felt] happy! [pause] It is a family tradition that with your first salary you've got to give yourself a present [smiles]. So, no problem with that, you can even spend it all! I put it aside for my driving licence! [both laugh] No, I just bought a pair of shoes. I spent 20 or 30 Euro on shoes, which I had never done before! So, you can imagine, and afterwards I even felt guilty because I always saved, I always looked at things that cost little!' (Margherita, F, 24, ME, U, IT)

As a consequence of limited resources, the interviewees present a short-term perspective when asked about their financial plans. Most of them do not manage any savings.

The sustainability of living standards, the strategies implemented by respondents to pursue economic independence, and the ways in which they perceive the economic disadvantage of their precarious position in the labour market are strongly influenced by participants' social origins. Those, who have a middle-class family background and greater support from parents seem to have fewer worries about precariousness and are more able to use coping strategies, as in the case of 26-year-old Lara. Even though formally unemployed, she is highly educated and has rich employment experience. At the time of the interview, in addition to private lessons, Lara is teaching an intensive English course once a week at a middle comprehensive school. Thanks to the strong economic, moral, and housing support from her mother, Lara sees her precarious teaching experience as fulfilling. While talking about her job, she emphasises the dimension of self-realisation, doing what she likes, as well as social and cultural exchange. In the future, she is considering moving to France, which in her perception, offers greater opportunities for growth, such as gaining a PhD.

Conclusions

In short, in Italy an increasingly restrictive labour market and the spread of precarious jobs have led to considerable insecurity which young people have to face by renouncing housing autonomy, relying on family support, and cultivating a short-term perspective. Polish interviewees struggle with low levels of income that, in many cases, are insufficient to allow them to leave their parental homes and start independent life.

However, interviewees do not seem to be passive subjects at the mercy of events. On the contrary, they are social actors who, within the limited scope for action available to them, implement countless practices and micro-strategies in their daily lives with which they save, set aside, reduce consumption, and make choices. Our interviewees are, overall, skilled in managing their economic income and resources of various kinds, however limited they may be: many work and strive to save, but more to buffer periods of non-work and meet immediate needs than to embark on life projects.

By economic autonomy, the interviewees mean the possibility of and ability to satisfy their needs with their own resources, and they define their needs mainly in terms of small personal daily necessities. Youth economic autonomy is shaped by their expected standard of living, available resources (for example, a flat of their own flat or cheap accommodation), the availability of parental support and willingness to accept it, and self-determination and individual skills.

The heterogeneity of the interviewees' perceptions of their own economic situation raises questions about the possibility of defining clear and objective criteria for economic autonomy, and this cannot be traced back entirely to either the type of employment contract, the level of income, or to its stability.

Economic autonomy is mainly defined subjectively by the Italian or Polish young people as a capacity for self-determination, but within the limits of the daily management of available resources. The respondents perceive and represent themselves as autonomous in that they are able to decide for themselves by defining their own training and work paths, by combining more resources, by managing their daily lives, and ultimately by developing their own system of preferences, even though they have to be economically dependent on their parents. It should be repeated once more: the interviewees do not have the option of supporting themselves and providing for their own sustenance through work.

In the interviewees' view, autonomy is not only about economic independence but also a more general capability – that is, it encompasses knowing how to manage one's needs and problems without asking for any help from both a practical and psychological point of view. They feel relatively autonomous, because they are able to act independently when making choices that concern only themselves.

Moreover, our results confirm the findings of some authors (Molgat, 2007; Mary, 2014; Manzoni, 2016) that the status of adulthood is not represented subjectively in terms of achieving specific transitions or markers (leaving the parental home or forming one's own family) and a stationary social position, but it is associated with certain personal qualities such as maturity or a sense of responsibility. Financial independence is linked to self-perceived adulthood, but – as mentioned – it is not always or necessarily the outcome of a stable entry into the labour market.

It must be underlined that neither Italian nor Polish youth have access to unemployment benefits when they are looking for their first job. In both countries, passive labour market policies do not target unemployed youth who are trying to enter the labour market for the first time. They cannot accumulate enough social security benefits to claim financial support. However, Polish youth are targeted by active policy measures – mainly paid internships that provide them with symbolic remuneration and give them the opportunity to gain necessary work experience. In Italy, because most interviewees have atypical contracts, they cannot access social protection. Few of them rely on policies and public institutions. A few have an internship as part of Italy's youth guarantee programme, but their judgement of that experience is very negative. Some elements of the Italian institutional and economic context play a significant role as vulnerability factors and have to be considered important disadvantages. Territoriality continues to be crucial in Italy: living in the south is a risk factor because it increases the probability of being unemployed, exposed to poverty and material deprivation, and living in a jobless family.

Individuals show high levels of socio-economic vulnerability, because they seem to be in a very precarious balance focused on a short-term perspective. Some are involved in a patchwork of various jobs that take them away from important domains such as self-care and interpersonal relationships, whereas others maintain economic autonomy solely through the adoption of a lifestyle characterised by sacrifice and self-imposed limitations. Youth in both countries adopt similar strategies to sustain their economic autonomy. The widespread inability among the interviewees to project themselves into the future and plan for this is an important factor in their vulnerability. The future seems to be plannable only in the short term, and this triggers a devaluation of long-term time references and their limited opportunities for agency. As a result, it seems as if the main risk young people are exposed to is that they will not be able to achieve the economic stability that will allow them to plan their social biography independently in a full sense. A generation that has no tomorrow is a generation that feels excluded from the possibility of taking on those responsibilities that society attributes to adult roles. In fact, limited autonomy, even for those who have higher educational qualifications, can be translated into the risk of exclusion from adult roles.

References

Armano, E., Bove, A. and Murgia, A. (eds) (2017) *Mapping Precariousness, Labour Insecurity and Uncertain Livelihoods: Subjectivities and Resistance*, London: Routledge.

Aspalter, C., Jinsoo, K. and Sojeung, P. (2009) 'Analysing the welfare state in Poland, the Czech Republic, Hungary and Slovenia: an ideal-typical perspective', *Social Policy and Administration*, 43(2): 170–85.

Bandura, A. (1989) 'Human agency in social cognitive theory', *American Psychologist*, 44(9): 1175–84.

Baranowska, A. and Gebel, M. (2010) 'The determinants of youth temporary employment in the enlarged Europe: do labour market institutions matter?', *European Societies*, 12(3): 367–90.

Barbieri, P. (2011) 'Italy: no country for young men (and women)', in H.P. Blossfeld, S. Buchholz, D. Hofäcker and K. Kolb (eds) *Globalized Labour Markets and Social Inequality in Europe*, Basingstoke: Palgrave Macmillan, pp 108–46.

Bello, B.G. and Cuzzocrea, V. (2018) 'Introducing the need to study young people in contemporary Italy', *Journal of Modern Italian Studies*, 23(1): 1–7.

Bertolini, S. (2011) 'The heterogeneity of the impact of labour market flexibilization on the transition to adult life in Italy: when do young people leave the nest?', in H.P. Blossfeld, D. Hofäcker and S. Bertolini (eds) *Youth on Globalised Labour Market: Rising Uncertainty and its Effects on Early Employment and Family Lives in Europe*, Opladen, Farmington Hills: Verlag Barbara Budrich, pp 163–86.

Bertolini, S., Goglio, V., Moiso, V. and Torrioni, P.M. (2018) 'Leaving home in insecure conditions: the role of labour market policies and the housing market in Europe', *Studies of Transition States and Societies*, 10(3): 9–27.

Blossfeld, H.P., Klijzing, E., Mills, M. and Kurz, K. (eds) (2005) *Globalization, Uncertainty and Youth in Society*, London: Routledge.

Bogumil, P. (2015) 'Securing Poland's economic success II: labour market and product specialisation – is there a link', *ECFIN Country Focus*, 12(4): 1–8.

Brougham, R.R., Jacobs-Lawson, J.M., Hershey, D.A. and Trujillo, K.M. (2011) 'Who pays your debts? An important question for understanding compulsive buying among American college students', *International Journal of Consumer Studies*, 35(1): 79–85.

Bruckner, H. and Mayer, K.U. (2005) 'De-standardization of the life course: what it might mean? And if it means anything, whether it actually took place?', *Advances in Life Course Research*, 9(1): 27–53.

Buchholz, S., Hofäcker, D., Mills, M., Blossfeld, H.P., Kurz, K. and Hofmeister, H. (2009) 'Life courses in the globalization process: the development of social inequalities in modern societies', *European Sociological Review*, 25(1): 53–71.

Bynner, J. (2005) 'Rethinking the youth phase of the life course: the case for emerging adulthood', *Journal of Youth Studies*, 8(4): 367–84.

Chambers, R. (1989) 'Editorial introduction: vulnerability, coping and policy', *IDS Bulletin*, 20(2): 1–7.

Corijn, M. and Klijzing, E. (eds) (2001) *Transitions to Adulthood in Europe*, Dordrecht: Kluwer Academic Publisher.

Côté, J.E. and Levine, C.G. (2002) *Identity Formation, Agency, and Culture: A Social Psychological Synthesis*, Mahwah: Lawrence Erlbaum Associates Publishers.

Ebralidze, E. (2011) 'Labour market regulation and perceived job insecurities in the early career: do Danish employees worry less?', in H.P. Blossfeld, D. Häfacker and S. Bertolini (eds) *Youth on Globalized Labour Markets,* Opladen, Farmington Hills: Verlag Barbara Budrich, pp 93–118.

Elzinga, C.H. and Liefbroer, A.C. (2007) 'De-standardization of family-life trajectories of young adults: a cross-national comparison using sequence analysis', *European Journal of Population*, 23(3–4): 225–50.

Emirbayer, M. and Mische, A. (1998) 'What is Agency', *American Journal of Sociology*, 103(4): 962–1023.

Eurostat (2016) 'Population and social conditions. Youth', Available from: http://ec.europa.eu/eurostat/data/database

Eurostat (2017) 'Population and social conditions. Youth', Available from: http://ec.europa.eu/eurostat/data/database

Fenger, H.M. (2007) 'Welfare regimes in Central and Eastern Europe: incorporating post-communist countries in a welfare regime typology', *Contemporary Issues and Ideas in Social Sciences*, 3(2): 1–30.

Freeland, J. (ed) (1991) 'Dislocated transitions: access and participation for disadvantaged young people, young people's participation in post-compulsory education and training', in *The Australian Education Council Review Committee*, vol. 3, Canberra: Australian Government Publishing Service, pp 161–224.

Galland, O. (1991) *Sociologie de la Jeunesse: L'Entrée Dans la Vie*, Paris: Armand Colin.

Galland, O. (2000) 'Entrer dans la vie adulte: des étapes toujours plus tardives mais resserrées', *Économie et statistique*, 337–8(1): 13–36.

Granaglia, E. and Bolzoni, M. (2016) *Il Reddito di Base*, Rome: Ediesse.

Hareven, T.K. (1994) 'Aging and generational relations: a historical and life course perspective', *Annual Review of Sociology*, 20(1): 437–61.

Hartley, J., Jacobsson, D., Klandermans, B. and Van Vuuren, T. (1991) *Job Insecurity*, London: Sage Publications.

Hawkins, R.L. (2005) 'From self-sufficiency to personal and family sustainability: a new paradigm for social policy', *The Journal of Sociology & Social Welfare*, 32(4): 77–92.

Kelly, P. (2001) 'Youth at Risk: processes of individualization and responsibilisation in the risk society', *Discourse: Studies in the Cultural Politics of Education*, 22(1): 23–33.

Lee, J. and Mortimer, J.T. (2009) 'Family socialization, economic self-efficacy, and the attainment of financial independence in early adulthood', *Longitudinal and Life Course Studies*, 1(1): 45–62.

Lewandowski, P. and Magda, I. (2017) 'Temporary employment, unemployment and employment protection legislation in Poland', in A. Piasna and M. Myant (eds) *Myths of Employment Deregulation: How It Has Not Created Jobs and Not Reduced Labour Market Segmentation*, Brussels: ETUI, pp 143–63.

Liefbroer, A.C. and Toulemon, L. (2010) 'Demographic perspectives on the transition to adulthood: an introduction', *Advances in Life Course Research*, 15(2–3): 53–8.

Manzoni, A. (2016) 'Conceptualizing and measuring youth independence multidimensionally in the United States', *Acta Sociologica*, 59(4): 362–77.

Mary, A.A. (2014) 'Re-evaluating the concept of adulthood and the framework of transition', *Journal of Youth Studies*, 17(3): 415–29.

Mills, M.C. and Blossfeld, H.P. (2005) 'Globalization, uncertainty and the early life course: a theoretical framework', in H.P. Blossfeld, E. Klijzing, M. Mills and K. Kurz (eds) *Globalization, Uncertainty and Youth in Society*, London, New York: Routledge, pp 1–24.

Misztal, B. (2011) *The Challenges of Vulnerability. In Search of Strategies for a Less Vulnerable Social Life*, London: Palgrave Macmillan.

Molgat, M. (2007) 'Do transitions and social structures matter? How "emerging adults" define themselves as adults', *Journal of Youth Studies*, 10(5): 495–516.

Rokicka, M., Kłobuszewska, M., Palczyńska, M., Shapoval, N. and Stasiowski, J. (2015) *Composition and Cumulative Disadvantage of Youth across Europe*. EXCEPT Working Papers, WP No. 1. Tallinn: Tallinn University, Available from: https://www.except-project.eu/working-papers/

Saraceno, C. (2011) *Family Policies, Concepts, Goals and Instruments*. Carlo Alberto Notebooks, Working Paper No. 230. Turin: Collegio Carlo Alberto.

Schwartz, S.H., Côté, J.E. and Arnett, J.J. (2005) 'Identity and agency in emerging adulthood: two developmental routes in the individualization process', *Youth and Society*, 37(2): 201–29.

Shanahan, M.J. (2000) 'Pathways to adulthood in changing societies: variability and mechanisms in life course', *Annual Review of Sociology*, 26(1): 667–92.

Silva, J.M. (2012) 'Constructing adulthood in an age of uncertainty', *American Sociological Review* 77(4): 505–22.

Sverke, M., De Witte, H., Näswall, K. and Hellgren, J. (2010) 'European perspectives on job insecurity: editorial introduction', *Economic and Industrial Democracy*, 31(2): 175–8.

Sverke, M., Hellgren, J. and Näswall, K. (2002) 'No security: a meta-analysis and review of job insecurity and its consequences', *Journal of Occupational Health Psychology*, 7(3): 242–64.

Tosi, M. (2017) 'Age norms, family relationships, and home-leaving in Italy', *Demographic Research*, 36(9): 281–306.

Walther, A. (2006) 'Regimes of youth transitions: choice, flexibility and security in young people's experiences across different European contexts', *YOUNG*, 14(2): 119–39.

Xiao, J.J., Chatterjee, S. and Kim, J. (2014) 'Factors associated with financial independence of young adults', *International Journal of Consumer Studies*, 38(4): 394–403.

Yodanis, C. (2005) 'Divorce culture and marital gender equality: a cross-national study', *Gender and Society*, 19(5): 644–59.

10

The role of informal social support for young people in unemployment and job insecurity in Italy, Estonia, and Germany

Antonella Meo, Roberta Ricucci, Christoph Schlee, Jelena Helemäe, and Margarita Kazjulja

Introduction

Several studies have shown that young people in Europe are experiencing increased labour market exclusion and job insecurity (Baranowska and Gebel, 2010; Armano et al, 2017). Even if they find a job, they are exposed to the risk of precarious lives, because their entry-level positions are characterised by insecure contracts and/or low wages (Rokicka and Kłobuszewska, 2016). Young people experience an increasing number of transitions during their working careers because of intertwined economic and social trends. These transitions are not only in the field of paid labour, from one job to another, but also throughout other activities and work, from education or unemployment to work. The term 'navigation' can be used as a conceptual metaphor to describe the resulting experience of managing several transitions into a precarious opportunity structure (Fagan et al, 2012).

In this framework, some scholars (Hardgrove et al, 2015) have investigated how young people negotiate uncertainty in the labour market by showing how their ability to navigate through changing opportunities is enabled by social and family support. Even though these supportive relationships seem to be increasingly important for young people, they have yet to be explored adequately.

According to recent literature on social policy, the welfare state's role in giving protection from new social risks is weakening, especially for young people. Many scholars have suggested that paying attention to the role of the family allows a clearer picture of the position of young adults to emerge (Majamaa, 2011). Other scholars, in contrast, have stressed the importance of non-kin ties as a source of support (Conkova et al, 2018).

Furthermore, a better understanding of the specific interaction between formal and informal support in young people is becoming crucial. This chapter enquires whether the role of informal social support is widespread in Estonia, Germany, and Italy, and whether it is turning into a compensatory mechanism for many economically vulnerable young people. Hence, the chapter investigates the role of family, friends, and social networks in supporting young people as they transition through the labour market across different institutional contexts and welfare regimes. By exploring the functions of social relationships, it provides empirical evidence for the crucial relevance of informal social support during these transitions. Analysing this issue provides a qualified representation of youth vulnerability in relation to new social risks and of how young people overcome job insecurity.

Theoretical considerations

In the literature, 'social support' is defined as the (potential) exchanges between network ties that are perceived as being helpful (Dykstra, 2017). Scholars have introduced the contrast between informal and formal support to distinguish between support from members of personal networks and that received from professionals (Conkova et al, 2018). However, support has been understood mainly as an informal resource, as unpaid help provided by family ties and/or non-kin ties, because it does not involve professional or institutional interventions (Thoits, 1995).

The concept of social support was originally used when referring to social relationships in the context of studies on health and well-being (Barrera and Ainlay, 1983). Early researchers conceptualised social support as 'a generalised resource available from one's network of parents, friends, acquaintances, neighbours (the social network) that helped one to deal with everyday problems or more serious crises' (Walker et al, 1993: 71).

Although there is no common definition of the main types of social support, supportive resources can be described as emotional or providing companionship (nurturance, sense of belonging), tangible (for example, financial assistance), or informational (advice) (Wellman, 1992).

Some scholars have shown that support provision is affected not only by the number, but also by the quality of social relationships (Silverstein et al, 1995). The link between support and network structure or network density is complex: a bigger or denser network is not necessarily better. For instance, low-density networks are those that most often provide resources such as companionship, whereas denser networks are most often able to mobilise resources for material support or care in the case of illness (Walker et al, 1993).

Regarding informal support, one key issue is generational interdependence (Brandt, 2013; Brandt and Deindl, 2013). There is strong empirical evidence for the ongoing relevance of families in young people's lives. In this regard, some scholars are very critical of the youth-as-transition approach that undermines the significance for youth of their family relationships by focusing on the assumptions of linear trajectories and independence from parents (Wyn et al, 2012).

Only a few comparative studies have analysed (potential) non-kin support, showing that to better understand the role of kin and non-kin, it is important to distinguish among different types of support (Gelissen et al, 2012; Conkova et al, 2018). For instance, advice and help when looking for a job tend to be non-kin types of support. In particular, these studies have revealed that in the north and west of Europe, for example, there is a higher probability that people turn to non-kin ties for this kind of help, whereas a common pattern cannot be found in the south and east of Europe.

As highlighted in previous research, degrees and cultures of informal social support vary across Europe (Bohnke, 2008). How macrolevel processes shape support exchanges is a key issue. Scholars in this field of inquiry have shown that different factors come into play. What are crucial are macro or structural variables such as the economic performance of a country, labour market characteristics, and, of course, the welfare regime and welfare state tradition.

In the literature, as mentioned, one way to approach the patterns of social support is to associate and compare them with the role of the welfare state in different countries. The two main kinds of social support – informal and formal – relate to each other in different ways. The provision of support through social relationships, according to some studies, is viewed as a compensation for the absence or inadequacy of welfare provisions (Pichler and Wallace, 2007).

The term 'transfer regime' (Albertini et al, 2007) has been introduced to analyse cross-national findings on intergenerational exchanges, thereby highlighting the correspondence with established classifications of countries based on the decommodification of public transfers and services (Esping-Andersen, 1990).

In contrast, some scholars have highlighted differences between cultural contexts by focusing on the role of the values of autonomy and independence and on the norms of family obligations (Kalmijn and Saraceno, 2008). Norms seem to be very important when people have to decide between receiving help from either kin or non-kin. Individualistic values seem to predict the choice of informal (non-kin) rather than formal (professional) support. This latter finding confirms the thesis that individualism operates through the notion of independence. The generosity or restrictedness of public provisions differentially releases or necessitates normative obligations in interdependent family relationships (Aassve et al, 2013; Dykstra, 2017).

The question of how far cross-national differences reflect differences in either welfare state systems or culture is addressed repeatedly in the literature (Dykstra, 2017): institutional, structural, and cultural factors are dependent upon one another across countries, and this explains why it is difficult to disentangle their effects.

Concerning country differences, previous research reveals the existence of a north/west–south/east division, with Southern European countries characterised by the highest levels of family reliance and very little informal support outside the family (Marckmann, 2017). If social support is more important in the south and east of Europe where welfare provisions are weaker, social support in the south is mainly in the form of family support; whereas in the east, informal support outside the family is also important (Pichler and Wallace, 2007). In fact, in Southern European countries, social capital is concentrated in the family. The family represents the first reference for those needing a loan or help with a personal problem. However, in Eastern Europe, both friends and family are important. In Nordic countries and Western Europe, there might be less need for informal support because the welfare state is more highly developed. As highlighted, the more extended de-familiarisation in the Nordic countries means that friends and associates have an enhanced role (Pichler and Wallace, 2007). In the Baltic region, informal networks are vital. However, Dykstra and Fokkema (2011) have found considerable intra-national variability in family solidarity patterns and express caution against presuming that countries have a single dominant pattern of social support.

In addition to the context effect, patterns of social support within an individual's network are also expected to vary over the life course. Specifically, recent research on social support has mainly included the elderly and help provided by adult children for their parents. Family members become essential as caregivers through performing duties for their parents or younger siblings (Schenk et al, 2014). Against this background, this chapter investigates the young interviewees' experiences of having received – from family, friends, and others – resources to face insecure employment and living conditions, as well as their expectations of receiving support in case of need, by framing them in three different countries: Estonia, Germany, and Italy.

Research questions, aims, and data

This chapter aims to develop two main lines of inquiry. The first addresses characteristics, sources, and goals of social support by considering young people's experiences, expectations, and subjective assessments. How are young people in insecure positions in the labour market supported by their social networks? What kind of informal social support (emotional or companionship/tangible/informational) do they receive? What is the role of family, friends, and social networks in supporting young people as they transition through the labour market? Are these supportive resources perceived as crucial in achieving their autonomy, given their weak attachment to the labour market? How do both feelings of being supported and feelings of being socially included or excluded emerge from the interviews? How are they interconnected?

The strategic importance of informal support in analysing young people's vulnerability to the risks of unemployment and precarious work is clear, because it exploits both the availability of a network and the ability of young people to activate it when needed. Indicators regarding support are usually based on the experience of having received support in case of need and on expectations of receiving support. The experience of support shows that a network is available and that it works. Of course, social networks may not only support but also constrain individual actions and outcomes. However, the expectation of being able to receive support in case of need (for example, when urgently needing a sum of money) can be considered an indicator of trust in one's own network, and thus of feeling socially included (Olagnero et al, 2008). In this framework, the link between the availability of supportive resources and feelings of being socially included or excluded is an important issue that deserves to be explored in greater depth, although it has not been adequately examined in the literature on young people.

The second line of analysis developed in this chapter concerns the role of informal support in relation to formal support, possibly identifying different patterns in the three contexts considered. What is the role of social support in relation to formal or institutional support for young people in Estonia, Germany, and Italy?

The degree to which parents and relatives support young adults in their families can be considered as a function of their needs, because these needs are shaped mainly by the labour market and the level of social protection coverage provided by the welfare state. Therefore, where the role of the welfare state is weaker, stronger forms of informal networking and social support can be expected. As mentioned, the combination of informal and formal social support can take different forms: they can complement, substitute for, or compete with each other.

The discussion of these issues is based on scrutinising all the interviews collected by the EXCEPT project (see Chapter 1 in this volume) in the three selected countries.

Institutional contexts

The interaction between social support and context is a complex phenomenon that requires improved understanding in comparative sociological research: indeed, structural features affect personal ties, the availability and types of resources exchanged through the links, and the expectations that people have of them.

The countries focused on in this analysis were chosen because they represent different paths of interaction between informal and formal support. The latter can be traced back to different institutional settings and welfare regimes. However, at the same time, young people's circumstances with respect to the labour market and solidarity networks also differ between the three countries.

Germany as a conservative welfare state, Italy as a Southern European state fitting the Mediterranean welfare model, and Estonia as a post-socialist liberal Baltic welfare state, differ in political measures and programmes in various fields. Compared to Italy and Estonia, Germany provides stronger state support through unemployment benefits and targeted policies for young people. It has, in fact, a long tradition of highly developed active labour market policies (ALMPs).

In contrast, Italy has a low level of investment in ALMPs, no income support for those looking for their first job, and no adequate social safety measures to protect those suspended between one temporary contract and another. Nonetheless, when considering how far policies focus on preventive measures or are purely reactive to manifest problems or part of a structural policy action, it is clear that over the time span considered, the Italian Government has increased its investment in supporting passive labour market policies (PLMPs), while scaling back ALMPs (Istat, 2018). Because of the economic downturn which began in 2008, resources have been concentrated more on containing emergencies (workers in their mid-50s at risk of job loss; welcoming asylum seekers) than on creating new opportunities for the unemployed (especially young people). However, measures related to strengthening skills and training or the creation of early career paths are planned to support young people. Nonetheless, the lack of national policies reveals the high jeopardisation of measures addressing young people across the country with huge differences in opportunities from region to region.

Estonia has recently changed its attitude toward developing ALMPs (Bertolini et al, 2018). Indeed, the latest OECD report on Estonia shows 'resources allocated to active labour market policies have increased in recent years, but remain one of the lowest among OECD countries. Around a half of that spending goes on the public employment service itself, which is double that of the EU average' (OECD, 2018a: 88).

The severe financial and labour market crisis of the past decade has shaped the economic fabric of several European countries. Italy and Estonia fit in this scenario, whereas Germany remains an exceptional case with a low rate of unemployment and the highest level of expenditure on both ALMPs and PLMPs (OECD, 2018b, 2018c). Despite this, data on the lives of 'emerging adults' (Smith et al, 2011) and in particular those at risk of being marginalised reveal a darker side. There are huge differences across Germany and within the federal states (Bundesagentur für Arbeit, 2017) which deserve more attention. The other countries, unfortunately, reveal a more negative story. Becoming adult is 'beset with real problems, in some cases troubling and even heartbreaking problems' (Smith et al, 2011: 3). These include being unemployed, not being in education, employment, or training (NEET), and migration. Despite several institutional attempts, scars from the 2008–09 economic crisis have not fully healed in Italy due to the strong economic downturn. In Estonia, in contrast, efforts have been made to overcome the consequences of the recession (OECD, 2016). Nonetheless, negative consequences of changes in the labour market during the crisis fell disproportionally on youth, the poorly educated, and ethnic non-Estonians and non-Italians (Masso and Krillo, 2011; Ambrosini and Panichella, 2016). As in Italy, matching skills and jobs is becoming a growing concern in Estonia; there is no demand for the skills of the unemployed on the labour market, whereas the education system faces challenges in providing the right skills, thereby hampering the school-to-job transition. If Germany seems to stand outside this framework, the other two countries, from a glance at labour market characteristics, seem to share the following characteristics: gender imbalance, significant territorial inequalities, labour market segmentation, precariousness, and mismatching skills.

Tackling youth unemployment still represents a crucial issue in the public debate in which the link between education, occupational skills, and on-the-job training emerges. However, as Hofäcker (2017: 15) has pointed out:

> the socio-economic situation of youth not only depends on institutions that influence the mere occurrence and duration of labour market uncertainty, but also on how the welfare states treat such periods and 'buffer' negative socio-economic outcomes, e.g. through public benefits and transfers ... Earlier research has highlighted, that a developed system of unemployment insurance is able to reduce the negative effects of unemployment, which may be due to the immediate effect of public transfers. At the same time, generous unemployment benefits may allow individuals a longer job search period by which they can optimize their search results.

This is the German case, Italy is opposite, with Estonia resembling Italy more than Germany.

Nevertheless, several socio-economic indicators and qualitative research data reveal the consistency of informal support in all the chosen countries. If in Estonia and Italy this kind of support substitutes – or complements – the more limited public initiatives, in Germany it tries to moderate the impact of social origin on entering both the educational system and the labour market. Italy still represents the leading country in the Mediterranean welfare model in which parents continue to be the greatest resource in the transition to adulthood. Notwithstanding this, as recent research findings have pointed out, the effects of the economic downturn on families and severe cuts in financing public services are a common trend in several European countries, alongside an increasing mistrust in public institutions, mainly among young people. Taking into account social class and educational capital, it seems clear that those who have fewer cultural and economic resources have trouble finding the right way to ask for help, filling out applications to obtain formal support, and getting information on the latest policies and institutional procedures (OECD, 2018b). This is why, in all three countries, the youth–public institutions nexus is weakened, leaving room for other informal support based primarily on family, friends, and acquaintances.

Social support: types, sources, and functions

Evidence suggests that informal social support plays an important role in the precarious lives of young people in all three countries. Turning to the family, friends, and social networks in order to receive various forms of support proved to be a widespread experience among the young people interviewed, and it was one of the specific strategies they adopted in their efforts to cope with labour market exclusion and job insecurity. However, there were significant differences between the interviewees' experiences of receiving informal support in all three countries.

Solid family support characterised the Italian interviewees, confirming previous research highlighting that family solidarity is very important in Southern Europe (Bohnke, 2008; Majamaa, 2011). As mentioned, high rates of unemployment and precarious employment, low levels of social protection, and the very heavy impact of the 2008 economic crisis are factors that contributed to explaining the difficulties young people encountered in supporting themselves. Although the deterioration of living conditions as a result of the 2008–09 economic crises, as well as the welfare state crisis, has intensified the pressure on families by compromising their ability to redistribute resources for the benefit of their weakest members, family support still represents a key element in young Italians' survival strategies as they transition through the labour market. The vast majority of the interviewees referred to parents as the main, if not exclusive, source of support. Both their experiences and expectations relied mostly on the family of origin.

In Estonia, most of the interviewees in insecure job positions in the labour market used some form of informal social support, many of them combining it in a number of ways with various kinds of formal support and/or unofficial work. In the interviews, they mentioned their families of origin, but also partners and their families, friends, and acquaintances as support providers.

In Germany, although support received from parents featured in emergencies (such as illness), the family network as a source of support was less relevant in the interviewees' lives compared to interviewees in the other two countries. Moreover, whereas Italians rarely made reference to friends and acquaintances in the interviews, they were mentioned more often as sources of support in Estonia and in Germany.

It is interesting to investigate what kind of support this is and look at its characteristics. In all three countries, support was primarily material. In Italy and Estonia, it was primarily financial help and provision of housing that seemed to influence young people's options when dealing with the consequences of labour market insecurity. Most of the young Italian women and men who participated in the interviews were unable to live independently or to maintain themselves financially on the income from their jobs. They still lived with their parents and relied on them for their day to day living expenses, wholly or partially, just like the majority of young people in Italy. This housing arrangement made it possible to make ends meet and to accumulate the kind of resources that provide a buffer against financial pressures as they navigate through the labour market. In Italy, they were not eligible to receive any kind of unemployment benefits, despite being unemployed. However, they turned to their parents for help, not only when they were unemployed but also when they were working. Moreover, as in many cases wages were not enough for them to live on, living with their parents allowed them to cover their basic needs, to invest in training and advanced education, and to cushion periods of unemployment, thereby freeing them from the demands of having to pay their own living expenses.

> 'I think I'm quite comfortable to the extent that I can be independent and I do not run the risk of having to face emergency situations, at least in the short term [pause] despite the fact I'm twenty-eight, I do not suffer too much from the fact that I still live with my parents. Since I live with my parents, my housing expenses are almost non-existent [pause] except for my personal expenses, the small daily satisfactions, I can save money.' (Dario, M, 28, HE, TE, IT)

> 'They [his parents] are always available for me and I'm too, if there is no help within the family, to whom one could ask for being supported?' (Giacomo, M, 20, LE, TE, IT)

As Giacomo and Dario showed, cohabitation with parents was, for many, quite satisfactory. Family relationships were often described as quite good. Giulia did not receive money from her parents, but by the same token, she did not contribute to household expenses, and her mother did all the housework.

> 'I'm fine at home with my mum because she cooks and washes and I don't have to do all those things. I say that's fine [pause] My mum has never asked me for money, but she has said "you do not give money but you put money aside, so I don't have to help you, you do not help me with the household expenses."' (Giulia, F, 26, HE, TE, IT)

The expectation of receiving help from parents – mainly housing and economic support – was widespread among the Italian interviewees.

In a familial context such as Italy, young people felt bound by normative and cultural obligations of interdependence in family relationships. The Italian interviewees expected support from their parents, but in many cases, especially among the working class, they assumed that they were bound by reciprocity. To give an example, Camilla helped her parents by helping out with their medical expenses if she had the chance. Graziano's family helped him to cope with his unemployment. His parents paid him a few euros when he helped his father in his self-employed activity from time to time. Sometimes, they gave him a little pocket money. In addition to this, sometimes Graziano helped his parents out by paying for their expenses.

However, in Italy family seemed to lie at the centre of an apparent paradox. On the one hand, living in the parental home was a protective factor and it allowed young people to save money to cope with job insecurity and to build more stable pathways of integration into the labour market, despite their limited economic resources due to frequent episodes of unemployment and precarious and poorly paid jobs. On the other hand, it seemed to entail a dependence on their parents, and this weighed heavily on some interviewees. Erika, for example, stressed that she very much wanted to leave her mother's home and to live with her present boyfriend, but without a job, this was not possible:

> 'I wish I had my own home! I greatly wish this! To live with my boyfriend, to create a family, even only to cohabit without getting married; just me and him, not like we are doing now, that from time to time he comes to my mother's house and stays with us for some days, but we are not alone. We are in good company with my mother, but that is another thing.' (Erika, F, 29, LE, NEET, IT)

Informal financial support for Estonian interviewees depended on familial resources and young people's stage of transition to adulthood. Familial support ranged from being totally financially dependent on parents to receiving some money in case of need. Families with more resources could afford to pay children's study loans or even, in a few cases, a loan for an apartment.

> 'My mom reached her retirement now and continued working, she still works, and then she decided to pay back my study loan, because I actually couldn't imagine how I had managed that now

[pause] But my mom raised that €4,000 and paid the study loan off, it was for her conscience.' (Mari, F, 29, HE, U, EE)

Disadvantaged families were only able to provide their children with small sums of money and not on a regular basis (for example, for special events such as children's birthdays). The social class of the family also mattered: families with substantial resources tended to provide more economic support to their children to enable them to pursue higher education, whereas families with scarce resources struggled to support them beyond lower level secondary education. Some interviewees who were not receiving informal financial support at the time of the interview, had received support earlier in their lives and were certain that they would get support from their families in case of need (see also Reiska et al, 2018).

Only a few interviewees had attained financial and housing autonomy and could rely mainly on themselves. Jevgeny (M, 29, ME, NCJ, EE) exemplified such a path to adulthood. He did not know much about his father, and his mother had found it hard to manage her own life. Jevgeny had to start earning money to support himself when he was 15. He had acquaintances who had helped him in the past, but when asked where would he turn in the case of unemployment, Jevgeny answered "to myself".

In Estonia, informal support in the form of co-residency depended on the youth's stage of transition to adulthood. In the interviews, this type of support refers to those who were preparing for the transition to adulthood, especially to those aged between 18–22.

'I have lived on my parents good will so to say, [laughs] so, my parents are starting to be fed up with me not working [laughs], but it is, mother's love, father's love are so big that they don't want to kick their son out.' (Peep, M, 25, LE, U, EE)

However, for some young adults, negative experiences in the labour market had forced them to resort to this type of support by going to live with their parents or with their partners' parents (their 'transition to adulthood' had been interrupted). In sum, living separately from the family of origin in Estonia was often a sign of significant progress towards adulthood and less reliance on help from the family of origin.

Some interviewees (those who had 'delayed adulthood' by remaining in the parental home) contributed to the household budget, but only occasionally, depending on their income at the time. Estonian interviewees who lived separately from their parents tended not to ask their parents for assistance with accommodation costs. Sharing housing costs with a partner (in one way or another) seemed to be a norm for interviewees, except for cases in which one of the partners had no income to contribute. At the time of the interview, only a few interviewees lived with friends and shared housing expenses. Overall, the lack of state policy to support housing autonomy brought about a wide range of strategies to gain and maintain housing autonomy, but almost all of these strategies presupposed the availability of informal support.

In Estonia, interviewees only turned to acquaintances or friends for material support when they were unable to access this help from their or their partners' families of origin. Like many Italian interviewees, some Estonian respondents also pointed out that their parents provided them not only shelter but also emotional support. Anna, for example, returned for a short time to her parents' home when labour market insecurity coincided with the breakdown of her engagement. The parental home represented what another interviewee called a 'mental refuge' – that is, a place to find emotional stability and think about how to proceed in life.

> 'Basically, I couldn't make sense of it all anymore so I decided to move back to my parents' home in the country for the summer [pause] Well, to put it briefly, the picture got too fuzzy. I felt that I can't manage it all anymore, well, alone.' (Anna, F, 29, HE, U, EE)

In all three countries, interviewees frequently mentioned emotional support in coping with their insecure position in the labour market, and also in coping with other negative events:

> 'My parents have always been present, that's been really helpful, they've really supported me a lot, they listened, they get me to talk, let it all out, it's a type of support that's always been there at home.' (Margherita, F, 24, ME, U, IT)

However, overall in Estonia, unlike in Italy, respondents who received informal social support mixed the help of different supporters. First, the family of origin, then partners and their families, friends, and acquaintances. It is interesting to note that the trust in informal support was so widespread: also the interviewees who found their jobs through the internet stated that (good) jobs were available only, or predominantly, through acquaintances.

Many Estonian interviewees reported that they had received informal help in the form of information sharing (for example, providing links to websites on the internet, 'inside' information on job offers in a company), advice (in filling out their curriculum vitae or application letters for jobs), references for jobs, or even being offered work in acquaintances' companies.

The experiences of the German respondents were to some extent similar to those of the Estonian respondents. Many of them talked about informal support received from several people, mostly family members such as parents and grandparents, but also from partners and friends. If most financial and emotional support seemed to be provided by the family of origin, other close social relations such as friends were more likely to provide companionship, informational support and a feeling of belonging:

> 'Relatives, acquaintances, friends. Those first people who simply help me get over the hurdles or something like that.' (Fabian, M, 22, ME, TE, DE)

In the German interviews, many mentioned advice on different areas of life (for example, assistance in filling in applications to the employment agency), support in job searches, establishing contacts with employers and firms, or in the application process (advice on writing job applications), and different favours in the form of financial and also emotional support. Whereas the Italian interviewees stressed the crucial role of parents for material and housing support, the repertoire of types of help received was more extensive in the interviews with young Germans and included informational and emotional support to improve their work situation and find a job or vocational training to help them stand on their own feet in the future.

In particular, an important issue that emerged in the German interviews was the sense of belonging provided by friends. Turning to these supportive relationships can be interpreted as young people's strategy for both achieving well-being in insecure situations and coping with the risk of social exclusion:

> 'Whenever I am outside and meet my friends, then mainly just to escape everything for somewhat an hour or two. To think about something else.' (Marc, M, 24, LE, U, DE)

In this regard, family members often supported emotionally, by giving advice, and materially by providing financial resources. The general possibility for young adults to fall back on informal support is a protective factor; indeed due to this informal support they can cope with the financial insecurity or other dimensions of social exclusion:

> 'Well [pause] yes, as naive as it sounds, but I think as soon as a problem occurs, I would give my mom a call or something like that [laughs] and say something like "What am I supposed to do?"' (Lisa, F, 25, ME, U, DE)

In Germany as well, informal support turned out to be one of the decisive factors on the road to independence for many interviewees. Autonomy, on the one hand, and mainly informal support on the other, might seem to be two conflicting concepts. However, for all the countries examined, it emerged that informal support on the trajectory to complete autonomy was crucial for many young adults in insecure life situations. In other words, it seemed impossible for young people to cope emotionally with insertion into the labour market without informal support.

Informal and formal support

Whereas the Italian interviewees stressed the role of parents given the lack of formal support, in Germany and in Estonia, many young adults in the sample combined formal (such as unemployment benefits) and informal (including economic but also emotional) support to help them cope with their situations in times of job insecurity or unemployment.

Indeed, it appears clear – as several authors have already pointed out – that informal support plays a role even in those contexts (such as Germany) in which institutional and formal support are widespread. All the young people interviewed in Italy, Germany, and Estonia followed similar patterns when describing the resources and support they received from non-institutional actors. General themes were consistent across employment situation, family size, household composition, and area of residence. Although some differences were noted, as described in the following paragraphs, the types of resource and support that participants mentioned were similar across demographic categories, gender, and countries: from financial aid to housing, from sharing information to offering emotional support.

Moving along an ideal line from the lack of any relation with institutional support to combined use of both formal and informal resources, we can start explaining what happens when young people are only able to rely on informal support.

First of all, in the case of interviewees who had not yet started their independent lives, support provided by the family of origin was the most comprehensive and was accepted without question. Sometimes, on the other hand, informal support was only provided when there were clear and strong barriers to accessing social benefits, and young people did not meet the necessary criteria to access formal support. In this case, even if there was pressure to become autonomous according to the subjective mood that young people were in, parents' material support became necessary in order to have some pocket money.

Indeed, some of the Germans interviewees were simply too young to qualify for unemployment benefits. They were dependent on their parents, who have a legal obligation to take care of their children financially up to the age of 25 years if they are themselves employed and able to support them. Due to this, parents play a substitution role for the state. Young people under 25 only receive the full amount of unemployment benefit if they no longer live in their parents' household. If their parents are also unemployed, all young people up to 25 years who live in the parental home are included in the community of needs, and the parents receive formal support to cover the entire family. Hence, the younger individuals in the sample tended to receive informal monetary support from their parents, which came indirectly from the state if their parents were also unemployed.

For many young people, formal financial support (unemployment benefits) seemed to be the most important support when in a financially insecure life situation. For some, informal support served as a supplement, and in cases when no formal support was provided, informal support (especially financial) through one's own social network was essential.

In the German context, more than in the other two countries, informal support seemed necessary but was not altogether welcomed. For young people living in a social context in which moving out of their parents' home and becoming autonomous represented a key turning point towards adulthood, being in need of financial and emotional support was perceived negatively. In particular, those who were unemployed and received unemployment benefits reported that they were socially stigmatised – they felt 'guilty' and 'being considered as useless'. Support from their own family and social networks seemed to be less problematic and more normatively recognised in comparison to institutional support. However, informal support was not always perceived as good.

> 'I mean [pause] when you get to know someone for the first time or something and then you first have to say, "Yes, I'm

unemployed" [grows quiet] so it's always been "But why? Are you lazy?" or stigmatised, something like that. You always get put into a category like that and [pause] that's when I think that he just doesn't know anything about it.' (Katrin, F, 27, LE, U, DE)

In other words, in the German context difficulties in achieving an autonomous life were aggravated in some cases by a social context that blamed youth, who were not in control of their lives, for not knowing how to manage them:

'Basically, I am ashamed of that.' (Klaus, M, 29, ME, U, DE)

In Estonia, it is not necessary to lose a job to gain access to unemployment allowance: young people who have studied, or been on parental leave for at least 180 days during the last year, are also eligible to receive an unemployment allowance. A waiting period (two months) is applied for those who have just finished their studies and are entering the labour market for the first time. The payment of €150 per month (in 2016) is insufficient to manage financially if the young person aims to gain at least some economic autonomy. These conditions make a difference for those with or without informal support. Thus, for those who are still in the parental nest, an unemployment allowance is just additional pocket money, the waiting period is of no practical importance. But for young people who interrupted their studies to look for a job because of strained economic conditions in the parental home, getting an unemployment allowance without a waiting period is an essential precondition to make ends meet. They still need some additional income, but for them, taking up short-term work for additional income is felt to be too risky, because it is forbidden to work during the period the person receives an unemployment allowance, and they often opted for some undeclared work (see Reiska et al, 2018).

Young parents were one of the groups among Estonian interviewees for whom combining both formal and informal support was an essential strategy for coping with labour market uncertainty. For most young people, parenthood is the important marker of adulthood. For many of them, especially women, parenthood is also associated with a sharply increased risk of dependence (employers' discrimination, need for informal practical help with babysitting, and so on). It is a period when all kinds of formal support are especially welcome, even though they are rarely adequate.

However, there is at least one other case in which young people refer only to informal support: when 'going to services or asking for them' was perceived as useless, a waste of time. It occurred especially when there was a high level of mistrust towards public services and the search for formal help was out of the question. As several interviewees stressed in Italy, there was widespread mistrust of institutions and their doings.[1] Discussing these services and social benefits meant collecting negative feelings towards public institutions that the interviewees may well have never visited: narratives based on word of mouth seemed to be most important.

In Estonia, attitudes towards the Unemployment Insurance Fund (UIF) differed greatly depending on the resources available to interviewees and their place of residence. Those with stronger informal support who lived in (bigger) towns were more critical towards UIF: for example, Aleksandr, who lived in the capital city of Estonia, did not believe in the possibility of finding a job through UIF, because the jobs offered there were those that "nobody wants".

> 'Such jobs, you go to the UIF and they send you straight to hell where nobody wants to work, where there are no conditions, where there is nothing. The UIF does not give you anything, it is all only on paper. They offer you this and that, but nobody wants to go there. There is no money and the work is awful. That's it, I think there is no point in going to the UIF at all.' (Aleksandr, M, 26, ME, NCJ, EE)

In contrast, those living in the countryside without informal support appreciated institutional support, particularly from the UIF. For example, Maili, a young mother who lived in the countryside, was very grateful:

> 'I have gotten a lot of help from the UIF. They referred me and helped me, recommended some courses for me and helped to find jobs [pause] So, they really helped me a lot, the UIF really helped me a lot.' (Maili, F, 18, LE, U parental leave, EE)

Moreover, in Estonia, criticism was related mainly to the range of available jobs and not towards the UIF as an institution as such. This criticism was not blind prejudice, but rather based on personal experience or the experience of friends.

However, several interviews showed how young people tried to manage a kind of patchwork of support. Intertwining welfare benefits with informal support required skill and a proactive attitude towards interactions with public services and institutions. Nevertheless, this relationship was neither easy nor obvious. Interviewees in all three countries (only some in Estonia) identified the following crucial factors that negatively affected the relationship with the various welfare benefits: language barriers; limited knowledge of what policies supporting youth were available and to what extent they worked; stereotypes about the inefficacy of public services; and a lack of empathy between the older generation of employees and the younger generation of recipients.

However, thanks to advice obtained from their informal networks (both parents and friends), young people developed their skills in dealing with bureaucracy and cutting back their living costs. Resorting to welfare benefits or cutting their own spending could have a negative effect on their self-esteem and their perception of themselves as adults who are able to cope with current socio-economic challenges.

Conclusions

Findings show idiosyncrasies and common trends when discussing the extent to which young people manage different types of support. For many interviewees in Italy, staying with their parents was a natural strategy for coping with job insecurity and economic uncertainty; for others, it was a necessity. This result is consistent with the literature (Iacovu, 2010). Even today, paraphrasing Kohli et al (2010), cohabitation is the Southern European way of transferring resources from parents to children (Dystra, 2017): a widespread recourse to parents, mainly for housing and economic support, offsets weak institutional support.

In Estonia, combining different informal and formal sources of support and taking on undeclared work seems to be the most common coping strategy for young people. For certain groups of young people, it is parents, siblings, or relatives who are the first port of call, even for those who are 'either receiving unemployment allowance or had received it in the past' (Bertolini et al, 2018: 90). In this Baltic country, according to the young people interviewed, obtaining support from one's partner or parents was an essential requirement for coping with labour market insecurity, because state welfare support was not considered sufficient. Even those who managed on their own income still mentioned parents as a backup.

Although in Germany the formal support provided by the state is relevant, several respondents highlighted the crucial role played by informal support in their insecure life situations, one of the decisive factors on the road to independence for many. Besides formal state support in the form of unemployment benefits, informal support can be described as an additional and often necessary form of help. As in the Estonian case, respondents in Germany reported receiving a wider spectrum of support and stressed the importance of information and emotional support in tandem with material support.

Therefore, despite the differences, a transversal trait emerges: informal support seemed to be an important protective factor and coping strategy for dealing with financial insecurities and the risk of social exclusion. However, even when formal support existed (in whatever form, ranging from training activities to improving skills to attending information sessions, from unpaid internships to following job-seeking guidelines), the help of parents, friends, and acquaintances remained necessary for those who had formed families of their own, as well as those who had left the parental household and were living alone or sharing. In all of these cases, the interplay between formal and informal support was essential, and in Estonia, undeclared work was also an important element. Interestingly, the importance of informal support in young people's lives did not just apply to the unemployed as many interviewees who experienced job insecurity such as temporary contracts or undeclared employment were unable to support themselves on their own earnings.

Two crucial issues emerged when discussing the role of informal support in relation to formal support – the availability of informal social support as a driver of inequality among young people, and the side effects of informal support on its recipients.

Concerning the link between informal support and inequalities, it is necessary to look at the parental household. Findings confirm that the economic and cultural background of the family and its capacity to provide support was a very important variable in young people's lives. Those who had a supportive and resourceful family did not feel themselves under economic strain: when their parents' financial resources were good, not only could they cover young people's personal expenses, but they could also help young people to save towards independence and make plans for the future. In contrast, interviewees with less supportive and resourceful families were forced to make sacrifices and live with self-imposed limitations. In fact, when the family of origin was affected by deprivation and material hardship and experienced low standards of living, young people's living conditions were strained by their very limited economic resources. Without a supportive family (financially, in kind by offering meals and a sofa to sleep on, and emotionally) or a dense and helpful social network, unemployment – and the subsequent lack of income – could represent a serious barrier to full participation in the community. Nonetheless, cohabitation with parents could also have a detrimental effect in that young people became dependent on their parents which could put them at risk of social exclusion. Social class still plays a role. The parental economic situation was a key variable in the young people's perceptions of well-being and autonomy. Educational level was also very important: in all three countries, young people with a low level of education and a lack of skills faced greater difficulties in entering the labour market permanently and regularly, and they were particularly in need of financial support (in both Estonia and Italy, they were often pushed into undeclared work). In many cases, those with low levels of education tended to belong to more deprived families and social networks.

The second issue, the side effects of receiving help, explores young people's negative perceptions of being dependent on support. If informal social support is a protective factor, young people can perceive being dependent on other people as a heavy burden. Most explicitly in Germany and to a lesser extent in Estonia, respondents perceived a direct link between a low standard of living, unemployment or precarious employment, and the experience of social disqualification. In Italy, paradoxically the country in which the process of becoming autonomous seems to be never-ending, this link was not perceived so negatively. This did not emerge as an issue in the interviews, and the Italians seemed to cope with it without major concerns and impact on their self-esteem. Finally, another transversal trait deals with the role played by associations and non-governmental organisations in all the three countries. Their activities appear as a hidden support in the Estonian and Italian samples, because young people don't distinguish between private and public organisations.

In the German case, in contrast, their presence emerged as contact with social workers from different institutions (advice, support, writing CVs). This is another transversal trait. In the internet age, with a maximum availability of information along with off- and online resources to activate in order to receive support, the closest ties seem to be the unique solutions for overcoming problems, dealing with the uncertainty of life, facing difficulties in saving, and dealing with troubles on a psychological level. This is not just the case in a familial country such as Italy. It is also the case in Estonia and Germany.

Note
[1] The latest OECD report (2018c) on Italy continues to confirm this attitude.

References
Aassve, A., Cottini, E. and Vitali, A. (2013) 'Youth prospects in a time of economic recession', *Demographic Research*, 29(36): 949–62.

Albertini, M., Kohli, M. and Vogel, C. (2007) 'Intergenerational transfers of time and money in European families: common patterns, different regimes', *Journal of European Social Policy*, 17(4): 319–34.

Ambrosini, M. and Panichella, N. (2016) 'Immigrazione, occupazione e crisi economica in Italia', *Quaderni di Sociologia*, 72: 115–74.

Armano, E., Bove, A. and Murgia, A. (eds) (2017) *Mapping Precariousness, Labour Insecurity and Uncertain Livelihoods: Subjectivities and Resistance*, London: Routledge.

Baranowska, A. and Gebel, M. (2010) 'The determinants of youth temporary employment in the enlarged Europe: do labour market institutions matter?', *European Societies*, 12(3): 367–90.

Barrera, M.J. and Ainlay, S.L. (1983) 'The structure of social support: a conceptual and empirical analysis', *Journal of Community Psychology*, 11(2): 133–43.

Bertolini, S., Deliyanni-Kouimtzi, K., Bolzoni, M., Ghislieri, C., Goglio, V., Martino, S., Meo, A., Moiso, V., Musumeci, R., Ricucci, R., Torrioni, P.M., Athanasiades, C., Figgou, L., Flouli, A., Kostouli, M. and Sourvinou, M.N. (eds) (2018) *Labour Market Insecurity and Social Exclusion: Qualitative Comparative Results in Nine Countries.* EXCEPT Working Papers, WP No. 53, Tallinn: Tallinn University, Available from: https://www.except-project.eu/working-papers/

Bohnke, P. (2008) 'Are the poor socially integrated? The link between poverty and social support in different welfare regimes', *Journal of European Social Policy*, 8(2): 133–50.

Brandt, M. (2013) 'Intergenerational help and public assistance in Europe', *European Societies*, 15(1): 26–56.

Brandt, M. and Deindl, C. (2013) 'Intergenerational transfers to adult children in Europe: do social policies matter?', *Journal of Marriage and Family*, 75(1): 235–51.

Bundesagentur für Arbeit (2017) 'Arbeitslosigkeit im Zeitverlauf: Entwicklung der Arbeitslosenquote (Jahreszahlen): Deutschland und Bundesländer', Available from: https://statistik.arbeitsagentur.de/Statistikdaten/Detail/Aktuell/iiia4/laender-heft/laender-heft-d-0-xlsx.xlsx

Conkova, N., Fokkema, T. and Dykstra, P.A. (2018) 'Non-kin ties as a source of support in Europe: understanding the role of cultural context', *European Societies*, 20(1):131–56.

Dykstra, P.A. (2017) 'Cross-national differences in intergenerational family relations: the influence of public policy arrangements', *Innovation in Aging*, 2(1): 1–23.

Dykstra, P.A. and Fokkema, T. (2011) *Ties between Parents and their Adult Children: A Western European Typology of Late-Life Families*. Multilinks Deliverable 5.3. The Hague: Netherlands Interdisciplinary Demographic Institute.

Esping-Andersen, G. (1990) *The Three Worlds of Welfare Capitalism*, Cambridge: Policy Press.

Fagan, C., Kanjuo-Mrčela, A. and Norman, H. (2012) 'Young adults navigating European labour markets', in T. Knijn (ed) *Work, Family Policies and Transitions to Adulthood in Europe*, London: Palgrave Macmillan, pp 130–54.

Gelissen, J.P.T.M., van Oorschot, W. and Finsveen, E. (2012) 'How does the welfare state influence individuals' social capital?', *European Societies*, 14(3): 416–40.

Hardgrove, A., McDiwell, L. and Rootham, E. (2015) 'Precarious lives, precarious labour: family support and young men's transitions to work in the UK', *Journal of Youth Studies*, 18(8): 1057–76.

Hofäcker, D. (ed) (2017) *Medium-Term Economic Consequences of Insecure Labour Market Positions*. EXCEPT Working Papers, WP No. 12, Tallinn: Tallinn University, Available from: https://www.except-project.eu/working-papers/

Iacovu, M. (2010) 'Leaving home: Independence, togetherness and income', *Advances in Life Course Research*, 15(4): 147–60.

Istat (2018) Rapporto Annuale del Paese 2018, Roma; Istat.

Kalmijn, M. and Saraceno, C. (2008) 'A comparative perspective on intergenerational support: responsiveness to parental needs in individualistic and familialistic countries', *European Societies*, 10(3): 479–508.

Kohli, M., Albertini, M. and Künemund, H. (2010) 'Linkages among adult family generations: evidence from comparative survey research', in P. Heady and M. Kohli (eds) *Family, Kinship and State in Contemporary Europe, Vol. 3: Perspectives on Theory and Policy*, Frankfurt, New York: Campus, pp 195–220.

Majamaa, K. (2011) 'Dismissed intergenerational support? New social risks and the economic welfare of young adults', *Journal of Youth Studies*, 14(4): 729–43.

Marckmann, B. (2017) 'All is not relative: intergenerational norms in Europe', *European Societies*, 19(4): 466–91.

Masso, J. and Krillo, K. (2011) *Labour Markets in the Baltic States During the Crisis 2008–2009: The Effect on Different Labour Market Groups*, The University of Tartu Faculty of Economics and Business Administration, Working Paper 79. Tartu: Faculty of Economics and Business Administration, University of Tartu.

OECD (2016) *Employment Outlook 2016*, Paris: OECD.
OECD (2018a) *Economic Survey: Estonia*, Paris: OECD.
OECD (2018b) *Economic Survey: Germany*, Paris: OECD.
OECD (2018c) *Economic Survey: Italy*, Paris: OECD.
Olagnero, M., Torrioni, P. and Saraceno, C. (2008) 'Patterns of sociability in the enlarged EU', in J. Alber, T. Fahey and C. Saraceno (eds) *Handbook of Quality of Life in the Enlarged European Union*, Abingdon: Routledge.
Pichler, F. and Wallace C. (2007) 'Patterns of formal and informal social capital in Europe', *European Sociological Review*, 23(4): 423–35.
Reiska, E., Roosmaa, E.L., Oras, K. and Taru, M. (2018) *Young Adults in Insecure Labour Market Positions in Estonia -the Results from a Qualitative Study*. EXCEPT Working Papers, WP No. 23, Tallinn: Tallinn University, Available from: https://www.except-project.eu/working-papers/
Rokicka, M. and Kłobuszewska, M. (eds) (2016) *The Short-Term Economic Consequences of Insecure Labour Market Positions in EU-28*. EXCEPT Working Papers, WP No. 10, Tallinn: Tallinn University, Available from: https://www.except-project.eu/working-papers/
Schenk, N., Dykstra, P., Maas, I. and Van Gaalen, R. (2014) 'Older adults' networks and public care receipt: do partners and adult children substitute for unskilled public care?' *Ageing & Society*, 34(10): 1711–29.
Silverstein, M., Parrott, T.M. and Bengtson, V.L. (1995) 'Factors that predispose middle-aged sons and daughters to provide social support to older parents', *Journal of Marriage and Family*, 57(2): 465–75.
Smith, C., Christoffersen, K., Davidson, H. and Snell Herzog, P. (2011) *Lost in Transition: The Dark Side of Emerging Adulthood*, Oxford: Oxford University Press.
Thoits, P.A. (1995) 'Stress, coping, and social support processes: where are we? What next?', *Journal of Health and Social Behaviour*, Spec No.: 53–79.
Walker, M.E., Wasserman, S. and Wellman, B. (1993) 'Statistical models for social support networks', *Sociological Methods & Research*, 22(1): 71–98.
Wellman, B. (1992) 'Which types of ties and networks provide what kinds of social support?', *Advances in Group Processes* 9: 207–35.
Wyn, J., Lantz, S. and Harris, A. (2012) 'Beyond the "transitions" metaphor: family relations and young people in late modernity', *Journal of Sociology*, 48(1): 3–22.

11

How young people experience and perceive labour market policies in four European countries

Roberta Ricucci, Chiara Ghislieri, Veneta Krasteva, Maria Jeliazkova, Marti Taru, and Magdalena Rokicka

Introduction

There is a growing concern about the socio-economic situation of young people, especially in those countries hit by the 2008 financial crisis (Eurofound, 2014; European Commission, 2016). As outlined by several studies, youth are more likely to be excluded from the labour market than prime age workers and to work under less favourable conditions (Banerji et al, 2014; International Labour Organization, 2015, 2017). It is no accident that the young are called the losers in a globalising world (Blossfeld et al, 2005). Therefore, it is important to find out not only what kind of counselling, job guidance, and other forms of support are available to them in various European countries, but also how they evaluate these policy tools. Are these initiatives and services in line with the expectations and needs of young people? How do these policy measures shape labour market prospects and future employment? Such questions are linked to the correspondence between, on one hand, young people's goals, expectations, and anticipated career path, and, on the other hand, the way policies address them.

This chapter is organised as follows: after providing information about the theoretical framework, it describes the main aspects of the national contexts in the chosen countries. It then presents the aims of the analysis. These are used as a basis to formulate the research questions and present the data used. Based on a comparative data analysis, results illustrate how young people use policies and perceive them. The final section discusses these results and summarises the findings while providing some policy suggestions.

Theoretical considerations

Several studies have highlighted the many facets and the complexity of today's youth, in terms of a list of 'lacks' that makes this generation of 'grown-up children' appear choosy and passive compared with previous generations, but they are also portrayed as 'more active, more enterprising, and more inclined to work' (Beaudry et al, 2015: 383). As a whole, the levels of complexity that confront young people in all societal domains seem to require targeted policies and practices such as, for example, guidance and support in planning their lives (Shore and Tosun, 2019). The frequent transitions from one insecure job to another, the discontinuities in educational paths, the enrolment in training courses and, above all, work path constraints need to be taken into account in guidance practice, and career counselling practices should activate and encourage the exploration of possible selves (Oyserman et al, 2006). Indeed, the guidance practices designed to sustain a job search must therefore help young people to reflect on their 'key assets' (Parker, 2007) in order to help them match their motivations and skills with the work activities needed by the contexts in which they live. Lack of job orientation, the need for the right information, quest for counselling, and tutorship in choosing educational, training, and job paths are common issues across countries (CEDEFOP, 2015). In this framework, it seems that European youth need more attention and concrete answers on how to fulfil their job aspirations, and, overall, how they can establish an autonomous life. These needs are part of the relationships between young people and institutions (schools, employment services, career offices, consultant agencies) at the local level, where young people live and try to develop their skills and job opportunities. Indeed, the outcome of the match between youth and their future in the labour market is a matter for local institutions, and these are the actors in charge of implementing national measures in actions and projects (Boeri and Jimeno, 2015). The interweaving derived from different regulatory actions and various authorities in terms of policies for the younger generation is therefore multilayered and complex across countries. Over time, there has been greater centrality on the local level, whose effective autonomy is being challenged by the weakness of the available resources (Ruano and Profiroiu, 2017; Pastore, 2018). In terms of financial resources and as a transversal topic, the progressive reduction in the transfer of resources from the centre to the periphery has highlighted how the decision (and the possibility) to intervene on each level in the approach to policies for young people is tied increasingly to the development of positive synergies between local authorities and private institutions (sometimes associations and civil society organisations) in each territory. In line with this way of managing the topic, the theoretical framework of this chapter is based on the street-level bureaucracy concept (Lipsky, 2010) that makes it possible to study the mechanisms and channels of formal state support in the form of active and passive labour market policies (ALMPs and PLMPs).

As explained by Lipsky (1980), the concept of street-level bureaucracy is built on two contradictory meanings. On the one side, bureaucracy is a set of procedures and rules imposed by the authorities to guarantee equal access to public services for all citizens who should be treated alike in their entitlement to welfare and benefits. On the other side, the street level conveys direct interactions in which individual needs and characteristics are accounted for, and certain decisions are at the discretion of public servants. As suggested by Lipsky, in street-level bureaucracy, routines and practices are adjusted so that they meet the personal needs and requirement of clients – citizens using public services. Public servants have to obey the rule of law, governmental regulations, and procedures. However, they also have a certain degree of autonomy regarding how they enforce these general rules and policies. Because citizens have direct contact with front-line public servants, the assessment of public servants' performance is associated with the evaluation of government authority and institutions per se. Therefore, one could expect that how youth assess particular labour market policies cannot be viewed in isolation from their personal experiences or the experiences of their peers with the staff at employment offices who are responsible for implementing these programmes and providing these services. While aware of this close relationship, this study will try as far as possible to disentangle the assessment of policies from the assessment of their implementation by public servants. Although there are some analyses and meta-analyses on the efficacy of active labour market policies (ALMPs; see Kluve, 2006; Caliendo and Schmidl, 2016) that highlight the relationship between investment and the effects of ALMPs on education and employment, only a few studies have considered the opinions – the voice – of young people with respect to policy (Ariely, 2013; Shore and Tosun, 2019). However, these opinions are important in understanding the causes of the relationship (positive, negative, or zero) between the policies and the developments and conclusions for which they were carried out.

For example, Caliendo and Schmidl (2016) have highlighted the need to evaluate the return on investment relative to the expenditure made by countries on ALMPs. The authors examined the effectiveness of a range of ALMPs (training courses, job search assistance and monitoring, subsidised employment, and public work programmes) on integration into the first integration in the labour market and further involvement in education, which were the two main objectives of the ALMPs. . Despite only a few partial data, this article highlights that the effectiveness of job search assistance (with and without monitoring) was overwhelmingly positive, whereas the effectiveness of training and wage subsidies was mixed, and of public work programmes was negative. However, Caliendo and Schmidt conclude that evidence on the impact of ALMPs on further education and on the quality of employment is scarce, and that further research is needed. The present study responds to this need, exploring the perceptions and assessments of policies by young Bulgarians, Estonians, Italians, and Poles.

Institutional contexts: different countries, different policies?

Labour market policy in **Poland** was formulated at the beginning of the 1990s. This coincided with a demographic peak and thousands of young people entering the labour market. Since then, different policy measures and instruments have been introduced to alleviate youth unemployment (which reached 42 per cent in 2002 among 15- to 24-year-olds). Together with economic, demographic, and political changes, these measures led to a decline in the unemployment rate, including among young people, to 14 per cent in 2017 (Eurostat Database, 2018).

Labour market policy in Poland is formulated by central government, which delegates its operation to regional and local administrations. Public employment services are decentralised and operate mainly on a regional (*Voivodship*) and a county level (*Poviat*). Poviat labour offices are responsible for registering the unemployed and paying unemployment benefits. There are also other labour market institutions: the Voluntary Labour Corps (OHP –specialised public institution acting on a national and local level), private job agencies, social partners, and local partnerships. EU priorities and incentives are extremely important in providing a framework for ALMP. Two of these are worth mentioning: the Youth Guarantee Scheme (YGS) and the Youth Employment Initiative.

Initiatives and programmes designed for young people in Poland change rapidly, and sometimes they are available only in specific regions. Long-term observations of youth labour market incentives in Poland show that internships are the main type of policy measure – 14.8 per cent of young unemployed (under 25 years) took part in internships in

2015 (Polish Ministry of Labour and Social Policy, 2015). In addition to internships, other popular measures are training, internship vouchers, training vouchers, and mobility vouchers (Zapala-Wiech, 2018).

In **Estonia,** provision of active labour market initiatives was launched in 1993. Between 1993 and 2009, developing and carrying out ALMP measures was the responsibility of the Estonian Labour Market Board established in 1990. On 1 May 2009, the Labour Market Board was reorganised and became the Estonian Unemployment Insurance Fund (EUIF). Hardly any youth-specific active labour market measures have been developed since the early 1990s. Before 2009, the number of ALMPs in general was low; there were no specific measures targeting young people. In 2009, a measure called 'Job Club' was introduced; in 2010 it was seen as an action specifically addressing, or at least more suitable for, young people (Siimer and Malk, 2010). The measure stopped running in 2018, after a similar service was offered by different measures. Estonia implemented the YGS initiated by the European Commission in 2015 through eight activities (My First Job; Workshops Directed to Youth; Introducing Labour Market and Working Life; Youth Guarantee Support System; Youth Prop-Up Programme; Youth Summer Work Brigades; Mobile Workshops to Introduce Selected Professions to Young People; Youth Initiatives; and Community Practice). Of the eight, the measure 'My First Job', which is administered by the EUIF, has the largest budget. This is a subsidised job programme that also has a subsidised job training component. Each young unemployed person enrolled in the measure will receive a sum of €2,500 that can be used to finance participation in one or more labour market training courses. Whether or not an unemployed person will actually participate in a course and which depends not only on the needs of the person as identified and agreed by the case manager, but also on the availability of courses. The job training component has been used by a minority of persons enrolled in the measure. The *Tugila* or 'Youth prop-up' programme is another policy initiative related to the YGS. What it does, essentially, is that youth workers using appropriate outreach methods attempt to identify young people who are unemployed and too discouraged to help themselves, or in need of support because of other life circumstances. The function of these youth workers is to encourage the young people, to counsel them, and, when necessary, to put them in touch with a specialist they consider most relevant in the particular case. This could be an EUIF case manager or it could also be a psychologist. This measure was initiated by the Estonian Youth Work Centre.

Italy stands out due to the high rate of unemployment among young people: 31.7 per cent in the 15 to 24 age range versus a European mean of 15.6 per cent (Eurostat Database, 2018; Istat, 2018). The 2008 crisis produced a need for new rules to regulate the labour market and to reduce the growing unemployment rate, especially among young people.

In 2015, the Jobs Act reform came into force, with the aim – according to the government – of addressing the growing rate of youth unemployment due to the negative effects of the financial crisis and supporting young people's insertion into a more globalised, competitive labour market. Despite these political statements, contractual insecurity did not diminish. On the contrary, the dark side of the coin emerged thanks to the opportunity for employers to modify workers' duties unilaterally on condition that new tasks are compatible with their level. Of course, flexibility increased and went beyond employment contracts and employers were able to act unilaterally, hampering the use of special 'vouchers' to pay seasonally (and at least daily or weekly workers).

In this context, both low- and high-skilled young people are paradoxically in the same quandary: the former due to their lack of skills, the latter due to a mismatch between their level of education and job opportunities.

The issue of youth unemployment has become central to the public debate in recent years and received the attention of policymakers. Almost daily, major national newspapers, magazines, and other mass media talk about cases of young unemployed people or young people with precarious jobs. Furthermore, the mass media rhetoric emphasises the 'brain drain' from Italy to other countries, speaking about the resurgence of Italian emigration (Ricucci, 2017). In recent years, internal mobility has increased as well (Svimez, 2017), recalling another key issue in the Italian context in which territorial differences still matter in the field of labour market policies, opportunities. and supports.

In **Bulgaria**, the adaptation of the labour market to transformation processes in the economy and society went through many serious difficulties. In the 1990s, labour market policies responded mainly through passive measures, proposing low benefit levels and adapting the regulatory frameworks to reduce the flow of registered unemployed. After 2003, in connection with the EU integration process, there was a shift to ALMPs based on various programmes and interventions aimed at various target groups. After 2010, the proportion of measures addressing young unemployed increased. In 2013, implementation of the YGS started and in the following year, special measures supporting young people were launched under the Youth Employment Initiative.

The overall formulation and coordination of labour market policies is highly centralised, while local labour offices register the unemployed, pay unemployment benefits, and implement different ALMPs. The targeted programmes try above all to provide a chance for young people by facilitating their transition into working life. However, most of the measures do not prioritise the most vulnerable groups among youth, and the support provided is often limited in duration. Furthermore, ALMPs aimed at reducing youth unemployment often have a compensatory function because of deficits in other public spheres and have to adopt the role of a corrective mechanism with a wide coverage. This is particularly true for inactive young people with little or no education. To be effective, active labour market measures need to replicate the whole process of institutional socialisation that has failed in the past. Hence, active labour market measures achieve different levels of effectiveness depending on their target subgroups among the group of jobless youth.

In summary, despite differences in the national economic contexts and labour market policies, similarities can be found in the four countries, particularly in the mobilisation of efforts to implement ALMPs, the implementation of common EU programmes such as the YGS, and the balance between centralised impacts and local activities. Additionally, in all four countries, young people cannot count on an organic, national, policy framework dedicated to them. Although younger generations are targeted by various initiatives, both legislative and operational, policy tools aimed directly at young people often have to be sought in the cracks among different, more general, measures. For example, these refer to the school system, the labour market, housing, and social policy in general.

Aims and research questions

Since 2008, the global financial crisis has affected specific employee groups; among these, young people and immigrants can be considered to be the most vulnerable. Indeed, scrutinising policies across several European countries reveals that young people have increasingly become the target group for ALMPs in numerous countries (O'Higgins, 2015; Pastore, 2017; Bjørn et al, 2019). In hard times, the role of public policies in supporting unemployed people is crucial (European Commission, 2017). The set of policies that can be taken into account range from activities in schools to orientation services, from counselling support to specific initiatives within the employment centres. Availability of such activities matters significantly in favouring the insertion of youth in the labour market when they are developed in coordination with an updated institutional framework with trained operators and personnel in charge who manage such activities in the local contexts that have been reshaped so severely by the crisis (van der Velden and Wolbers, 2003; Breen, 2005).

In view of this, it is essential to investigate how labour market policy measures are assessed by young people; what, from their perspectives, are the main weaknesses? Which areas could benefit potentially from improvements? A comparative approach based on interviews with young people from four European countries is useful in addressing these issues. This chapter focuses on the subjective feelings about different labour market policies and about the functioning of labour market institutions expressed by young people. It also identifies which factors encourage young people to use the support of labour market institutions and which hinder or prevent them from using such support. Bulgaria, Estonia, Italy, and Poland are the case studies: this selection is driven by the differences in both the situation of youth on the labour market and the different political institutions and labour market approaches in these countries. The chapter also investigates how far members of the Facebook generation, growing up in the post-Cold War era within the trend of progressive EU enlargement and widespread European citizenship, are defining shared requests and ways of thinking that go beyond borders. On the contrary, what national and local traits still define the relationship between the policies introduced and their use among youth?

The main aim of this chapter is to analyse the subjective assessments of young people from four European countries regarding the support they have received from the state in periods when they were unemployed or looking for a job. Based on the theoretical background, previous research, and the national contexts, the main research questions guiding the analysis in this chapter are:

1. How do young people assess the labour market policies and the activities offered by employment offices?
2. What factors encourage or discourage young people's use of labour market institutions?

Answers to these questions have led to suggestions emerging from reports by young people on their experiences, together with their socialisation on the labour market in the family, at school, and/or within their peer group.

Data and methodology

The analysis in this chapter is based on interviews with young people conducted as part of the EXCEPT project. The empirical material is composed of 186 qualitative interviews conducted in the four countries concerned: 43 in Bulgaria, 53 in Estonia, 50 in Italy, and 40 in Poland (Table 11.1).

Among the 186 qualitative interviews, 97 are with young people who have been involved in ALMPs (21 in Bulgaria, 29 in Estonia, 27 in Italy, and 20 in Poland) and 89 are with young people who have not had experience of ALMPs (22 in Bulgaria, 24 in Estonia, 23 in Italy, and 20 in Poland).

From a methodological point of view, reference is made to the full sample in the four scrutinised countries: this takes into account both those who have been involved with public services or have participated in a specific policy addressed to them, and those who have never had contact with employment services. The arguments for including those who have been involved in active labour market measures are clear: the analysis of their attitudes, satisfaction, and dissatisfaction can enrich understanding of the correspondence between young people's expectations and their real experience. At the same time, in order to evaluate attitudes towards employment offices, it is also important to investigate why other young people have not engaged with the measures, whether as a result of a lack of available programmes, unwillingness, or other reasons.

Young people's assessment of labour market policies in the four countries

The interviews with young people from the different countries about their interactions with employment offices reveal similarities and differences. The following subsections compare and analyse the

Table 11.1: Number of interviewees according to involvement in ALMPs

Involvement in ALMPs	Bulgaria	Estonia	Italy	Poland
Involved	21	29	27	20
Not involved	22	24	23	20
Total	43	53	50	40

nuances of their experience in different countries in regard to each research question.

How do young people assess labour market policies and activities offered by employment offices?

For most interviewees, evaluation of the programmes in which they were included is shaped mainly by the success they have in finding a job afterwards. Very often, young people express a positive attitude towards the training and internship opportunities they receive. However, they are disappointed when the end of the programme comes and they are without a job again. A number of interviews in each country reveal that the transition from internship provided by the state to employment is very difficult or impossible, especially in villages and small towns. Some Polish young people mention that the internship was neither in their field of specialisation nor did it lead to a full-time job contract. For example, Michalina participated in five internships organised by the poviat labour office. All of them were at the same local police station, but she still cannot get a job there and is waiting for one of the staff members to retire. In small towns with limited employment opportunities, the transition from internship into permanent employment is almost non-existent. The majority of respondents have had placements as interns in different public administration offices, but these offer only a few vacancies and very low employment turnover:

> 'It's like, some friend of somebody's friend is going to leave the job, so they are already sending their daughter to the appropriate faculty, to graduate and to take this place.' (Michalina, F, 26, HE, TE, PL).

Similar dissatisfaction with internships is expressed by Bronek, currently on an internship at the poviat labour office. When asked whether he is gaining new skills, he says:

> 'I wouldn't call this "learning". All the things I am doing right now ... I could do before.' (Bronek, M, 20, ME, U, PL)

Several interviewees in Estonia had received individual career training aimed at improving the efficacy of their job applications. Their evaluation is quite negative: this training focuses on fairly general aspects of applying for a job and in the case of applying for an actual job, other factors such as former experience and education play a more important role. This is also reflected in the interviewees' opinions.

I: Writing your CV ...
R: Yes, a sort of general stuff.
I: Was this helpful?
R: Well, maybe a bit for my CV although my CV was ok already before [the interviewee is referring to time before that training] ...
I: What about job interview training, was it useful for the interview?
R: I am not sure. In fact, it was the recruiter who gave me feedback [the interviewee is saying that it was not the case manager from the UIF who gave him feedback]. (Mati, M, 26, ME, U, EE)

Although interviewees do not see the training as very significant in the context of finding a job, it is still clear that opinions about training are polarised. Some of the interviewees are satisfied with the training, whereas others are negative. Those with a positive outlook see their experience as helpful and encouraging, whereas others consider it to have been a waste of time which had given them nothing useful. A positive experience is described in the following excerpt:

'Well, it was on how one finds a job, or something. How to put together a CV, communicate with people, search for a job, all this stuff. And this, this course, well it encouraged me indeed. That I indeed could search for a job and try and see what happens.' (Helena, F, 23, LE, U, EE)

This interviewee did in fact apply for a job, and from the perspective of assessing the usefulness of the UIF service, the quote shows that it was an encouraging experience.

A negative reaction to a course offering information is expressed in the following excerpt.

R: I have attended some sort of information lectures.
I: What do you think of those?
R: I think, these were a complete waste of time. One was some sort of handicraft; I have no idea why I was sent there. And then another one was on entrepreneurship. Hm. But this too

was only some group play and games. And lasted four hours only, I gained nothing from there. (Marju, F, 27, LE, U, EE)

Obviously, this interviewee is not satisfied with the use of her time. Nor has she acquired skills that would improve her future outlook. And it is also clear that she did not benefit from the content of the course.

The EUIF also subcontracts training providers in specific areas such as beauty services (for example, hairdressing, cosmetics), construction, computer programming, and so forth. Unlike careers advice, general preparation for applying for a job and the like, these courses prepare unemployed people to perform specific jobs. The decision to finance attendance at a course like this will be taken jointly by the case manager and the job seeker after having analysed the job seeker's situation, competencies, wishes, and preferences as well as the labour market situation. Hence, it is only natural that the majority of interviewees express satisfaction with the professional training they receive.

However, a recurring theme in the interviews in Estonia is the jobseeker's expectation that they would receive training to improve/obtain specific skills such as coding or offering beauty services.. This theme emerges from interviews with some unemployed who had a fairly clear idea of the field of training they wanted to enter, whereas others did not express such a strong inclination toward a specific area. The areas the job seekers were interested in included, for instance, computer programming, beauty services, and entrepreneurship training. There was little interest in attending babysitting or customer servicing training:

> 'I have been applying for a training since [pause] January [given the date of the interview, it was two months ago] [pause] but I don't have these €1,500 to pay for the training. ... It is a programming school, it is [pause] HTML, CCS, Javascript, it is an introductory training.' (Mari, F, 29, HE, U, EE)

Some of the interviewees express discontent with the content of the courses they had attended, because they found the courses useless in terms of acquiring concrete skills that would help them get a job:

> 'Through the EUIF, I took part in a training course on entrepreneurship. It was useful, in some sense, but at the same time I had a feeling as if sitting there had been a waste of time. Well, anyway, it was at least some activity.' (Toivo, M, 28, ME, U, EE)

In Italy, among young people with a low level of academic qualifications and an impoverished family environment, a certain vagueness emerges when they speak about policies, social benefits, and social welfare. Often these issues are met by strong statements and negative feelings that turn out to be inaccurate or based on word of mouth.

Young people frequently give up on relations with special services, on initiatives that could help them, because they are conditioned by a negative prejudice that focuses on the importance of social ties: the latter supports are seen to be more helpful and reliable than the guidance guaranteed by public institutions. Employment services appear to be living on another planet. Young interviewees report the discrepancy between their daily lives and the suggestions they receive from job counsellors. In a rapidly changing labour market environment, employers pay attention not only to formal education but also to the wide range of soft skills that can be developed through various experiences.

Some interviewees in Italy cite friends' negative experiences with the employment services. These stories have increased young people's disillusionment with public institutions, and they hark back to a kind of golden age in which students found jobs just after having got their diplomas.

Nonetheless, those Italian young people who – thanks to an active employment policy (for example, the YGS) – were able to turn the corner in their professional lives are very satisfied. For 24-year-old Margherita, the Youth Guarantee experience was a turning point because it gave her opportunities and self-confidence.

> 'It gave me a little more confidence than just going in blindly [pause] the fact that they looked after me, that I always had someone to speak to about certain things gave me a little more confidence and made it possible for me to have a much longer work experience, instead of working for 4 days I managed to stay on for 6 months, that at least. And in fact, I worked in the restaurant there.' (Margherita, F, 25, ME, U, IT)

It should be underlined, however, that several young people distinguish between YGS, which they appreciate because it is directed specifically towards them, and other more general related services. Whereas feelings about the former are mixed, the latter are, for the most part, roundly criticised.

One significant factor that shapes the youth assessment of ALMPs is the personal interaction of young people with employees in the state institutions. Many interviewees in Estonia, for instance, express positive reactions to the EUIF services and case managers with whom they have been in contact. In particular, they say in the interviews that they appreciate the practical help they received in terms of finding a suitable job or a training course.

> 'The EUIF has helped me so much. They guided and assisted me, advised certain training courses, helped to search for jobs and [pause] well, helped to consider which job I could apply to, what would be a suitable job for me. Altogether, the EUIF has helped me so much.' (Maili, F, 18, LE, U, EE)

Some of the reactions are simply general assessments of the case manager. However, it can be difficult to distinguish between views about an actual case officer and the services offered by the EUIF. So, even if the interviewees mention only case managers, they could not have expressed this attitude outside the range of services offered by the EUIF itself, independently of the characteristics of an individual case manager:

> 'They are very nice, trying to help.' (Stella, F, 24, ME, U, EE)

> 'A very nice consultant.' (Anna, F, 29, HE, U, EE)

Sometimes, however, relationships external to the unemployment status and the relationship between an unemployed person and the EUIF might play an important role:

> 'The current case manager, she came through family relationships, she firmly holds me trying to find me an easy life.' (Peep, M, 25, LE, TE, EE)

A reaction that repeatedly surfaces from interviews in Estonia is dissatisfaction with case managers. This irritation addresses the level of enthusiasm and energy that case managers devote to helping and assisting the unemployed – it is often perceived as being too limited. According to some interviewees, case managers simply ask what unemployed young people have done to find a job, instead of offering adequate help and assistance to help them find a job.

> 'But those experienced ones [the interviewee is referring to consultants] – so, what will you do? Will you write me an

application? So, you just leave and drop it there. It was just like that – I felt like writing an application that I want to give up totally. And there you just feel how you are regarded as inferior.' (Aleksandr, M, 26, ME, U, EE)

Another characteristic of the counselling process at the EUIF that is mentioned repeatedly as negative is frequent changes of case managers. Quite a lot of interviewees mention that during the time they had been in interaction with the EUIF, their counsellor has changed several times. This means that each time a young person meets a new officer, she or he needs to start telling her or his story all over again right from the start. As a result, the meeting is spent on giving an overview of the situation, not on addressing substantive issues with the unemployed young person. However, for some, the change of counsellor has actually meant a positive change, because the new counsellor was more active and more eager to help the particular young person, and as a result, they found a job or a training course.

> 'It turned out that I changed consultants five times and, in the end, a young girl, still an apprentice, was assigned my case. She was of my age approximately and we started to interact and communicate intensively and it turned out so that she very soon found a suitable training course for me. Without any problems at all.' (Deniss, M, 28, ME, U, EE)

Several interviewees also mention that case managers are too strict with them, to the extent that may even be perceived as harsh. However, this perceived strictness and harshness is evidently a result of case managers following internal rules of service provision in the EUIF and their control over the counselling process.

R: Yes, I have now new case manager who is much harsher to me.
I: What do you mean, much harsher?
R: Well, she requires that I would do more when looking for a job, but I am very pessimistic about that [pause] In the first place, you see, I am not so very keen on listening to that boss and secondly, I would like to minimise working in my life. (Georg, M, 23, LE, U, EE)

Among the services the EUIF in Estonia offers are apprenticeship positions, voluntary work, and work practice. Although these jobs do not come with an employment contract, they still involve a legal relationship between the person who does the work and the organisation that provides it. Although their main purpose is to support getting people ready for work, they also have the potential to evolve into an employment contract. These services receive a positive assessment from the interviewees.

The lack of adequate personal support tailored to individual young people in Bulgaria and the formalism and bureaucracy of the employment offices often explain the negative attitudes of young Bulgarians:

'The assistance provided by public employment services is inadequate. Services are not personalised and do not take into account both health condition and individual preferences of the job seeker.' (Mira, F, 24, ME, U, BG)

'Well, because the organisation itself so to speak is one system that simply is mostly doing nothing or offers you some jobs that you're not interested in, you have no desire, and they say – well we had offered him – he does not want anything.' (Kiro, M, 28, HE, PE, BG)

Young Bulgarians who have engaged in policy measures share some positive and some negative views about the programmes. The evaluations of the various ALMPs depend on the personal experience, prospects provided, and the relevance of the program to the young person.

When the programmes provide job opportunities which match the young person's level of education or training, evaluations are positive.

'Definitely positively, because, I suppose you know that when you graduate it is very difficult to get a job because most employers require you to have some experience, on one hand. On the other hand, they want you to be young. This is pretty hard, so I'm glad there is such a programme and thanks to it I could find work.' (Daria, F, 22, HE, PE, BG)

When the programmes are short term and provide no follow up, they are often considered meaningless and just ticking boxes. Negative views are often related to doubt about whether the programmes will lead to job offers.

'Yes, I think that I need more security [pause] I think it's important to have security in your personal life and at work, because it has a very big impact on the human psyche and way of life. As an employee of the programme, I have a job for nine months, yes, I have a job that I like, which is not irrelevant. Any contracts, it is not specifically about contracts, but it is another thing to know that you are in a permanent job, and another thing to know that you are under a programme. Things are different.' (Donna, F, 24, HE, TE, BG)

'Duration, yes [pause] It is something which I'm worried about because after that it is not clear what is going to happen [pause] I have to go through the same path [pause] to register myself at the employment office, to get an unemployment benefit and after that [pause] uncertainty.' (Katya, F, 29, HE, TE, BG)

Still, the most common reason for negative assessments of ALMPs and labour offices in Bulgaria, both for those involved with them and those not involved, is the low pay.

'Young people can find a job, but existing jobs are not well paid. Remuneration is not sufficient and adequate, and, therefore, these factors prevent young people from making a decision to establish their own families. As another option, unfavourable labour market conditions force young people to leave the country in search of better working conditions and higher salaries [pause] The public authorities at central and local level [the municipality] can change this situation, but in fact are not willing to do that: Where there's a will, there's a way.' (Koko, M, 27, HE, TE, BG)

What factors encourage or discourage young people's use of labour market institutions?

One common feature of the interviewees from the four countries is that few of them met the eligibility criteria for unemployment benefits or other forms of social support when needed.

Very few Polish interviewees were receiving unemployment benefits (PLMPs). The eligibility criteria seem specifically to limit access to this form of support to young people or recent school leavers. Unemployment benefits are available for a person who has been employed for at least 365 days during the previous 18 months, paid all social contributions, and received at least the minimum wage. The amount of unemployment benefit varies slightly depending on previous tenure; however, the maximum level of unemployment benefit is around 800 zł (which is about 40 per cent of the minimum wage) for the first three months, and then it decreases by 20 per cent. What is worth mentioning is that the amount does not depend on previous earnings and is based on the minimum wage.

R: Last year, for sure [pause] I was getting the benefit for half of a year.
I: And then after this half-year benefit, did you have some other form of support? [pause]
R: No, they were just calling me, asking whether I'm looking through the offers, and I do, but nobody wants me. (Konrad, M, 23, ME, U, PL)

The following interview extract is an example of the relationship between young people and the employment office in Italy. Dario, a young 28-year-old man, lives in Catania (in Southern Italy), is highly educated, and has a permanent part-time job:

'That's pretty much the million-dollar question [smiling] in the sense that I think we'll try for a while to find the perfect recipe. I don't know, I would not be able to respond with an honestly great idea, because then I think that the difficulties, in this historic phase, are also linked a little to economic difficulties in general. In times of economic prosperity maybe, you know, one thing leads to another.' (Dario, M, 25, HE, TE, IT)

Only very few young people in Bulgaria receive unemployment benefits due to the inadequate and restrictive eligibility criteria. Some of the young people who have children of their own receive child allowances (family benefits) but these are considered very low.

'Children allowances are 37 leva [around €19] and do not cover even kindergarten. They cover nothing. Absolutely nothing. At least they should make them so that you can pay the fee in kindergarten. There are paid 60 leva per month, and they give 37 leva and now the food at school has to be paid and when you don't have maternity allowances [benefits during maternity leave for a child] and very low minimum wage.' (Tina, F, 28, HE, U, BG)

Others receive heating support in the winter:

'We received once 130 leva and after that 260 leva. This is a total of 400 leva per year for heating support. In winter we pay 130 to 140 leva per month for electricity.' (Vania, F, 23, ME, U, BG)

However, some of those interviewed doubt the opportunities to receive social assistance, because this is connected with certain conditions that should be covered.

'Then they will send me 15 days to sweep streets in order to continue to receive aid. The bad thing is, that there is nowhere to drop off your child, thus you cannot go to sweep. Otherwise, I receive 37 leva for the bigger child and 50 leva for the smaller one. A total of 87 leva [around 44 Euro] monthly. If the children do not have immunisation, I will not get even this money.' (Vania, F, 23, ME, U, BG)

'The adequacy of social assistance benefits is very low and at the same time beneficiaries are required to perform community service 14 days per month [pause]. This is [pause] in my opinion this is a mockery with the people's work.' (Victor, M, 28, ME, PE, BG)

The respondents from Poland rarely mention social assistance benefits and they do not seem to play any important role for them. However, for the majority of young people, obtaining free health insurance is one of the main incentives for registering at the local employment office.[1]

Coverage of social benefits by the state during training and internships offered by ALMP is a very important factor in programme participation for some of the young people. In Poland, for instance, trainees in internship schemes, available for registered unemployed people for up to 12 months, get social and health insurance and a monthly remuneration equal to 120 per cent of unemployment benefits. According to some of our respondents, this is a very useful form of support.

'These internships here in our sector, it's a very good thing, because without such internship, to get somewhere straight away, it's probably really difficult. So, I think it's a cool thing. Me, myself, I really learned a lot during all these internships, really a lot. So, for me it was a very useful thing, because without it I don't think I would get in here.' (Ewa, F, 30, HE, TE, PL)

The same is true in Estonia: young people who have registered at the EUIF but do not want and are not planning to work turn down all information on available jobs. The reasons this group give for registering at the EUIF include the availability of health insurance, unemployment transfers, and the possibility of receiving labour market training.

One of the main reasons that young people feel discouraged about using labour market institutions is their low level of trust that they will get any help from them. This attitude is found in the interviewees in all four countries.

Young Poles have low trust in public administration in general and hold negative stereotypes about employment institutions. Anna, like other Poles, is clearly unwilling to consider the services provided by the labour office, because she recalls the bad experiences of her father at labour offices, and does not count on any support coming from official sources. Gabrysia, for example, has not applied for housing allowance although she is entitled to it, because she has problems facing clerks at any public administration office:

'Well me, if I am just supposed to go to some institution or just to some office, I just get sick three days before. So I just can't manage all these things.' (Gabrysia, F, 23, ME, TE, PL)

This might be a typical attitude inherited from the previous generation and parental experiences of socialism when public administration was mainly seen as a hierarchical and authoritarian element of state control and not as a client-friendly provider of public policy and support.

Moreover, young people who claim that they are not interested in seeking state support stress the importance of self-reliance in adult life as a form of independence:

'Just a formality [registering as an unemployed in the city council]. If everyone would count on something, well ... no, I don't count on it.' (Gabrysia, F, 23, ME, TE, PL)

Interviewees in Estonia have mixed reactions to the information[2] on job opportunities that have opened up through the EUIF. One clearly articulated and common reactions to information on job opportunities is that "there is nothing suitable for me, no job I would be willing to take". Reasons for not taking a job vary, however, and are often linked to the job seeker's life circumstances; for example, mothers of young babies clearly have specific job requirements that are compatible with their care responsibilities.

Young people in Estonia searching for a convenient job and good working conditions are also selective about information from the

EUIF. Their job expectations include that they are interesting and exciting, easily accessible, carried out in normal working hours, and in a specific location.

Generally speaking, young people interviewed in Bulgaria do not consider labour market policies to be an important contribution to their well-being or likely to help them find appropriate jobs. Young people who are not involved usually assess these policies negatively:

> 'I will apologise for what I will say but [pause] in my point of view the state does not do anything.' (Milena F, 21, ME, U, BG)

> 'I do not trust public employment services [pause] I have many friends who are registered there [pause] but nothing happened.' (Boris, M, 26, LE, U, BG)

Some of the young people registered at the labour office have never been offered any programme or training:

> 'I registered two years ago and they never offered me anything.' (Valyo, M, 21, LE, U, BG)

> 'I've been registered for a period of one year and they still haven't suggested a job offer corresponding to my field of studies [pause] So I'm doubtful.' (Kornelia, F, 26, HE, TE, BG)

Others feel that programmes cannot offer what they need:

> 'If there is something and it will help me start working as a hairdresser or as a sous-chef at good pay, I would go.' (Valya, F, 20, ME, U, BG)

> 'No, I have not dealt with that [pause] It never crossed my brains to register. Otherwise, a friend told me to register there and I told him all right I will sign, but I didn't go [pause] I don't know them. I haven't got friends who found a job this way. I would take advantage of existing programmes provided I liked the pay.' (Stefan, M, 21, ME, U, BG)

> 'I know nothing about those programmes and I don't need them. I can't become a street cleaner because that's what you have to do following some kind of employment programme. I don't know what else they have to offer. I've heard something

about educational programmes that offer professional learning courses but the programme members are trained to become waiters, cooks, or to get computer skills and I don't need those skills. A programme to help me find the proper internship corresponding to my education would be good for me now. If there is such a programme, but I don't know if there is any.' (Ani, F, 24, HE, U, BG)

A very decisive factor for participation in ALMP is the (lack of) information about the LM programmes and the opportunities given by the ALMPs. Most young people in the Polish sample have very limited knowledge of existing labour market policies, especially when they have no previous experience with labour market institutions. However, this changes when they are unsuccessful in searching for jobs themselves and they register at the local employment office.

R: I didn't believe that you can find work through the city council, to be honest.
I: And now something has changed, that sometimes it works out?
R: Well, something yes ... [laughs] [pause] There is this support for young people. There are many programmes, there are some vouchers, there is also this programme supporting employers of people below the age of 30 [pause] and there are these internships here, as well, also as a form of a support. (Łukasz, M, 29, HE, TE, PL).

In Bulgaria, there are grounds to believe that the main reason why the most vulnerable young people do not participate in measures and programmes offered by public employment services is their lack of awareness of the available options. Another reason why some of them do not participate is the belief that state support is for people in need who do not have any other means of coping with their situation.

In Italy, the lack of concrete information that is readily available and expressed in comprehensible (that is, not bureaucratic) and accessible language is often cited negatively. The employment service, in particular, is seen as remote from young people. In their perceptions, these services are rooted in the past, whereas serious employee training efforts are needed.

Indeed, young people in Italy do not really understand what employment services do and, in general, they think that there is a lack of information about the policies and benefits that might be available.

'There's an unbelievable queue [to gain access to the employment office], you have to be there at 7am to register in two minutes [pause] If it was online it would be easier, but [pause] and [pause] there are two employment offices, it depends on where you live, and [pause] What can I say, you register [pause] I don't really understand what they do, I mean, ok, they register you, but then.' (Margherita, F, 25, ME, U, IT)

Discussion

There are a number of similarities in the opinions voiced by young people starting with a lack of trust in institutions. It is evident that young people do not rely too much on the help received from labour offices. Part of this might be explained by the general distrust of public administration, negative stereotypes regarding the functioning of these institutions, and insufficient knowledge about available policy measures. On the other hand, young people assess the activities of the labour offices on the basis of the results achieved. If and when an adequate job is offered, young people seem ready to forgive institutions for their weaknesses. However, when the interaction does not result in an adequate job offer, the purpose of the interaction remains obscure and this leads to negative assessments.

It is important to underline that in all the countries under scrutiny, there are young people among those interviewed who are involved in specific programmes offered by the labour offices and they are satisfied with the support provided. However, these are usually exceptions and not the rule. Second, such personal histories are not well known and could hardly be used as examples by other young people. Another common problem concerns the scarcity of concrete information that is both readily available and expressed in accessible language. In several cases, young people who have been in touch with local labour offices stress the bureaucratic ritualism and excessive focus on rules and regulations as a barrier to the effectiveness of these institutions. Furthermore, several public operators confirm numerous critical points in the performance of their work. Criticisms include the impersonal approach and unhelpful support from advisers. Often, young people receive job offers that do not match their qualifications or their specific personal situations – for example, a car mechanic receiving a job offer for unskilled manual work as a house renovator, or a young mother with small children offered work in a liquor store open at night. One particular issue linked to this point and raised by various interviewees is frequent changes in employment advisers in the course of the process.

Demand was widespread with regard to expectations in receiving specific, concrete and helpful training. This is especially relevant for some interviewees who have a fairly clear understanding of the field of training they would like to enter. Nonetheless, even those who do not have clear expectations regarding a specific kind of training expect a training to not just be for the sake of the training, but that it should lead to an appropriate job offer. When that does not happen, evaluation of the activities of labour offices is quite negative. Most of the young respondents stress the need for better educational counselling to help them to to choose the right educational path according to their skills and attitudes.

Another interesting theme relates to counselling practices: according to many interviewees in all four countries, services should be more focused and address teenagers in schools; and the high school and university curriculum should give students more practical experience and prepare them better for the labour market. Asked what they would change, several point to the need for university studies to be better adjusted to the labour market, and for a greater exchange of experiences between employers, students, and universities. On the other hand, many interviewees find that labour market institutions are somewhat outdated or obsolete, and that more dynamic and innovative approaches are needed to transform them into more client-friendly and modern institutions.

Young people stress the level of benefits and the difficulties in gaining them due to bureaucratic barriers. In some countries (Bulgaria and Estonia), this happened in a very explicit way while, in other cases, in a hidden way (Poland and Italy); in this last case, it mostly regarded interviewees involved in specific programmes. It has to be said that some young unemployed people are pressurised into registering at labour offices for other purposes than finding work, for example, to gain health insurance, to receive child allowance, heating support, and so forth. However, this hardly contributes to better assessments of the work of the employment offices. Rather, this is seen as an obligation to be met, but assessments depend on offering an appropriate job.

Interviews therefore reveal that both male and female young people in all these countries have rational expectations of the labour offices: (a) that they should receive an offer proposing an appropriate and good quality job, or training followed by an appropriate job offer; and (b) that interactions with staff in the labour offices should follow established standards for quality work with a client-centred attitude, clear concern, and helpful advice tailored to their personal situation. These are also the basic directions for improvements in the studied field.

Conclusions

This chapter extends the literature on school-to-work transitions by investigating the role of policies in support of labour market insertion. It contributes to the literature on policy evaluation in three respects. First, previous comparative research has often evaluated policies in terms of their outcomes. This study uses qualitative material based on policy recipients' experiences, thus allowing a more dynamic analysis of how the issue of having (or not having) a job interplays with other crucial issues. Second, the use of interviews carried out in four countries with the same questionnaire makes it possible to compare and contrast perceptions on the same topics while controlling for potential context effects on the interviewees.

Finally, although the relationship of youth labour insertion to social and gender inequality has been a central issue in this research field, the perspective of the unemployed has been largely neglected despite several EU policy documents and initiatives developed to address them (European Commission, 2012, 2014).

Regardless of the different national contexts, many similarities emerge across the sample when young people from the four different countries assess labour market policies and the activities of labour offices. In addition, although some nuances are derived for the different countries, it should be stressed that experiences are problematic in all four countries. In every country, personal contact with staff in the labour offices are often unsatisfactory; few young people are motivated to turn to employment agencies. Offering appropriate or relevant and good quality jobs is crucial here. Crucial for policymakers, however, should be findings that confirm a lack of trust in state institutions to help improve young people's situation and help them find jobs. Many interviewees describe employment offices as the last place they would go to look for a job. In some cases, the negative attitude is based on the opinions of friends and family rather than on any personal experience. Despite this, many interviewees share that they have been registered in the employment office for a long time but never received a job offer or any kind of support. At the same time, many young people do not know about the existence of programmes and measures that the state offers to facilitate inclusion in the labour market. Supporting young people toward labour insertion means working on different levels and with a wide range of actors and institutions.

The educational paths and the business organisations, local youth services, and all the departments (from housing to financial aid for setting up a new business) should be involved in planning and updating coherent and coordinated policies. Among these, it is inevitably the educational system that young people stress. Indeed, even when expressed in different ways, the core message is the same: if policies are to be efficacious, it is important to look at school and its role in training students in the right skills, and the need to update school curricula in line with the skills and competencies needed in a changing world.

However, it is not just schools and the labour market that appear to be separate worlds for young people. In all four countries (and in others, according to the literature), it is the school system that is failing to supply a solid cultural basis offering knowledge and competences for interacting with a complex, rapidly changing, and unpredictable world of work. In addition to the need to update teaching programmes, guidance services should be implemented to spread both knowledge and awareness of how helpful various services, initiatives, tools, and opportunities can be, and to try to overcome the perception that it is only *social connections together with someone's influence that matter*. The interviewees seem to have clearly understood that there is a need to go beyond bureaucratic scrutiny of education, and they stress the importance of recognising informal educational and work experience (for example, odd jobs, voluntary work) in developing professional skills. The feeling of being mistreated and undervalued in both regular and irregular jobs is another theme that cuts across interviews in all four countries.

In the already negative scenario depicted in the interviews, things are potentially even worse for those in certain groups. The situation of those who are NEET or belong to specific risk groups such as immigrants, people with disabilities, or part of the minorities who are often unwelcome in certain countries appears more complex than that of young people who have diplomas or degrees and who do not suffer from multiple institutional discrimination. To the recipients, employment services seem ill- prepared to overcome stereotypes and develop more friendly and understandable policies in both their procedures (the way they train their operators) and their relations with entrepreneurs and other key figures on the labour market.

In summary, the findings highlight that labour policies must be able to address the circumstances and requirements of those they are intended to serve, and inform individualised and targeted practices based on the range of requirements of the young people involved: standard practices have not met the support needs young people who are unemployed or in insecure employment. The services provided are simply perceived as bureaucratic and remote from the young people they are designed to serve. Finding a balance between individualised practices and cost compatible with public spending is the real challenge facing many countries in the coming years.

Notes

1. In Poland, registered unemployed people can still use the public health system, and this is considered a measure of protection. Few people in our sample used this as an additional benefit while working informally as manual workers in small factories.
2. Through online portals, emails sent directly to registered unemployed people, information delivered at the counselling sessions, and information obtained at job fairs.

References

Ariely, G. (2013) 'Public administration and citizen satisfaction with democracy: Cross-national evidence', *International Review of Administrative Sciences*, 79(4): 747–66.

Banerji, A., Saksonovs, S., Lin, H. and Blavy, R. (2014) *Youth Unemployment in Advanced Economies in Europe: Searching for Solutions*. International Monetary Fund Staff Discussion Note, SDN/14/11, Washington: International Monetary Fund.

Beaudry, P., Green, D.A. and Sand, B.M. (2015) 'The declining fortunes of the young since 2000', *American Economic Review*, 104(5): 381–86.

Bjørn H., Schoyen, M. and Sirovátka, T. (eds) (2019) *Youth Unemployment and Job Insecurity in Europe: Problems, Risk Factors and Policies*, Cheltenham: Edward Elgar Publishing.

Blossfeld, H.P., Klijing, E., Mills, M. and Kurz, K. (2005) *Globalization, Uncertainty, and Youth in Society: The Losers in a Globalizing World*, Abingdon: Routledge.

Boeri, T. and Jimeno, J.F. (2015) 'Unemployment in Europe: what does it take to bring it down?', *Paper Prepared for the European Central Bank Forum on Central Banking*, Available from: https://www.ecb.europa.eu/pub/conferences/ecbforum/shared/pdf/2015/boeri_paper.pdf

Breen, R. (2005) 'Explaining cross-national variation in youth unemployment: Market and industrial factors', *European Sociological Review*, 21(2): 125–34.

Caliendo, M. and Schmidl, R. (2016) 'Youth unemployment and active labor market policies in Europe', *IZA Journal of Labor Policy*, 5(1): 1–30.

CEDEFOP (2015) *On the Way to 2020: Data for Vocational Education and Training Policies. Country Statistical Overviews*, Thessaloniki: CEDEFOP.

Eurofound (2014) *Social Situation of Young People in Europe*, Luxembourg: Publications Office of the European Union.

European Commission (2012) *EU Youth Report, EU Youth Strategy 2010–2018*, Luxembourg: Publications Office of the European Union.

European Commission (2014) *Investing in People: EU Funding for Employment and Social Inclusion*, Luxembourg: Publications Office of the European Union.

European Commission (2016) *EU Youth Report 2015*, Luxembourg: Publications Office of the European Union.

European Commission (2017) *European Semester Thematic Factsheets: Active Labour Market Policies*, Luxembourg: Publications Office of the European Union.

Eurostat Database (2018) 'Unemployment by sex and age: annual average', Available from: http://appsso.eurostat.ec.europa.eu/nui/show.do?dataset=une_rt_a&lang=en

International Labour Organization (2015) *Global Employment Trends for Youth 2015: Scaling up Investments in Decent Jobs for Youth*, Geneva: ILO.

International Labour Organization (2017) *Global Employment Trends for Youth 2017: Paths to a Better Working Future*, Geneva: ILO.

Istat (2018) *Rapporto Annuale 2018: La Situazione del Paese*, Rome: Istat.

Kluve, J. (2006) *The Effectiveness of European Active Labor Market Policy*. IZA Discussion Papers, No. 2018, Bonn: Institute of Labor Economics (IZA).

Lipsky, M. (1980) *Street-Level Bureaucracy: Dilemmas of the Individual in Public Services,* New York: Russell Sage Foundation.

Lipsky, M. (2010) *Street-Level Bureaucracy: Dilemmas of the Individual in Public Services: 30th Anniversary*, New York: Russell Sage Foundation.

O'Higgins, N. (2015) *Youth Unemployment*. IZA Policy Paper, No. 103, Bonn: Institute of Labor Economics (IZA).

Oyserman, D., Bybee, D. and Terry, K. (2006) 'Possible selves and academic outcomes: how and when possible selves impel action', *Journal of Personality and Social Psychology*, 91(1): 188–204.

Parker, D. (2007) *The Self in Moral Space: Life Narrative and the Good*, Ithaca: Cornell University Press.

Pastore, F. (2017) 'Getting it right: youth employment policy within the EU', *CESifo Forum*, 18(2): 26–33.

Pastore, F. (2018) *Why is Youth Unemployment So High and Different Across Countries?* IZA World of Labor, Article no. 420. Bonn: Institute of Labor Economics (IZA).

Polish Ministry of Labour and Social Policy (2015) 'Sprawozdanie MPiPS-01 o rynku pracy za rok 2015: Compare with Sytuacja na rynku pracy osób młodych w roku 2015, Sytuacja na rynku pracy osób młodych - yearly reports 2009–1015', Available from: http://www.mpips.gov.pl/analizy-i-raporty/raporty-sprawozdania/rynek-pracy/sytuacja-na-rynku-pracy-osob-mlodych/

Ricucci, R. (2017) *The New Southern European Diaspora: Youth, Employment and Migration*, Lanham: Lexington.

Ruano, J.M. and Profiroiu, M. (eds) (2017) *The Palgrave Handbook of Decentralisation in Europe*, Cham: Palgrave Macmillan.

Shore, J. and Tosun, J. (2019) 'Personally affected, politically disaffected? How experiences with public employment services impact young people's political efficacy', *Social Policy and Administration*, 53(7): 958–73.

Siimer, K. and Malk, L. (2010) *Noored Töötud Eesti Tööturul*. Teemaleht Sotsiaalministeeriumi toimetised. Working Paper 4, Tallinn: Sotsiaalministeerium.

Svimez (2017) *Rapporto Svimez Sull'Economia del Mezzogiorno*, Bologna: Il Mulino.

Van der Velden, R. and Wolbers, M. (2003) 'The integration of young people into the labour market: the role of training systems and labour market regulation', in W. Müller and M. Gangl (eds) *Transition from Education to Work in Europe: The Integration of Youth into EU Labour Markets*, Oxford: Oxford University Press, pp 186–211.

Zapała-Więch, J. (2018) *Youth Employment Policies in Poland*. EXCEPT Working Papers, WP No. 25, Tallinn: Tallinn University, Available from: https://www.except-project.eu/working-papers/

PART III

Labour market insecurity and the socio-economic consequences for youth

12

Can labour market policies protect unemployed youth from poverty? A cross-European comparison

Małgorzata Kłobuszewska, Marta Palczyńska, Magdalena Rokicka, Jędrzej Stasiowski, Kadri Täht, and Marge Unt

Introduction

Economic deprivation and poverty are often related to what has increasingly been referred to as multiple disadvantage (Kieselbach et al, 2001; Berthoud, 2003; McDonald and Marston, 2005). This could be described as a bidirectional relationship in which deprivation during early socialisation leads, for example, to early school leaving and subsequently to unemployment, whereas unemployment (Cantó-Sanchéz and Mercader-Prats, 1999) or labour market insecurity (Pavis et al, 2000; Clasen and Goerne, 2011) increase the risk of economic deprivation and poverty among youth. The latter risk is higher when access to welfare is restricted or non-existent (Saltkjel and Malmberg-Heimonen, 2017) and when the family of origin is, for whatever reason, unable to support its offspring.

Previous studies on youth poverty (Aassve et al, 2006, 2013; Scarpetta et al, 2010) have pointed out various risk factors for material deprivation among youth, and a central one of these is unemployment. Most studies find that, on average, early youth unemployment has serious negative effects on incomes: young adults experiencing labour market exclusion face a significantly higher risk of poverty and material deprivation (Aassve et al, 2006; Rokicka and Kłobuszewska, 2016). Moreover, as well as the short-term effect, young adults experiencing unemployment in their early careers may become 'scarred' with respect to their future careers and face issues such as increased risk of unemployment or reduced earnings (see for example Arulampalam, 2001; Steijn et al, 2006; Schmillen and Umkehrer, 2013). Next to the material dimension, the negative effect of unemployment has also been observed on a psychological level resulting in negative expectations of future employment prospects (Knabe and Rätzel, 2011), reduced life satisfaction (Wulfgramm, 2014), career dissatisfaction (Helbling and Sacchi, 2014), reduced subjective psychological well-being (Alvaro and Garrido, 2003), and reduced self-esteem (Sheeran et al, 1995).

When trying to explain youth deprivation and poverty, the main focus of previous research has been on individual or social origin characteristics (Aassve et al, 2006) such as family structure (Berthoud, 2003; Kangas and Palme, 2000), or on labour market factors such as unemployment or low pay (Pavis et al, 2000). However, a growing body of research is pointing out that in order to better understand the distribution and accumulation of (economic) disadvantage, structural factors should also be taken into consideration (Aassve et al, 2002, 2013; Saltkjel and Malmberg-Heimonen, 2017). Previous studies have demonstrated a relationship between macroeconomic characteristics of a country and that country's distribution of income levels. For example, the lower the wealth of a country (measured in GDP) the higher the levels of poverty and deprivation. Likewise, the higher the unemployment rate – particularly long-term unemployment – in a country, the higher the levels of poverty or deprivation (Aassve et al, 2013; Duiella and Turrini, 2014). At the same time, studies show that both poverty rates and labour market factors such as unemployment, which are risk factors for youth poverty, tend to vary across countries (Cantó-Sanchéz and Mercader-Prats, 1999; Aassve et al, 2006). The same also applies to the association between financial resources and deprivation levels, as shown in a study by Nolan and Whelan (2010) who analysed the variability in poverty and social exclusion levels in Europe. A study by Kenworthy (2011) has also shown a modest negative relationship between the size of social policy expenditure and material deprivation, although that effect varies across countries.

One plausible explanation for this varying effect is the variability in the countries' institutional contexts. Individual life courses are socially embedded in the macroinstitutional and structural context that defines the set of opportunities and constraints to which individuals respond (Mayer, 2009; Buchmann and Kriesi, 2011). Whereas the institutional and structural context is shaped fundamentally by policies that vary strongly across countries, national institutional settings and policies have a moderating effect on how risks of labour market exclusion among young people translate into risks of social exclusion (Mills and Blossfeld, 2003). In other words, the major detrimental consequence of unemployment is a lack of personal income that translates directly into a deterioration of the financial situation along with material deprivation, which can be alleviated not only by informal support but also by specific policy measures. However, in the same way that policies vary across countries, youth in different countries also vary in the extent to which they experience both the risks as well as the outcomes of economic hardship. Saltkjel and Malmberg-Heimonen (2017) have demonstrated that the negative effect of unemployment on the risk of both material deprivation and income poverty is mediated significantly by the welfare generosity level of a country. The central policy measures intended to shape the labour market situation and, respectively, the effect of labour market insecurities on young people's economic situation are passive and active labour market policies (PLMPs and ALMPs) (Gallie and Paugam, 2000). These are also the central focus of interest in the current chapter.

The aim of the study presented here is to understand the moderating effect of ALMPs and PLMPs on the (negative) effect of unemployment on the economic situation of young people. It does this by drawing on cross-sectional microdata from the EU-Statistics on Income and Living Conditions (EU-SILC) survey from 2013. The first part of the chapter gives an overview on the association between individuals' economic situation and the country institutional context based on previous research. Then, hypotheses are formulated on the moderating effect of ALMPs and PLMPs. The second part of the chapter discusses the data and data-related issues and presents the findings of the study. The chapter closes with a summary of the findings and a short discussion.

The moderating effect of labour market policies on the economic situation of unemployed youth

One of the central 'equalising effects' on the dispersion of income highlighted in previous studies is the generosity of a country's welfare system and existing (social) policies (Korpi and Palme, 1998; Kenworthy, 1999; Bäckman, 2009; Brady et al, 2009). Access to welfare resources can modify the extent to which individual disadvantages in one area relate to disadvantages in another (Fritzell and Lundberg, 2007). Welfare systems provide benefits and services to meet individuals' needs (Kenworthy, 2011) and influence individuals' and households' income and consumption (Nelson, 2012). In other words, existing policy measures (via the provision of services, benefits, and so on) can buffer the impact of income loss or low income associated with unemployment (Saltkjel and Malmberg-Heimonen, 2017), thereby reducing the known negative effect of labour market exclusion on individuals' economic situations. Saltkjel and Malmberg-Heimonen (2017) have demonstrated that welfare generosity moderates the risk of both material deprivation and income poverty. For example, they found that among individuals who experienced long-standing illness and either low levels of education or non-employment, the absolute inequalities in material deprivation decreased with increasing welfare generosity. The results of their study indicated lower absolute levels of both material deprivation and income poverty among disadvantaged individuals in generous welfare states. A study by Bárcena-Martín et al (2013) has demonstrated that welfare generosity is associated with material deprivation among individuals living in households in which the household reference person faces socio-economic disadvantages such as low level of education and lack of full-time paid work. Furthermore, Brady et al (2009) have shown a significant association between welfare generosity in interaction with low education level and individual-level income poverty.

Gallie and Paugam (2000) have pointed out that the main measures against employment-related exclusion are PLMPs (for example, unemployment benefits) and ALMPs (such as training). Contributory benefits such as unemployment benefits are generally designed to uphold accustomed standards of living and provide various degrees of income security. Respectively, the more those excluded from the labour market are eligible for any type of benefit (insurance or means-tested), the lower should be their risk of poverty. Moreover, the level of financial compensation should affect the situation of the unemployed directly, with higher levels of compensation creating conditions more similar to being at work and lowering significantly the stigmatisation associated with unemployment. Thus, it is expected that:

Hypothesis 1: In a country with a higher contribution to PLMPs the negative effect of labour market exclusion on young people's financial situation will be reduced.

Since the 1990s, there has been a general shift in Europe from PLMPs to ALMPs (Barbier, 2005). The main assumptions behind this shift (for more details see Malmberg-Heimonen, 2005) are: (a) self-sufficiency in relation to welfare benefits is a precondition for individual welfare and for the welfare of the state (Goul Andersen and Jensen, 2002); (b) welfare dependency in the longer term promotes poverty, inequality, and long-term unemployment, and unemployment benefits can have a disincentive effect on job search and re-employment (Torfing, 1999); and (c) generous replacement rates increase the level of minimum wages, and this, in turn, decreases an individual's financial incentive to seek re-employment (Torfing, 1999; OECD, 2014). The latter led to various activation measures such as setting incentives for participation in active policy measures or individual activation plans based on an assessment of needs and agreements on the labour market integration of excluded youth. The fundamental objective of most ALMPs has been to prevent unemployment becoming long term and thereby leading to social exclusion. The International Monetary Fund (2009) argues that well-designed training programmes in more than 90 countries have had a significant impact on the livelihoods of workers excluded from the labour market. Thus, it could be expected that the poverty gap between the employed and the unemployed will be smaller in countries with a higher productive potential and a higher employability of the whole workforce due to more substantial investments in active labour market policies, including those for the young unemployed. This translates into the following hypothesis:

Hypothesis 2: In a country with a higher contribution to ALMPs, the negative effect of labour market exclusion on young people's financial situation will be reduced.

Methodological strategy

Method and data

The present analysis is based on cross-sectional microdata from EU-SILC gathered in 2013. Because it focuses on youth, the present sample is restricted to young people aged 16 to 29 years who are not in education or training. Young people who are doing military service are also excluded from this analysis. Due to problems of missing data for specific countries or variables, the number of countries included in the analysis varies from 23 to 26.

To address the issue of the impact of the labour market status on the economic situation of youth while taking into account cross-country variation and the moderating effect of country policies and labour market settings, the study applies multilevel modelling with country random intercepts and cross-level interactions (Snijders and Bosker, 1999). The first level of the analysis is based on individual and household information; the second level is defined by country characteristics.

The results of estimating linear probability models are presented for a subsample of youth who live apart from their parents and for the whole youth population. This distinction is motivated by previous empirical studies indicating that leaving the parental household is associated with a higher risk of poverty (Aassve et al, 2006) but lower unemployment

(Cordón, 1997). Three different definitions of the dependent variables are used in order to capture the hypothesised effects at both the individual and the household level. Moreover, on the household level, both subjective and objective indicators of households' economic situation are used. This makes it possible to check the robustness of the results and see if they hold regardless of the particular measure of economic situation used in the analysis.

The analysis starts with the objective measure of the respondents' household financial situation. The risk of poverty is defined as a binary variable that is equal to 1 when the respondent's household equivalised disposable income (after taxes and transfers) is below 60 per cent of a country's median disposable income. This measure refers to the income reference period. For most EU countries, this is a fixed 12-month period (the preceding calendar or tax year). For the UK, the income reference period is the current year, and for Ireland, it is collected for the previous 12 months. The measure of risk of poverty, although easy to define, is very sensitive to country differences and year-to-year changes. Thus, this indicator provides questionable results in times of economic boom or sharp recession when the median income itself can change considerably (Jenkins et al, 2012).

Whereas the first measure describes the economic situation of the whole household, the second indicator focuses on personal economic situations. It is based on a set of questions referring to the respondent's ability to cover the costs of the following activities: getting together with friends/family (relatives) for a drink/meal at least once a month, regularly participating in a leisure activity, and spending a small amount of money each week on yourself. If a respondent was unable to do at least one of these three actions for financial reasons, she or he is treated as being excluded from social life, and the variable takes the value 1. In other cases, the variable is equal to zero. Thus, this indicator measures the level of a respondent's exclusion from social life due to financial reasons.

The third dependent variable is a subjective measure of a household's overall economic condition. It is based on the following question from the EU-SILC questionnaire: 'Thinking now of your household's total income, from all sources and from all household members, would you say that your household is able to make ends meet?' The respondent can choose on a scale ranging from *with great difficulty* to *very easily*. The present analysis constructed a binary variable that is equal to 1 if the household can make ends meet with difficulty or great difficulty. In other cases, the variable takes the value 0.

The focus of this analysis is on the labour market status of the young person. It analyses the situation of unemployed versus employed youth. Information about unemployment is based on questions about the number of months spent in unemployment during the income reference period. If a person was unemployed for at least seven months, she or he is assigned an unemployed person status. If a person was working (in different kinds of employment, also self-employment) for at least 7 months during the income reference period, she or he is treated as being employed.[1] This definition is parallel to the one applied to monthly information gathered in the EU-SILC: if somebody spends more than two weeks of the month in a certain labour market status, this status is reported as her or his main economic activity. The constructed binary variable is then equal to 0 for an unemployed respondent, and 1 for an employed respondent.

The selection of control variables is based on the results of the descriptive analysis presented by Rokicka and Kłobuszewska (2016). Because two of the three dependent variables are related to the household level, it is necessary to control for the composition of the household and the situation on the labour market of its members (which influences the economic situation of the whole household). This makes the results for young people in this data set as precise as possible. Hence, the following control variables are included in the analysis: age groups (16–24 years and 25–29 years), sex, educational attainment, immigration status, living arrangements (living with parents, children, partner/spouse in the same household), and household work intensity status.[2]

A set of macrolevel indicators is used to address the issue of the moderating impact of policies, institutions, and a country's economic situation.

Regarding the hypotheses, two macroindicators are used that show the level of a country's public expenditures on ALMPs and PLMPs. Eurostat calculates both measures as an expenditure on a given type of labour market policy in thousands of euros (purchasing power standards or PPS) divided by the number of unemployed and inactive people. Nonetheless, ALMPs and PLMPs are very broad categories which look very different across the EU, and it is important to acknowledge the substantial differences between them.

PLMPs are defined as out-of-work income maintenance and support. This includes different types of unemployment benefits such as unemployment insurance and redundancy compensation. ALMPs are more diversified and include many types of policy measure. In the present study, the scope of the indicator was narrowed to the ALMP measures that might impact on the economic situation of the unemployed. This included the following categories of active labour market policies: training (institutional training, workplace training, alternative training, and special support for apprenticeships), employment incentives (recruitment incentives, employment maintenance incentives, job rotation, and job sharing), sheltered and supported employment and rehabilitation, direct job creation, and start-up incentives.[3]

Additionally, the second-level controls for GDP per capita are derived from the Eurostat database. This is computed as the PPS in euros by dividing GDP by the mid-year population. The poverty level and the subjective feeling of economic difficulties in a society depend on a country's economic performance. Thus, GDP might be considered as a measure of a country's economic performance and could be a proxy for the wealth of a society. Divided by the country's population, it approximates the average standard of living. Controlling for GDP per capita makes it possible to use nominal values of policy indicators (expenditures on labour market policies).

Sample and descriptive findings

As depicted in Table 12.1, an average of 18 per cent of youth in the present sample live in households that are at risk of poverty. Around 28 per cent claim that they are excluded from social life for financial reasons, whereas more than 37 per cent live in households that are struggling to make ends meet.

The distribution of outcome variables among youth living independently from their parents is similar to that of the general youth population. Young people living outside the parental household are slightly more likely to live under the poverty line than youth in general, and they have a similar level of social exclusion to youth in general. However, they seem to be more optimistic in their subjective assessment of the financial situation of their households.

However, as depicted in Table 12.2, youth from those two types of household differ substantially in regard to their labour market status, personal characteristics, and family characteristics. Only 14 per cent of youth living independently are unemployed compared to 23 per cent among those still living with their parents. Young people living independently are also older (only 28 per cent of them are under the age of 25 years in comparison to 50 per cent in the overall sample), and they are more likely to have tertiary education, an immigrant background, a partner, and dependent children. Results show that these two groups differ markedly: the situation of younger adults depends more often on the financial situation of their parents, so even if there

Table 12.1: Summary statistics of dependent variables

	All types of households			Household without parents		
	Risk of poverty	Ends met with difficulty	Exclusion from social life	Risk of poverty	Ends met with difficulty	Exclusion from social life
Mean	0.180	0.375	0.285	0.193	0.295	0.280
Standard deviation	0.384	0.484	0.451	0.395	0.456	0.449

Source: Authors' own calculations based on EU-SILC.

Table 12.2: Summary statistics of independent variables

	All types of households		Household without parents	
	Mean	SD	Mean	SD
Unemployed	0.230	0.421	0.141	0.348
Aged 18–24	0.504	0.500	0.287	0.452
Lower secondary	0.205	0.404	0.184	0.387
Tertiary	0.242	0.428	0.312	0.463
Female	0.465	0.499	0.595	0.491
Immigration status	0.071	0.256	0.117	0.321
Living with parents	0.654	0.476	–	–
Living with children	0.178	0.382	0.425	0.494
Living with partner	0.283	0.450	0.741	0.438
Household work intensity	2.942	0.832	3.119	0.863
ALMP expenditure (thousands of euros)	1.52	1.47	1.52	1.47
PLMP expenditure (thousands of euros)	3.17	2.65	3.17	2.65

Note: SD = standard deviation.

are more unemployed young people in the first group, their households are less exposed to poverty than households of young people living independently. Thus, the decision to analyse the mitigating role of policies separately by household type seems to be supported by the data.

Because of the finding that the rate of unemployment of young people differs by type of household, descriptive statistics were investigated further by calculating the mean value of the financial indicators among young with different labour market status and

Figure 12.1: Household financial indicators by employment and household type

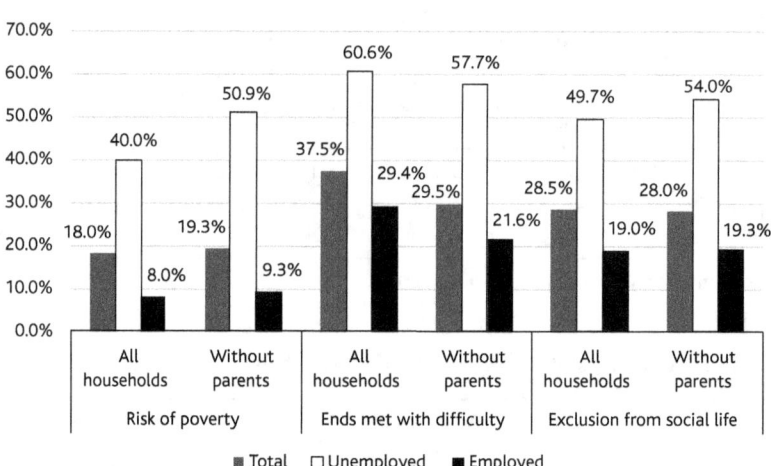

Source: Authors' own calculations based on EU-SILC

household type (see Figure 12.1). Regardless of the household type, the financial situation of unemployed youth is always worse than that of their working counterparts. As expected, unemployed youth outside the family household are more likely to be at risk of poverty than unemployed youth in general (10 percentage point difference). They are also more likely to be excluded from social life (4 percentage point difference), yet surprisingly, they express lower financial distress than the households of unemployed youth in general.

In this sample of countries, average expenditure on PLMP (€ 3,349) is twice as high as average expenditure on ALMP (€ 1,712). Although the amount is adjusted for a country's price differences using PPS, there are visible country variations in this respect. The highest expenditure on PLMP is in Belgium, Ireland, and the Netherlands (above € 7,300) and the lowest in Latvia, Poland, and Romania (less than € 450). Smaller variations are found for ALMP expenditure, with Denmark, Luxembourg, and Sweden spending more than € 4,800, and Hungary, Latvia, and Romania spending less than € 250 per person wanting to work.

Moderating effect of labour market policies on situation of unemployed youth: empirical findings

Table 12.3 reports results on the relationship between youth unemployment and young people's household and personal financial situation based on the 2013 wave of EU-SILC. It presents three

Table 12.3: Economic situation of unemployed youth: moderating role of PLMP and ALMP (all households)

	Model 1	Model 2	Model 3	Model 4	Model 5	Model 6
	Risk of poverty	Risk of poverty	Ends met with difficulty	Ends met with difficulty	Exclusion from social life	Exclusion from social life
Unemployed	0.165***	0.148***	0.088***	0.092***	0.228***	0.211***
Exp. on PLMP	−0.012**		−0.021		−0.011	
Unemployed # exp. on PLMP	−0.018***		−0.009***		−0.017***	
Exp. on ALMP		−0.011		−0.060**		−0.021
Unemployed # exp. on ALMP		−0.027***		−0.025***		−0.028***
Age 16–23 (binary)	0.035***	0.035***	0.020***	0.020***	0.012*	0.012*
Education: lower secondary	0.115***	0.114***	0.131***	0.131***	0.125***	0.124***
Education: tertiary	−0.036***	−0.036***	−0.111***	−0.112***	−0.100***	−0.100***
Sex: female	0.007	0.007	0.014**	0.014**	0.029***	0.029***
Immigrant	0.080***	0.081***	0.051***	0.053***	0.071***	0.073***
Lives with parent	−0.128***	−0.128***	−0.010	−0.010	−0.066***	−0.066***
Lives with children	0.020***	0.020***	0.055***	0.056***	0.068***	0.068***
Lives with partner/spouse	−0.056***	−0.056***	−0.057***	−0.058***	−0.011	−0.011
Household work intensity status	−0.154***	−0.154***	−0.116***	−0.116***	−0.083***	−0.083***
GDP per capita	0.0004	−0.0005	−0.007*	−0.003	−0.005	−0.005
Constant	0.676***	0.677***	0.932***	0.876***	0.646***	0.637***
Log likelihood	−6984.8	−7003.6	−15975.0	−15964.9	−11289.7	−11300.5
Country variance	0.002 (0.001)	0.002 (0.001)	0.015 (0.004)	0.012 (0.003)	0.014 (0.004)	0.014 (0.004)
Observations	29,550	29,550	29,550	29,550	24,381	24,381
N of countries	26	26	26	26	23	23

Notes: * $p < 0.05$, ** $p < 0.01$, *** $p < 0.001$. + UK and EL excluded from Models 1–6 (lack of data on LMP expenditures); ++ CZ, DK, and SI excluded from Models 5–6 (lack of dependent variable). Base category: for unemployed – employed; for age 16–23 – age 24–29; for education level – secondary education; for immigrant – born in the country; for lives with parent – lives without parent; for lives with children – lives without children; for lives with partner/spouse – lives without partner/spouse.

indicators of financial hardship: being at risk of poverty, having difficulty in making ends meet (both on the household level), and being excluded from social life for financial reasons (on the individual level).

The direct negative effect of youth unemployment on personal or household financial situation is strong and robust across all specifications. Households with unemployed young people have a substantially higher probability of being in poverty (0.11 higher than for those with employed young people for the average levels of PLMP and ALMP expenditures,[4] see Models 1–2) and of having difficulty in making ends meet (0.05–0.06 higher than those with young employed for the average levels of PLMP and ALMP expenditures, see Models 3–4). Young unemployed people also have a higher probability of exclusion from social life compared to young workers (0.16–0.17 higher for the average levels of PLMP and ALMP expenditures, see Models 5–6).

Models 1, 3, and 5 test the hypotheses on the moderating role of PLMPs whereas Models 2, 4, and 6 focus on the moderating role of ALMPs, for three indicators of socio-economic disadvantage: being at risk of poverty, having difficulty in making ends meet, and being excluded from social life for financial reasons. In line with Hypothesis 1, for countries that make a higher contribution to PLMPs, the negative effect of youth unemployment on their financial situation is reduced. A one standard deviation increase in the PLMP contribution is predicted to reduce the probability of poverty in unemployed youth by 0.03–0.05 depending on the measure of financial hardship. This is a significant decrease that halves the effects of unemployment in the case of household indicators. Across Models 2, 4, and 6, there is also a mitigating effect of a country's ALMP expenditure on the effect of unemployment on all analysed measures of financial difficulty. This confirms Hypothesis 2. A one standard deviation increase in ALMP contribution is predicted to reduce the probability of poverty in the unemployed by 0.04, independent of the measure analysed.

Interestingly, the expenditure on PLMPs also reduce the probability of household poverty for employed youth with the effect being significant for the objective household indicator: risk of poverty. For the effects of ALMPs on households with employed youth, the pattern is similar, but statistically significant only for the subjective household indicator: difficulty in making ends meet. These results suggest that households with working youth also benefit from labour market policies, probably because other household members are eligible to take advantage of these policies.

To test the robustness of these findings, Table 12.4 reports the results of the analysis for individuals who do not live with parents. As most

Table 12.4: Economic situation of unemployed youth: moderating role of PLMP and ALMP (households without parents)

	Model 1	Model 2	Model 3	Model 4	Model 5	Model 6
	Risk of poverty	Risk of poverty	Ends met with difficulty	Ends met with difficulty	Exclusion from social life	Exclusion from social life
Unemployed	0.211***	0.173***	0.159***	0.156***	0.134***	0.141***
Exp. on PLMP	−0.011**		−0.014		−0.010	
Unemployed # exp. on PLMP	−0.018***		−0.016***		−0.006	
Exp. on ALMP		−0.011		−0.050**		−0.023
Unemployed # exp. on ALMP		−0.014*		−0.033***		−0.018*
Age 16–23 (binary)	0.039***	0.039***	0.002	0.002	0.008	0.008
Education: lower secondary	0.090***	0.089***	0.124***	0.123***	0.127***	0.126***
Education: tertiary	−0.033***	−0.033***	−0.109***	−0.110***	−0.110***	−0.111***
Sex: female	−0.007	−0.007	0.008	0.008	0.038***	0.038***
Immigrant	0.060***	0.061***	0.056***	0.058***	0.076***	0.077***
Lives with children	0.024***	0.024***	0.071***	0.070***	0.063***	0.063***
Lives with partner/spouse	−0.074***	−0.073***	−0.065***	−0.065***	−0.024**	−0.024**
Household work intensity status	−0.147***	−0.147***	−0.084***	−0.084***	−0.091***	−0.091***
GDP per capita	0.002	0.001	−0.006	−0.003	−0.005	−0.004
Constant	0.629***	0.633***	0.779***	0.731***	0.682***	0.665***
Log likelihood	−2653.2	−2668.5	−5305.1	−5299.8	−4266.7	−4265.4
	0.001 (0.000)	0.002 (0.001)	0.013 (0.004)	0.011 (0.003)	0.013 (0.004)	0.013 (0.004)
Observations	11,809	11,809	11,809	11,809	9,714	9,714
N of countries	26	26	26	26	23	23

Notes: * $p < 0.05$, ** $p < 0.01$, *** $p < 0.001$. UK and EL excluded from model (lack of data for LMP expenditures). CZ, DK, and SI excluded from model (lack of dependent variable). Base category: for unemployed: employed; for age 16–23: age 24–29; for education level: secondary education; for immigrant: born in the country: for lives with parent: lives without parent; for lives with children: lives without children; for lives with partner/spouse: lives without partner/spouse.

of the data on poverty and material deprivation are collected on a household basis, they are sensitive to household composition. In the households with parents, the effects of youth unemployment may be buffered by parents' higher income. Running the analyses on the subsample of youth living independently from parents can exclude this effect at least in part. Overall, results are qualitatively very similar to those reported for the total sample. As expected, the direct negative effect of being unemployed on the financial situation of the household is stronger for youth living without parents, but this group has a lower probability of exclusion from social life than youth overall. Moreover, higher PLMP and ALMP contributions buffer the negative effect of unemployment on young people's economic situation.

The results of almost all individual-level control variables are robust for the three indicators analysed. Looking at the demographic characteristics, individuals with a higher level of education have a lower probability of living in a household at risk of poverty and of being excluded from social life for financial reasons. Younger individuals (aged 16 to 29 years in this sample) have a higher probability of economic hardship when controlling for household composition. Also being a woman and an immigrant increases the probability of financial difficulty. In line with findings from other studies (for example, Iacovou and Berthoud, 2001; Aassve et al, 2006), household composition is an important determinant of poverty and material deprivation. Living with parents or a partner/spouse protects young people from economic hardship, whereas living with children increases the risk.

Conclusions

The aim of the present study was to analyse the moderating effect of ALMPs and PLMPs on the negative effect of unemployment on young people's economic situation. For this a subsample of cross-sectional microdata from EU- SILC from 2013 was used.

The central findings of the study can be summarised as follows. First, they confirm that youth unemployment is associated with a worse household economic situation. In other words, young adults who are unemployed are, compared to those in employment, more likely to experience economic hardship measured in both objective and subjective ways. However, it is important to bear in mind that lack of financial resources might also be considered as one of the causes of problems with finding employment. Thus, the observed relationship might be bidirectional and suggest an ongoing circle of social exclusion – unemployment causes poverty and poverty constrains opportunities to find a stable job.

Second, results confirmed that in countries with higher expenditures on PLMPs, the negative impact of unemployment on the economic situation of youth is reduced. The same moderating effect was also identified for ALMPs – higher expenditure on ALMPs decreases the size of the negative effect of youth unemployment on young people's personal and household financial situation. However, because there is no detailed information on respondents' participation in labour market programmes or measures, one cannot say how much of this is a direct effect of receiving unemployment benefits and participation in training or apprenticeships, and how much is an indirect effect. Higher expenditure on labour market policies might also be interpreted as an indicator of more generous welfare systems that protect both unemployed and employed youth against poverty. The latter suggestion also seems to be supported by the findings: the data show that countries with higher expenditure on labour market policies have lower levels of young people in poverty.

Third, results indicate that higher expenditure on PLMPs is especially important for young people who are not living in their parents' households. In general, the moderating effect of PLMPs and ALMPs for unemployment on young people's risk of economic hardship holds for both those still living with their parents and those living outside the parental home. However, this effect is much stronger for households in which young people live apart from their parents. This, again, suggests that in countries with higher expenditure on PLMPs, unemployed young people are more likely to benefit from such measures or to receive other forms of financial support in other policy areas (for example, housing or health).

Another relevant contribution of the current study lies in the use of different types of poverty measure – objective and subjective – to assess the economic situation of young people. Two of these measures – household risk of poverty and subjective assessment of household economic situation – allow an assessment of the economic situation of young people on the household level. In order to measure the economic situation at the individual level more directly, a measure of respondents' exclusion from social life due to financial reasons was introduced. Findings suggest, however, that this indicator works rather as a proxy for individual economic autonomy. In general, findings show that unemployed young people are more likely to experience financial problems in covering the costs of various social activities (getting together with friends, participating in a leisure activity, regularly spending a small amount of money on oneself). Surprisingly, however, this effect is considerably stronger among young people living with their parents who theoretically might be able to count on their parents' financial support. This paradox could be explained by financial autonomy, which is greater among young people who do not live with their parents. Despite encountering economic problems, they are more likely to be in charge of their (modest) financial resources.

To summarise, the current study shows that welfare generosity (measured here as investment in PLMPs and ALMPs) is negatively associated with youth household income poverty and material deprivation. In a more generous welfare state context, young adults excluded from the labour market have lower risks of poverty and material deprivation.

Notes

[1] It is necessary to take into consideration that such a definition focuses more on the long-term unemployed, whereas those with short periods of unemployment (less than 5 months) are considered to be employed. Particularly in countries with open labour markets, this might underestimate the actual incidence of unemployment.

[2] The household work intensity status shows the overall labour market situation of household members. According to the Eurostat definition, this measure is based on the total number of months that all working-age household members have worked during the income reference period divided by the total number of months the same household members could have worked in the same period theoretically.

[3] Although this study focuses on youth unemployment, due to the lack of comparative EU statistics it was not possible to use indicators of ALMP spending on youth. It is not just the structure of ALMPs that differs by country; they also have different eligibility criteria with different definitions of youth or the young population.

[4] The means and standard deviations of PLMP and ALMP expenditures can be found in Table 12.2.

References

Aassve, A., Billari, F.C., Mazzuco, S. and Ongaro, F. (2002) 'Leaving home: a comparative analysis of ECHP data', *Journal of European Social Policy*, 12(4): 259–75.

Aassve, A., Cottini, E. and Vitali, A. (2013) 'Youth prospects in a time of economic recession', *Demographic Research*, 29(36): 949–62.

Aassve, A., Iacovou, M. and Mencarini, L. (2006) 'Youth poverty and transition to adulthood in Europe', *Demographic Research*, 15(2): 21–50.

Alvaro, J.L. and Garrido, A. (2003) 'Economic hardship, employment status and psychological wellbeing of young people in Europe', in T. Hammer (ed) *Youth Unemployment and Social Exclusion in Europe: A Comparative Study*, Bristol: Policy Press, pp 173–92.

Arulampalam, W. (2001) 'Is unemployment really scarring? Effects of unemployment experiences on wages', *The Economic Journal*, 111(475): 585–606.

Bäckman, O. (2009) 'Institutions, structures and poverty: a comparative study of 16 countries, 1980–2000', *European Sociological Review*, 25(2): 251–64.

Barbier, S.C. (2005) 'The European employment strategy: a channel for activating social protection?' in J. Zeitlin, P. Pochet and L. Magnusson (eds) *The Open Method of Co-Ordination in Action: The European Employment and Social Inclusion Strategies*, Brussels: Peter Lang.

Bárcena-Martín, E., Lacomba, B., Moro-Egido, A.I. and Pérez-Moreno, S. (2013) 'Country differences in material deprivation in Europe', *The Review of Income and Wealth*, 60(4): 802–20.

Berthoud, R. (2003) *Multiple Disadvantage in Employment: A Quantitative Analysis*, York: Joseph Rowntree Foundation.

Brady, D., Fullerton, A.S. and Cross, J.M. (2009) 'Putting poverty in political context: a multi-level analysis of adult poverty across 18 affluent democracies', *Social Forces*, 88(1): 271–99.

Buchmann, M. and Kriesi, I. (2011) 'Transition to adulthood in Europe', *Annual Review of Sociology*, 37(1): 481–503.

Cantó-Sanchéz, O. and Mercader-Prats, M. (1999) *Poverty among Children and Youth in Spain: The Role of Parents and Youth Employment Status*. Studies on the Spanish Economy, Working paper no. 46, Madrid: Fundación de Estudios de Economía Aplicada.

Clasen, J. and Goerne, A. (2011) 'Exit Bismarck, enter dualism? Assessing contemporary German labour market policy', *Journal of Social Policy*, 40(4): 795–810.

Cordón, J.A.F. (1997) 'Youth residential independence and autonomy: a comparative study', *Journal of Family Issues*, 18(6): 576–607.

Duiella, M. and Turrini, A. (2014) *Poverty Developments in the EU after the Crisis: A Look at Main Drivers*. ECNIF Economic Briefs 31. Brussels: European Commission Directorate General for Economic and Financial Affairs.

Fritzell, J. and Lundberg, O. (2007) 'Health inequalities and welfare resources', in J. Fritzell and O. Lundberg (eds) *Health Inequalities and Welfare Resources: Continuity and Change in Sweden*, Bristol: Policy Press, pp 1–18.

Gallie, D. and Paugam, S. (eds) (2000) *Welfare Regimes and the Experience of Unemployment in Europe*, Oxford: Oxford University Press.

Goul Andersen, J. and Jensen, P.H. (2002) 'Changing labour markets, welfare policies and citizenship: an introduction', in J.G. Andersen and P.H. Jensen (eds) *Changing Labour Markets, Welfare Policies and Citizenship*, Bristol: Policy Press, pp 1–14.

Helbling, L.A. and Sacchi, S. (2014) 'Scarring effects of early unemployment among young workers with vocational credentials in Switzerland', *Empirical Research in Vocational Education and Training*, 6: 1–22.

Iacovou, M. and Berthoud, R. (2001) *Young People's Lives: A Map of Europe*, Colchester: University of Essex, Institute for Social and Economic Research.

International Monetary Fund (2009) *Global Monitoring Report 2009: A Development Emergency*, Washington DC: World Bank.

Jenkins, S.P., Brandolini, A. and Micklewright, J. (2012) *The Great Recession and the Distribution of Household Income*, Oxford: Oxford University Press.

Kangas, O. and Palme, J. (2000) 'Does social policy matter? Poverty cycles in the OECD countries', *International Journal of Health Services*, 30(2): 335–52.

Kenworthy, L. (1999) 'Do social welfare policies reduce poverty? A cross-national assessment', *Social Forces*, 77(3): 1119–40.

Kenworthy, L. (2011) *Progress for the Poor*, Oxford: Oxford University Press.

Kieselbach, T., Heeringen, K. and La Rosa, M. (2001) *Living on the Edge: An Empirical Analysis on Long-Term Youth Unemployment and Social Exclusion in Europe*, Opladen: Leske+Budrich.

Knabe, A. and Rätzel, S. (2011) 'Scarring or scaring? The psychological impact of past unemployment and future unemployment risk', *Economica*, 78(310): 283–93.

Korpi, W. and Palme, J. (1998) 'The paradox of redistribution and strategies of equality: welfare state institutions, inequality and poverty in the Western countries', *American Sociological Review*, 63(5): 661–87.

Malmberg-Heimonen, I. (2005) 'Integration into work through active labour market policies in different welfare state regimes', in H. Bradley and J. Hoof (eds) *Young People in Europe: Labour Markets and Citizenship*, Bristol: Policy Press, pp 223–38.

Mayer, K.U. (2009) 'New directions in life course research', *Annual Review of Sociology*, 35: 413–33.

McDonald, C. and Marston, G. (2005) 'Workfare as welfare: governing unemployment in the advanced liberal state', *Critical Social Policy*, 25(3): 374–401.

Mills, M. and Blossfeld, H.P. (2003) 'Globalization, uncertainty and changes in early life courses', *Zeitschrift für Erziehungswissenschaft*, 6(2): 188–218.

Nelson, K. (2012) 'Counteracting material deprivation: the role of social assistance in Europe', *Journal of European Social Policy*, 22(2): 148–63.

Nolan, B. and Whelan, C.T. (2010) 'Using non-monetary deprivation indicators to analyse poverty and social exclusion in rich countries: lessons from Europe?', *Journal of Policy Analysis and Management*, 29(2): 305–25.

OECD (2014) *OECD Employment Outlook 2014*, Paris: OECD Publishing.

Pavis, S., Platt, S. and Hubbard, G. (2000) *Young People in Scotland: Pathways to Social Inclusion and Exclusion*, York: Joseph Rowntree Foundation.

Rokicka, M. and Kłobuszewska, M. (2016) *The Short-Term Economic Consequences of Insecure Labour Market Positions in EU-28*. EXCEPT Working Papers, WP No. 10, Tallinn: Tallinn University, Available from: https://www.except-project.eu/working-papers/

Saltkjel, T. and Malmberg-Heimonen, I. (2017) 'Welfare generosity in Europe: a multilevel study of material deprivation and income poverty among disadvantaged groups', *Social Policy & Administration*, 51(7): 1287–310.

Scarpetta, S., Sonnet, A. and Manfredi, T. (2010) *Rising Youth Unemployment During the Crisis: How to Prevent Negative Long-term Consequences on a Generation?* OECD Social, Employment and Migration Working Papers No. 106, Paris: OECD Publishing.

Schmillen, A. and Umkehrer, M. (2013) *The Scars of Youth: Effects of Early-Career Unemployment on Future Unemployment Experience*. IAB Discussion Paper 6/2013, Nuremberg: Institute for Employment Research.

Sheeran, P., Abrams, D. and Orbell, S. (1995) 'Unemployment, self-esteem, and depression: a social-comparison theory approach', *Basic and Applied Social Psychology*, 17(1): 65–82.

Snijders, T.A.B. and Bosker, R.J. (1999) *Multilevel Analysis: An Introduction to Basic and Advanced Multilevel Modeling* (1st ed), Los Angeles; London; New Delhi; Singapore; Washington DC: Sage Publications.

Steijn, B., Need, A. and Gesthuizen, M. (2006) 'Well begun, half done? Long-term effects of labour market entry in the Netherlands, 1950–2000', *Work, Employment and Society*, 20(3): 453–72.

Torfing, J. (1999) 'Workfare with welfare: recent reforms of the Danish welfare state', *Journal of European Social Policy*, 9(1): 5–28.

Wulfgramm, M. (2014) 'Life satisfaction effects of unemployment in Europe: the moderating influence of labour market policy', *Journal of European Social Policy*, 24(3): 258–72.

13

Unemployment and job precariousness: material and social consequences for Greek and Italian youth

Lia Figgou, Martina Sourvinou, Christina Athanasiades, Valentina Moiso, and Rosy Musumeci

Introduction

There is a growing body of literature on the consequences of unemployment and job precariousness in both Europe (Karanikolos et al, 2013; Berneo, 2014; O'Reilly et al, 2015) and beyond (Poverty and Employment Precarity in Southern Ontario [PEPSO], 2013; Posel et al, 2014). This research interest seems to derive from the fact that the economic crisis was followed by an increased unemployment rate in many national contexts (Eurostat, 2015). Furthermore, the last decade has been characterised by an immense increase in precarious employment in the labour market that is affecting sectors and groups that had seemed to be insulated from this in the past (Hatton 2011; Standing, 2011).

However, even within this body of research, studies on the socio-economic consequences of labour market insecurity and exclusion for young people are rather infrequent compared to the large amount of research on poverty and deprivation in other age groups. This scarcity is striking, given that young people have been disproportionally affected by increases in the unemployment rate. Furthermore, they constitute a group with certain characteristics, and their risk position – in terms of the socio-economic implications of job insecurity – may differ substantially from that of the general population (Hofäcker et al, 2017). This chapter aims to address this research lacuna by focusing on data derived from interviews with young people in two national contexts: Greece and Italy.

Theoretical considerations

Existing research on the socio-economic consequences of labour market exclusion and insecurity has revealed the multifaceted nature of the phenomenon (Boon and Farnsworth, 2011; Dowler and O'Connor, 2012). Measures of income poverty and/or material deprivation have been used to investigate the socio-economic disadvantage of either individuals or entire households. Research has been based on either *objective* poverty and deprivation indicators or the *subjective* perceptions of social actors on their socio-economic situation (Hofäcker et al, 2017). Moreover, authors have highlighted the interrelation/intersection between the material and the social and psychosocial implications by elaborating on the ways in which poverty gets under the skin and into the minds of those affected through processes of 'embodied deprivation' (Hodgetts et al, 2007: 714).

Since 2009, the European Union's set of commonly used social indicators has included measures of material deprivation (Deutsch et al, 2015). This term refers to a state of serious economic strain defined as the enforced inability to attain the material standards that most people consider to be desirable or even necessary to lead an adequate life (Whelan et al, 2008; Guio et al, 2016).[1] According to Eurostat data, one out of six members of the European Union population was materially deprived in 2015. The highest proportions were in Bulgaria (49.1 per cent) and Greece (40.8 per cent), with more than half of the materially deprived persons in these countries facing severe deprivation. Similarly, more than half of those considered to be materially deprived in Italy experienced severe material deprivation (although overall, the country was ranked in the middle of the range for European countries). Greece was also among the countries with the largest increase in the proportion of materially deprived people during and following the economic crisis and particularly between the years 2014 and 2015.[2]

The attempt to construct absolute criteria for assessing deprivation is essential to obtaining reliable comparative data from different contexts. It has, however, certain limitations. It is well known that deprivation may be relative, and the feeling of being deprived may be the result of comparisons between oneself and others. Relative deprivation is, in short, the perceived discrepancy between personal status and the status of some relevant other(s). It is the belief that a person is deprived (or entitled to something) based on a comparison to someone else (Davies, 1969). According to relative deprivation theory (Crosby, 1984), the greater the discrepancy between the outcomes people achieve and the outcomes to which they feel entitled, the greater are their feelings of relative deprivation – and this, in turn, implies greater damage to their well-being (Fryer, 1998). Entitlement to certain outcomes may be constructed through recourse to social (group level) identity (Tajfel and Turner, 1986). A common finding in the research is that people experience the feeling of being disadvantaged in relation to a reference group. According to Brand and Simon Thomas (2014), economic decline as a result of unemployment may cause a strong feeling of deprivation among more advantaged families whose peers are similarly advantaged and for whom job displacement and subsequent economic decline are a significant shock. Likewise, contexts of widespread unemployment, although associated with severe economic loss, may decrease the probability of internalising blame and the social stigma associated with job loss.

Furthermore, (relative) deprivation may also be the result of comparisons between one's economic status at present and one's past situation. Hence, experiences and feelings of deprivation may be relative, arising from temporal comparisons (Clark et al, 2001; Brand, 2015). In other words, the sharp increase of deprivation in some national contexts (for example, Greece) during the recent economic upheaval may reflect not only the equally sharp decrease of income as a result of massive unemployment and austerity measures, but also the huge difference between one's situation at present in comparison with the past.

The impact of unemployment and job insecurity is not limited to economic decline; it also extends to family and social life and includes considerable short-term and long-term non-economic consequences not only for individuals and households but also for entire communities. Households and individuals who have to deal with enduring unemployment or uncertainty face challenges in starting or maintaining a family, in forming or maintaining friendships, in getting involved in community life, in enjoying recreational activities during their leisure time, or in maintaining a healthy way of life (Brand, 2015; Lewchuk et al, 2015). Moreover, they face psychological and physical distress, and, more often than not, they also have to cope with societal pressures and stigmatisation.

Studies exploring the impact of unemployment on family life have documented an increased risk of family tension and family disruption (Jahoda et al, 1971; Davis and Von Wachter, 2011). Another strand of research on the harmful effects of parental unemployment and job uncertainty on children has indicated a higher likelihood of school dropout and suspension (Johnson et al, 2012), low educational achievement (Kalil and Wightman, 2011), as well as erratic and low income of the children in adulthood (Page et al, 2007).

The relationship between enduring unemployment, resignation, and lack of participation in social and community life has been emphasised repeatedly. It was exposed dramatically in the seminal Marienthal study (a deep ethnographic analysis of everyday life in a community outside of Vienna ridden by the worldwide economic crisis of the 1930s) undertaken by Jahoda and her colleagues almost a century ago (Jahoda et al, 1971). By analysing everyday discourses and practices, these authors delivered an influential work that has contributed to the understanding of subjectivity in unemployment and emphasised that prolonged deprivation, far from causing a rebellious reaction, may lead to despair and resignation (Fine, 2016).

But what was a surprise for political activists and social scientists in 1933 seems to constitute common knowledge nowadays. Research has indicated repeatedly that displaced workers are significantly less likely to participate socially in both formal and informal contexts including community groups, youth organisations, charities, and social gatherings with friends (Brand and Burgard, 2008; Rüdig and Karyotis, 2013). As Putnam (2000) put it, the strain of uncertainty, psychological distress, (unwanted) geographic mobility, but also reduced social trust and the loss of commitment to social reciprocity, vitally contribute to decreased levels of social participation.

Although research on the socio-economic consequences of unemployment is proliferating, much of it remains restricted to using a top-down approach. With some exceptions (Hodgetts et al, 2007; PEPSO, 2013), most studies on the economic and social consequences of job displacement and precarity apply quantitative methods and predefined categories and concepts. In contrast, this chapter will mobilise the tools and concepts of qualitative research in an attempt to explore the ways in which young (Greek and Italian) interviewees themselves construct their experience of labour market exclusion and/or uncertainty, and to identify the material and social consequences this has for their daily lives and future planning.

Institutional context

The two contexts focused on in this analysis, Greece and Italy, have many similarities. They are both considered to share values and norms that characterise the so-called 'Southern European social model' (Karamessini, 2015) and they have been affected strongly by the recent economic crisis. However, they also differ in terms of the structure and growth of their economies as well as in terms of the specific repercussions of the economic recession (Eichorst and Neder, 2014).

Youth unemployment rates, as well as precarious forms of employment, have increased dramatically in both countries in the 'era of crisis'. Unemployment in Greece in July 2017 amounted to 21.0 per cent, with youth (18–25) unemployment being almost double (42.8 per cent) that of the general population, thereby constituting the highest youth unemployment rate in the EU (Tsekeris et al, 2015). In the same period, the youth employment rate in Italy (reaching 35 per cent) was higher than that across all age groups (11.2 per cent) and that of youth in other European countries (OECD, 2018). A notable characteristic of unemployment in Italy is regional differences, with the higher rates of youth unemployment affecting the southern regions of the country (Leonardi and Pica, 2015). In general, young people have to face difficulties that were not common in past generations, and their situation deserves to be explored in depth (Bello and Cuzzocrea, 2018). Nevertheless, it is not only widespread unemployment that afflicts Greek and Italian youth, but also the spread of insecure forms of employment. In Greece, temporary employment has exceeded permanent forms of employment, with atypical employment increasing as a result of market deregulation and policies to promote flexibility (Gialis and Tsampra, 2015). Joblessness, skill mismatch, and unemployment among highly educated young people have resulted in a massive emigration of highly qualified youth, a phenomenon that is well known as the 'brain drain' (Labrianidis, 2014). In Italy, fixed-term contracts grew disproportionately among young adults (Eurostat, 2020). The economic crisis, however, is not the only cause: several labour market reforms have been introduced since the end of the 1990s with the aim of increasing flexibility without linking these new types of contract to adequate forms of social protection and institutional support. The spread of temporary employment increasingly made the search for 'well-protected' and stable jobs more difficult, resulting in fragmented and discontinuous work paths for most young people (Bertolini, 2011).

Both countries also suffer from a constant decrease in GDP. However, in Greece, the rapid fall in GDP between 2008 and 2014 (25.9 per cent) as a result of the financial problems and the strict austerity measures that followed the 'bailout' deals with the 'troika' of the European Commission, European Central Bank, and International Monetary Fund has produced a humanitarian crisis. According to other commentators, the impoverishment of 35 per cent of the population within a period of four years can be equated with the repercussions of the great depression of the 1930s (Karamessini, 2015). Italy, on the other hand, is witnessing a phenomenon of hidden poverty. Italian GDP is diminishing under austerity measures (Engler and Klein, 2017), and in the absence of a minimum income scheme, young Italians often need to rely on their families – something that causes increased financial difficulties for thefamily and enforces their dependency on parents (Saraceno, 2015).

Finally, both Greek and Italian welfare are characterised by fragmentation in entitlements, gaps in social protection, and familialism. Conditions in Greece deteriorated because the rapid increase in unemployment and the fall in economic activity seriously undermined the social insurance system and, in particular, health care coverage. Statistics from the Hellenic Labour Inspectorate reveal that almost 40 per cent of people working in precarious and/or low quality jobs do not have social or health insurance. Within this context, the family is expected to serve as a social shock absorber (Karamessini, 2015) and protect its members from exposure to severe social and financial risks (Papadopoulos and Roumpakis, 2013). Italy is also considered to have a 'familistic' welfare system. Family is expected to be (and in fact is) the main protective factor against social and financial risks, although differences can be spotted between the south and the north (León and Migliavacca, 2013).

Research questions and aims

Focusing upon the two national contexts briefly sketched earlier, the present study aims to explore how the experience of unemployment, job insecurity, and their implications are constructed in the discourse of young people. The approach is based on the assumption that lay people do not necessarily structure and give meaning to their experiences by using the same categories that social scientists apply in their macrosocial approach to social reality. Thus, by adopting a bottom-up approach, the purpose of this chapter is (a) to document the ways in which the material and social consequences of labour market exclusion are constructed by social actors themselves; (b) to highlight the complicated nature of the everyday experience of unemployment and precarity, and (c) to indicate relations and intersections between concepts while reconsidering existing categories and binaries.

Data and methodology

Sample

The analytic material is derived from 90 semi-structured interviews conducted for the EXCEPT project (see Chapter 1 in this volume). The Greek sample consisted of 40 interviews with 20 men and 20 women of whom 19 were aged 18 to 24 years and 21 were aged 25 to 30 years. Sampling focused mainly on cntral and northern Greece, areas both urban and rural in which the unemployment rate is considerably and constantly high. When it comes to the education level, according to the ISCED scale, seven of the interviewees had low education level (ISCED 0-2), 21 had medium level (ISCED 3-4), and 12 had high education level (ISCED 5-8). In terms of employment status, the sample included nine young people in temporary employment (TE), 10 in non-contractual jobs (NCJ), 15 unemployed (U), and six not in education, employment, or training (NEET). It is worth noting that seven of the total sample were immigrants.

The Italian sample consisted of 50 interviews with 31 interviewees living in northern Italy and 19 in the south. The overall sample was balanced in terms of gender. With respect to age, 25 interviewees were aged 18 to 24 years, while the other 25 were aged 25 to 30. Regarding their educational level, most (26 out of 50) had medium education level (ISCED 3-4), 12 had high education level (SCED 5-8) and 12 had low educational level (ISCED 0-2). Regarding their employment status, 17 had temporary employment (TE), 21 were unemployed (U) or working in non-contractual jobs (NCJ), six were NEET, and another six had permanent employment (PE).

Interviews

Interviewees were recruited through both formal (career counselling services, public employment offices, and training institutions) and informal channels. All interviews took place between November 2015 and July 2016 and lasted from 45 to 120 minutes. In nearly all cases, interviewers first contacted the potential interviewees via telephone and informed them about the research aims in general and the interview procedure in particular. On the day of the interview, the interviewers explained the procedures regarding confidentiality and requested consent to record the interview. Finally, they asked the interviewees to fill out and to sign the consent forms. The interview outline included questions asking directly about interviewees' current economic situation and about savings and financial planning. They were also asked directly about the consequences of unemployment and precarity for their living conditions and future plans and expectations.

Analytic procedure

A thematic analysis (Braun and Clarke, 2006) was conducted on the interviews with the assistance of ATLAS.ti 8. The construction of the codebook was both theory driven and inductive. The initial coding phase was data driven, whereas the grouping of codes into themes was both theory driven and guided by the prevalence of these themes across the data set. This phase also used both a semantic approach (focusing mainly on explicit meanings) and a latent approach (taking into account underlying assumptions and implicit relations between data categories).

Findings

Material deprivation and economic strain

At some point in the interview, all interviewees (both Greek and Italian) expressed their concerns about the implications of income shortage and/or instability for their lives. Some of them vividly described the challenges they currently faced, whereas others expressed their fears about the near future and the possibility of having to face unexpected costs. More specifically, all Greek interviewees discussed economic strain as part and parcel of their daily lives and emphasised their inability to face unexpected expenses. Characteristic is the following extract from the interview with Dimos, a young man who works (without a contract) in a small family business. In the interview extract quoted here, Dimos, who lives with his unemployed girlfriend, highlights how difficult it is for them to make ends meet when they rely solely on his own basic income:

> 'Uh if something happens out of the blue and you need money, this thing keeps you back [pause] it has happened to me to owe money for electricity for half a year, because something else had come up, my fridge broke down and I had to fix it.' (Dimos, M, 29, ME, TE, EL)

Most Greek interviewees express their concern that if a serious health problem were to occur, they would not have the means to pay for their treatment. The interviewer invited Valeria, a young woman who at the time of the interview had a temporary non-contractual job at a pharmacy, to evaluate her current employment situation. She reports:

'Uhm [pause] I don't believe my money is enough mhm because if a sickness comes up, I cannot afford the cost. Of course, sickness can be the flu [laughs] which is okay. For something, more serious that may involve hospitals and so, money is not enough.' (Valeria, F, 24, ME, TE, EL)

Greek young people refer to their inability to cover health expenses and their tendency to postpone a visit to a doctor unless they face really serious health problems. The majority of interviewees depict particular medical treatments (such as dental treatment) as totally inaccessible. Young people whose work trajectories have been characterised by precariousness and income instability emphasise their inability to organise their expenses and engage in any type of financial planning. In the following extract, Victoria, who was unemployed at the time of the interview, talks about her past employment experiences when she was working in modelling as a freelancer.

'The bad thing with it [working as a freelancer] is that you don't earn a standard amount of money per month, so that you can organise your expenses, and some months may go great while on others you may earn nothing.' (Victoria, F, 27, HE, U, EL)

According to some Greek interviewees, one reason why their budget management is extremely challenging is having to pay back existing debts. Debts accumulate during periods of unemployment, and the low-paid jobs that follow these periods do not provide the financial resources to manage existing debts without accumulating new ones.

But although the previous findings apply to the vast majority of the Greek sample, there were also some cases in which Greek interviewees narrated stories of extreme poverty and deprivation, talking about their difficulty in covering basic needs such as food or electricity. Asimakis, an interviewee who lives under extreme poverty conditions, vividly describes his situation:

'I'm deprived of, first of all, of the most basic things. Food. Let's say a steak, to have a steak in a Sunday meal. We reached the point of seeing it [a meal that includes meat] as a miracle.' (Asimakis, M, 24, LE, NEET, EL)

According to the interviewee himself, long-term unemployment and absence of family support have contributed to his situation. Extreme poverty in the parental family and lack of familial support seem to constitute an important risk factor for Foteini. In the following extract, Foteini describes the conditions of extreme poverty that she and her family had to face when her father's small business closed down as a result of the economic crisis. The interviewee, who was unemployed at the time of interview, is particularly eager to find any (type of) job in order to cover her own needs and to support her family financially.

> 'We have spent many years without electricity [pause] it was really hard and I don't think that any kid should be forced to go through this thing [lower voice], because we owned a gift shop and it didn't do well, and we ended up in a thing where we had no electricity, we had to eat from the soup kitchen.' (Foteini, F, 20, ME, U, EL)

The majority of Italian interviewees, on the other hand, do not narrate stories of extreme deprivation. In general, they mention cutting back on what they deem to be unnecessary expenses such as holidays or leisure activities, but they do not represent themselves as being materially deprived, maintaining that they are in a position to cover their more urgent needs.

> 'Basically, what do I need, apart from the rent? It's not that I'm a big spender, nothing else than eating a sandwich, when I'm out, or a beer. I also don't travel much. If I do, I'll take a train and I'll stay with friends who can host me.' (Carlo, M, 26, LE, TE, IT)

Of course – in common with the findings from the Greek study – low pay or work and income discontinuity represent important risk factors for economic strain for Italian youth as well. In many cases, their income allows them to cover only their basic daily needs, and the only buffer against deprivation is family support. Hence, in common with the Greek context, family economic background is a very important protective factor against the most severe implications of unemployment and precarity.

Living in the south of Italy where the percentage of population at risk of poverty is almost double the national rate (Istat, 2016) seems to constitute a differentiating factor between Italian respondents. Youth from the south maintained that both they and their families had been affected by the crisis, and they face its implications in their everyday lives. Gaia was unemployed at the time of the interview and she was unable to rely on her family, because her father (an electrician) was also affected by the economic crisis (seven years later). As Gaia says:

> 'When he [the father] comes back home, he brings shopping bags full of fruit because old people sometimes pay him this way. Sometimes people also pay him with bad cheques. We have found our bank account empty many times.' (Gaia, F, 24, ME, U, IT)

Tamara was also unemployed, as were her father and her brother. Her mother is a housewife, but she sometimes works irregularly, taking care of an old woman without a regular labour contract:

> 'My mom has now got a job. She takes care of an elderly lady, aged 88. She is saving some money, in order to buy a car. A car would be very useful. We go everywhere on foot, even when we need to go to the doctor!' (Tamara, F, 23, ME, U, IT)

Long-term financial planning and the time perspective

Unemployment and precarity also impact on young people's ability to make long-term financial plans. Income poverty and/or instability make it extremely difficult for both the Greek and the Italian respondents to save money and to make long-term financial arrangements and plans – something that has dramatic implications for different phases of the respondents' lives. As Stavros, a Greek young man who works on a temporary basis as a supply teacher in the public sector puts it, he earns some money every now and then, and when the work comes to an end, he starts to worry until the next temporary appointment comes through:

> 'I know that this year, I will work until June, I will earn some money and then again I will start to worry. So, there is no room for long-term plans.' (Stavros, M, 28, HE, TE, EL)

Lack of long-term planning in general and retirement plans in particular can be found in Greek interviewees' accounts of the problematic aspects of the Greek social insurance system. The rigours of acquiring social insurance puzzle them. Olek, a second-generation immigrant to Greece from Ukraine, has been working to support himself since completing his compulsory education. He has changed jobs many times, but he has not received any insurance or employment stamps as evidence of his work experience. He describes this situation as being the rule in the Greek market, and that causes worries for the future.

> I: Regarding your employment is there anything that concerns you?

R: It does concern me that I will never get pensioned, because I do not have the employment stamps needed and they [pause] they don't give you any out there. (Olek, M, 26, HE, U, EL)

Italian interviewees also maintain that they are unable to do much for their economic future. In fact, they do not earn enough to be able to save or invest. Furthermore, they point out that they do not think about retirement plans. Having a pension seems a rather remote objective that is difficult to achieve. Hence, investing in a pension and paying contributions means simply *losing money*:

'I would work, I would work again, paid under the table. Anyway, I won't get the pension myself. So why should I give them the money? To pay someone else's retirement benefits?' (Mara, F, 30, ME, U, IT)

To sum up, the majority of both Greek and Italian interviewees seem to pay attention to short-term economic consequences and to be oriented towards the present. Their inability to plan for the future results, according to interviewees' accounts, in a focus on the present, on immediate needs and short-term goals, and on lowering one's expectations. This 'present-time' orientation demonstrates not only an inability to have control over the future but also distrust towards it. The following quotes from Mara, a young Italian woman, and Dimos, a Greek interviewee, are examples of the present-focused perspective of youth:

'At this moment I don't see any future [pause] it's bad to say so, but it's like that. The money, really, the money makes the future.' (Mara, F, 30, ME, U, IT)

'As I told you I live thinking only of the present [pause] I always think that yes, in the future nothing is for granted. I may be left without a job, for example.' (Dimos, M, 29, ME, TE, EL)

In many cases, intergenerational comparisons illustrate the lack of future perspectives among young people. In the following extract, Mary, a young Greek woman, compares her life with that of her parents. She claims that they lived a 'full' life while she stands still due to unemployment:

I: Mhm. So, you think your parents have been living better? You think it was better back then?

R: Yes, yes. Much better. They had a job, the opportunity to dream, and the potential to make their dreams come true. (Mary, F, 26, ME, U, EL)

In the same way, Italian interviewees feel deprived compared to their parents, but not compared to their peers with whom they share the situation of precariousness.

Implications for family life

The lack of adequate financial resources, and therefore of autonomy, not only raises the risk of severe economic deprivation, but also affects social and family relationships. The majority of Greek and Italian interviewees report on the consequences for family life caused by financial strain. For example, Valeria sees the everyday tensions in her family as natural in the context of financial hardships:

I: Did you have any other sort of income?
R: No. No, no, uuh I was strained with uuh the reactions in my home, which were natural but they didn't do any good [pause] when there is no income, there is a negative atmosphere, fights, complaints. (Valeria, F, 24, ME, TE, EL)

Italian youth living with parents also reported some cases in which the family climate is affected by economic hardship, with quarrels between family members on how to use the little money they earn being part of their daily routine. Tamara, for example – quoted earlier when commenting on the material consequences for their family of her father's job loss – also maintains that her relationship with him has become really difficult to deal with:

'I can't talk with my father. We don't get on well. With my mother, yes: since we have the same opinion about many things.' (Tamara, F, 23, ME, U, IT).

As far as relationships with partners are concerned, research has shown that precarious employment, non-standard working hours, and irregular work schedules may make it difficult to co-ordinate shared leisure time between couples, and that this has implications for the sustainability of relationships (Craig and Brown, 2014). Partnership relations also seem to be affected by the disruption of the male breadwinner/female caregiver model and the increase in women's 'market-related resources'

(Fuwa, 2014). In the following extract, Thomas expresses concerns over the implications of the fact that his partner seems to be the main bearer of the financial burden of the household:

I: Does your partner have a steady job?
R: She has a steady job, yes, and unfortunately, she shoulders more expenses than me, which is very stressing.
I: For you?
R: Yes. She herself hasn't touched on the issue but you can comprehend that it is an issue. Maybe not for her, but for the people around us. (Thomas, M, 28, HE, NCJ, EL)

Precarious employment can shape and limit important life decisions including partnership formation, where to live, when to start a family, and many other choices that can affect the quality of life of individuals and households. Many of our interviewees maintain that they may decide to live with partners and gain some of the benefits of marriage, including sharing housing costs. However, making strong commitments seems unrealistic, given their uncertain future. Thanos, who was unemployed at the time of interview, states that starting a family is an issue that worries him and his friends:

'We would like a family, but nowadays it's so hard to think about it, even if you have a relationship that's going towards this direction uuh it's hard. I mean, your job is not for sure these days.' (Thanos, M, 27, ME, U, EL)

Along the same lines, Andrea, a young Italian man, says that he is very reluctant to start a family given his poor and unstable income; and he constructs this situation as being common for people of his age.

'I really like to have a family, but how can you support a family on €800 a month from precarious work? I hope we won't go back to the Middle Ages when they would choose for you a partner who had money.' (Andrea, M, 24, ME, TE, IT)

Maintaining friendships and social bonds, participating in social life

Precarity and economic hardship seem to affect the social life of interviewees. As previous research indicates (Lewchuk et al, 2015), income instability lessens the chances of being involved in social activities and being engaged with the community. Therefore, it increases the chances of social isolation. The workplace can function as a social network in which friendships might occur. Hence, when a person is unemployed or employed under precarious conditions, the likelihood of forming social bonds is limited. In the following extract, Thaleia, a Greek interviewee, considers that forming new friendships constitutes one of the positive aspects of having a job.

> 'Maybe those who aren't in the working field don't have the chance to meet new people. That's because, when you work, you meet people, you mingle with them and necessarily you have some common interests. I still have contacts with people from my last job. We go for a coffee, we share our news.' (Thaleia, F, 24, HE, U, EL)

Interviewees also pointed out that unemployment and precarity can affect existing friendships, because of the financial incapacity to participate in social activities and to follow social norms. They pointed out that material deprivation is often accompanied by feelings of shame. Gedi, a young immigrant living in Greece, vividly describes how poverty penetrates social life:

> 'I can't go out like a normal person to drink a coffee with my friends. I don't go out. If you don't work, you can't do anything, you go out with your friends, they drink a beer, but you don't have a euro in your pocket, you get mad.' (Gedi, M, 28, LE, NEET, EL)

Along the same lines, Mara who had no income of her own at the time of the interview, argues that she cannot have any social life. Having a social life, she maintains, always implies costs that she cannot afford:

> 'I cannot buy any Christmas presents, because I cannot afford it. I'd like to go to the theatre, but with what money? So, these are all things that, anyway... force you to stay at home, in the end, to become antisocial.' (Mara, F, 30, ME, U, IT)

The fact that young people are forced to withdraw from friendships and social life due to economic hardship seems to produce a vicious circle, because according to their own accounts, friends constitute a very important source of support. According to our interviewees, even if it is not a source of information on how to get a job, the social network remains an important source of material and emotional support.

Being deprived of basic rights and reluctant to claim them

Another important outcome of living in conditions of prolonged uncertainty, according to youth interviewees, is the fear of claiming one's rights. As other commentators have argued, unemployment and precarity may result not only in deprivation of economic rights but also of civil, cultural, and political rights *de iure* and *de facto* (Standing, 2014). Job insecurity leads to compromise and accepting less because of the fear of long-term unemployment. Complaints about the way in which the labour market situation can result in deprivation of rights are evident in interviews in both countries, albeit more frequently in the Greek context – something that, given the rate of youth unemployment, is to be expected. Kiriaki, a young Greek woman, maintains:

> 'I believe that everyone is afraid of demanding their rights, because we know that if we demand anything, we won't continue working or we won't even be hired, so we keep our mouths shut. We don't ask for anything, because the boss will say "If you don't accept what I'm giving you, I can find someone else" [pause] there is so much unemployment.' (Kiriaki, F, 29, HE, NCJ, EL)

Greek interviewees draw comparisons between the pre- and post-crisis labour market. Gedi talks about how he used to bargain for better wages. However, in recent years, he accepts a job under any (in many cases humiliating) circumstances.

> 'Now you can't [bargain] [pause] heads down. Back then you would say "I want this money". If they didn't give you, you would go elsewhere mhm now they just don't give you. Now they say uuh "Do you want that? If you don't, don't come."' (Gedi, M, 28, LE, NEET, EL)

Nevertheless, interviewees do not construct their reluctance to claim their rights as some type of resignation. Instead they represent it as a decision imposed on them by the fact that precarious work constitutes the only alternative to unemployment. Exploitation and precarious conditions are not constructed as an exception; they are represented as a generalised work regime. Within this regime, youth do not have a choice. The only alternative to precarious employment is unemployment (Kesisoglou et al, 2016).

Interviewees also emphasise that, in order to make claims, they have to meet certain requirements such as having formal employment status (a contract) or having been employed for a certain period of time. Entitlement to (most) employment rights is a consequence of being fully integrated into the labour market. Thus, under conditions of insecurity, it is very difficult to make claims. Emma, a young Italian woman, says:

> 'At the *** [4-star hotel on the ski slopes] I replaced a member of the staff for two weeks [pause]. No contract. He paid me €50 for two weeks of work [pause], I was finishing work at two o'clock at night, starting again at six, four hours to sleep [pause] but anyway at that moment I had nothing in my hand.' (Emma, F, 20, ME, TE, IT)

Hence, the result is a vicious circle: precarity makes claiming one's rights difficult or even impossible, and by the same token, gives birth to further exploitation and uncertainty. In some cases, interviewees maintain that after having worked for a couple of weeks, they were 'fired' without notice and told that they would not be paid because they had just completed a trial period. This was the case for Olek, quoted in the following extract:

> 'I had spent two, two and a half weeks working there, when I told them to give me my money, they said "Uh no, you were on a trial period."' (Olek, M, 26, HE, U, EL)

The interviewees are willing to make a lot of compromises in order to obtain a job: Francesca was advised not to say she had a child when she was called again for a job through a private agency. Her daughter was only 3 months old and Francesca needed to work because she did not receive any type of institutional support:

> 'I was only 19, I was told: "No one is ever gonna bother keeping you there, if you have kids." My daughter was so little – 3 months! She was 3 months old. I could have stayed longer with my daughter! Of course. But obviously since I didn't have a contract, I didn't have the opportunity to go on maternity leave or anything.' (Francesca, F, 23, LE, TE, IT)

For other Greek and Italian youth, working without payment is something that they themselves offer to do in periods of prolonged unemployment in order to improve their job prospects. This is the only way, according to some interviewees, to obtain the work experience that employers commonly ask for:

'Of course, I was looking for a job. I was looking in newspapers and I was asking people, but it was hard. If you don't have work experience, they will not hire you [pause] So, after that I started working voluntarily at a cafeteria, without payment. I worked for a whole summer without being paid.' (Matina, F, 22, ME, TE, EL)

'Honestly, I can adjust myself to everything. You know even if I don't get paid, I'll do it all the same, rather than staying at home, being paid or not!' (Isa, F, 22, ME, U, IT)

In most cases, the interviewees themselves admit that this strategy seems to have negative implications, not only for the individual lives of the young employees themselves, but also for further deregulation of the labour market. Young people end up with insignificant short-term work experience which does not substantially improve their employment prospects. On the other hand, willingness to work under any conditions harms individual self-esteem and reinforces exploitation.

Conclusions

This chapter considered the material and social consequences of unemployment and job precariousness as constructed subjectively in interviews with Greek and Italian young people. Findings reveal that the implications are drastic and complex and affect many aspects of respondents' private and social lives. As far as the Greek interviewees' construction of their economic and material situation is concerned, the analysis confirmed what has been documented repeatedly in other studies (Karanikolos et al, 2013; Tsekeris et al, 2015): Greek society is experiencing a deep humanitarian crisis with tremendous effects. Thus, the most vulnerable of the interviewees narrated stories of severe deprivation and poverty such as having to live without enough food, heating, and electricity for long periods of time. The majority of Italian young people, on the other hand, did not represent themselves as being severely materially deprived. The relatively infrequent narratives of severe deprivation in the Italian sample come from interviewees located in the south of the country where the effects of the economic crisis seem to be more salient. Italian youth, however, also face the material implications of unstable income and fragmented and discontinuous working paths that allow them to cover only their essential basic needs (Bertolini, 2011).

In both contexts, family is constructed as a potential source of support, and the material situation of youth is related closely to the financial situation of the parental family. In Italy, parental material support appears to constitute the most important protective factor against the harshest implications of income poverty and/or instability, creating a phenomenon of 'hidden poverty' (Saraceno, 2015). In Greece, on the other hand, where unemployment in the general population has reached dramatic proportions, let alone the high youth unemployment rate, other family members, including parents, are also affected by unemployment and low work intensity, and the family cannot always protect young people from severe social and financial risks (Papadopoulos and Roumpakis, 2013).

Both Greek and Italian interviewees, even if the latter do not construct their financial situation as being extremely harsh, express their complete inability to engage in any type of financial planning, and they construct access to pension and future financial security as an objective that they will never achieve. Consequently, they avoid considering the future and prefer to work 'under the table' – something that affects interviewees' 'employment capital' and has multifaceted negative implications for different aspects of their life (Thomas et al, 2013). Interviewees' tendency to focus on the present and to distrust the future seems to echo the results of other studies on the economic crisis and its repercussions on the general population. According to the Eurobarometer (2014), a high percentage of Greek (almost 65 per cent) and Italian (42 per cent) people argue that as a result of the crisis and its repercussions, they refrain from dreaming about or making plans for the future. Other authors have argued that, as a result of the austerity in Southern Europe, new ways of approaching temporality have emerged (Knight and Stewart, 2016). According to these authors, austerity differs from poverty or underdevelopment, because it applies to situations in which social actors or communities that used to enjoy higher standards of living have to cope with a new situation. In these situations, the linear course of events, which characterises the modern collective representation of reality, gives way to temporal comparisons and 'plunges societies into the converse of counterfactual history in which one is invited to ask, "what if the past had happened differently?"' (Knight and Stewart, 2016: 3). Intergenerational comparisons that contrasted the present situation of youth with that enjoyed by previous generations were common in our interviewees' accounts. These comparisons involve both temporal and intergroup dimensions, and they make explicit the complexity of the construct of subjective (relative) experience of poverty/deprivation and the difficulty in operationalising it.

Apart from employment capital, the interviewees' social capital is also affected by unemployment and labour market exclusion (Van Oorschot et al, 2006). As other commentators have stressed (Jahoda, 1981), employment is associated not only with visible material benefits but also with latent benefits such as a time structure, social contacts, and personal status. Interviewees maintain that the workplace gives them the chance to meet new people and to form social bonds and friendships. In contrast, during periods of unemployment, they become totally isolated. Furthermore, involvement in social life is conditional upon one's ability to spend; and poverty may in some cases have implications that violate social norms. Personal and family life are presented as influenced in various ways by a precarious work life and by unemployment. First, employment insecurity, unpredictable work schedules, and varying income flows increase tensions at home and make it difficult to sustain relationships. Second, due to insecurity, long-term binding decisions are necessarily postponed (Buchholz et al, 2008). Finally, another consequence situated within the social and political sphere of the interviewees' lives has to do with the violation of certain rights and entitlements. They tend to maintain that they are reluctant to claim their employment rights and tolerate labour exploitation because the only alternative to poor employment conditions and precarity is unemployment (Kesisoglou et al, 2016).

In conclusion, these findings from interviews with young people in two Southern European countries situate the material and social implications of unemployment and precarity in the context of the recent economic turmoil in line with existing literature. The bottom-up perspective adopted here, however, serves to highlight complex relations and intersections between constructs that are usually contrasted and operationalised in existing literature (temporal vs group comparisons, individual vs household deprivation), and this perspective emphasises new forms of subjectivity and agency (Gershon et al, 2011; Standing, 2011). Of course, given the nature of qualitative research, it is necessary to recognise that although these findings may be valid in the specific context in which they are set, their generalisation is limited. However, some of the intersections between constructs that have been indicated here may have some validity beyond the specific microsocial context and confirm the need to give prominence to lay discourses and subjective experiences at times of ever-growing inequality (Fine, 2016).

Notes
[1] This refers particularly to the inability to afford items and activities such as a washing machine, TV, telephone, car, holidays once a year, and keeping one's home adequately warm. It also includes enforced inability to pay unexpected expenses and being confronted with payment arrears (for example, mortgage or rent, utility bills).
[2] https://ec.europa.eu/eurostat/statistics-explained/index.php/Glossary:Material_deprivation

References

Bello, B.G. and Cuzzocrea, V. (2018) 'Introducing the need to study young people in contemporary Italy', *Journal of Modern Italian Studies*, 23(1): 1–7.

Berneo, N.G. (2014) *Unemployment in Southern Europe: Coping with the Consequences*, London: Routledge.

Bertolini, S. (2011) 'The heterogeneity of the impact of labour market flexibilization on the transition to adult life in Italy: when do young people leave the nest?', in H.P. Blossfeld, D. Hofäcker and S. Bertolini (eds) *Youth on Globalised Labour Markets: Rising Uncertainty and its Effects on Early Employment and Family Lives in Europe*, Opladen and Farmington Hills: Verlag Barbara Budrich, pp 163–87.

Boon, B. and Farnsworth, J. (2011) 'Social exclusion and poverty: translating social capital into accessible resources', *Social Policy & Administration*, 45(5): 507–24.

Brand, J.E. (2015) 'The far-reaching impact of job loss and unemployment', *Annual Review of Sociology*, 41: 359–75.

Brand, J.E. and Burgard, S.A. (2008) 'Job displacement and social participation over the life course: findings for a cohort of joiners', *Social Forces*, 87(1): 211–42.

Brand, J.E. and Simon Thomas, J. (2014) 'Job displacement among single mothers: effects on children's outcomes in young adulthood', *American Journal of Sociology*, 119(4): 955–1001.

Braun, V. and Clarke, V. (2006) 'Using thematic analysis in psychology', *Qualitative Research in Psychology*, 3(2): 77–101.

Buchholz, S., Jabsen, A., Kurz, K., Marold, J., Schmelzer, P. and Blossfeld, H.P. (2008) *Globalization, Economic Restructuring and Increasing Uncertainty in Old Age: A Theoretical Framework*. flexCAREER Working Paper Series. Bamberg: Universität Bamberg.

Clark, A., Georgellis, Y. and Sanfey, P. (2001) 'Scarring: the psychological impact of past unemployment', *Economica*, 68(270): 221–41.

Craig, L. and Brown, J.E. (2014) 'Weekend work and leisure time with family and friends: who misses out?', *Journal of Marriage and Family*, 76(4): 710–27.

Crosby, F. (1984) 'Relative deprivation in organizational settings', *Research in Organizational Behavior*, 6: 51–93.

Davies, J.C. (1969) 'The J-Curve of rising and declining satisfactions as a cause of some great revolutions and a contained rebellion', in H.D. Graham and T.R. Gurr (eds) *The History of Violence in America: A Report to the National Commission on the Causes and Prevention of Violence*, New York: Bantam, pp 690–730.

Davis, S.J. and Von Wachter, T.M. (2011) 'Recessions and the costs of job loss', *Brookings Papers on Economic Activity*, 43: 1–72.

Deutsch, J., Guio, A.C., Pomati, M. and Silber, J. (2015) 'Material deprivation in Europe: which expenditures are curtailed first?', *Social Indicators Research*, 120(3): 723–40.

Dowler, E.A. and O'Connor, D. (2012) 'Rights-based approaches to addressing food poverty and food insecurity in Ireland and UK', *Social Science & Medicine*, 74(1): 44–51.

Eichorst, W. and Neder, F. (2014) *Youth Unemployment in Mediterranean Countries*. IZA Policy Paper, No. 80. Bonn: Institute of Labor Economics (IZA).

Engler, P. and Klein, M. (2017) 'Austerity measures amplified crisis in Spain, Portugal, and Italy', *DIW Economic Bulletin*, 7(8): 89–93.

Eurobarometer 81 (2014) 'Public opinion in the European Union', European Commission, Directorate General for Communication, Available at: https://ec.europa.eu/commfrontoffice/publicopinion/archives/eb/eb81/eb81_publ_en.pdf

Eurostat (2015) *Being Young in Europe Today*, Luxembourg: Publications Office of the European Union.

Eurostat (2020) 'Annual Employment statistics', Available from: https://ec.europa.eu/eurostat/statistics-explained/index.php/Employment_-_annual_statistics

Fine, M. (2016) 'Commentary on Part III: Political discourse and practice', in C. Howarth and E. Andreouli (eds) *The Social Psychology of Everyday Politics*, London: Routledge, pp 253–60.

Fryer, D. (1998) 'Labour market disadvantage, deprivation and mental health', in P.J.D. Drenth, H. Thierry and C.J. de Wolff (eds) *Handbook of Work and Organizational Psychology*, Hove: Psychology Press, pp 215–27.

Fuwa, M. (2014) 'Work–family conflict and attitudes toward marriage', *Journal of Family Issues*, 35(6): 731–54.

Gershon, I., Cohen, A.J., Ho, K., Sanders, T., Sykes, K., Wright, S. and Gershon, I. (2011) 'Neoliberal agency', *Current Anthropology*, 52(4): 537–55.

Gialis, S. and Tsampra, M. (2015) 'The diverse regional patterns of atypical employment in Greece: production restructuring, re/deregulation and flexicurity under crisis', *Geoforum*, 62: 175–87.

Guio, A.C., Marlier, E., Gordon, D., Fahmy, E., Nandy, S. and Pomati, M. (2016) 'Improving the measurement of material deprivation at the European Union level', *Journal of European Social Policy*, 26(3): 219–333.

Hatton, E. (2011) *The Temp Economy: From Kelly Girls to Permatemps in Postwar America*, Philadelphia: Temple University Press.

Hodgetts, D., Radley, A., Chamberlain, K. and Hodgetts, A. (2007) 'Health inequalities and homelessness: considering material, relational and spatial dimension', *Journal of Health Psychology*, 12: 709–25.

Hofäcker, D., Schadow, S. and Kletzing, J. (2017) *Long-Term Socio-Economic Consequences of Insecure Labour Market Positions*. EXCEPT Working Papers, WP No. 16. Tallinn: Tallinn University, Available from: https://www.except-project.eu/working-papers/

ISTAT (2016) 'Annual report: the atate of the nation', *Annual Report*, Rome: ISTAT.

Jahoda, M. (1981) 'Work, employment and unemployment: values, theories and approaches in social research', *American Psychologist*, 36(2): 184–91.

Jahoda, M., Lazarsfeld, P.F. and Zeisel, H. (1971) *Marienthal: The Sociography of an Unemployed Community*, Chicago: Aldine-Atherton.

Johnson, R.C., Kalil, A. and Dunifon, R.E. (2012) 'Employment patterns of less-skilled workers: links to children's behavior and academic progress', *Demography*, 49(2): 747–72.

Kalil, A. and Wightman, P. (2011) 'Parental job loss and children's educational attainment in black and white middle-class families', *Social Science Quarterly*, 92(1): 57–78.

Karamessini, M. (2015) 'The Greek social model: towards a deregulated labour market and residual social protection', in D. Vaughan-Whitehead (ed) *The European Social Model in Crisis. Is Europe Losing its Soul?* Geneva, Cheltenham: ILO and Edward Elgar, pp 230–88.

Karanikolos, M., Mladovsky, P., Cylus, J., Thomson, S., Basu, S., Stuckler, D. and McKee, M. (2013) 'Financial crisis, austerity, and health in Europe', *The Lancet*, 381 (9874): 1323–31.

Kesisoglou, G., Figgou, L. and Dikaiou, M. (2016) 'Constructing work and subjectivities in precarious conditions: psycho-discursive practices in young people's interviews in Greece', *Journal of Social and Political Psychology*, 4(1): 24–43.

Knight, D.M. and Stewart, C. (2016) 'Ethnographies of austerity: temporality, crisis and affect in Southern Europe', *History and Anthropology*, 27(1): 1–18.

Labrianidis, L. (2014) 'Investing in leaving: the Greek case of international migration of professionals', *Mobilities*, 9(2): 314–35.

León, M. and Migliavacca, M. (2013) 'Italy and Spain: still the case of familistic welfare models?', *Population Review*, 52(1): 25–42.

Leonardi, M. and Pica, G. (2015) 'Youth unemployment in Italy', in J.J. Dolado (ed) *No Country for Young People? Youth Labour Market Problems in Europe*, London: CEPR Press, pp 89–104.

Lewchuk, W., Lafleche, M., Procyk, S., Cook, C., Dyson, D., Goldring, L., Lior, K., Meisner, A., Shields, J., Tambureno, A., and Viducis, P. (2015) *The Precarity Penalty: Poverty and Employment Precarity in Southern Ontario*, Ontario: McMaster University.

O'Reilly, J., Eichhorst, W., Gábos, A., Hadjivassiliou, K., Lain, D., Leschke, J. and Russell, H. (2015) 'Five characteristics of youth unemployment in Europe: flexibility, education, migration, family legacies, and EU policy', *SAGE Open*, 5(1): 1–19.

OECD (2018) *Youth Unemployment Rate*, indicator, viewed 22 June 2018.

Page, M., Huff Stevens A. and Lindo, J. (2007) 'Parental income shocks and outcomes of disadvantaged youth in the United States', in J. Gruber (ed) *The Problems of Disadvantaged Youth: An Economic Perspective*, Chicago: University of Chicago Press, pp 213–35.

Papadopoulos, T. and Roumpakis, A. (2013) 'Familistic welfare capitalism in crisis: social reproduction and anti-social policy in Greece', *Journal of International and Comparative Social Policy*, 29(3): 204–24.

Posel, D., Casale, D. and Vermaak, C. (2014) 'Job search and the measurement of unemployment in South Africa', *South African Journal of Economics*, 82(1): 66–80.

Poverty and Employment Precarity in Southern Ontario (PEPSO) (2013) 'It's more than poverty: employment and precarity and household well-being', Available from: https://www.unitedwaygt.org/document.doc?id=91

Putnam, R.D. (2000) 'Bowling alone: America's declining social capital', in L. Crothers and C. Lockhart (eds) *Culture and Politics*, New York: Palgrave Macmillan, pp 223–34.

Rüdig, W. and Karyotis, G. (2013) 'Beyond the usual suspects? New participants in anti-austerity protests in Greece', *Mobilization: An International Quarterly*, 18(3): 313–30.

Saraceno, C. (2015) *Il Lavoro Non Basta: La Povertà in Europa Negli Anni Della Crisi*, Milan: Feltrinelli Editore.

Standing, G. (2011) *The Precariat: The New Dangerous Class*, London: Bloomsbury Academic.

Standing, G. (2014) 'The precariat', *Contexts*, 13(4): 10–12.

Tajfel, H. and Turner, J. (1986) 'The social identity theory of intergroup behavior', in W.G. Austin and S. Worche (eds) *The Social Psychology of Intergroup Relations*, Monterey: Brooks/Cole, pp 33–47.

Thomas, H., Boguslaw, J., Chaganti, S., Atkinson, A. and Shapiro, T. (2013) *Employment Capital: How Work Builds and Protects Family Wealth and Security*. Leveraging Mobility Series, Waltham: Institute on Assets and Social Policy.

Tsekeris, C., Pinguli, M. and Georga, E. (2015) 'Young people's perception of economic crisis in contemporary Greece: a social psychological pilot study', *Crisis Observatory Research Paper*, 19: 1–26.

Van Oorschot, W., Arts, W. and Gelissen, J. (2006) 'Social capital in Europe: measurement and social and regional distribution of a multifaceted phenomenon', *Acta Sociologica*, 49(2): 149–67.

Whelan, C.T., Nolan, B. and Maitre, B. (2008) *Measuring Material Deprivation in the Enlarged EU*. ESRI Working Paper No. 249. Dublin: Economic and Social Research Institute.

14

Syntheses of long-term socio-economic consequences of insecure labour market positions for youth in Europe[1]

Dirk Hofäcker, Sina Schadow, and Janika Kletzing

Introduction

As a result of the projected ageing of Europe's population, the sustainability of public pensions has become one of the most important political issues in recent decades, because the number of pension recipients is increasing while the number of pension contributors is decreasing. Hence, the period over which pension recipients receive pension payouts is expected to increase in many OECD countries (Chomik and Whitehouse, 2010). Pay-as-you-go pension systems, which are common across Europe, face increasing difficulties in ensuring their current and future sustainability.

These difficulties were already acknowledged in a report published by the World Bank in 1994, entitled *Averting the Old Age Crisis: Policies to Protect the Old and Promote Growth*. Here, it was argued that in the face of ageing populations, three-pillar pension systems should be established that combine standard public pensions with additional savings into both occupational and private pension plans. Up to now, many European countries have established such three-pillar pension systems, though with significant cross-national variations in the relative importance of the three pillars. At the same time, the generosity of public pensions, which previously accounted for the 'lion's share' of old-age income, has generally decreased – for example, by reducing the gross pension replacement rate and increasing the retirement age (OECD, 2013). With the implementation of the three-pillar pension model, responsibility for ensuring a sustainable income in old-age has been shifted increasingly away from public authorities and on to individuals. This creates intergenerational inequalities, because – unlike today's pensioners who still retire with good public pensions – almost all young Europeans will retire under the new three-pillar pension system (Ebbinghaus and Gronwold, 2011). Hence, reforms of public pensions will affect young people in particular who are increasingly expected to invest in occupational and private pension plans as early as possible to ensure their future old-age income (Hofäcker and Blossfeld, 2011).

At the same time, employment conditions have changed substantially for European youth whose employment paths have become increasingly insecure. Young people frequently experience long-term unemployment and are also disproportionately found in atypical employment such as fixed-term contracts, platform working, or (fake) self-employment in the gig economy, which often pays lower wages than those for the regularly employed (Rokicka et al, 2015). The impact of employment uncertainty is likely to decrease young people's capacity to save for their old age. Because the employment path has become more unpredictable, young people may find it difficult to commit themselves to long-term binding financial investment plans that require continuous contributions.

Taking all these factors into account, young people in Europe will be increasingly dependent on additional income in old age due to the cuts to public pensions. However, the current labour market situation is making it increasingly difficult for them to save towards pension income (Hofäcker et al, 2017). In the long-term, employment uncertainties such as periods of fixed-term employment could accumulate into substantial pension gaps. This suggests a more negative view of atypical types of employment, which previous studies have shown to be less detrimental in the short term (Rokicka and Kłobuszewska, 2016) or to act potentially as a stepping stone to secure employment in the medium-term (Hofäcker, 2017).

Against this background, this chapter aims to systematically address the long-term socio-economic consequences of insecure labour market positions such as unemployment or atypical employment for future pension prospects, considering all three pension systems: *public*, *occupational*, and *private*.[2] These long-term socio-economic consequences will be analysed from both demand- and supply-side perspectives. On the *demand side*, it will investigate how far young people are aware of the increasing need to invest in occupational and private pension plans together with their actual saving behaviour. Are young Europeans building up savings for old age and, if not, what prevents them from doing so? On the *supply side*, it will investigate how far young people – if interested – have access to such pension schemes and how they treat periods of employment uncertainty with regard to their future pension entitlements.

This investigation employs a mixed-methods approach. The methodological approaches used will be presented separately for the demand and the supply side.

Demand side

For the demand-side perspective, quantitative data are taken from a Flash Eurobarometer of 2008 (European Commission, 2009) and the European Social Survey of 2006 (ESS Round 3, 2006). These include single indicators on savings behaviour, though with a focus on the overall population rather than on youth.[3]

Furthermore, interviews were conducted with experts from different fields and professions in six EU countries (Estonia, Germany, Italy, Poland, Sweden, and the United Kingdom [UK]) as well as the Ukraine. The selected countries – drawn from EXCEPT member states – represent different types of welfare system: conservative (Germany), Southern European (Italy), liberal (UK), social-democratic (Sweden), and Eastern European (Estonia, Poland, and the Ukraine) (Esping-Andersen, 1990). These countries differ widely in their general welfare logic (Myles and Peirson, 2001) and in the structure of their three-pillar pension systems.

One of the main reasons for expert interviews was that although there are some data on public pension savings for youth, cross-national comparative evidence about occupational and private pension schemes is scarce. This is due not least to the fact that the structure and management of occupational and private pension plans differ widely among European countries and are also often based on individual negotiated contracts rather than 'standard models'. Faced with this variety, experts can take the role of specialist 'informants' who possess specific knowledge about the structure and administrative process and procedures for these schemes (Gläser & Laudel, 2010). Expert interviews were used to provide a deeper insight into the reasons behind the savings behaviour of young people in all three pension pillars. In light of the relative importance of each pension pillar and the complexity of the national pension systems, at least three interviews were conducted per country.

Quantitative results

To investigate the importance attributed to savings by youth in Europe, Figure 14.1 displays results from a question included in a Flash

Figure 14.1: General importance attributed to savings in European countries: young people (15–39 years) versus full (non-retired) sample in 2008

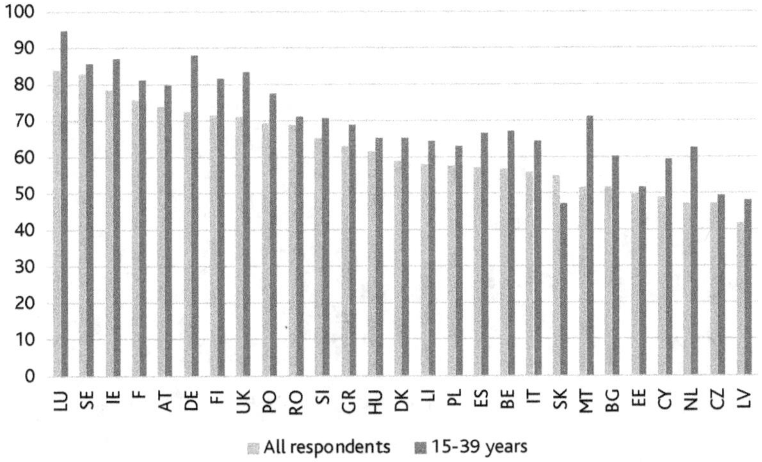

■ All respondents ■ 15-39 years

Note: Question wording: 'Thinking of the time when you retire, would you consider saving money or taking up insurance in case you become dependent' (Yes/No/Don't know).
Source: Flash Eurobarometer 247 (authors' own calculations)

Eurobarometer study in 2008. This asked respondents: 'thinking of the time when [they] retire, would [they] consider saving money or taking up insurance in case that [they] become dependent', with the response categories 'yes' or 'no'.[4] Figure 14.1 shows the proportion of the full (non-retired) sample reporting individual readiness to save compared to respondents aged up to 39 years.[5]

Results provide clear evidence of a high level of readiness to make additional savings among European youth, ranging from 80 to 90 per cent in countries such as France, Ireland, Luxembourg, and Sweden to between 50 and 60 per cent in some Eastern European countries (Bulgaria, Czech Republic, Estonia, and Latvia), but also the Netherlands and Cyprus. Notably, this readiness is often slightly higher among younger respondents than among the overall population. Despite their temporal distance from retirement, young people seem well aware of the need to make additional provision in a changing pensions landscape.

Figure 14.2 goes beyond the mere readiness to save by focusing on actual savings behaviour. Data originate from the third wave of the European Social Survey 2006 in which respondents were asked 'are you currently saving or have ... saved in the past specifically in order to live comfortably in your old age?' The figure reports the percentage

Figure 14.2: Own savings to live comfortably in old age: young people (15–29 years) versus full (non-retired) sample in 2006

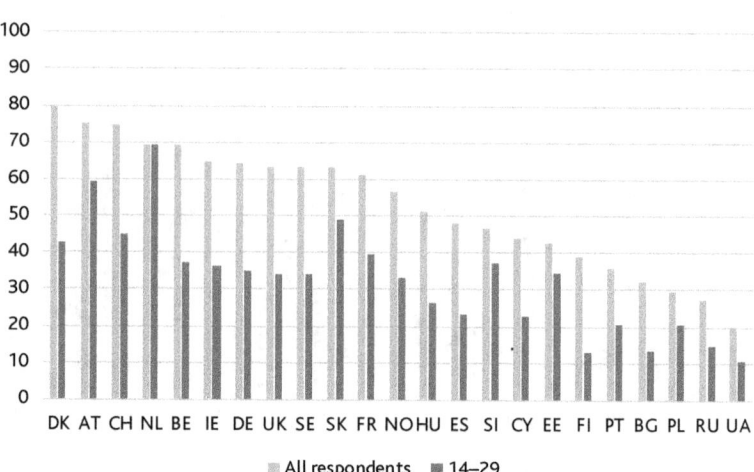

of respondents making own savings, again contrasting young people (respondents aged up to 29 years) with the entire population.[6]

In contrast to the readiness to save (see previous discussion), Figure 14.2 shows a clear gap in actual savings between younger people and the overall population. Overall, the proportion of people who save varies widely between around three quarters of the population in countries such as Austria, Denmark, the Netherlands, and Switzerland, and one third or less in a number of Eastern European countries. In contrast, less than half of young people effectively have savings, with particularly low levels in Eastern and Southern European countries. A more detailed breakdown of figures among youth (see Hofäcker et al, 2017) shows that savings behaviour is particularly low among young people in fixed-term employment, suggesting that it is not only their age, but also their insecure labour market situation that prevents young people from saving for the longer term. As other research such as Tosun et al (2019) has shown, young people may also be discouraged from further savings by their perceptions of their own financial situation which they view as being worse than that of the previous generation.

Findings from expert interviews: financial literacy of youth

Besides the delaying effect of insecure employment on pensions as reported previously, experts from different European countries indicated that the financial literacy of youth — that is, their understanding of multi-pillar pension systems and their key characteristics — could be another factor that keeps young people from putting savings into occupational or private pension plans. Most interviewed experts claim that the financial literacy of young people in Europe seems to be low in general (see Moiso, 2017; Schadow, 2017; Stasiowski, 2017; Unt and Reiska, 2017).

> 'It's a problem that many people, especially young people — no matter which country you look at — are not well prepared to make financial decisions.' (EXP02, Germany)

In particular, young people with a low level of education apparently face difficulties in making rational financial decisions because they often do not possess the necessary knowledge about pension systems.

> 'I do not know if children in Poland are taught to save money [pause] I do not know if a lower secondary school graduate who goes to high school has any idea what the interest rate is on credit, how much it costs him to borrow like this [pause] why it is worth having some savings.' (EXP03, Poland)

These findings are in line with those of other studies reporting low levels of financial literacy across the population as a whole (Lusardi and Mitchell, 2011b) and for young people in particular (Lusardi et al, 2010; Garg and Singh, 2018), and showing that financial literacy correlates highly with socio-demographic characteristics such as educational background (Lusardi and Mitchell, 2011b; Garg and Sigh, 2018).

Without doubt, increasing individual responsibility for one's own pension provision and the associated investment in financial markets increase the importance of financial education (Lusardi and Mitchell, 2011a), especially when the market for pension plans is highly complex as in Germany, Italy, and Poland (Moiso, 2017; Schadow, 2017; Stasiowski, 2017). However, it is questionable how far financial literacy alone can improve the situation and lead to greater engagement in occupational or private pension savings plans. On the one hand, information provided about different occupational and private pension schemes is inconsistent, and this makes comparisons difficult even for the financially literate (for Germany, see Schadow, 2017). On the other hand, it is problematic to estimate the future development of global financial markets over a time horizon of about 30 or 40 years even for experts or rating agencies (Fachinger, 2018). Furthermore, financial literacy can do little to improve the situation when the possibility of putting savings into additional pension programmes is limited by low and unpredictable income.

Supply side

Attention now shifts from young people's understanding of the need for pension savings to the supply side – that is, the type of pension schemes offered to young people and how they treat employment uncertainties. In this respect, the initial focus will be on *public* pension systems that still make up the major pillar of pension income in European countries. To this end, stylised institutional data will be used from various cross-national databases such as the Mutual Information System on Social Protection in Europe (MISSOC, 2016) or the OECD Pension at a Glance Report (OECD, 2015). The analyses here consider existing regulations for the period 2014–15 whenever possible. For occupational and private pension schemes, again findings from the expert interviews were utilised (for the methodological approach, see earlier discussion).

Characteristics of public pension systems

One key characteristic of public pension systems is that they are in principle universal – that is, they cover the entire population of a country. In some countries, certain groups such as the self-employed, are exempt from public pensions and have their own old-age insurance schemes.

The following typology developed from the literature and data focuses on how employment uncertainties influence future pension outcomes. Pension systems are expected to be less 'youth-friendly' when periods of employment uncertainty effectively reduce the extent of pension rights, or when they endanger eligibility for pensions in general. Four dimensions regarded as key components of public pension systems are considered here (see Hofäcker et al, 2017: 42ff.): the assessment basis, the qualifying period, the treatment of periods of unemployment, and the treatment of periods of childcare. For each dimension, each national public pension system is classified as being either favourable for youth (3), partly favourable for youth (2), or unfavourable for youth (1).

- The **assessment basis** of a pension scheme reflects the calculations on which pensions are computed. As marginal cases, they can be based on either the *amount* or the *length* entirely decoupled from a contribution logic when a flat-rate basic pension is paid out. It is assumed here that the stronger the logic of proportionality with contributions, the more negatively such systems will penalise youth with employment interruptions, lower wages, or less stable wages. Based on this assumption, one can classify countries in which pension systems depend solely on the level of previous contributions as being unfavourable (1), those in which means-tested minimum pensions are targeted at specific individuals as partly favourable (2), and those in which later benefits are not means-tested and entirely independent of previous working life as being favourable for youth (3).

- A pension's **qualifying period** refers to the minimum requirement in contribution years to become eligible for a pension. It can be assumed that the higher the number of years required, the more difficult it will be for those with employment interruptions to reach eligibility. Again, countries can be clustered into three groups based on their actual distribution within Europe: those with a qualifying period of up to five years are considered as favourable for youth (3), those with a qualifying period of between six and 15 years as being partly favourable (2), and those with more than 15 years as being unfavourable (1).
- Whereas the previous dimension refers to the more general logic of pension systems, countries can also differ regarding how employment interruptions are treated as contribution periods when calculating pension benefits. The more comprehensive they are, the less disadvantageous they are to young people with discontinuous careers. On the one hand, this concerns **periods of unemployment.** Countries in which unemployment spells are not considered at all or are considered only for minimum pension entitlements are assumed to be the most disadvantageous for youth (1). Countries in which pension benefits are considered only for a first period of unemployment and/or are considered at a rate of up to 80 per cent of previous contributions are assumed to be partly favourable (2), whereas those in which pension benefits are paid continuously at higher rates are considered to be favourable (3).
- A similar approach is applied for **periods of childcare**. Countries that do not consider such interruptions when calculating pension benefits, that factor them in at 25% of normal contributions or less, or that restrict the consideration of such contributions to one year are considered unfavourable (1). Countries that consider childcare breaks for a period between one and three years are assumed to be partly favourable (2), and those that consider them for more than three years or consider them close to previous earnings are taken as being favourable (3).

Figure 14.3: Consideration of employment uncertainty in public pension systems: composite index

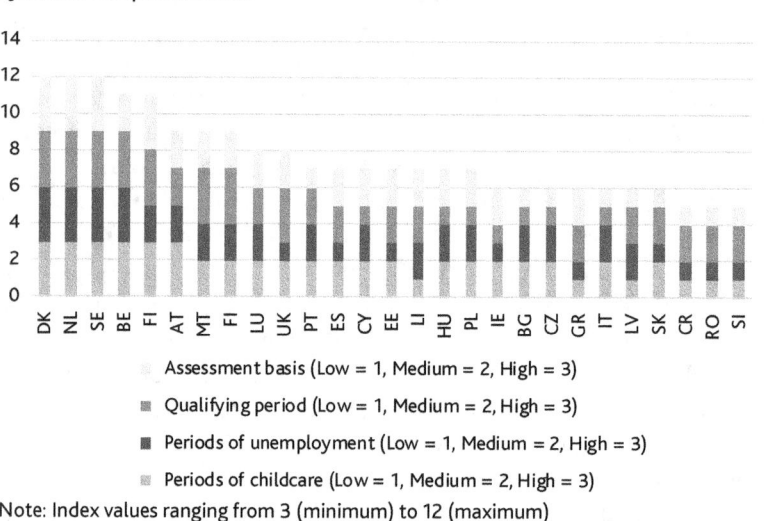

Note: Index values ranging from 3 (minimum) to 12 (maximum)
Source: Authors' own illustration based on MISSOC, 2016, OECD, 2015, and EGGSI, 2011

Data from cross-national institutional databases were examined systematically and values for 2014–15 were assigned to countries based on the typology. Values for the single dimensions were then added up to form a composite unweighted index value (see Figure 14.3).

Figure 14.3 shows the respective results for European countries, reflecting both the overall index value as well as values for the single dimensions. It is clear that European countries vary substantially in their consideration of employment uncertainties for public pension benefits. On the one hand, in a number of mostly Central and Northern European countries (with the single exception of Malta as a Southern European country), various characteristics of the national pension system account for labour market uncertainties of youth positively, and this is reflected in high index values. In *Denmark*, for example, the basic pension shows no connection to previous earnings (score of 3 for assessment basis), and there is also no minimum number of years required for qualifying for a pension (score of 3 for qualifying period). Contributions for periods of unemployment and childcare are paid at up to double the amount of standard contributions (score of 3 for consideration of unemployment respectively childcare). In contrast, in a number of Eastern European countries in particular, the situation for young people facing employment uncertainty seems to be particularly unfavourable with regard to their future public pension rights.

One possible drawback of the focus on institutional differences in considering employment uncertainties applied here without considering the actual incidence of such uncertainties, is that if employment uncertainties are not widespread, the outlined pension consequences may apply to only a small group of youth. However, further evidence shows that particularly in countries in which, for example, unemployment is accounted for comprehensively when calculating public pensions, youth unemployment rates are comparatively low with values roughly between 10 to 25 per cent (see Hofäcker et al, 2017). Vice versa, the highest unemployment rates are found particularly in countries where unemployment is accounted for least favourably(Hofäcker et al, 2017). This suggests a *negative* relationship between the consideration of unemployment uncertainties and their incidence among youth. In other words, in contexts in which youth unemployment is a major problem, unemployment will have severe consequences for young people's income in later life because employment interruptions are not accounted for in pension calculations.

Findings from expert interviews

Public pensions

The findings in the previous section focused on the consideration of employment uncertainties for *public* pensions. In the following, this information is supplemented with evidence from the qualitative expert interviews. For virtually all countries in the sample, experts expected that the (gross) pension replacement rate would decrease in the future (see Merritt, 2017; Moiso, 2017; Schadow, 2017; Stasiowski, 2017; Unt and Reiska, 2017). At the same time, the retirement age is rising almost universally. The increase in potential contribution years, however, is likely to be "eaten up" (EXS01, Germany) by employment interruptions, particularly in countries in which periods of unemployment are not considered in calculating public pensions. In sum, these developments imply that young people will need to work longer to receive relatively less (Schadow and Kletzing 2017). As occasional evidence suggests, however, youth are not always aware of this projected decrease (Stasiowski, 2017).

Experts also highlighted that there are still several groups that are not covered by mandatory insurance, particularly in flexible employment forms that apply disproportionately to youth. In some countries (in the present set, Germany, Poland, Sweden, and the Ukraine), the *self-employed* are not mandatorily covered by public pensions or, where they have the possibility of voluntarily joining the scheme, can choose to reduce their contributions; an option that is used widely (see Choi, 2009; ifo Institute, 2015; Nikolaieva and Vakhitova, 2017; Schadow, 2017; Stasiowski, 2017; Strandh, 2017).

Occupational pensions

Expert interviews also allow an assessment of current trends in the second pillar – occupational pensions – and their implications for the future income of young people in old age. One main advantage of occupational pensions is that future pension rights are often co-financed by employers, thereby increasing the amount of pension payouts. In the UK, for example, employers often double the amount that employees contribute to occupational pensions.

> 'A lot of employers do give more than the minimum. And often double what people put in up to a set amount. For example, if the employee puts in 2 per cent they will give 4 per cent. Usually up to 8 or 10 per cent.' (EXP02, UK)

Occupational pensions are much more common in established welfare states (Germany, Italy, Sweden, and the UK), whereas in the relatively new welfare states of Eastern Europe (such as Estonia and Poland), such second-pillar pensions schemes do not exist or are of only minor importance.

Notably, when occupational pensions are not made mandatory, they frequently have only rather low coverage rates due to restrictive access conditions. The coverage rate of occupational pension plans is naturally limited, because they do not cover the *self-employed* or *unemployed*. Furthermore, even among the dependent employees, occupational pensions effectively apply only to those on regular work contracts, whereas the *atypically employed* are often not covered (Moiso, 2017). In Germany, occupational pensions have a wider coverage, but are frequently used as a human resource policy instrument and thus are often offered only to higher-skilled employees in internal labour markets (Schadow, 2017). Even in the UK in which an auto-enrolment into occupational pensions[7] has recently been established for new working contracts, specific groups of employees such as those with *zero-hour contracts*, *low-waged* employees, or those on *fixed-term contracts* with a duration of less than three months are still excluded from occupational pension plans, (see Merritt, 2017). Only in Sweden do occupational pensions cover about 90 per cent of Swedish employees. However, they are not common in the health sector in which many Swedish young people work nowadays (Strandh, 2017).

Pensions portability can be an issue for occupational pensions – that is, savings from these schemes are often not portable between sectors and employers internationally or even on a national level (Schadow, 2017). If the transfer of pension entitlements between different occupational pension schemes is possible, such transfers often have high transaction costs.

Furthermore, occupational pension plans are frequently connected to a minimum qualifying period. Particularly young people on fixed-term contracts may find it hard to fulfil the qualifying periods because of their frequent *job mobility*. This problem of portability could also affect successful and highly mobile young people who may accumulate savings in multiple occupational pension plans, yet with only low or no revenues (Hofäcker, Schadow and Kletzing, 2017). Furthermore, one main disadvantage of occupational pension plans is also that in contrast to public pensions, contributions cease during periods of unemployment or childcare, effectively punishing employment interruptions.

Even for young people enrolled in occupational pension plans, the effectiveness of savings in the second pillar to ensure a sustainable income in old-age has deteriorated dramatically since the financial crisis in 2008. Since then, many good schemes with high revenues – often defined benefits schemes in which revenues are guaranteed – have closed to new members (Merritt, 2017; Moiso, 2017; Schadow, 2017). Hence, young people in Europe face specific disadvantages in the second pillar, because their savings conditions are worse in comparison to those of older generations. As one expert strikingly put it:

> 'Previously, there were more promises for occupational pensions and also higher promises.' (EXP06, Germany)

Private pensions

Private pensions are individual investment accounts that are offered by insurance companies and based on individually negotiated contracts. In some countries, such plans are subsidised generously by tax benefits, as with the so-called 'Riester Pension' in Germany (Schadow, 2017).[8] The expert group report that all countries had implemented third-pillar private pension plans and that there are explicit state subsidies in Estonia, Germany, Italy, Poland, and the UK. In comparison to occupational pensions, there are no access conditions and virtually all individuals are advised to invest in such schemes to complement public pensions. The only exception is Sweden where private pension plans intended for some risk groups such as the self-employed or migrants, or for people who have frequent interruptions in their career due to unemployment or periods of childcare (Strandh, 2017).

One main finding from the expert interviews in all countries in which they were conducted is that the use of private pension plans seems to vary strongly with educational and financial background. In most countries, private pensions are used disproportionally frequently by high earners and higher educated people. Experts pointed out that the observed problems of distribution could arise from, on the one hand, the strong connection of private savings to individual resources. On the other hand, especially experts in Germany indicated that high earners will benefit more from tax benefits than low earners, because their tax load is particularly high (Schadow, 2017). But not only income and educational backgrounds seem to be a strong predictor of participation in private pension plans. Experts claimed that it is especially young people who do not often participate in such schemes (Moiso, 2017; Schadow, 2017; Stasiowski, 2017; Unt and Reiska, 2017). On the one hand, they claimed that young people normally have low wages at the beginning of their careers that naturally limit their ability to sacrifice some savings for pension products. On the other hand, retirement seems to be a remote topic.

> 'The main problem we see in pensions with young people is that they are not interested in pensions when they are 18, 19, or in their 20s; they have other things they want to spend their money on, and retirement seems an awfully long way away and you sort of think, I'd rather go out and have a few beers tonight. It's too far away to be of interest.' (EXP02, UK)

Furthermore, particularly in well-established welfare states, the private pension market has reached a high level of complexity and increasingly lacks transparency (Merritt, 2017; Moiso, 2017; Schadow, 2017). Considering the generally low financial literacy of young people, it is nearly impossible for them to make rational investment decisions. As a consequence of this situation, if they join such a scheme at all, many young people simply join the first scheme they are offered by their consultants without comparing different pension products:

'You could say, they give themselves into the hands of the consultants. Do what you want with me.' (EXP04, Germany)

Particularly the young *unemployed* may not be able to pay contributions to private schemes. Even when private pension plans offer the possibility of lowering the contributions or pausing them, times of no or lower contributions will negatively affect future revenues from such schemes. For young people on *fixed-term contracts,* the assumption of continuous contributions could also be a barrier that may prevent them from committing themselves to long-term financial investments, because they also need their savings for transition times between working contracts.

'To have a decent supplementary pension they have to have so much money [pause] that young people do not have! ... if young people save in a pension fund, they will get their money back when they retire, while there are other products they can withdraw when needed.' (EXP03, Italy)

Furthermore, in countries such as Estonia in which the poverty rate is high, private pension products will not ensure additional incomes for old age, because the potential of savings is low, which is why many people will not be covered by such schemes.

Like occupational pensions, private pension plans were hit hard by the financial crisis and that has dramatically reduced their effectiveness in ensuring future income in old age (Antolin and Stewart, 2009), because interest rates still have not recovered ten years after the crisis. Private pension products in Eastern Europe were particularly badly affected. In the Ukraine, the financial crisis has left the stock market for private pension products largely 'dead' (Nikoleiva and Vatikova, 2017).

Policy recommendations

From the previous discussions, it emerges almost unanimously that today's youth is in a very difficult situation with regard to future pension outcomes. Up to now, none of the three pension pillars have adapted to employment flexibilisation and increasing labour market mobility.[9] For youth in uncertain labour market positions, this means that it has become increasingly difficult to invest in savings for old age. Nevertheless, from our consideration of overall trends and single country results, some more general challenges and policy conclusions can be derived that could help to improve the situation of young people in the future.

One basic problem for the future savings of young people is that the three pension pillars – even public pensions – do not in effect offer universal coverage. In order to protect 'weaker groups' of young people at the margins of or outside the labour market, public pensions should be reinforced to ensure they really are universal by including groups such as the self-employed or atypical workers in compulsory insurance schemes.

Another problem is that the overrepresentation of young people in atypical employment, especially at the beginning of their careers, leads to difficulties in accessing secondary and third-pillar schemes. Access conditions for both occupational and private pension schemes should be made more flexible for the self-employed or those in atypical employment as young people will need savings in all three pillars to provide a sustainable pension income in old age.

Restricted portability of different pension plans in cases of high job mobility was also identified as a major problem for youth. This may apply on either a national or international level, as national differences in pension systems can make the international transfer of pensions difficult. Thus, old-age savings problems arise not only for young people in precarious work situations but also for mobile and successful young people with sufficient earnings. Partly in response to this, the EU has recently proposed the *Pan-European Personal Pension Product (PEPP)*[10], intended as a move towards solving the problem of portability. The major advantage of the PEPP product is that it represents an EU-wide pension plan with portable entitlements. Furthermore, the PEPP programme does not change with employment status. This 'open access' circumvents the problem of various existing private pension plans. Nevertheless, as already described at the beginning, it may well be that it is primarily successful young people who benefit from this new type of product.

However, the present findings strongly suggest that there is no one-size-fits-all solution for all countries. Especially for countries in Eastern Europe or some Southern European countries, different solutions have to be developed that take the country-specific context into account. The implementation and maintenance of a three-pillar pension system rests on specific requirements including stable labour market conditions, stable financial markets, low poverty and unemployment rates, and relatively stable political conditions. Those conditions are often not met in Eastern European countries, either because of high youth unemployment rates or limited budgets that make it difficult for governments to support multi-pillar pension systems. This is particularly critical in the Ukraine (Nikoleiva and Vatikova, 2017). Enforcing pension privatisation could make their situation even worse, because transitions to funded pension systems frequently imply an increasing burden on government finances in the short to medium term (Orenstein, 2011). Case studies in Poland (Stasiowski, 2017) and the Ukraine (Nikoleiva and Vatikova, 2017) showed that in countries in which such systems were not securely established, the 2008-09 financial crisis further increased the burden of pension schemes on public finances. Under these conditions, stabilising the labour market and financial situation must take first priority before further reforms of the pension system.

For countries in which the aforementioned preconditions in terms of labour market conditions, financial markets and political conditions are fulfilled, the case studies suggest that there are at least two best-practice examples in countries which have reformed their pension systems in a way that makes them more sustainable with regards to old-age security for today's youth: Sweden and the UK. Both countries have developed differential multi-pillar pension systems, yet both options rely on intrinsically different policy assumptions about responsibility for the maintenance of such a system.

In Sweden, the public pension system combines different types of pensions – universal and private – directly within the public pillar: the income-based pension system covers all employees and the self-employed. A quasi-private 'premium pension' is added, into which employees can invest 2.5 per cent of their taxable income. In this pillar, Swedes can choose to invest their money in five of more than 700 funds, including independent fund managers as well as one offered by the National Swedish pension fund (Strandh, 2017). Effectively, 90 per cent choose this 'default' option provided by the Swedish government (Barr, 2013: 78). A third subpillar is the 'guaranteed' pensions provided through the government as a minimum pension to those on low incomes. In addition to this differentiated public pillar, occupational pensions cover 90 per cent of the population, and are jointly governed through collective bargaining between unions and employers. The third pillar consists of private insurance and savings solutions, but its importance is clearly decreasing. Taken together, Sweden has differentiated its pension system into a multi-pillar system that includes public, occupational, and private components. Yet, the role of the state in the governance and administration of these funds has remained high. The offer of a private 'default fund' in the first pillar has reduced the complexity of choice that frequently overburdens (young) individuals in their pension choices. The Swedish model thus combines sufficient security through a multi-pillar pension structure with state-based governance of pensions that facilitates young people making lasting decisions for security in their old age.

The *UK's* pension system consists of three pillars: a public pension ensuring basic security through modest replacement rates, an occupational pension, and an additional private pension (Merritt, 2017). The peculiar feature of the UK pension system lies in the construction of the occupational pillar. The British government decided in 2017 that by 2018, every employer must automatically enrol its employees in an occupational pension plan,[11] thus making second-pillar pensions available for larger groups of employees. Employers will make additional pension contributions supplementing those of their employees which will increase the amount of savings and spread responsibility to different actors. Young people are then 'released' from the sole burden of making long-term binding decisions for old age that are particularly hard to take under conditions of labour market uncertainty (Hofäcker et al, 2017).[12] Individuals can 'opt out' of this occupational pension system, but have to do this deliberately. The coverage of this pension pillar had risen to 84 per cent of eligible employees in 2017 (DWP, 2018), whereas opt out rates have remained modest with little difference according to salary (DWP, 2014). The 'default' occupational pension equally secures more and differentiated savings for young people in an insecure labour market. Yet, unlike Sweden, the key responsibility has shifted more toward the free market of employer–employee negotiations on occupational pensions and individual deliberation about investing in such schemes rather than relying primarily on state governance.

Yet, even in these two policy models, a relative disadvantage remains for weaker groups of young people in both the UK and Sweden (Hofäcker et al, 2017). This may result from one of the main problems of funded pension provisions, because the tight link between pension payouts and paid contributions tends to discriminate against people in weaker labour market positions. Thus, funded pension provisions always involve problems concerning social inequalities that they do not and cannot compensate adequately, thus making the future of old-age security one of the most important social issues faced today.

Notes

[1] This chapter presents a synthesis of results from the analysis of long-term socio-economic consequences of insecure employment. More detailed information is available in Hofäcker et al (2017).

² Though it may be interesting to look at further long-term outcomes of employment uncertainty – on, for example, career progression, acquisition of poverty, or physical or mental health – this chapter is restricted to an analysis of the consequences within different types of pension systems. This is either because these aspects have been covered in other parts of the EXCEPT project (physical/mental health) or are very difficult to trace empirically given their large variation across countries (property ownership or firms, career patterns).

³ It was necessary to go back to this older data as a rough proxy, because, up to now, hardly any cross-national comparative data are available on young people's savings behaviour apart from some national studies such as the German SAVE study (Börsch-Supan et al, 2009). Furthermore, these focus mainly on the general attitudes of populations towards pension systems and their legitimacy (for example Bechert and Quandt, 2010).

⁴ The item was asked as part of a larger item battery focusing on post-retirement behaviour without a clear temporal focus on the proposed behaviour. This makes it somewhat difficult to link the item directly to the current individual savings behaviour of non-employed persons. Yet, in the absence of alternative indicators, this item is used in the following as a rough proxy indicator of the importance attributed to savings for old age going beyond mere pension savings.

⁵ Given small sample sizes on the national level, the age window had to be opened up to 39 years.

⁶ Higher sample sizes allowed the use of a narrower age bracket for this indicator.

⁷ The auto-enrolment rule was implemented in 2017. Since 2018, all employees over 22 years of age are automatically enrolled in an occupational pension scheme. Employees can also decide to opt out within 30 days (for more detailed information, see Merritt, 2017).

⁸ The 'Riester Pension' is a specific state-subsidised private pension plan with tax benefits. The state funding consists of supplements from the state (€178 from 2018 on per year for each contract and €300 per year for every child born from 2008) and tax benefits (the contributions to the Riester Pension are tax free). Taxes have to be paid on pension payouts from private pension plans in retirement. To receive the full state funding, people should invest 4% of their yearly gross income, otherwise the state funding will decrease according to the amount of investment.

⁹ However, previous results were based on the extrapolation of existing standards and trends in contemporary pension systems. Naturally, these standards are not necessarily stable, so there is also the opportunity for changes that could improve the socio-economic situation for youth (Hofäcker et al, 2017).

¹⁰ For information see: https://ec.europa.eu/commission/news/new-pan-european-personal-pension-products-2017-jun-29_en

¹¹ This group includes employees who are over 22 and under state pension age and earn more than £10,000 a year (Merritt, 2017: 69).

¹² However, a sizeable number of young people will not be covered by this reform, because they are self-employed or on zero-hour contracts which are both still largely excluded from occupational pensions.

References

Antolín, P. and Stewart, F. (2009) *Private Pensions and Policy Responses to the Financial and Economic Crisis*. OECD Working Papers on Insurance and Private Pensions, No. 36, Paris: OECD Publishing.

Barr, N. (2013) 'The pension system in Sweden', *Report to the Expert Group on Public Economics* 7, Stockholm: Ministry of Finance.

Bechert, I. and Quandt, M. (2010) *ISSP Data Report Attitudes towards the Role of Government*, GESIS Monograph Series Vol. 6, Bonn: GESIS Leibniz Institute for the Social Sciences.

Börsch-Supan, A., Coppola, M., Essig, L., Eymann, A. and Schunk, D. (2009) *The German SAVE Study: Design and Results*, Mannheim: Mannheim Research Institute for the Economics of Aging (MEA).

Chomik, R. and Whitehouse, E. (2010) *Trends in Pension Eligibility Ages and Life Expectancy, 1950–2050*. OECD Social, Employment and Migration Working Papers No. 105, Paris: OECD Publishing.

Choi, J. (2009) *Pension Schemes for the Self-Employed in OECD Countries*. OECD Social, Employment and Migration Working Papers No. 84, Paris: OECD Publishing.

DWP [UK Department of Work and Pensions] (2018) *Workplace Pension Participation and Savings Trends of Eligible Employees: Official Statistics 2007 to 2017*, London: DWP.

DWP [UK Department of Work and Pensions] (2014) *Automatic Enrolment Opt Out Rates: Findings from Qualitative Research with Employers Staging in 2014*. Ad hoc research report No. 9, London: DWP.

Ebbinghaus, B. and Gronwold, M. (2011) 'The changing public-private pension mix in Europe: from path dependence to path departure', in B. Ebbinghaus (ed) *The Varieties of Pension Governance: Pension Privatization in Europe*, Oxford: Oxford University Press, pp 23–53.

Esping-Andersen, C. (1990) *The Three Worlds of Welfare Capitalism*, Cambridge: Polity Press.

ESS Round 3 (European Social Survey Round 3 Data) (2006) *Data File Edition 3.7. NSD*, Norway: Norwegian Centre for Research Data. Data Archive and distributor of ESS data for ESS ERIC, doi:10.21338/NSD-ESS3-2006.

European Commission (2009) *Flash Eurobarometer 247 (Family Life and the Needs of an Ageing Population)*, Brussels: The GALLUP Organisation. GESIS Data Archive, Cologne. ZA4883 Data file Version 1.0.0, https://doi.org/10.4232/1.4883.

Fachinger, U. (2018) 'Die Altersvorsorge in Deutschland: Einige Anmerkungen zu Mehrsäuligkeit, Abdeckungsgraden und staatlicher Verantwortung', *Sozialer Fortschritt*, 67(11–12): 929–54.

Garg, N. and Singh, S. (2018) 'Financial literacy among youth', *International Journal of Social Economics*, 45(1): 173–86.

Gläser, J. and Laudel, G. (2010) *Experteninterviews und qualitative Inhaltsanalyse*, Wiesbaden: VS Verlag.

Hofäcker, D. (ed) (2017) *Medium-Term Economic Consequences of Insecure Labour Market Positions*. EXCEPT Working Papers, WP No. 12, Tallinn: Tallinn University, Available from: https://www.except-project.eu/working-papers/

Hofäcker, D. and Blossfeld, H.P. (2011) 'Globalization, uncertainty and its effects on early family and employment lives: an introduction', in H.P. Blossfeld, D. Hofäcker and S. Bertolini (eds) *Youth on Globalised Labour Markets: Rising Uncertainty and its Effects on Early Employment and Family Lives in Europe*, Leverkusen Opladen: Verlag Barbara Budrich, pp 69–92.

Hofäcker, D., Schadow, S. and Kletzing, J. (eds) (2017) *Long-Term Socio-Economic Consequences of Insecure Labour Market Positions*. EXCEPT Working Papers, WP No. 16, Tallinn: Tallinn University, Available from: https://www.except-project.eu/working-papers/

ifo Institute (2015): 'DICE database 2015: Pension rules for the self-employed in the EU 2014', *ifo Institute*, Available from: http://www.cesifo-group.de/DICE/fb/8j3SM8j2

Lusardi, A. and Mitchell, O.S. (2011a) *Financial Literacy and Planning: Implications for Retirement Wellbeing*, NBER Working Paper 17078, Cambridge: National Bureau of Economic Research.

Lusardi, A. and Mitchell, O.S. (2011b) 'Financial literacy around the world: an overview', *Journal of Pension Economics & Finance* 10(4): 497–508.

Lusardi, A., Mitchell, O.S. and Curto, V. (2010) 'Financial literacy among the young', *Journal of Consumer Affairs*, 44(2): 358–80.

Merritt, R. (2017) 'Country-case study of the United Kingdom', in D. Hofäcker, S. Schadow and J. Kletzing (eds) *Long-Term Socio-Economic Consequences of Insecure Labour Market Positions*. EXCEPT Working Papers, WP No. 16, Tallinn: Tallinn University, pp 64–72, Available from: https://www.except-project.eu/working-papers/

MISSOC (2016) Mutual Information System on Social Protection database, Available at: http://ec.europa.eu/employment_social/missoc/db/public/compareTables.do

Moiso, V. (2017) 'Country-Case Study of Italy', in D. Hofäcker, S. Schadow and J. Kletzing (eds) *Long-Term Socio-Economic Consequences of Insecure Labour Market Positions*. EXCEPT Working Papers, WP No. 16, Tallinn: Tallinn University, pp 79–88, Available from: https://www.except-project.eu/working-papers/

Myles, J. and Peirson, P. (2001) 'The comparative political economy of pension reform', in P. Peirson (ed) *The New Politics of Welfare State*, New York: Oxford University Press, pp 305–33.

Nikolaieva, O. and Vakhitova, H. (2017) 'Country-case study of Ukraine', in D. Hofäcker, S. Schadow and J. Kletzing (eds) *Long-Term Socio-Economic Consequences of Insecure Labour Market Positions*. EXCEPT Working Papers, WP No. 16, Tallinn: Tallinn University, pp 117–23, Available from: https://www.except-project.eu/working-papers/

OECD (2013) *Pensions at a Glance 2013: OECD and G20 Indicators*, Paris: OECD Publishing.

OECD (2015) *Pensions at a Glance 2015: OECD and G20 Indicators*, Paris: OECD Publishing.

Orenstein, M.A. (2011) 'Pension privatization in crisis: death or rebirth of a global policy trend?', *International Social Security Review*, 64(3): 65–80.

Rokicka, M., Kłobuszewska, M., Palczyńska, M., Shapoval, N. and Stasiowski, J. (2015) *Composition and Cumulative Disadvantage of Youth across Europe*. EXCEPT Working Papers, WP No. 1, Tallinn: Tallinn University, Available from: https://www.except-project.eu/working-papers/

Rokicka, M. and Kłobuszewska, M. (2016) *The Short-Term Economic Consequences of Insecure Labour Market Positions in EU-28*, EXCEPT Working Papers, WP No. 10. Tallinn University, Tallinn, Available from: http://www.except-project.eu/working-papers/

Schadow, S. (2017) 'Country-case study of Germany', in D. Hofäcker, S. Schadow and J. Kletzing (eds) *Long-Term Socio-Economic Consequences of Insecure Labour Market Positions*. EXCEPT Working Papers, WP No. 16, Tallinn: Tallinn University, pp 53–63, Available from: https://www.except-project.eu/working-papers/

Stasiowski, J. (2017) 'Country-case study of Poland', in D. Hofäcker, S. Schadow and J. Kletzing (eds) *Long-Term Socio-Economic Consequences of Insecure Labour Market Positions*. EXCEPT Working Papers, WP No. 16, Tallinn: Tallinn University, pp 89–104, Available from: https://www.except-project.eu/working-papers/

Strandh, M. (2017) 'Country-case study of Sweden', in D. Hofäcker, S. Schadow and J. Kletzing (eds) *Long-Term Socio-Economic Consequences of Insecure Labour Market Positions*. EXCEPT Working Papers, WP No. 16, Tallinn: Tallinn University, pp 73–78, Available from: https://www.except-project.eu/working-papers/

Tosun, J., Arco-Tirado, J.L., Caserta, M., Cemalcilar, Z., Freitag, M., Hörisch, F., Jensen, C., Kittel, B., Littvay, L., Lukeš, M., Maloney, W.A., Mühlböck, M., Rainsford, E., Rapp, C., Schuck, B., Shore, J., Steiber, N., Sümer, N., Tsakloglou, P., Vancea, M. and Vegetti, F. (2019) 'Perceived economic self-sufficiency: a country- and generation-comparative approach', *European Political Science*, 18(3): 510–31.

Unt, M. and Reiska, E. (2017) 'Country-case study of Estonia', in D. Hofäcker, S. Schadow and J. Kletzing (eds) *Long-Term Socio-Economic Consequences of Insecure Labour Market Positions*. EXCEPT Working Papers, WP No. 16, Tallinn: Tallinn University, pp 105–16, Available from: https://www.except-project.eu/working-papers/

World Bank (1994) *Averting the Old Age Crisis: Policies to Protect the Old and Promote Growth. Summary*, Washington, DC: World Bank.

15

Conclusions: Integrating perspectives on youth transitions and the risk of social exclusion

Sonia Bertolini, Vassiliki Deliyanni-Kouimtzi, Michael Gebel, Dirk Hofäcker, and Marge Unt

Most previous research in this area has addressed the drivers of youth job insecurity and especially youth unemployment. Gathering and implementing knowledge to prevent youth unemployment and support youth pathways out of temporary jobs is a highly relevant research activity. Moreover, there is also an urgent need to understand the consequences of such individual-level labour market insecurities, because unemployment along with extended periods of temporary employment, including a chain of mini-jobs, are a widespread phenomenon among youth. Likewise, policies need to be evaluated not only in terms of their ability to tackle youth labour market vulnerability per se, but also regarding the role these policies play in mitigating the consequences of labour market insecurity on other dimensions of young people's lives. This book extends the limited amount of previous European comparative research in this field (see, for example, Blossfeld et al, 2005; Gallie, 2013; Vossemer et al, 2018; Stasiowski and Kłobuszewska, 2018; Högberg et al, 2019a, 2019b; Hvinden et al, 2019; Täht et al, 2020). The chapters of this book do not follow the same line of analysis for all countries, but take more of a comparative approach providing systematic in-depth insights into the different consequences of individual-level labour market insecurities in Europe for the risks of social exclusion of youth. Starting from a shared multilevel theoretical model, the book approaches this research topic empirically from a multimethod and European comparative perspective. The aim is to promote comparative qualitative research by adding to the almost non-existent qualitative literature on young people's own perceptions of labour market insecurity from a comparative perspective.

Taking both a short- and a long-term perspective, this book examines the microlevel effects of young people experiences of labour market exclusion in their early careers on a multitude of outcomes reflecting the risk of social exclusion: (a) the development of their health and well-being, (b) their chances of gaining autonomy by leaving the parental home and gaining economic independence from their parents, as well as (c) their economic situation in terms of risks of poverty, material deprivation, and eligibility for social security. It investigates the coping strategies and compensatory mechanisms available to young people who are having to deal with negative consequences on both the micro- and the mesolevels. On the macrolevel, it studies the role of *labour market, economic, family, housing, and social policies* in either aggravating or mitigating the negative effects of labour market insecurities.

This chapter reviews these findings against the background of the three main research questions, addressing the multifaceted consequences of labour market insecurities, coping strategies, and policies that are effective in mitigating the negative consequences. It summarises the findings and conclusions in response to each of these three questions. The final section offers a critical discussion of the limitations of this study and outlines potential directions for future research.

Research Question 1: Consequences of labour market insecurities

The first research question focuses on the multifaceted individual-level consequences of labour market insecurities for young people's risk of social exclusion. The following will highlight the main findings and conclusions structured along the three dimensions of risk of social exclusion: namely, youth well-being and health, autonomy, and socio-economic consequences.

Well-being and health

One central aspect of social inclusion is the subjective well-being of young people, and there is a growing body of research aiming to obtain a better understanding of how this along with youth's health is affected by labour market insecurities (Fryer, 2000; Thern et al, 2017; Vancea and Utzet, 2017). The present book delivers complementary findings and further insights into these effects. For example, the results of quantitative analyses in various chapters (Chapter 2, Nizalova et al; Chapter 3, Baranowska-Rataj and Strandh; Chapter 4, Lauri and Unt) show that unemployment and job insecurity reduce life satisfaction and happiness compared to being employed and in a secure job, with the effect of unemployment being stronger than the effect of job insecurity. There is also variation in effects depending on which outcome variable is considered. Negative effects of unemployment and job insecurity are larger for life satisfaction than for happiness; and effects vary substantially across countries. Next to the negative effects on subjective well-being, Baranowska-Rataj and Strandh's findings (Chapter 3) reveal that becoming unemployed is also associated with significantly poorer self-rated health. These findings from quantitative analyses are in line with in-depth insights from qualitative analyses. For example, Schlee et al (Chapter 5) illustrate how being unemployed or in insecure jobs relates to the malaise, worries, and anxiety of young people.

The adverse effects of a lack of jobs may go beyond the individuals who become unemployed and also affect their closest family members – that is, their partners (Baranowska-Rataj and Strandh, Chapter 3). Analyses reveal that it is not only individual, but also partner's unemployment that is associated with statistically significantly poorer health in both women and men.

Interestingly, the analyses shed light on potential gender differences. The effect of unemployment on life satisfaction and happiness is stronger in young men, whereas the effect of insecure employment on life satisfaction and happiness is relatively stronger in young women. Put differently, the state of being unemployed seems to be more detrimental for the well-being of males, whereas having an insecure job is more detrimental for the well-being of females. Results also suggest that unemployment has a considerably larger effect on young men than insecure employment, whereas the difference between the two effects is much smaller in young women.

Gender-specific findings also reveal that while becoming unemployed is also associated with significantly poorer self-rated health for all, the transition into inactivity is associated with a negative effect only among men. Detailed analyses by Baranowska-Rataj and Strandh (Chapter 3) show that after controlling for unobserved heterogeneity, the impact of both unemployment and inactivity weaken but remain statistically significant among men but no longer play a major role among women. Regarding the spillover health effects, Baranowska-Rataj and Strandh (Chapter 3) show that the effects of partners' transitions into unemployment are stronger on women than on men, implying that the impact of unemployment on health in partners is gendered. That is, the association is stronger on women's health in the case of a male partner's unemployment, whereas the association on men's health when a female partner is unemployed is only half as large.

What are the drivers of loss of well-being in the case of labour market vulnerability? Investigations of the causal mechanisms by Nizalova et al (Chapter 2) via quantitative analysis highlight that the effects of unemployment and job insecurity on life satisfaction and happiness cannot be attributed to the loss of income alone, although this is theoretically one of the main expected causal mechanisms. Likewise, results reported by Baranowska-Rataj and Strandh (Chapter 3) show that the negative effects of a partner's unemployment on individual health still prevail, even after controlling for the change in household income. In contrast, controlling for a partner's health eliminates the effect of a partner's unemployment on individual health.

Partial and indirect insights into the causal mechanisms can also be gained from the qualitative study on the meaning of work (see Chapter 5, Schlee et al; Chapter 6, Roosmaa et al). Results show that young people still see work as an important source of identity and one young man even described it as '*the engine of life*'. Work has a manifest function as a provider of financial resources. However, next to a salary, almost all interviewed young people emphasised other aspects of work. Latent intrinsic functions of work such as an interesting, self-fulfilling job or having good relations with colleagues and supervisors are reported as well. Work is seen not only as a source of income, but is also associated with dignity, self-worth and stability, as well as autonomy in general and especially autonomy from parents. Being without a job for a long time is related to strong fears about the future in different institutional contexts. Moreover, young people in a context with low overall unemployment describe stigmatisation as a mediator between unemployment and well-being.

Autonomy: transition to adult life as a dynamic process

The chapters in Part II of this book scrutinise the process of leaving the parental home, which is traditionally a central marker of adulthood (Corijn and Klijzing, 2001). Housing autonomy is linked closely to but not coincident with economic autonomy. In line with previous literature (Blossfeld et al, 2011), the chapters in this book demonstrate that social exclusion from the labour market and job insecurity postpone the transition toward autonomy. However, it is also crucial to note that insecurity in the labour market not only postpones leaving the parental nest (Goglio and Bertolini, Chapter 7) but also renders it more complex.

Housing autonomy still carries a high value for youth. However, in respect to becoming adult, leaving the parental home is not universally considered to be an important step towards adulthood – or, at least, not the only way to become an adult – in a time of economic constraint. Moreover, housing and economic autonomy are no longer coincident for young people's transition toward self-perceived adulthood (Chapter 8, Bertolini et al; Chapter 9, Meo et al).

Different modalities of becoming adult emerge from the qualitative insights. Vulnerable labour market conditions such as low incomes in Bulgaria, long spells of unemployment in Greece, and precarity in Italy, together with the fact that young people in these countries generally have no access to unemployment insurance (because of contributive systems in all three countries), have made prolonged cohabitation with parents the norm (Chapter 8, Bertolini et al). Young people can remain in the parental home for long periods, they can live in the same house but apart from their parents, they can return to the parental home in case of need, or form a family but still live in the same house as their parents. For instance, in Bulgaria, Greece, and Italy, young people usually believe that moving out of the parental home implies starting a new family. This is undoubtedly a very traditional notion of the transition to adult life which is still prevalent in these countries, at least perceived as an ideal life path. In reality, the lives young people live can differ dramatically from their aspirations. Due to economic constraints in Bulgaria, for instance, vulnerable young people tend to live with their parents even after they get married. Although young people in Bulgaria aspire to autonomy, they prioritise their well-being over housing autonomy, for example.

Thus, as a *consequence of labour market insecurity, housing autonomy is no longer so central*, especially for Mediterranean and Eastern European countries, and *new modalities of becoming autonomous and adult are emerging*.

The second dimension of autonomy, financial independence, is linked to self-perceived adulthood and is perceived as a desired outcome. Meo et al (Chapter 9) show how even if they gain a foothold in the labour market, young people do not attain financial independence. Their narratives demonstrate that economic autonomy is a fuzzy concept shaped by individual assessments of the balance between available resources and personal needs and goals. When young people are unable to support themselves and to provide for their own livelihood through work, they redefine economic autonomy creatively and diminish its scope. They see it as a capacity for self-determination while still living in the parental home. In such cases, interviewees define economic autonomy as the possibility of and ability to satisfy their needs within their own resources, by defining their needs mainly in terms of small personal daily necessities.

However, the interviewees perceived and represented themselves as autonomous, in that they were able to decide for themselves by defining their own training and work paths, by managing their daily lives, and ultimately by developing their own system of preferences, even though they had to remain economically dependent on their parents. As a possible consequence of increasingly scarce job opportunities, it appears that job uncertainty pushes them to dwell only in the present. For many young people today, being independent means having to deal with problems and decisions on a day-to-day or short-term basis and, from an economic point of view, being able to cover one's own leisure expenses plus a little on top. A process of *redefining the concept of autonomy* is taking place. Young people's definition of autonomy is increasingly limited in space and time.

As a consequence of the process of redefining autonomy, the findings presented in the qualitative chapters do not identify risks of social exclusion for young people in the traditional sense of the concept, but rather as *risks of exclusion from adult roles*. Young people in these countries do not feel themselves excluded socially in relative terms, because their situation is similar to that of their friends. However, they behave as if they were socially excluded. They feel excluded from policies and limited in their ability to stand up for their rights when working in insecure jobs, and this gives rise to further exploitation and uncertainty. Then they mainly use exit strategies, they find refuge in the private sphere and in the family of origin (Chapter 10, Meo et al; Chapter 11, Ricucci et al; Chapter 13, Figgou et al).

Socio-economic consequences

The underlying assumption in this book is that labour market insecurities (through both labour market exclusion and insecure jobs) may also impair the socio-economic situation of young people due to the absence of or fluctuations in income from work. Compared to youth in safe, well paid and continuous jobs, these young people are relatively disadvantaged in material and financial terms.

In the short-term economic situation, as Kłobuszewska et al's quantitative analysis (Chapter 12) demonstrates, the major detrimental consequence of unemployment is a lack of personal income. This translates directly into a deterioration of young people's financial situation and material deprivation, and it also manifests itself in a higher risk of exclusion from social life. Since the Great Recession, youth aged 16 to 29 who are not in education or training and cannot get a foothold on the labour market are twice as likely to be at risk of poverty compared to employed young people. Unemployed youth assess their subjective economic situation as being fragile because they often have greater difficulty in making ends meet than employed youth. However, after controlling for household structure, the analysis no longer suggests gender-specific poverty is a risk among young people. It is the presence of children that increases both the objective and the subjective poverty risk, whereas living with parents or a partner mitigates it.

Following the dynamic life course perspective, Hofäcker et al (Chapter 14) extend the view to the long-term consequences of labour market problems in the early stages of young people's careers. The negative impacts of unemployment are not restricted to the immediate situation; unemployment also increases the future risk of poverty for young people. Chapter 14 highlights how, particularly in countries with high youth unemployment, public pension systems barely take account of gaps in employment or pension contributions when calculating future pension entitlements. The dynamic life course perspective is also important for accounting for differences in the short term and consequences in the long term. Whereas in the short term the socio-economic consequences of temporary employment are modest compared to unemployment, they are more detrimental in the long term. Savings behaviour is negatively affected for young people in fixed-term employment, and this is particularly harmful to their socio-economic situation in the long term. Fixed-term employees are rarely included in occupational pension plans, contributing further to a higher risk of poverty in old age.

Concern about the long-term consequences of current labour market insecurity is vividly expressed in the narratives of Greek and Italian youth (Figgou et al, Chapter 13) who describe their complete inability to engage in any type of financial planning. They see a pension and future financial security as impossible objectives to achieve. The institutional analysis of pension systems and expert interviews across Europe (Hofäcker et al, Chapter 14) demonstrate that until now, public, occupational and private pension pillars have not adapted to employment flexibilisation and increasing labour market mobility. Hence, results highlight a paradoxical situation for young people in Europe. In the context of recent reforms and developments, they will depend increasingly on additional income in old age due to cuts in public pensions; yet, the current labour market situation makes it increasingly difficult or impossible for them to contribute to other savings or pension schemes.

Research Question 2: Coping strategies

The second research question asks what coping strategies and compensatory mechanisms on the individual and mesolevel young people use to face the consequences of labour market insecurity. According to Schlee et al's qualitative analysis (Chapter 5), it becomes evident that the individual impact on well-being depends strongly on individual coping strategies. The coping strategies young people use include optimistic thinking and either ignoring or whitewashing the current insecure situation in order to avert the potentially negative influence on their own well-being (emotion-focused); or they search for jobs and write applications to counter uncertainties resulting from financial limitations or a lack of meaning in their lives (problem-focused).

Apart from individual-level coping strategies, family and social networks are very important moderators on the mesolevel. The family and social relations are used as a protective factor or to provide financial help (for instance, when formal support is not available or insufficient), and sometimes advice and emotional support. Next to the family, public services and various youth organisations also play a role. Generally, a number of coping strategies are combined in a latent or undifferentiated way. However, the mesocontext can also have detrimental moderating effects. For example, family conflicts and the dissolution of parental households exacerbate the situation for young people experiencing labour market insecurities (see Meo et al, Chapter 10). Shore and Tosun (2017) have reported negative assessments of public employment services by young people in Germany, although this country is often highlighted as an exemplary case for good youth labour market outcomes. The qualitative insights into youth experiences with and perceptions of public services illustrate some of the triggers for their negative assessment of public employment services such as the perceived bureaucratic ritualism, excessive focus on rules and regulations, and an impersonal approach which may further exacerbate the feeling of stigmatisation (Chapter 11, Ricucci et al).

Adjusting personal feelings of autonomy to the available opportunities and/or cohabitating with a partner are the most common strategies young people use to cope with the existing situation, especially those living in societies in which young people typically leave their parental homes early. The findings of Bertolini et al (Chapter 8) and Meo et al (Chapter 9) provide insights into the 'late-exit' countries, revealing that postponing housing autonomy is often used as a mechanism to help avoid the consequences of unemployment and to facilitate the process of gaining financial autonomy.

Regarding socio-economic consequences, and in line with previous findings, the chapters in Part II show that household composition is an important determinant of poverty and material deprivation for young people. Kłobuszewska et al (Chapter 12) demonstrate that living with parents or a partner/spouse protects against economic hardship whereas living with children increases this risk. Meo et al (Chapter 10) and Figgou et al (Chapter 13) shed more light on the interplay of coping mechanisms on the individual level by investigating the experience of receiving support from family, friends, and others to help them face insecure employment. For young people, parental resources and support are crucial in pursuing the path toward adulthood and counterbalancing the lack of job and income. Hence, the material situation of young people is closely related to the financial situation of the parental family. Broadly speaking, the biggest difference between unemployed and employed youth is their ability to participate in social life. Qualitative evidence reported by Figgou et al (Chapter 13) provides in-depth insights into the narratives of Greek and Italian youth and shows how unpredictable work schedules and varying income flows are constructed as having drastic and complex implications for social life, and how these relate back to heightened anxiety about the future. Vulnerable young people do not have sufficient resources to keep up with the lifestyle of friends who are better off. Although friends invite them and pay for them, such relationships are hard to maintain due to shame and, more broadly, a strong social norm favouring mutual reciprocity in social relationships. The forced withdrawal from friendships and social life is one of the mechanisms which contributes to a vicious circle, because friends – especially working friends – are an important source of information, material support, and emotional support; and without such support, it is more difficult to obtain a job. The second important mechanism contributing to this vicious circle is that young people in insecure and especially in informal jobs find it difficult to claim their rights – and this gives birth to further uncertainty. Young people are willing to make many compromises to get or keep a job, and this effectively silences their voices, even in extremely precarious work situations.

However, it is also important to describe the interplay between the meso- and the macrolevel in different contexts. For instance, in Greece and Italy, interviewees stressed above all the role of their parents given the lack of formal support, whereas in Estonia and Germany, many young adults in the sample combined formal (such as unemployment benefits) and informal (economic and other) supports to cope with their situations in times of job insecurity or unemployment. Indeed, it appears clear that informal support and the parental family in particular play a role even in those contexts (such as Germany) in which institutions and formal support are widespread and deeply consolidated.

Research Question 3: Policies effective in mitigating the negative effects

The third research question addressed in this book examines which policies are effective in mitigating the negative effects of labour market insecurities for young people at risk of social exclusion. This question introduces the macrolevel into the multilevel model. Yet, in doing so, the interest is not primarily in the direct effect of macrolevel institutions on social exclusion (that is, an analysis of whether institutions directly influence the overall *degree* of labour market exclusion in European countries), but far more in the moderating effect of institutions –the ways in which nation-specific institutions strengthen or weaken the effect of unemployment and employment uncertainty on the different outcome variables examined in this book (health, well-being, autonomy, and socio-economic situation). This research question is approached in various ways: using broad comparative survey data, authors estimate multilevel regression models in order to identify the general moderating effect of specific types of institution through interaction effects. This focus is supplemented by small-N comparisons of countries purposefully selected to identify the effects of concrete institutional regulations more closely both quantitatively and qualitatively. Finally, qualitative comparative analysis (QCA) is used to better understand the effects of specific institutional constellations (rather than single institutions) in moderating the consequences of labour market uncertainty for youth. The results of this differential approach can be summarised as follows:

Nation-specific institutions matter for youth, because they moderate the consequences of labour market uncertainty in various respects. This is shown, for example, when Goglio and Bertolini (Chapter 7) demonstrate that even though experiencing unemployment generally delays youth transitions out of the parental home, the degree to which this negative effect on an individual's autonomy materialises depends on the type of labour market regulation. Particularly in countries with segmented labour markets (such as those in Central and Southern Europe), the delaying effect of unemployment is high. In a similar way, Lauri and Unt (Chapter 4) show that the negative effect of unemployment on life satisfaction is moderated by passive labour market policies (PLMPs) – that is, the degree to which life satisfaction declines depends on the material support provided through state policies. Hence, negative effects of labour market uncertainty on the life situation of young people are not uniform across countries, but differ depending on nation-specific institutions. From a policy perspective, these findings inherently mean that *policies matter*, and that the repercussions of labour market uncertainty for youth can, in principle, be shaped through the implementation of policies.

In many cases, it is not single institutions that moderate the negative effects of unemployment and employment uncertainty, but rather the mutual interplay between different types of institution. In other words, institutional effects are those of institutional packages rather than single stand-alone policies. This finding stands out particularly in the QCA performed by Lauri and Unt (Chapter 4). They show that in many of the Nordic countries, it is the interplay of strong ALMPs and PLMPs (the so-called 'universal route') that may account for the more modest drop in life satisfaction for the unemployed. In Spain and Portugal, a similar effect is achieved through a combination of PLMPs and extended family support. In contrast, the reliance on ALMPs alone, as practised in the 'capacitating route' taken by liberal countries, cannot moderate the negative effects of becoming unemployed to the same degree.

The effects of policies are not restricted to those impacting on the immediate situation of young people, but are also linked to long-term social security programmes. As Hofäcker et al (Chapter 14) show, the negative long-term effects of unemployment and uncertain jobs on future social security savings can be mitigated by policies that foster employer-based social security (as in the UK) or integrate young people into state-governed multi-pillar pension systems (as in Sweden). Policymakers are thus advised to consider not only the immediate effects of political reforms, but to design more far-reaching 'life course policies' that also promote individual welfare in a long-term perspective.

Results also show that, in many respects, public policies need to be contextualised within their broader societal setting. This general conclusion applies in multiple respects:

First, public policies may not be seen as the only provider of welfare for youth. In providing for youth, it may be necessary to consider the entire welfare triangle of Esping-Andersen (1990) and additionally involve the family and the market. The previous section has already highlighted the contribution of family and private networks to diminish the effects of employment uncertainty. Hofäcker et al (Chapter 14), in contrast, also highlight that employer-provided occupation pension schemes – that is, support through the market – may help to mitigate the negative consequences of labour market uncertainty for future pension savings.

Second, the effect of welfare policies needs to be viewed in the light of more general economic conditions. As Nizalova et al (Chapter 2) show, a favourable economic situation, as reflected in high GDP, moderates the negative effects of insecure jobs on the health and well-being of youth. On the other hand, in countries with high unemployment, being in an insecure job may not be perceived as being as detrimental as it is in countries with low unemployment, because gaining employment of any sort may already be perceived as a relative success under difficult conditions.

Third, the effect of public policies does not depend solely on further structural factors such as other welfare providers or the general economic setting. It is also embedded in a broader cultural context. Baranowska-Rataj and Strandh (Chapter 3), for example, demonstrate that the negative effects of unemployment on a partner's health depend on the country-specific cultural context. Particularly in countries with a patriarchal culture manifesting in a male breadwinner norm, the negative effects of unemployment loom largest.

When considering the impact of policies, policymakers are thus advised not only to take into consideration the effects of policies 'in general', but also to be sensitive to their embeddedness in a broader cultural context.

The previous remarks already point to the more general conclusion that there are no easy 'standard' policy solutions to improve the situation of youth. As Ricucci et al (Chapter 11) highlight, young people themselves have little trust in 'standardised' institutional approaches, but prefer individualised approach to ensure that their situation will be treated with the necessary specificity. Hence, future policies will need to pay specific attention to the demands of youth, particularly of those affected most seriously by labour market uncertainty. Furthermore, there also seems to be no one single 'policy role model' towards which countries may orient themselves when developing appropriate policies. As Lauri and Unt (Chapter 4) show, even within the previously uniform social-democratic model of Scandinavian states, some have gone on to follow differential reform pathways in recent years. Hence, when trying to implement successful policies, policymakers will will need to consider a complex set of contextual factors. Further research at the national and international level is needed in order to better understand the mutual interrelationships of these factors.

Limitations and directions for future research

Studying the aforementioned questions in order to understand consequences for young people often confronts researchers with limitations in the *availability of longitudinal data* (Gebel et al, 2018). First, there are no truly pan-European comparative longitudinal data on youth. Very few European countries such as Germany, Sweden, and the UK provide good longitudinal data (either survey or administrative data). In contrast, Eastern and Southern European countries (for example, Estonia, Greece, and Italy) are often largely under studied due to a lack of recent longitudinal data on youth transitions and/or longitudinal cohort studies. Furthermore, comparative longitudinal analyses require longer term panel studies that focus particularly on youth on an internationally comparative level. Such data would allow better comparisons of life course trajectories and lead to a better understanding of how policy and labour market circumstances affect well-being, health, and other outcomes. Longitudinal data may also help in investigating long-term effects –for example, the analysis of young people's future social security on which research to date is rather scarce. Such analyses may deliver innovative suggestions for truly life course-oriented policies that would increase the inclusiveness of society. When taking short to medium and long-term perspectives, it is important to identify future risks and opportunities and make *appropriate policy recommendations.*

Acting in the present has consequences in the long term and young people are not always aware of this. From a macro point of view, it is very important for policymakers to consider the long-term socio-economic consequences for youth. Temporary contracts have a considerably smaller effect on well-being and autonomy than unemployment. However, a slow and fragmented entrance into the labour market seriously hinders young people's capacity to save and contributes to future inequalities in pension entitlements. These inequalities can be compensated by suitable policies and a responsive welfare state system. For these reasons, this book shows that it is important to design more far-reaching 'life course policies' that also promote individual welfare in a long-term perspective.

The findings also highlight the vital need to better integrate qualitative and quantitative data. The combination of these two kinds of data had allowed us as researchers to individuate new modalities of transition to adult life, both in terms of objective conditions and subjective perceptions of the process and decision making. Mixed methods research would benefit particularly from qualitative longitudinal data sets which can track agency and change in different aspects of well-being, autonomy, and socio-economic consequences over time and make a significant contribution to life course analyses.

The current COVID-19 pandemic, and the great individual and collective uncertainty about the present and the future associated with it, will certainly have an additional impact on young people. Many countries are already experiencing rising unemployment and decreasing labour force participation. However, the first wave of the COVID-19 crisis has been cushioned at least partially by strong fiscal responses from the EU and most European countries (Eurofound, 2020; ILO, 2020). The uniqueness of the situation generated by COVID-19 is that collective and individual uncertainty are strongly interconnected, and this leads to an escalating reinforcement of uncertainties. The health crisis is clearly affecting older cohorts more directly, whereas it exposes younger cohorts more to the economic and social crisis because joblessness and its consequences escalates faster for young people than for the rest. A recent blog by Eurofound (2020) shows that youth unemployment has risen more quickly and that young people feel that it is more likely that they will lose their jobs in coming months. The restrictions on social interaction have also been particularly detrimental to young people, as they were more at risk of depression than the rest of population during the lockdown in April 2020 (Eurofound, 2020). The collective uncertainty caused by the COVID-19 crisis is likely to impact on young people's already undermined ability to make long-term and binding decisions, on their ability to imagine and plan for the future.

It is too early for any concrete analysis, but it seems plausible to assume two possible outcomes of the COVID-19 crisis. On the one hand, rising uncertainties may mean that risks for youth as well as the social inequalities in facing these risks may grow even further – that is, there will be differentiated socio-economic impacts in the different European countries due to variations in the ability to prevent risks. Some recent trends point in this direction. In many countries, protection increased for those with permanent contracts through the extended layoff prohibition as a precondition for state support throughout the early lockdown period. The same did not take place for those who had temporary contracts or engaged in new forms of work like gig workers. In this way, young people and young adults working with this kind of temporary contract, especially in countries with segmented labour markets, face even higher risks of labour market exclusion.

However, the pandemic could also redesign new borderlines and new forms of social inclusion and exclusion. Throughout the early pandemic period, teleworking has been expanding as well as use of digital technology. Moreover, the pandemic has highlighted the value of essential services that preserve basic societal functioning. This change could generate more negotiating power for those essential but undervalued workers and contribute to more overall equality in society. This change also has the potential to generate new opportunities for young people to enter the labour market, and to valorise their abilities to use digital technologies. However, such developments require political will, and in the case of digital working, they also require national governments to make major investments in education, lifelong learning and the digital infrastructure. Without such investments, international differences between countries, as well as inter-individual inequalities between young people with varying human capital in the affectedness by labour market uncertainties and their negative effects, may increase only further.

References

Blossfeld H.P., Hofäcker D. and Bertolini, S. (eds) (2011) *Youth on Globalised Labour Markets: Rising Uncertainty and its Effects on Early Development and Family Lives in Europe*, Opladen: Verlag Barbara Budrich.

Blossfeld, H.P., Klijzing, E., Mills, M. and Kurz, K. (eds) (2005) *Globalization, Uncertainty and Youth in Society*, London: Routledge.

Corijn, M. and Klijzing, E. (eds) (2001) *Transitions to Adulthood in Europe*, Dordrecht: Kluwer Academic Publishers.

Eurofound (2020) *ERM Report 2020: Restructuring Across Borders*, Luxembourg: Publications Office of the European Union.

Fryer, D. (2000) 'Unemployment and mental health: hazards and challenges of psychology in the community', in K. Isaksson, C. Hogstedt, C. Eriksson and T. Theorell (eds) *Health Effects of the New Labour Market*, New York: Kluwer Academic/Plenum Publishers, pp 11–23.

Gallie, D. (ed) (2013) *Economic Crisis, Quality of Work, and Social Integration: The European Experience*, Oxford: Oxford University Press.

Gebel, M., Hofäcker, D., Jeliazkova, M., Schadow, S., Täht, K. and Unt, M. (2018) *Proposal for Future Research Based on EXCEPT Project*. EXCEPT Working Papers, WP No. 58, Tallinn: Tallinn University, Available from: https://www.except-project.eu/working-papers/

Högberg, B., Strandh, M. and Baranowska-Rataj, A. (2019) 'Transitions from temporary employment to permanent employment among young adults: the role of labour law and education systems', *Journal of Sociology*, 55(4): 689–707.

Högberg, B., Voßemer, J., Gebel, M. and Strandh, M. (2019b) 'Unemployment, well-being, and the moderating role of education policies: a multilevel study', *International Journal of Comparative Sociology*, 60(4): 269–91.

Hvinden, B., O'Reilly, J. and Schoyen, M.A. (2019) *Negotiating Early Job Insecurity. Well-Being, Scarring and Resilience of European Youth*, Cheltenham: Edward Elgar Publishing.

International Labour Organization (2020) *ILO Monitor: COVID-19 and the World of Work* (2nd edn), Geneva: International Labour Organization.

Shore, J. and Tosun, J. (2017) 'Assessing youth labour market services: young people's perceptions and evaluations of service delivery in Germany', *Public Policy and Administration*, 34(1): 22–41.

Stasiowski, J. and Kłobuszewska, M. (2018) 'Does the context matter? Labour market characteristics and job satisfaction among young European adults working on temporary contracts', *Studies of Transition States and Societies*, 10(3): 51–67.

Täht, K., Xanthopoulou, D., Figgou, L., Kostouli, M. and Unt, M. (2020) 'The role of unemployment and job insecurity for the well-being of young Europeans: social inequality as a macro-level moderator', *Journal of Happiness Studies*, 21(7): 2355–75.

Thern, E., de Munter, J., Hemmingsson, T. and Rasmussen, F. (2017) 'Long-term effects of youth unemployment on mental health: does an economic crisis make a difference?', *Journal of Epidemiology & Community Health*, 71(4): 344–9.

Vancea, M. and Utzet, M. (2017) 'How unemployment and precarious employment affect the health of young people: a scoping study on social determinants', *Scandinavian Journal of Public Health*, 45(1): 73–84.

Vossemer, J., Gebel, M., Täht, K., Unt, M., Högberg, B. and Strandh, M. (2018) 'The effects of unemployment and insecure jobs on well-being and health: the moderating role of labor market policies', *Social Indicators Research*, 138(3): 1229–57.

Index

Page numbers in *italic* type refer to figures; those in **bold** type refer to tables. References to endnotes show both the page number and the note number (231n3).

A

active labour market policies (ALMPs) 2, 17, 19, 84, 85, 104–6, 146, 298, 301–2, 372
active labour market policies generosity (AG) 86, 95, 97
  capacity of 95
  in Estonia 244–5
  in Germany 244–5
  hypothesis 86
  interviewees according to involvement in **271**
  in Italy 116, 220, 244–5
  effect of labour market insecurities 297
  moderating role of **305**, **307**
  in Polish youth 217, 220
adulthood, transition to 166, 194, 215
  attaining economic autonomy 215
  as dynamic process 365–7
  family socialisation role 216
  leaving home of origin 11, 193
  markers 80, 166, 214, 215, 228
  role of family of origin 12
  see also housing autonomy
advanced intergenerational autonomy model 85
anxiety 20, 58, 123, 129, 364
apprenticeships 2, 118, 127, 130, 309
ATLAS.ti 8, 321
attribution theory 35–6, 52
auto-enrolment rule 357n7
autonomous living, transition to 200
autonomy 3, 5, 8, 10–11, 151, 169, 211, 214, 253, 365–7
  and adulthood 160
  advanced intergenerational 85, 86, 105
  financial 310
  high intergenerational 100
  meaning of work with 151
  relative intergenerational 85
  see also economic autonomy; housing autonomy
average marginal effect (AME) **176**, *177*

B

bidirectional relationship on deprivation 295
bottom-up approach *see* inductive approach
Bulgaria
  housing autonomy of young adults in 192–3, 203–4
  coping strategies 209–10
  leaving from parental home 193–4, 196–9
  models of welfare regime 192
  number of interviewees by age and housing status **198**
  prerequisites 204–6
  process of transition to adulthood 210
  labour market policy in 268–9
  counselling practices 286
  failure of school system 288
  interviewees according to involvement in ALMPs **271**
  lack of trust in institutions in youth 285–6
  leaving parental home 366
  material deprivation 316
  participation in public employment services 284
  unemployment benefits 280–1
  young people's assessment 278–9
Bulgarian National Youth Strategy 205
bureaucracy 257, 265
  employment offices 278
  street-level 265

C

capacitating route 86
capacitating support route 100
career outlook 143
case-oriented approach 16
Central and Eastern European (CEE) countries 144, 145
companionship 240–1, 243, 252
conservation of resources theory (COR theory) 32, 34–5, 51
control variables 38, 76n2, 301
  in baseline models 63
  effects 68

logistic regressions 173
coping 115, 116, 369
coping strategies 113, 114
  and compensatory mechanisms
    on macrolevel 3–4
    on microlevel 3
  for housing autonomy in times of
    labour instability 206–10
  on risk of social exclusion 369–71
  for well-being 120–1
    macrolevel 127–9
    mesolevel 125–7
    microlevel 121–5
covered support route 98
COVID-19 pandemic 375–6
  impact on youth labour markets 1–2
crossover effects in life course of young people 9, 60–1
cultural factors in life courses of young people 12, 13–14

D

deprivation 11
  economic 60, 295, 327
  in Greece and Italy 332–3
  material 296–7, 316, 322–5
  relative 317
  youth 296
de-standardisation of life courses 82
dissatisfaction with life 38, 41, 43, 45, 50–1, 53
diversity in European family systems 14

E

economic agency 217–8, 223, 225–6, 231
economic autonomy 10–11, 204, 214–15, 217, 233, 365–7
  institutional context 219–21
  see also housing autonomy
economic decline 317
economic deprivation 60, 295, 327
economic strain 258, 316, 322–5
economic trajectory, long-term 36, 37, 53
employer-provided occupation pension schemes 372
employment 60, 114
  opportunities 31, 141
  part-time 147, 226
  permanent 130, 272
  temporary 5, 31, 120, 169, 172, 185, 319, 321, 362
  uncertainties 341
    long-term outcomes 357n2
  see also unemployment; public employment services

employment protection legislation (EPL) 169, 170–3, 177–80, 184
  indicators 177, **179**
  Index 174
environmental clarity 143, 158, 161
equifinality 83, 87
equity 143, 156
Esping-Andersen's typology 14, 82, 145, 219, 372
Estonia
  career outlook and job security 146–7
  characterisation of national context **147**
  diversity in 14
  employment status **148**
  formal and informal supports 370
  income status of youth 145–6
  informal social support in 240, 247, 250
    ALMPs 244–5
    characteristics, sources, and goals 243
    combined informal and formal support 255–7
    emotional support 251–3
    financial support from family 249–50
    PLMPs 244–5
    role in relation to formal support 243–4
    socio-economic situation of youth 246
    supporting housing autonomy 251
    tackling youth unemployment 246
  labour market policy in 267
    ALMPs 146, **271**
    counselling practices 286
    failure of school system 288
    information on job opportunities 282–3
    job expectations 283
    lack of trust in institutions in youth 285–6
    registering at EUIF 282
    young people's assessment 272–4, 277–8
  lack of longitudinal data on youth transitions 374
  manifest functions of work 149–53
  private pension plans 352
  representing welfare state 145
Estonian Labour Market Board 267
Estonian Unemployment Insurance Fund (EUIF) 267, 274, 276–7
Europe 2020 strategy 2
European Central Bank 319

European Commission 319
European Platform against Poverty and Social Exclusion 3
European Social Fund Youth Opportunities Initiative 2
European Social Survey (ESS) 38, 40, 66, 342, 343
European Union policy initiatives 12
European Union Statistics on Income and Living Conditions (EU-SILC) survey 59, 62, 88, 173, 297
European Values Study (EVS) 66, 139, 144
European Values Survey *see* European Values Study (EVS)
Eurostat 173–4, 301
Eurostat Qualitative Reports of Labour Market Policy Statistics 92
Eurozone crises 1
EXCEPT project 16, 17, 19, 116, 129, 148, 271, 357n2
explanatory model 103
extended dependence model 84, 97
extended family model 83, 86–7, 98, 101, 104
extended family support route 98, 100–1, 104–5, 372
externally generated goals 143
extrinsic meanings of work 143–4

F

family allowances 13
family networks 247, 369
family residence models 84–5, 97
financial crisis in Europe, 2008–09 1, 2, 14, 31, 192, 263, 268, 269, 351, 353, 355
financial independence 10, 120, 216, 225, 231, 233, 366
financial literacy of youth in European countries 344–6
financial security by work 157
fixed-term contracts 13, 120, 130, 224, 319, 341, 350, 353
fixed-term employees 368
formal social support for young people 240, 241, 253–7

G

Gallie and Paugam's model 98
gender
 as determinant to leaving home 167
 gender-role attitudes 66, **67**, 70, **72–3**, **74**, 75
 gender-specific poverty 368
generational interdependence 241
generosity, 92
 of country's welfare system 297

of PLMP 90
of public pensions 340
of unemployment benefits 90, 116
generous replacement rates 298
Germany
 data and methodology 116–17
 formal and informal supports 370
 German dual vocational education and training system 130
 German SAVE study 357n3
 informal social support in 240, 247
 ALMPs 244–5
 characteristics, sources, and goals 243
 combined informal and formal support 253–5
 emotional support 251–3
 PLMPs 244–5
 role in relation to formal support 243–4
 socio-economic situation of youth 246
 tackling youth unemployment 246
 institutional context 115–16
 longitudinal data on youth transitions 374
 negative assessments of public employment services 369
 occupational pensions 350
 private pension plans 352
 Riester Pension in 351
 well-being and labour market insecurity 113–15
 coping strategies for well-being 120–9
 subjective perceptions and risk factors 117–20
 youth unemployment rates 112
Great Depression 31
Great Recession 1, 31, 73, 367
Greece
 formal support, lack of 370
 housing autonomy of young adults in 192–3, 201–3
 coping strategies 207–8
 family safety net for unemployed youth 196
 leaving from parental home 193, 197–9
 models of welfare regime 192
 number of interviewees by age and housing status **198**
 prerequisites 204–6
 process of transition to adulthood 210
 social capital of young people 195
 labour market insecurity in youth 368
 leaving parental home 366

longitudinal data on youth transitions, lack of 374
unemployment and precarity of youth in
　analytic procedure for research 321
　decrease in GDP 319–20
　economic strain 322–5
　fear of claiming one's rights 330–2
　humanitarian crisis in Greek society 332
　implications for family life 327–8
　interviews for research 321
　long-term financial planning and time perspective 325–7
　maintaining friendships and social bonds 328–30
　material deprivation 316, 322–5
　participating in social life 328–30
　relative deprivation 317
　sampling for research 320–1
　welfare system 320
　youth unemployment rates 319
guidance practices 264

H

health
　effects of unemployment in couples 60–2
　　distribution of contextual variables across countries **71**
　　effects of control variables 68
　　impact of individual and partner's unemployment **64–5**
　　means and proportions **69**
　　moderating role of gender roles 75
　　negative effects of lack of jobs 73, 74–5
　　policies for reducing societal consequences 75–6
　　random-effects models 67–8
　　research design 62–7
　　results for mediating role of reduced household income **66**
　　results for moderating factors **67, 72–3, 74**
　well-being and 363–5
Hodrick–Prescott filter (HP filter) 40, 45
hopelessness, sense of 117
household composition 253, 308, 370
housing autonomy 10–11, 167, 169, 173, 193, 194, 365–6
　coping strategies in times of labour instability 206–10
　country-specific institutional arrangements 168
　data and methodology 197–9, 173–5

EPL 169, 170–3, 177–80, 184
　indicators *177*, **179**
　gender role in 167
　institutional context 195–7, 207
　prerequisites 204–6
　labour market integration 166–7
　macrolevel factors 166–7, 170
　macrolevel indicators 169, 173, **175**
　as marker for transition to adulthood 192, 193
　meanings of 199–204
　negative moderating effect 184
　parental home, leaving 166, 167–8, 183, 193–5
　patterns of family formation 195
　public expenditure on housing policies 180–3
　indicators *181*, **183**
　public policies supporting 185, 173
　research questions 197
　results from multilevel regression 175–7
　theoretical background 170–3
　see also economic autonomy
hybrid models *see* random-effects models

I

income poverty 11, 325
　in Greek and Italian youth 325
　investigating socio-economic disadvantage 316
　negative effect of unemployment 297
　welfare generosity effect 297–8, 310
indicator-based approach 15
individual agency of young people 8
individual-level dynamic perspective 8
individual-level labour market insecurity, determinants of 4–5
individual life courses of youth 12, 166, 296
inductive approach 17
informal social support for young people 240, 241, 243
　combined with formal social support 253–7
　institutional contexts 244–6
　research questions, aims, and data 243–4
　strategic importance 243
　theoretical considerations 240–3
Inglehart, R. 159
institutional arrangements, country-specific 168
institutional effects on unemployment 372

institutional factors in life courses of young people 12, 13
intergenerational inequalities 340–1
International Labour Organisation (ILO) 39
International Monetary Fund 299, 319
intrinsic values or meanings 143
Italy
　ALMPs 146, 271
　　interviewees according to involvement **271**
　career outlook and job security 146–7
　characterisation of national context **147**
　data and methodology 116–17
　economic autonomy of youth in ALMPs 220
　　economic independence 225–8
　　economy and labour market institutions 219–20
　　educational level 218
　　job insecurity and 221–4
　　partially economically autonomous youth 228–32
　　subjective perspectives 217, 224–5
　employment status **148**
　failure of school system 288
　housing autonomy of young adults in 192–3, 199–201
　　coping strategies 206–7
　　latest-late model 196
　　leaving from parental home 193, 197–9
　　models of welfare regime 192
　　number of interviewees by age and housing status **198**
　　prerequisites 204–6
　　process of transition to adulthood 210
　income status of youth 145–6
　informal social support in 240, 247–8
　　ALMPs 244–5
　　characteristics, sources, and goals 243
　　emotional support 251–3
　　familial support 249
　　PLMPs 244–5
　　role in relation to formal support 243–4
　　socio-economic situation of youth 246
　　tackling youth unemployment 246
　institutional context 115–16
　interviewees' statements about work 151
　labour market insecurity 368
　labour market policy in 267–8
　　counselling practices 286
　　lack of trust in institutions in youth 285–6
　　participation in public employment services 284–5
　　young people's assessment 275–6
　lack of formal support 370
　lack of longitudinal data on youth transitions 374
　latent functions of work 153–9
　leaving parental home 366
　manifest functions of work 149–53
　Mediterranean welfare model 246
　occupational pensions 350
　private pension plans 352
　representing welfare state 145
　representing work values in 144
　unemployment and precarity of youth in
　　analytic procedure for research 321
　　decrease in GDP 319–20
　　economic strain 322–5
　　fear of claiming one's rights 330–2
　　implications for family life 327–8
　　interviews for research 321
　　long-term financial planning and time perspective 325–7
　　maintaining friendships and social bonds 328–30
　　material deprivation 316, 322–5
　　parental material support 333
　　participating in social life 328–30
　　sampling for research 320–1
　　welfare system 320
　　youth unemployment rates 319
　well-being and labour market insecurity 113–15
　　coping strategies for well-being 120–9
　　subjective perceptions and risk factors 117–20
　youth unemployment rates 112

J

Job Club 267
job insecurity 1, 9–10, 38, 50, 113, 114
　coping strategies to facing 113–15
　economic autonomy and 221–4
　effects on individuals' well-being 31–2, 35–6, 40, 50–1
　in Polish and Italian youth 217
　socio-economic consequences of 316

see also unemployment and job insecurity on well-being
joblessness *see* unemployment
job mobility 185, 351, 354
Jobs Act in Italy 268
job search assistance 13, 266

L

labour market exclusion 1, 8, 9, 169, 173, 295–6
　material and social consequences 320
　negative effect on young people's financial situation 298–9
　social consequences 6
　socio-economic consequences of 316
labour market insecurities 1, 295
　consequences of 363
　　socio-economic consequences 367–8
　　transition to adult life as dynamic process 365–7
　　well-being and health 363–5
　microlevel context 8, 9–11
　moderating macrolevel context 12–14, 19–20
　moderating mesolevel context 11–12, 20–1
　multi-method and European comparative approach 15–17
　multifaceted consequences 3–5
　policies effective in mitigating negative effects 371–3
　theoretical multilevel model 7–8, *9*
　well-being and 113–15
　　subjective perceptions and risk factors 117–20
labour market policies (LMPs) 13, 115–16
　aims and research questions 269–70
　in Bulgaria 268–9
　data and methodology 271
　in Estonia 267
　institutional contexts 266–9
　in Italy 267–8
　methodological strategy
　　household financial indicators *304*
　　method and data 299–302
　　sample and descriptive findings 302–4
　　statistics of dependent variables **303**
　　statistics of independent variables **303**
　moderating effect
　　on economic situation of unemployed youth 297–9
　　on situation of unemployed youth 304–8, **305**, **307**
　in Poland 266–7
　theoretical considerations 264–6
　variation across countries 296–7
　young people's assessment 271–2
　　policies and activities 272–9
　　use of labour market institutions 279–85
labour market uncertainties
　in European countries 112
　negative effects of 372
labour market vulnerability 365–6
latent functions of work 141, **142**, 143–5, 153
　latent extrinsic aspects of work 156–9, 161
　latent intrinsic aspects of work 153–6, 160–1, 365
　see also manifest functions of work
latest-late model 196
less stigmatisation route 87
life courses of young people 8, 12, 166, 296
　crossover effects 9, 60–1
　cultural factors 12, 13–14
　de-standardisation 82
　institutional factors 12, 13
　research 11
　structural factors 12, 13
life course perspective 368
life satisfaction (LS) 62, 82, 85, 107n15
　global judgements of 10
　effect of unemployment 88–9, *90*, 103–4, 364, 371
linear regression model 103–4, 174, 175, 178, 183
linked lives, principle of 11
logistic regressions 173, 175–6
log-odds based approach 106n4

M

macrocontextual strategies 114–15
macrolevel coping strategies 127–9 *see also* mesolevel coping strategies; microlevel coping strategies
Malmberg-Heimonen, I. 297
manifest functions of work 141, **142**, 144–5, 149–53, 159 *see also* latent functions of work
material deprivation 296–7, 316, 322–5
　investigating socio-economic disadvantage 316
　welfare generosity effect 297–8, 310
maturity 231, 233
　transition to 211
maturity, transition to 211
meanings of work 139–40
　concepts regarding **142**

latent functions of work 153–9
manifest functions of work 149–53
theoretical considerations 141, 143–5
Merton's paradigm of functional analysis 141, 148–9
mesolevel coping strategies 125–7 *see also* macrolevel coping strategies; microlevel coping strategies
microlevel coping strategies 121–5 *see also* macrolevel coping strategies; mesolevel coping strategies
minimisation process 98, 100–1
multimethod and European comparative approach 7, 15–17, 362
Mutual Information System on Social Protection in Europe (MISSOC) 346

N

National Swedish pension fund 355
nation-specific institutions 371–2
navigation 239
non-kin support *see* informal social support for young people
not in employment, education, or training (NEET) 1, 9, 17, 113, 196, 220

O

occupational pension systems 341, 350–1
OECD Pension at Glance Report 346
overqualification among youth 144

P

paid work 59–61, 70, 139, 144, 298
Pan-European Personal Pension Product (PEPP) 354
parental home, youths leaving 10, 107n15, 166, 183, 193–6, 199–201, 211, 215, 365
determinants of decision to 167–8, 170, 178
gaining autonomy through 3, 5, 8
relationship with parents 161n3
role of labour income in 152
parental unemployment and job uncertainty effects on children 37
partially economically autonomous youth 228–32
part-time contracts 120, 146–7
passive income support policies 128
passive labour market policies (PLMPs) 5, 13, 17, 19, 84, 106, 182, 298, 301, 371, 372
covered route 104

extended family route 104
high share of beneficiaries of unemployment benefits 95
in Italy, Estonia and Germany 244–5
effect of labour market insecurities 297
moderating role of **305**, **307**
negative effect of labour market exclusion 298–9
passive coverage (PC) 85
passive generosity (PG) 85, 92
pay-as-you-go pension systems 340
pensions portability 351
pension systems 341
occupational 341
private 341
public 368, 341–8, 349–50
three-pillar 340, 354–5
personal income, lack of 296, 367
pessimistic thinking 117
physical security at work 143, 159, 161
Poland
ALMPs 146, 271
interviewees according to involvement **271**
career outlook and job security 146–7
characterisation of national context **147**
economic autonomy of youth in ALMPs 217, 220
economic independence of youth 225–8
economy and labour market institutions 219–20
educational level 219
job insecurity and 221–4
NEET 220
partially economically autonomous youth 228–32
subjective perspectives of youth 217, 224–5
employment status **148**
failure of school system 288
income status of youth 145–6
labour market policy in 266–7
counselling practices 286
lack of trust in institutions in youth 285–6
participation in ALMP 284
social assistance benefits 281
unemployment benefits 279–80
young people's assessment 272
latent functions of work 153–9
manifest functions of work 149–53
private pension plans 352

Index

using public health system 289n1
representing welfare state 145
three-pillar pension systems in 355
policymakers 372, 373
post-retirement behaviour 357n4
poverty
  in Greece and Italy 332–3
  hidden 319, 333
  income 11, 298, 316, 325, 333
  risk of 3, 5–6, 8, 295, 296, 298, 300, 302, 304, 306, 308–9, 363
Poviat labour offices 266
precarity *see* unemployment—and job precariousness
predictability issues related to income 152
private pension systems 341, 351–3
problem-focused coping strategies 115, 116, 369
proportional reduction in inconsistency (PRI) 87
psychological support for interviewees 126
psychological well-being 113
public employment services 12, 13, 245, 266, 284
  negative assessments of 369
public expenditure on housing policies 180–3
  indicators *181*
public pension systems 368, 341, 349–50
  characteristics 346
    assessment basis 346–7
    pension's qualifying period 347
    periods of childcare 347, 348
    periods of unemployment 347
  employment uncertainty 348
  generosity of 340
  reforms of 341
  supply side perspective 346
  sustainability of 340
public policies 372
  supporting housing 185, 173
public regulation of labour market 13, 85
public social services 13
purchasing power parity value (PPP) 39
purchasing power standards (PPS) 95, 302

Q

qualitative comparative analysis (QCA) 15, 16, 87–8, 105–6, 107n12, 371, 372
quasi-private 'premium pension', 355

R

random-effects models 62, 67–8
recession and austerity measures 14
regression based approach 106n4
relative deprivation theory 33, 35, 316–17
relative intergenerational autonomy model 85
Riester Pension in Germany 351, 357n8
routes to youth well-being 81–3
  analytical framework 84–7
  configurational analysis 98–103
    empirical linkages between countries' combinations **99**
    sufficient routes to outcome **100**, **102**
  measurement and calibration
    dimensions in configurational comparison **91**
    of explanatory dimensions 90–8, **93–4**
    of outcome 88–90
    outcome dimension, explanatory conditions and crossover points **96**
  method 87–8

S

self-development 154–5
self-employment 249, 301, 341, 346, 350, 354
self-fulfilment 154
self-perceived economic autonomy 217
self-sufficiency 216, 298
small-N comparison 16, 19, 371
social exclusion 3
  coping strategies 369–71
  dimensions 6, 8–9
  indicator on expenditure for *181*, 181
  labour market insecurities, consequences of 4, 5, 363
  socio-economic consequences 367–8
  transition to adult life as dynamic process 365–7
  well-being and health 363–5
  limitations and directions for future research 373–6
  risk of 3, 8, 258, 296, 363
social identity theory 52, 114
social inclusion 3, 139, 363
Social Insurance Entitlements Dataset 107n10
social networks 18, 115, 125, 240, 243, 247, 329, 369

social norm of unemployment 70,
  72–3, **74**, 75
social security programmes 13, 372
social support 247–53
socio-demographics 89
socio-economic consequences 18,
  356n1, 367–8, 370, 374
  demand side perspective 341–2
  findings from expert
    interviews 344–6
  importance attributed to savings in
    European countries *343*
  quantitative results 342–4
  of insecure labour market
    positions 341
  of labour market exclusion and
    insecurity 316
  policy recommendations 353–6
  supply side perspective 341, 346
    characteristics of public pension
      systems 346–9
  of unemployment 318
socio-economic situation of youth
  10–12, 15, 19, 246, 263, 367, 371
spillover effects 60, 75
statistical techniques of multivariate data
  analysis 16
stigmatisation 86–7, 119, 125, 130, 365
  minimisation 90, 104
strain 60, 118, 119
  economic 316, 322–5
  of uncertainty 318
street-level bureaucracy concept 265
stress-free working environment 158
stress 58, 60, 115, 118, 128
structural factors in life courses of
  young people 12, 13
subjective attitudes of interviewees 124
subjective economic
  autonomy 223, 224
  at extreme poles of continuum 225–8
  partially economically autonomous
    youth 228–32
subjective well-being of young
  people 3, 5, 10, 88, 112, 113,
  130, 363–4
subprotective route 85
supportive supervision 143, 158
sustainability of public pensions 340
Sweden
  longitudinal data on youth
    transitions 374
  occupational pensions 350
  pension systems 355–6
  private pension plans 352, 355
  problems of funded pension
    provisions 356

T

theoretical multilevel model 7–8, *9*
three-pillar pension systems 340, 354–5
top-down approach *see*
  deductive approach
transactional stress theory 114
transitory business cycle
  fluctuations 36, 37, 53
tripolar typology, classical 145
Tugila see 'youth prop-up' programme
typology-based approach 15–16

U

unemployment (UE) 82, 89, 113, 117,
  122, 295, 319, 375
  allowance 255
  benefits 128
  consequence of 296–7
  effects on well-being 82–3, 88–90
  hypothesis 87
  information about 301
  job precariousness 315
    data and methodology 320–2
    fear of claiming one's rights 330–2
    implications for family life 327–8
    institutional context 318–2 and 0
    long-term financial planning and
      time perspective 325–7
    maintaining friendships and social
      bonds 328–30
    material deprivation and economic
      strain 322–5
    participating in social life 328–30
    research questions and aims 320
    theoretical considerations 316–18
  long-term 296
  negative consequences of 83, 84,
    97–8, 101, 104
  negative effect of 295–6, 306
  social norm of 70, **72–3, 74**, 75
  socio-economic consequences 318
  transition to 59, 67
  welfare regime 84
  see also employment
unemployment and job insecurity on
  well-being 31–2, 34, 112–14
  analysis results 41, 44–5, 50
  attribution theory 35–6
  COR theory 32, 34–5
  descriptive statistics for samples **42–3**
  empirical analysis 50
    main effects 50–1
    moderating effects 51–4
  gender-specific findings 365
  impact on adult life 363–4
  long-term economic trajectory 36, 37
  macrolevel moderators 39

microdata 38
microlevel variables 38–9
negative effects 364
relative deprivation theory 35
strategy for analysis 39–41
transitory business cycle fluctuations 36, 37
see also routes to youth well-being
Unemployment Insurance Fund (UIF) 256
United Kingdom (UK)
  longitudinal data on youth transitions 374
  pension systems 350, 352, 355–6
  problems of funded pension provisions 356
universalistic route to life satisfaction 85
universal route 104, 372

V

Voivodship 266
Voluntary Labour Corps (OHP) 266

W

work ethic *see* work obligation
work, latent intrinsic functions of 365
work obligation 59, 61, 66, **67**, 70
work-role centrality 34

Y

youth-as-transition approach 241
Youth Employment Initiative 266, 268
Youth Guarantee Scheme (YGS) 2, 266–9, 275
youth labour market problems 2, 4, 5
Youth on Move flagship initiative 2
'youth prop-up' programme 267
youth well-being 33–4, 37, 88
  and health 363–5
  identifying routes to 98–103
  job features related to 143
  and labour market insecurity in Italy and Germany 113–15
    coping strategies 120–9
    subjective perceptions and risk factors 117–20
  effect of micro-and macroindicators and interactions **44**, **48**–9
  moderating effects of macroeconomic indicators 45, 47
  unemployment effects on 82–3, 88–90
see also routes to youth well-being

Z

zero-hour contracts 350, 357n12

www.ingramcontent.com/pod-product-compliance
Lightning Source LLC
Chambersburg PA
CBHW071145070526
44584CB00019B/2667